# The Microsoft® Office Project 2007 Survival Guide

Lisa A. Bucki

THOMSON

COURSE TECHNOLOGY™

**Professional ■ Technical ■ Reference**

ISBN-10: 1-59863-284-1

ISBN-13: 978-1-59863-284-2

Library of Congress Catalog Card Number: 2006906797

Printed in the United States of America

07 08 09 10 11 TW 10 9 8 7 6 5 4 3 2 1

**Publisher and General Manager, Thomson Course Technology PTR**
Stacy L. Hiquet

**Associate Director of Marketing**
Sarah O'Donnell

**Manager of Editorial Services**
Heather Talbot

**Marketing Manager**
Heather Hurley

**Acquisitions Editor**
Mitzi Koontz

**Marketing Coordinator**
Adena Flitt

**Project Editor**
Sandy Doell

**Technical Reviewer**
Jack Dahlgren

**PTR Editorial Services Coordinator**
Erin Johnson

**Copy Editor**
Heather Kaufman Urschel

**Interior Layout Tech**
William Hartman

**Cover Designer**
Mike Tanamachi

**Indexer**
Katherine Stimson

**Proofreader**
Laura R. Gabler

THOMSON
COURSE TECHNOLOGY
Professional ■ Technical ■ Reference

Thomson Course Technology PTR, a division of Thomson Learning Inc.
25 Thomson Place ■ Boston, MA 02210 ■ http://www.courseptr.com

In loving memory of Bojangles, Danté, and Sweet Pea

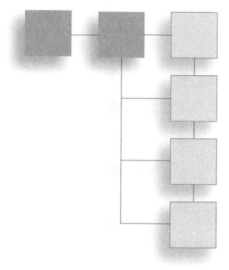

# ACKNOWLEDGMENTS

Writing the manuscript for a book like this consumes a significant chunk of time, so it's always a relief to know that the words and illustrations will be well taken care of by an expert publishing team. A fine group of people contributed their talents and efforts to turn my words and illustrations into the attractive, informative book you hold now in your hands. I first would like to thank Thomson Course Technology PTR Publisher and General Manager Stacy Hiquet for being receptive to the idea of publishing a Project book and for her ideas to open it up to a wider audience that includes students and adult learners. It was a pleasure to once again work with Project Editor Sandy Doell, whose laid-back personal style by no means clashes with her high-powered editing and process management skills. Thanks, Sandy. My thanks as well to Copy Editor Heather Kaufman Urschel and Technical Editor Jack Dahlgren, who both were invaluable in helping refine the words and techniques presented in the book. It was a pleasure to be working with both of these good professionals and nice people again. I'd also like to give a shout out to Designer Mike Tanamachi and the production team who created this great final product from the manuscript and graphics.

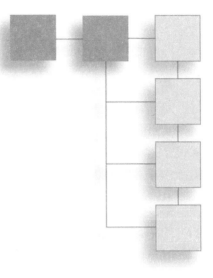

# About the Author

An author, trainer, and consultant, **Lisa A. Bucki** has been writing and teaching about computers and software for more than 15 years. She wrote *Managing with Microsoft Project* (multiple editions), *Learning Photoshop CS2, Dell Guide to Digital Photography: Shooting, Editing, And Printing Pictures, Teach Yourself Visually Microsoft Office PowerPoint 2007, Learning Computer Applications: Projects & Exercises* (multiple editions), and *Adobe Photoshop 7 Fast & Easy.*

Bucki has written or contributed to dozens of additional books and multimedia tutorials covering a variety of software and technology topics, including FileMaker Pro 6 for the Mac, iPhoto 2, Fireworks and Flash from Adobe, Microsoft Office applications, and digital photography. Bucki also spearheaded or developed more than 100 computer and trade titles during her association with the former Macmillan Computer Publishing (now a division of Pearson). Bucki has conducted Microsoft Project training sessions for nearly 10 years.

# ABOUT THE TECH EDITOR

**J**ack Dahlgren has been using and writing about Microsoft Project for nearly a decade. Prior to that, he worked extensively with other project scheduling tools. With an eclectic background in Architecture, Construction, and Hi-tech Product Development, he has adapted Project to suit a wide variety of scheduling problems. His three-step advice to those just learning the use of Project is to:

Understand what you want to do first; then use the tool to help you achieve that goal.

Try it out—use simple examples to figure out how things work.

Keep it as simple as possible but no simpler—you don't need to use every feature.

Jack also maintains a top-ranked web site and blog, which give examples of how to use Microsoft Project and, in particular, how to use VBA to get the most out of Project. You can read some of his writings on Project and Project Management at:

> http://zo-d.com/blog
>
> http://masamiki.com/project/

Jack would like to thank his wife, Kay, and three boys, Masao, Mikio, and Rikio, for being patient during the making of this book.

# TABLE OF CONTENTS

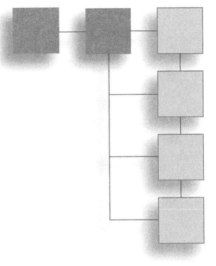

# Introduction: Meeting Microsoft Project

## Is This Book Right for You?

If you're looking for a book to teach you everything about the art and science of project management, put this one right down and back away slowly. This book does not endeavor to help you learn to become a professional project manager. For that, buy a project management how-to book over in the business books section.

If you've had a project thrust in your lap and have been asked to use Microsoft Project or want to try to use it to improve your results, buy this book now. (And please accept my thanks and appreciation for doing so!) *The Microsoft Office Project 2007 Survival Guide* will teach you the essential skills for using Microsoft Project, providing tips and hints about how Project can help you manage project progress more effectively. It also will present the type of real-world examples and techniques that apply to mainstream business people, not just technical professionals.

I've geared *The Microsoft Office Project 2007 Survival Guide* to help new Project users. You can count on this book to help you build a project plan, add the resources to get it done, nail down your budget, and track and share results. It will give you what you need to organize your plan and move forward, and it will help steer you away from the mistakes that beginners make. (And I've seen my Project students and clients make some doozies!) The end of every chapter includes Review Questions and hands-on Projects, so that you can reinforce your knowledge of key concepts and practice the skills you'll be using to build your own project plans.

With *The Microsoft Office Project 2007 Survival Guide*, you *can* survive learning to use Microsoft Project. Properly used, the program *can* help you survive and thrive in managing your projects. When you're ready to get started, turn to Chapter 1.

# Project and Windows Versions and This Book

Microsoft Project has been the leading project management program on the market for many years now. Microsoft Project is used in many different types of organizations and settings, from small non-profit groups to large aerospace manufacturers and commercial construction firms. Such a diverse user community means that Project is being used in a variety of ways in a variety of computer infrastructure settings.

## Project 2007 Versions

Like computer technology as a whole, Project has evolved in a variety of ways to better serve user demands, such as the increasing need for collaboration on projects. The most recent version of Microsoft Office Project is available in these separate versions serving different types of users:

- **Microsoft Office Project Standard 2007.** This basic Project version is for standalone users. If you're working in a small organization or group and only one or two people will be using Project, chances are this is the version that you'll have or choose to use. This version runs on the desktop or server versions of Windows, but the server is not required. If you're using this Project version, this book applies to you.

- **Microsoft Office Project Professional 2007.** This enhanced Project version can be used as a standalone program, or it can work with the server version of Project (described next) to facilitate team collaboration. It also can run on the desktop or server versions of Windows, depending on your needs and organizational computing infrastructure. If you're using this Project version, this book applies to you but only covers the standalone aspects of the program and not the high-level collaboration features.

- **Microsoft Office Project Server 2007 and Project Web Access.** Microsoft Office Project Server 2007 underpins the Microsoft Office Enterprise Project Management (EPM) Solution. What that means is that Project Server enables a team to share and manage projects collaboratively, where everyone can view the project information stored in a central location. Project Professional can access the project plan, or end users without Project can use Project Web Access, a viewer application. Project Server must be installed on a server version of Windows, and there are other enterprise software requirements. This book does NOT apply to Project Server or Project Web Access users.

## Windows Versions

At nearly the same time that it was updating Project, Microsoft released a new version of its Windows operating system: Windows Vista. Project Standard and Professional 2007 run on both Vista and XP versions of Windows.

The screen shots in this book show Microsoft Office Project Professional 2007 installed on Windows Vista (desktop). If you are using Project on Windows XP, your screen should look similar in most cases.

### Other Project Versions

Can you use this book if you're using an older version of Project Standard or Project Professional? Absolutely. Basic features of these standalone versions of Project have remained largely identical since the 2002 versions of Project. While some of the new features in Project 2007 will not be available if you are using an older version, those features represent only a minimal percentage of the content of this book.

## How This Book Is Organized

Even if you're not a professional project manager, using Project 2007's tools in the proper order will enhance your productivity and success. *The Microsoft Office Project 2007 Survival Guide* leads you through the proven project management process that Project has been designed to facilitate.

- Part 1, "Your First Look at Project Management and Project," gives you an overview of the project management practices that Project follows and introduces the terminology and concepts you'll need to know to work effectively in the Project program. You'll learn how the "home base" view of Project looks, how to take advantage of guidance built in to Project, and how to get help when you're stuck. The final chapter in Part 1 gives you a jump start, where you create, track, and report about an example project.

- Part 2, "Building a Project Plan," covers the actions you need to take to build a project plan file in Microsoft Project. You will learn to specify what will be done, in what order it should be done, how long it will take, who or what should be handling particular work, and what the costs add up to.

- Part 3, "Finalizing and Launching Project," explains how your focus and use of Project shifts when a project moves from the planning phase to the execution phase. You will see here how to review the project plan to make sure it's as realistic and accurate as possible, how to save initial plan information to use for later progress tracking, and how to track work to keep your project plan current.

- Part 4, "Reviewing and Sharing Results," provides you with experience in finding, viewing, printing, and otherwise sharing the valuable information in your project plan. You'll also see how to share information between other applications and Project how to share resources between project files, and you'll even learn to see how different project schedules compare.

The book concludes with three appendixes: one that covers key differences between Windows XP and Windows Vista, one that provides help in using Project to tackle special project planning situations, and a final one that provides answers to the chapter Review Questions.

## How To Use This Book

If you are brand new to Project and/or the project management process, I strongly recommend that you start with Chapter 1 and work through the chapters in order. In teaching Microsoft Project to business users, I have encountered many instances where a student thought he or she already knew how to use Project or had played around with it and thought it was obvious, only to cause themselves many hours of added work down the line because they had set up their project plans incorrectly. If you move through this book in order, you'll be able to set up a project plan correctly the first time, saving yourself later grief.

If you are in a desperate situation where you need to put together at least a basic project plan RIGHT NOW, go first to Chapter 3, "Jump Start: Create and Manage a Project." This chapter presents hands-on steps where you build and work with a basic project plan.

Along the way, you'll find special text elements that highlight key information.

When you see a *Gotta Know*, don't skip it! These boxes call your attention to information that is key, key, key!

*Missteps* identify common mistakes that new users make, so that you can avoid introducing problems into your project plan.

**Tips** provide shortcuts or hints for working more effectively.

*Notes* present additional technical details or steps that you may need.

Each chapter concludes with Review Questions and Projects to help you test and build on your new knowledge of Microsoft Project.

# PART ONE

# Your First Look at Project Management and Project

# CHAPTER 1

# The Project Management Process and Microsoft Project

This Chapter Teaches You How To:

- Understand how projects and project management differ from other business activities
- Follow the basic process used by professional project managers
- Know the key terms and concepts you'll need to work with Microsoft Project
- See how Microsoft Project follows the standard project management process
- Use Project in the way that will be of most benefit to your success

Here you are with Microsoft Office Project 2007 installed on your system for you to use for the first time. Whether you're raring to go or facing that first startup with a few reservations, rest assured you'll find the help you need in this book. Think of this first chapter as a first-day job orientation, where you'll get insight into your work to come with Project and learn more about the project management process.

## Help! The Boss Wants Project

Government finance and account gurus now consider "worker productivity" an important aspect of the economy to track and evaluate on a regular basis. Companies have long squeezed out more products and services by automating with robotics and computerized processes. But now, employee intelligence and production have become more of a focus, and that means businesses work harder to harvest the employee intelligence and capabilities that provide a competitive edge over other widget and gadget makers. In today's world-view, efficiencies and productivity gains come from giving experienced people the best overall tools—like Microsoft Project—to work smarter.

Although in the past only engineers, large commercial construction project managers, and software and Information Technology (IT) project managers used project management programs like Project, you now can find Project at work in a wide variety of organizations and job categories. For example, students I've taught and clients I've worked with have included:

- Educational administrators who needed to implement a new curriculum in a school system.
- Museum planners who needed to map out upcoming exhibits and schedules.
- Small construction companies who needed to provide project plans to fulfill government contract requirements.
- Health spa operators who needed to develop plans for implementing new services.
- Operators of a private park attraction who wanted a tool to plan and schedule maintenance upgrades.
- Administrative staff members responsible for working with engineers to update and publish project plans.
- Paper manufacturing company equipment operators and maintenance staff who needed to plan machine maintenance downtimes and communicate about those outages to management and others in the plant.
- Between-careers managers who wanted to add familiarity with Microsoft Project to their skill sets.

Some of the folks mentioned above identified Microsoft Project as a tool they wanted, and so they embraced the program with open minds. In other cases, the people I taught were more or less "ordered" to start using Project to document projects, no matter what levels of computer comfort or project management skills they had. Both types of students were able to learn the essentials and use Project to build project plans, and you can, too.

Even if learning Microsoft Project isn't the next new job skill you'd like to have, if you stay open to learning the process as presented in this book, you'll quickly be on the path to managing your projects to better results.

## What Are Projects and Project Management?

*Project management* is more than a résumé buzz word. Project management represents a field of study and body of information defining a growing professional discipline. The Project Management Institute (PMI) is the leading project management organization that develops the standards and models for professional project management, brought together in the *Project Management Body of Knowledge* (*PMBOK*). The group also administers conferences and project management training and certification programs. The fact that it constitutes an entire field of study might be your first clue to the fact that there's more to project management than checking off items on a To Do list.

If a project manager hands you a business card with "PMP" beside her name or title, that means she is a certified Project Management Professional who has completed thousands of hours of documented on-the-job task management, many months of document project management, PMI's rigorous education curriculum, and PMI's certification exam. Achieving the PMP designation represents a significant accomplishment for dedicated project managers.

Practically speaking, however, in most organizations, a project manager is anyone who is put in charge of leading a team to manage a series of activities designed to produce specific outcomes. You might think that that description applies to nearly anyone in your organization, *but* whether or not one is really acting as a project manager depends on whether the activities one is directing are actually projects.

A ***project*** is a series of activities leading to defined goals and deliverables achieved in a specified time frame. A project has a specific starting date and a specific ending date. A project may involve the activities of a team of people or may be a relatively complex series of activities completed by a single person. The team members may all come from one department, or they may include persons from many departments or even other companies. While a particular type of project may occur many times, ongoing activities are not considered projects. Nor are isolated To Do list items that involve a single person or activity. Table 1.1 provides a comparison list of example projects versus similar activities that are not projects.

 If you're curious about the professional field of project management and want to find books and other resources to learn more, go to www.pmi.org, the Project Management Institute's Web site. Other international organizations and standards also exist, such as the PRINCE2 approach widely used in the UK; to learn more about the PRINCE2 method and certifications, see http://www.prince2.org.uk/web/site/home/Home.asp. If you are entering a new job or career where project management skills and standards are a must, consult with others in the field and geographic location to learn which particular project management standards and practices apply. Wikipedia's entry about project management also lists different standards and standards organizations in the article at http://en.wikipedia.org/wiki/Project_management.

**Table 1.1**  Project...or Not?

| Project | Not a Project |
|---|---|
| Selecting or developing and implementing a new accounting system | Managing daily Accounts Payable tasks |
| Designing a new daily reporting system | Updating and running daily reports |
| Planning and holding a client seminar | Meeting with a client for an update |
| Planning and executing a company move to a new facility | Setting up an office for a new employee |
| Planning the maintenance team's work on a plumbing system upgrade | Creating the work schedule for the maintenance team |
| Planning and executing an equipment upgrade for a manufacturing line | Scheduling the production for a manufacturing line |
| Planning, writing, producing, and distributing a client newsletter | Writing a letter to a client |
| Planning and delivering a software upgrade to every employee's system | Repairing a software installation on a single system |
| Planning and building an addition to a facility | Cleaning the flooring in an office |
| Researching, purchasing, and deploying a new telecom system | Assigning or changing an employee's extension |

# What Steps Go into Managing a Project?

Whether done in a formal way or not, most organizations routinely follow what the Project Management Institute has defined as the "official" project management process, illustrated in Figure 1.1.

**Initiating.** This phase involves defining the overall scope of the project, including objectives (goals and deliverables), what the overall project due date will be, who the stakeholders are who will be involved in or affected by the project and its outcomes, what people and equipment will be available to contribute to the project, what the budget limitations are, and what other performance measures such as quality standards must be met. During this process, you try to identify underlying assumptions that might impact project outcomes in a positive or negative way, such as whether other departments can really make the type of contribution required. Before proceeding to the next phase, all stakeholders should agree on the project's parameters.

**Planning.** This crucial phase can make or break the project. During this phase, the project manager must detail the specific activities needed to achieve the project deliverables; define the specific people, equipment, and materials involved and the

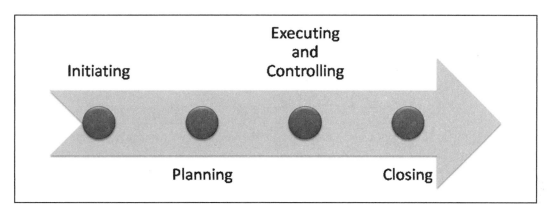

**Figure 1.1** Overall phases for managing a project.

cost for each; determine which people will handle which tasks; create the detailed schedule for all aspects of the work; identify how activities relate and may impact one another; and solidify the budget. Once the project manager believes that the project plan is thorough, complete, realistic, and accurate and will result in the required goals and deliverables, she should make sure that all stakeholders buy in to and agree to the plan. At that point, the project manager should secure formal approval and signoffs as required in her organization to proceed with the project, at which point work can begin.

Having to stop a project that's been poorly planned is ultimately more costly to an organization than spending more time on planning and consensus-building. Don't make the mistake of pushing a project forward if you haven't gotten all the information that you need, may have omitted key factors, or don't have agreement that the plan makes sense and is doable. Make sure that you and your organization make the tough choices to change direction and kill or revise the plan before work and expenditures begin.

**Executing.** Just before work begins, the project manager should make a record of the original project plan to use as a tool for later evaluation. The project manager should set up regular communication avenues to urge team members to complete work and to gather information about actual progress in completing project activities. Tracking tools can help gauge overall project progress.

**Controlling.** Controlling a project primarily happens concurrent with project execution (although you can think of discipline during the initiation and planning phases as control, too). As the project manager tracks progress, she needs to identify deviations from the original plan as quickly as possible and take corrective actions, such as reassigning work, seeking more tools to complete the work, adjusting the schedule based on changes, and managing and limiting budget issues. During this phase, the project manager must respond to and manage needed changes. Execution and control also involve reporting project progress to team members and stakeholders as required.

---

**Tip** *Scope creep* happens when a project somehow morphs to encompass more than its original goals and objectives. Part of your control role as project manager is to be on the lookout for scope creep, because it obligates you to deliver more results without necessarily receiving more time, dollars, or people power. If stakeholders genuinely want to change the scope of the project, estimate the increased cost, resource, and time requirements; get the proper sign-offs on the new scope; and replan the remainder of the project as required.

---

**Closing.** While this phase may be the least formal in any company's project management routine, some type of closure typically occurs when the project is declared finished and the project team members released from project obligations. The project manager should document lessons learned, either for herself personally or for the whole team, and provide final reports and documentation.

The professional project management discipline details numerous steps and official types of documents for planning and controlling a project. These include documents like a scope statement, project charter, statement of work, or scope change request. If your organization doesn't have any formal planning process whatsoever, you might want to explore putting some formal documents or processes in place. (A good project management book can help with this objective.)

Many organizations have other documents or systems that stand in for the types of documents called for by project management practices. For example, if a client issues a Request for Quote or Request for Proposal, that document and your response to it go a long way toward establishing the project scope, deliverables, schedule, budget, and resources needed to complete the work. The signed contract initiates the project execution, and client reporting requirements drive some aspects of control. The client's acceptance of and payment for the final work close the project's life cycle.

To increase your successful outcomes, be sure to formalize your project planning and management process, in whatever fashion applies in your organization and for your team. Project management doesn't just "happen." Applying discipline, consistency, objectivity, creativity, and (when needed) flexibility throughout the process will help you drive projects forward.

# Tasks, Resources, and Other Key Concepts

In developing a project plan, you will need to provide detailed answers to questions like "What work needs to be done?" and "Who or what is required to complete the work?" It is at this crucial juncture that the seeds of project failure can be planted. Many organizations and individual project managers fail to plan how and when work will be done in adequate detail. When work later begins and reveals the planning to have been incomplete and inadequate, the cost and pain to correct the situation can be tremendous. So, a successful project manager needs to bear down during the planning phase to create the best plan possible by answering the crucial questions.

"What work needs to be done?" The answer to this question is key, because you need to identify the project deliverables and then figure out the actions required to produce those deliverables. The project manager needs to break down the overall project activities (that will produce the deliverables) into discrete actions called *tasks* (Figure 1.2). Identifying all the tasks to complete, in detail, provides the project manager with a more accurate picture of the breadth of the work involved in the project. It also can help the project manager verify that the goals and deliverables for the plan can indeed be achieved or whether it would be appropriate to adjust the project's scope to make the project more realistic. The project manager also must arrange the tasks in the proper sequence and estimate the schedule for each task. In this way, the project manager begins to map out the overall project schedule.

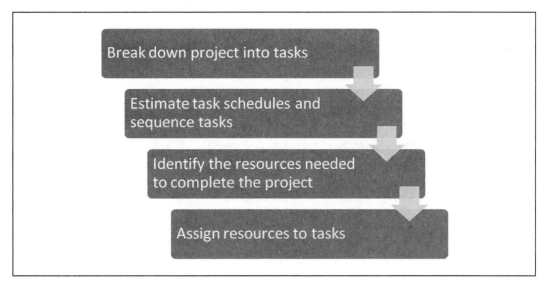

**Figure 1.2** The project manager needs to identify specific tasks and available resources during project planning.

"Who or what is required to complete the work?" In answering this question, the project manager needs to list the *resources*—team members, equipment, and consumable materials—required to complete the project. This list should be comprehensive, because if the project manager fails to plan for and request all the required resources during the planning phase, needed additional resources may not be available during project execution, which would seriously damage the team's overall ability to meet project commitments.

In continuing to build the plan, the project manager must make *assignments*: deciding which specific resource(s) will complete each particular task. During this process, the project manager can begin to identify the costs associated with using each resource, thus building the budget. If a resource can't work full-time for the team or has other scheduling limitations, his tasks may need to be rescheduled, which can change the overall project schedule.

A *task* is a specific activity with a start and finish point. A *resource* is a person, an item of equipment, or a quantity of material used to complete a task. An *assignment* occurs when you apply a resource to a task, indicating that the resource is responsible for or will be used in completing the task.

Identifying project tasks, resources, and assignments and building a detailed schedule provides the proper roadmap for project execution, control, and closure, reducing uncertainty along the way. If you as project manager take the time and have the discipline to do the detailed planning, you give your project and team a strong base to work from in the form of clear goals and objectives.

## How Does Project Fit into the Process?

If building a detailed list of tasks and resources sounds like a lot of work, well, that's a painful truth. But this is where Microsoft Office Project 2007 comes in. Project provides tools to facilitate the planning portion of the project management process. Project helps you list tasks and can calculate the overall project schedule; Project enables you to better visualize the plan and determine which tasks are more critical to project success. Because Project helps you develop a more detailed and thorough plan, you can better communicate about project requirements and progress.

Project provides specific views where you can build the list of project tasks and the list of project resources. You can establish how long it will take to complete each task and easily indicate how tasks relate. Once you've done so, Project calculates the project finish date for you. As you assign resources to tasks, Project can recalculate the project finish date for you to reflect the impact of the assignments you make. In the pop-up tip shown in Figure 1.3, Project has calculated a finish date of 4/17/07 for the project plan shown.

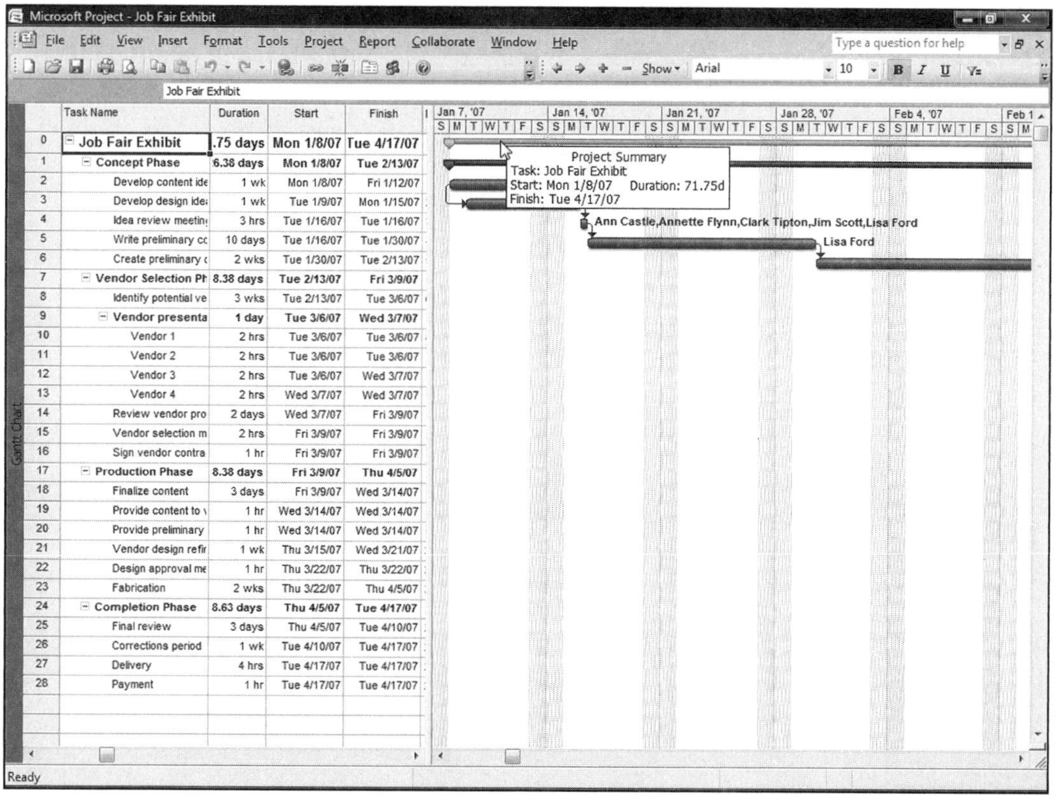

**Figure 1.3** Project calculates the overall project finish date for you.

While building a project plan remains a matter of putting in the required time and thought, once you've built the plan, you can take advantage of really powerful Project features to review the plan to ensure it's realistic and reasonable, and then execute and control the project:

- **Views to help you identify planning problems before work begins.** Project includes views where you can see whether you've assigned too much work to a resource during any time period, giving you the opportunity to correct that type of planning error before launching work on the project. You also can see which tasks are most important or critical to the overall schedule, so you can add resources to those tasks to have the greatest positive impact on the overall project completion date.

- **Tools to track work completed.** Project provides you with the flexibility to update completed work on tasks one by one, in groups, or in a somewhat automatic fashion.

- **Tools to reschedule work.** If work is not completed on schedule, Project enables you to reschedule multiple tasks based on the date when work will resume. When you use this feature, Project recalculates the schedule for related tasks automatically, so you can see the overall impact on your project's finish date. You can then take corrective action as needed to bring the project back on track.

- **A view to enable you to compare your current plan versus your original plan.** This feature enables you to pinpoint where and how your project may have gotten off track, again so that you can take corrective action.

- **Customizable views and reports that enable you to keep team members and stakeholders up to date.** Project can provide the information that various players want, so that you don't have to compile and develop reports by hand.

You may need to create multiple versions of a project plan before the executing phase begins. Use Project's views and features to do a thorough job of weeding out potential problems (and of course get input from others in the organization and team) before the work begins.

## How Do I Use Project to Manage for Success?

Project is no substitute for your human intelligence and experience. It can't build a project plan for you, and it doesn't put project execution on "autopilot." Still, Project lends tremendous value to you as project manager through some specific benefits you can realize by using it. With Project, you can:

- **Build the plan in greater detail than otherwise possible.** Although it's certainly possible to create a project plan on paper or with software tools not specifically geared for project management, Project gives you specific project management tools for building a detailed, comprehensive plan. With Project, you can drill down and capture all the necessary planning information, setting the stage for success. Even better, Project visually captures the relationship between different tasks and assignments, so you can immediately see how each task impacts others down the line.

- **Test "what-ifs" in detail.** Because Project can recalculate the entire schedule based on any change you make, you can test variations on your plan before finalizing the plan and beginning execution. In this way, you can pick what you believe to be the best possible schedule.

- **Build stakeholder buy-in on the plan.** Project enables you to present plan information that's both textual and graphical. Project plans not only look impressive, but they provide a clear indication that you have done your homework so stakeholders can buy in with confidence.

- **Execute and communicate to the plan.** Projects can get off track when a project manager doesn't communicate adequately with the team. Stakeholders also require care and feeding in the form of solid progress reports. Take advantage of Project's reports and views to supply information to team members and stakeholders at regular intervals as you execute the project.

- **Control and update the plan.** Track work with Project to make sure that the project plan is up to date. You should set regular intervals where you'll gather task updates from resources and update the plan with that information. Then, your project plan will always have the best information available for decision making, corrective action, or redirection. Likewise, review project budget and resource information at regular intervals to ensure the project is staying on budget and resources are pulling their weight.

- **Close and learn from the plan.** When a project concludes, the natural tendency is for lessons learned to fall by the wayside. However, with Project, you always can return to the final files from earlier projects to evaluate how long particular tasks took, how well particular resources performed, and how outcomes were affected by planning errors. Your lessons learned have been captured in the Project file, so you always can revisit them when planning your next project.

## Chapter Review

With any luck, the overview of the project management process, your role as project manager, and Project's role in the project management process presented in this chapter have made you eager to move on and learn more. This chapter explained the overall steps or phases in managing a project and why successful project managers emphasize project initiation and planning. After learning how tasks, resources, and assignments form the building blocks of any project plan, you explored how Microsoft Office Project 2007 provides the tools to help you put those building blocks together. Finally, the chapter passed on some advice about using Microsoft Project to manage your way to project success. Challenge yourself now with the Review Questions and Projects before moving on to the next chapter.

### Review Questions

Write your answers to the following questions on a sheet of paper.

1. What's the difference between a To Do list and a project plan?
2. What are the overall steps in managing a project?
3. What is a task?
4. What is a resource?

5. What is an assignment?

6. Name one phase or part of the project management process that Microsoft Office Project 2007 can help with.

## Projects

 To see example solution files created by completing the projects in this chapter, go to www.courseptr.com, click the **Downloads** link in the navigation bar at the top, type **Microsoft Office Project 2007 Survival Guide** in the search text box, and then click **Search Downloads**.

### Project 1

1. Take a sheet of paper and divide it into two columns.

2. In the left column, write down the five overall phases or stages of project management.

3. In the right column, write down at least two specific activities that might be part of that phase.

### Project 2

1. Think of a project you've handled on the job recently.

2. Draw each task for the project as a box on a sheet of paper, and write the name of the task in the box.

3. Draw lines between the task boxes to show which tasks followed from previous tasks.

### Project 3

1. Think of another project you've handled recently on the job or personally.

2. List the tasks performed to complete the project.

3. List the resources needed to complete the project.

4. To the right of each task, draw an arrow and then write the name(s) of the resource(s) from your resource list who handled the task.

# CHAPTER 2

# LEARNING PROJECT BASICS

This Chapter Teaches You How To:

- Start and exit Project
- Move around in the default view
- Display another view
- Display and use the Project Guide
- Use the Help system
- Find options settings for working with files and customizing the program
- Be aware of new features and other online resources

In terms of some of its tools, Microsoft Office Project 2007 works just like a lot of other programs. Yet Project also has some unique features and aspects that sometimes confuse new users a bit. This chapter will help you get comfortable with basic features and operations in Project so that you can work with confidence as you build your project plan. The chapter shows you how to start and close the Project program. You will learn about the parts of the default view in Project, as well as how to find information and display one of the numerous other Project views. The chapter teaches you how to use assistance tools like the Project Guide and Help and shares links to some other online resources that might be useful. The chapter also previews some of the new features in Project 2007.

# Starting Up and Shutting Down

Starting a program loads it into your computer's memory so that it's ready for you to use. As when you start many other programs, especially other programs in the Microsoft Office suite, starting Project opens a blank file onscreen by default. No matter whether you're using Project on the Windows XP or Windows Vista operating system, the startup steps are roughly the same:

1. Click the **Start** button on the taskbar in the lower-left corner of the screen, or press the Window key on the keyboard.
2. Click **All Programs**.
3. Click **Microsoft Office**.
4. Click **Microsoft Office Project 2007**.

The Windows Vista Start menu provides another fast way to open the program:

1. Click the **Start** button on the taskbar. If you see Microsoft Office Project 2007 in the left column of the Start menu, jump to Step 3.
2. Type **Project**. The text you type automatically appears in the Search text box, and the left column of the Start menu lists matching programs and files, as shown in Figure 2.1.
3. Click **Microsoft Office Project 2007**.

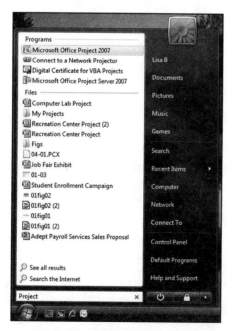

**Figure 2.1** Use the Search text box to find and start Project.

You can add a shortcut icon for starting Project to the Windows desktop. Just drag the Microsoft Office Project 2007 choice from any location on the Start menu to the desktop. You can then double-click the shortcut icon to start Project.

When you've finished your work in Project, you will want to close or exit the program. Closing the program closes any open files that you were working on to ensure that your work is properly secure. You can exit the Project program in one of three ways:

- Click **File** on the menu bar and then click **Exit**.
- Click the **Close (X)** button in the upper-right corner of the program window.
- Press **Alt+F4**.

If you've made changes to any open Project file that you haven't yet saved, Project prompts you to save, as shown in Figure 2.2. Be sure to click **Yes** each time Project displays the message to ensure you save your changes to all of the files that you had open. (Chapter 4, "Creating a Project Plan File and Calendar," provides more information about working with files in Project.)

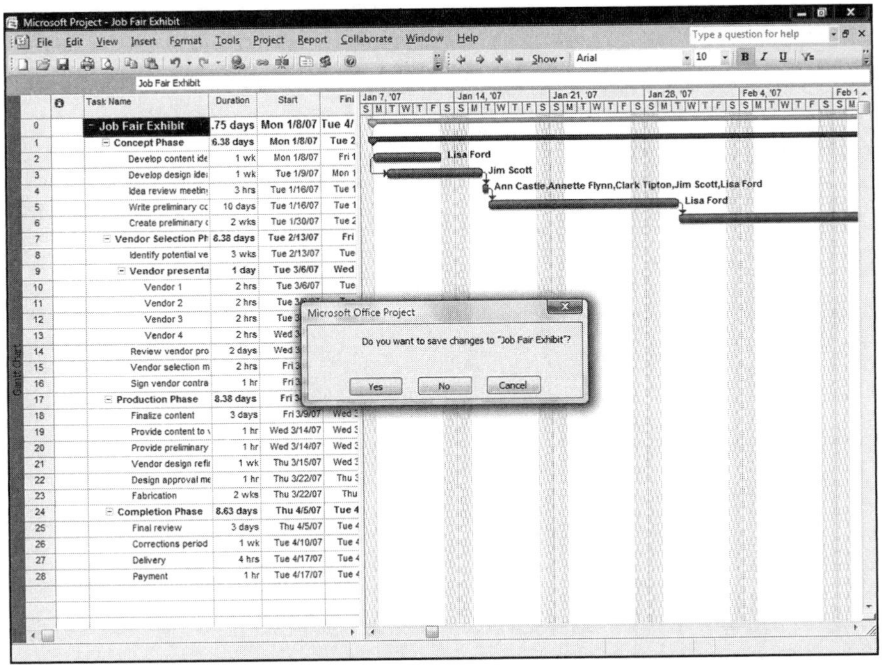

**Figure 2.2** You have the opportunity to save recent changes when you exit Project.

# Navigating the Gantt Chart (Default) View

Unlike most of the other applications in the Microsoft Office 2007 suite, Microsoft Project has maintained a more traditional Windows program appearance, in particular retaining the menu bar and toolbar structure used in the previous few versions of Office. So, if you're comfortable working in recent Office versions, you'll have a head start in learning to work in Microsoft Project.

Figure 2.3 shows you the Project program window with its default view, called the Gantt Chart view, displayed. The key features of the Project program include the following:

- **Title bar.** The title bar across the top of the window displays the name of the program as well as the name of the current project plan file.

- **Close (X) button.** Clicking this button at the far right end of the title bar closes the Project program. You can use the Minimize and Restore/Maximize buttons beside it to manipulate the size of the program window.

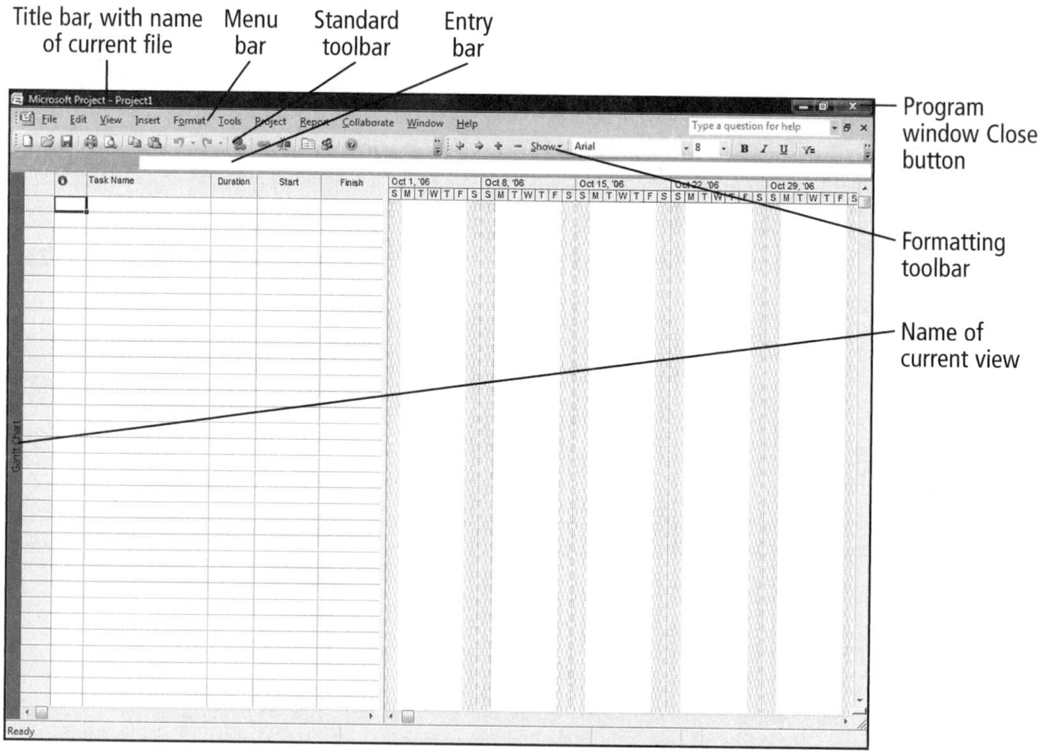

**Figure 2.3**  The default Project view is called the Gantt Chart view.

- **Menu bar.** This bar—just below the title bar—lists menus, or groups of commands, for working in Project. Click a menu to display its commands and then click a command in the list. Clicking a command might display a submenu from which you choose additional commands or a dialog box in which you specify additional choices for executing the command.

If you see a command in this book that reads along the lines of "Choose Tools, Options," that means to click the Tools menu, and then click the Options command.

- **Toolbars.** By default, Project displays two toolbars on the row below the menu bar: the Standard toolbar and the Formatting toolbar. (Toolbars can also appear on multiple, separate rows below the menu bar.) Each toolbar offers buttons and choices that enable you to execute changes directly rather than having to choose a menu command. Click a toolbar button to run its command. To see what a toolbar button does, move the mouse pointer over it; a yellow ScreenTip with the tool's name and any available keyboard shortcut appears.

The buttons displayed on any toolbar change based on usage, so if you or another person has been working with Project on your system, you may see different buttons than those shown in Figure 2.3. Also, keep in mind that some buttons become disabled based on the current action, such as when you are editing a cell.

- **Entry bar.** When you're working with the entry in a cell, you can make your changes either in the cell itself or here in this box.
- **Current view.** A thin bar along the left side of the window lists the name of the current Project view. You can check here to ensure you're working with the view that you want to use.

Project includes several toolbars, not just the two shown by default, and you need to know how to hide and display toolbars to work effectively in Project. Right-click a toolbar to display a menu of available toolbars, as shown in Figure 2.4. A check mark appears beside any currently displayed toolbar. Click the name of the toolbar to display (check) or hide (uncheck). To move a toolbar, you can drag it by its handle at the left end or by its title bar if the toolbar appears in its own window. Dragging a toolbar to any of the four sides of the screen docks the toolbar at that location. If you drag it off the toolbar row, the toolbar may snap into its own window. Double-click the window title bar to return the toolbar to the top of the screen. To see a menu of additional buttons you can display on a toolbar, click the **Toolbar Options** button at the right end of the toolbar.

Toolbar handle

Displayed (checked) toolbar

Toolbar Options button

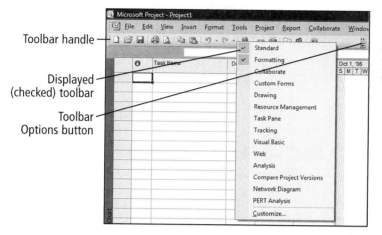

**Figure 2.4** Right-click a toolbar to see a menu that enables you to hide and display toolbars.

## Sheet and Chart and More

The Gantt Chart view consists of two sides with information (see Figure 2.5), and you need to understand how each side works in order to navigate and work comfortably in Project.

Select All button

Field name

Divider bar

Timescale

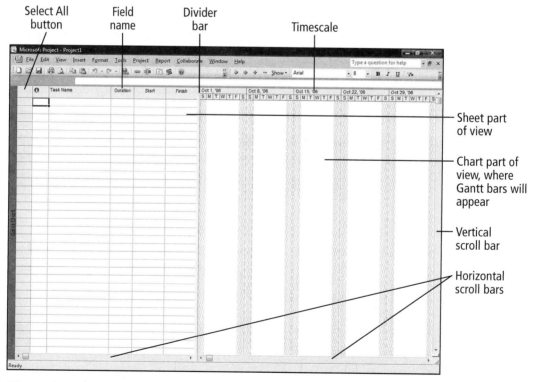

Sheet part of view

Chart part of view, where Gantt bars will appear

Vertical scroll bar

Horizontal scroll bars

**Figure 2.5** The Gantt Chart view offers two independent sides presenting information.

The left side holds a sheet portion of the view. Like a spreadsheet, a sheet view in Project divides information into rows and columns, with each bit of information held in an individual cell. The gray header cells across the top list the field or column names, which tell you what type of information appears in that column. The information for each task will appear on a single row, and when you add a task, its task ID number (task number) will appear in the gray row header cell to the left of the task name. You can click the **Select All** button where the row and column headings intersect (it's a plain gray box in the upper-left corner) to select all the cells in the sheet.

A *sheet* view holds a collection of rows and columns forming cells and resembles an Excel spreadsheet. The *field* or column name appears at the top of each column. Each row holds the information for a single task, and a *task ID number* (task number) appears to the left of the task name.

After you start adding tasks, a Gantt bar will appear for each task in the right side of the Gantt Chart view (see Figure 2.6). You can think of this side as the chart portion of the view. The timescale across the top of the view shows you the scheduled timeframe for each Gantt bar. This Gantt charting style has long been a preferred method of charting project schedules because it provides an easy way to see how tasks progress. By default, Project includes the name of the resource(s) assigned to each task beside the task Gantt bar, making it easier to identify which resources you need to follow up with as you manage the project.

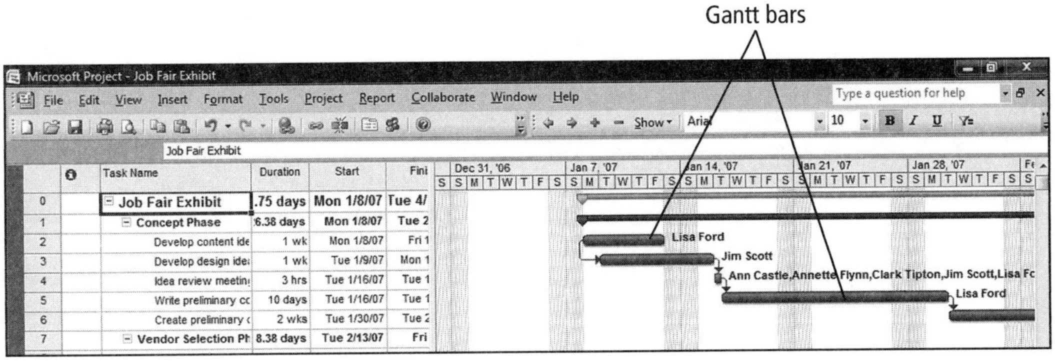

Gantt bars

**Figure 2.6** Gantt bars illustrate task schedules.

Notice in Figure 2.5 that the Gantt Chart view includes three scroll bars: the vertical scroll bar along the right and a horizontal scroll bar at the bottom of each side of the view. You can use the vertical scroll bar to scroll the project plan down and back up. The task sheet and Gantt bar information will stay in synch (on the same row) as you scroll up and down. You can use the horizontal scroll bars to scroll each pane to the right and back to the left.

## Displaying Gantt Chart Information with Scroll to Task and Go To

The first few times you engage in good planning and use Project to detail all the tasks necessary in a project, you might be surprised by how long the list is. Because Project gives you a central area for building the project plan, you can get a handle on projects of increasing complexity. You'll finally be able to illustrate all the work that goes into delivering the results that others in the organization want. Scrolling around through hundreds of tasks in a project plan consumes a lot of time, so Project provides some navigation shortcuts.

Scrolling down and clicking a task in the sheet portion of the Gantt Chart view doesn't automatically scroll the chart portion of the view to show the selected task's Gantt bar. This becomes a bothersome issue with projects that have a long overall timeframe. For example, you might have to scroll the chart portion of the view several pages to the right to see the Gantt bar for the task selected in the sheet pane at the left.

Project offers a Scroll to Task feature that enables you to snap the Gantt bar for any selected task into view in the chart pane of the Gantt Chart view. Here's how to use Scroll to Task:

1. Scroll down the project, if needed, and then click the task name of the task to select in the sheet (left) pane.
2. Press **Ctrl+Shift+F5**. Or, click the **Scroll to Task** button on the Standard toolbar. If the button doesn't appear on the toolbar due to your toolbar usage or screen resolution, click the **Toolbar Options** button for the Standard toolbar and then click the **Scroll to Task** button, shown in Figure 2.7.

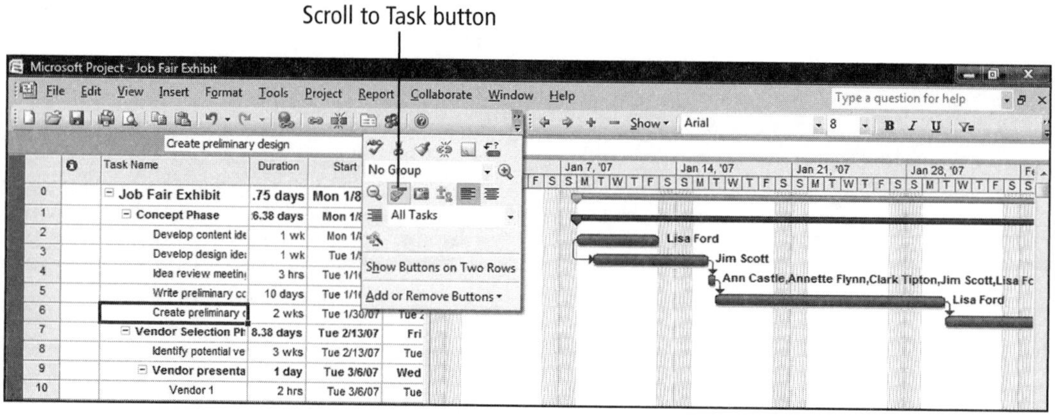

**Figure 2.7** Use the Scroll to Task button to display the Gantt bar for the selected task.

Figure 2.8 shows an example of how the Scroll to Task feature works. In the top portion of the figure, you can see that Task 6 is selected in the sheet, but its Gantt bar is not fully visible in the chart. The bottom portion of the figure shows how the view looks after Scroll to Task has been used to display Task 6's Gantt bar.

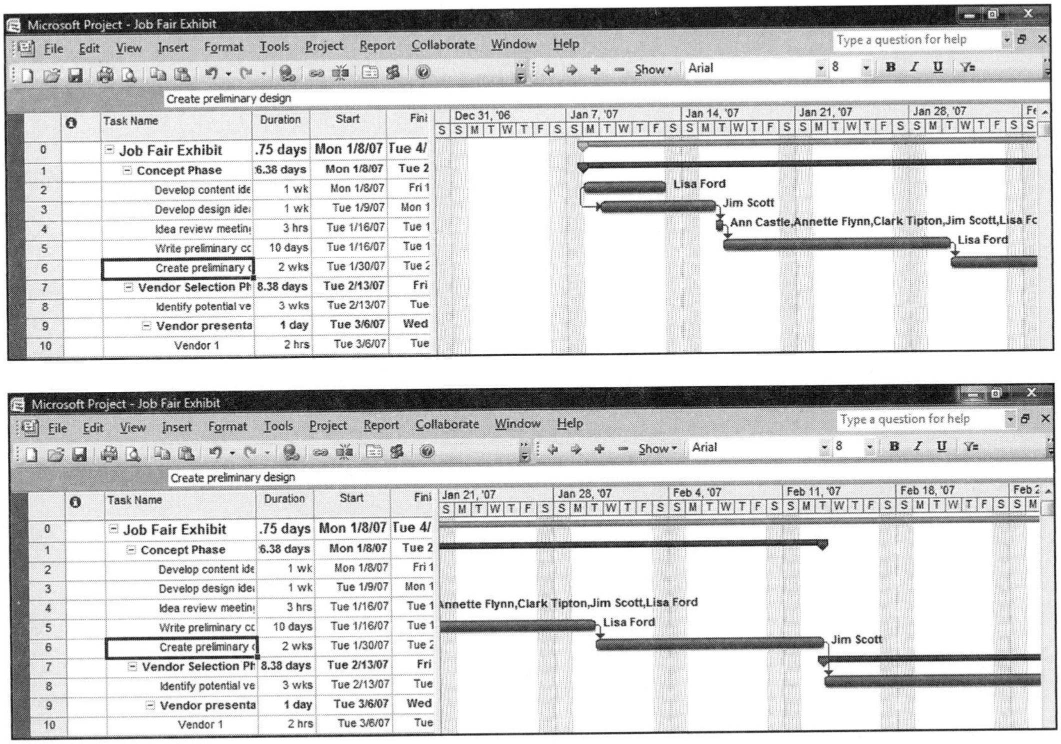

**Figure 2.8** Scroll to Task was used to display Task 6's Gantt bar (bottom).

Most beginning users are thrown by the fact that the chart portion of the Gantt Chart view doesn't automatically show the Gantt bar for the selected task. Get in the habit of pressing **Ctrl+Shift+F5** after you scroll the sheet portion of the view and click another task. That will ensure you're always seeing the Gantt bar for the current task.

The Go To feature enables you to jump to a task by entering its ID number. This process both shows the task's name in the sheet side of the Gantt Chart view and displays the task's Gantt bar in the chart side of the view. It can save a lot of time when you want to jump to a task that's either much later or much earlier in the project plan than the tasks you're currently viewing, because Project will scroll vertically to the task name and horizontally to its Gantt bar. To Go To a task:

1. Click the **Edit** menu and then click **Go To**. (Shortcut: **Ctrl+G** or **F5**.) The Go To dialog box appears.

You can display the Go To dialog box in most Office applications by pressing **F5**, so keep that handy shortcut key in mind.

2. Type the task ID number for the task that you want to select. As you can see in Figure 2.9, the number appears automatically in the ID text box of the Go To dialog box.

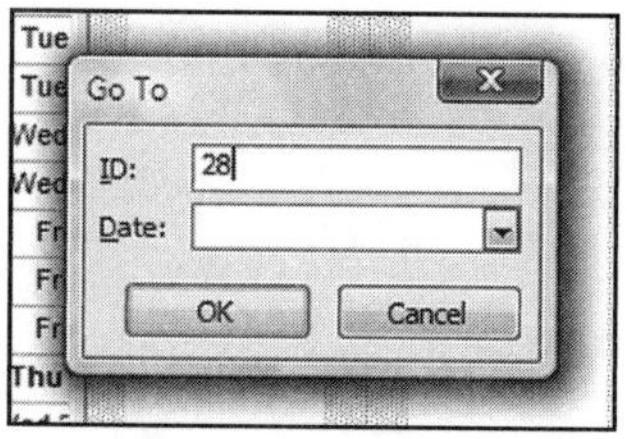

**Figure 2.9** Go To provides the fastest way to jump to a task—if you know the task ID.

3. Click **OK** or press **Enter**. Project displays the task row and its Gantt bar.

You can also use the Go To text box to scroll the chart portion of the Gantt Chart view to show the tasks scheduled on a particular date. In Step 2 above, enter the desired date in the Date text box and then click **OK**. Project scrolls the chart to the left or right to show the specified timeframe.

If you know all or part of a task's name and want to search by name, you can use the Find feature to jump to it. See "Saving Time with Find and Replace" in Chapter 9, "Enhancing Task and Resource Information," to learn how.

# Changing Views

In my years of conducting Project training classes and working one-on-one with Project users, I've learned that I can never emphasize finding and using Project views enough. The ability to display a view in Project takes on a great deal of importance because:

- Project stores or calculates dozens and dozens of fields of information. No single view can show all of this information onscreen at one time. So, as project manager, you need to be able to find the view that shows the information that you need to track and make decisions about your project.

- When you want to print information from Project, Project prints whatever view currently appears onscreen. So, as project manager, you need to be able to find the view that displays the information that team members and stakeholders need to see so that you can print and provide that information.

Although learning which view will work best for your needs in a given situation will take some time and exploration on your part, later parts of this book help by emphasizing what view to work in to perform project management activities and to find specific types of information. For example, when you want to see more detail about the tasks and schedules for individual resources, you can change to the Resource Usage view shown in Figure 2.10.

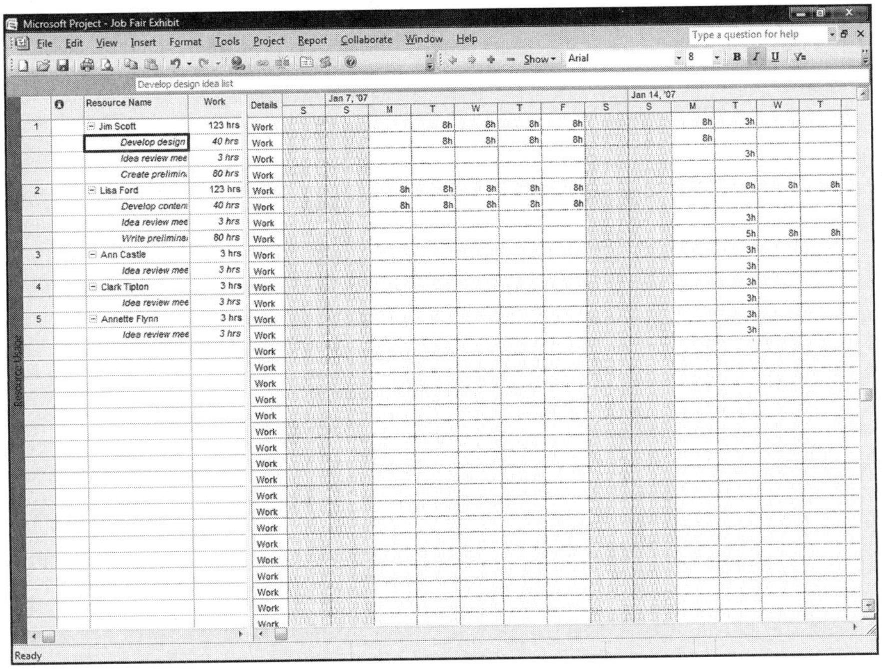

**Figure 2.10** You can change to the view that shows desired information, such as this Resource Sheet view.

Always remember that the View menu in Project (see Figure 2.11) serves as your home base for finding and working with the available views. Click **View** on the menu bar to open the View menu. The first eight choices in the View menu each represent a frequently used view. A check mark appears beside the name of the current view. You can click any of the views listed to display that view immediately. To display one of the many other views, use the More Views dialog box, discussed next.

| View | Insert | Format | Tools | Proje |
|---|---|---|---|---|
| | Calendar | | | |
| ✓ | Gantt Chart | | | |
| | Network Diagram | | | |
| | Task Usage | | | |
| | Tracking Gantt | | | |
| | Resource Graph | | | |
| | Resource Sheet | | | |
| | Resource Usage | | | |
| | More Views... | | | |
| | Table: Entry | | ▶ | |
| | Toolbars | | ▶ | |
| | Turn On Project Guide | | | |
| | View Bar | | | |
| | Hide Change Highlighting | | | |
| | Header and Footer... | | | |
| | Zoom... | | | |

**Figure 2.11** The View menu lists frequently used views and other viewing commands; click a view to display it.

If you don't mind giving up some of your screen real estate, you can display a View bar along the left side of the screen. The View bar includes an icon for each of the eight views listed at the top of the View menu, plus an icon for the More Views dialog box. Click an icon to display the view or open the dialog box. To display and hide the View Bar, click the **View Bar** command on the **View** menu.

## Using More Views

The More Views dialog box enables you to display any of the two dozen views built in to Project, as well as any custom views that you create to accommodate your project management and reporting needs. (Chapter 12, "Using and Printing Views," gives you the tools you need to go custom with views.) If the view that you want to display doesn't appear on the View menu, here's how you can access the view via the More Views dialog box:

1. Click **View** and then click **More Views**. The More Views dialog box appears.

2. Scroll down the Views list (see Figure 2.12) until you see the view you want.

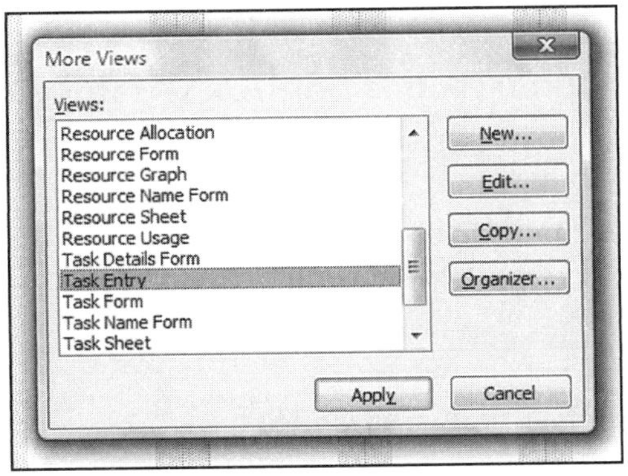

**Figure 2.12**
Choose a lesser-used view in the More Views dialog box.

3. Click the view in the Views list.

4. Click **Apply**. The dialog box closes and the view appears immediately.

## Changing Tables

One aspect of sheet views in Project differs significantly from working with a spreadsheet: the issue of tables. In Project, a table is a collection of different fields (columns) of information. For example, when you're entering new information about your tasks, you'll view an Entry table with basic task information (see the top of Figure 2.13). When you later want to review cost information on a task by task basis, you will want to see the Cost table (see the bottom of Figure 2.13). By offering different collections of fields as named tables, Project makes it easier for you to access and view the relevant fields (out of the dozens available) for particular project management tasks.

> The *table* controls which columns appear in a sheet. The default table for any sheet view is the Entry table.

You can move back and forth between the tables at will, rather than having to customize the sheet view or hide and redisplay columns. Use one of these methods to display the desired table:

- Click **View**, point to the **Table: (*Table Name*)** choice, and then click the name of the table to display.

- Right-click the **Select All** button and then click the table to display in the shortcut menu that appears (see Figure 2.14).

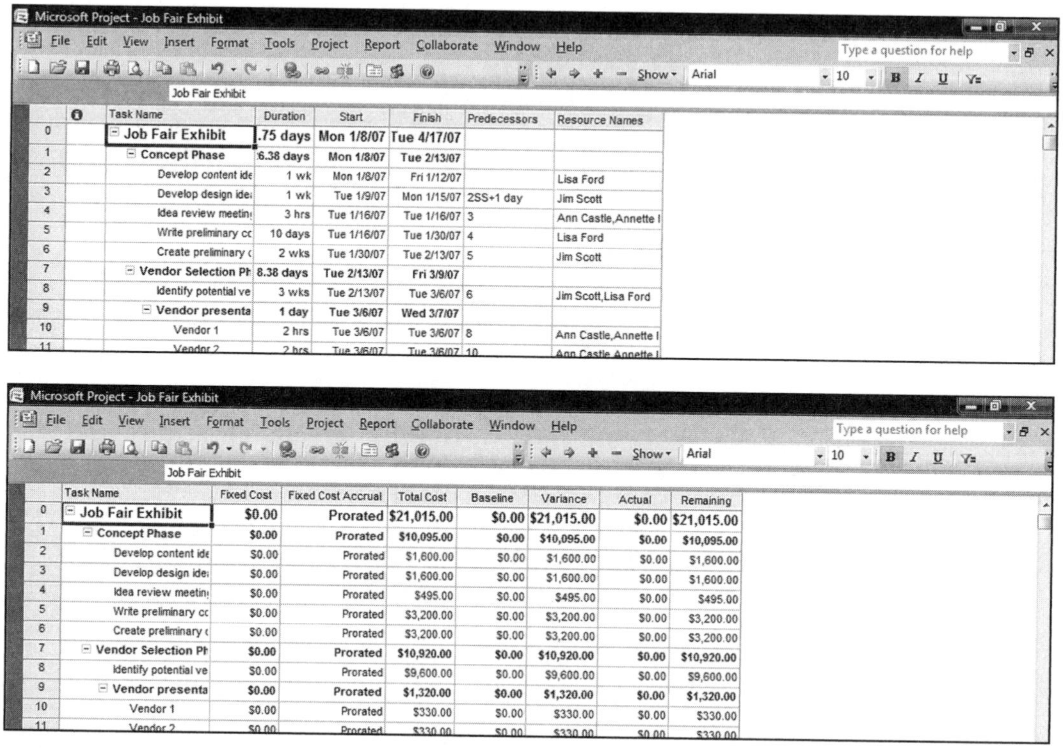

**Figure 2.13** This example compares the Entry table (top) and Cost table (bottom) in the Task Sheet view.

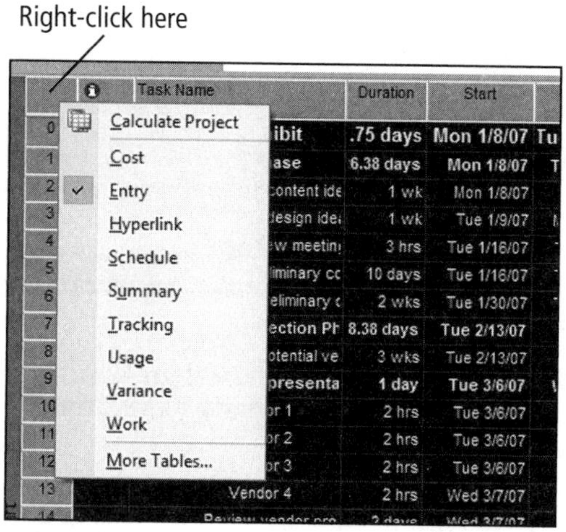

Right-click here

**Figure 2.14**
Choose another table from this shortcut menu.

Keep in mind that when you change to another table (or make changes to the fields shown in the table itself), those changes become part of the current view in the current file. So, if you will want to get back to the original view, keep notes about what changes you make, so that you can undo them later. Even better, create a custom table or custom view, as described in Chapter 12, "Using and Printing Views," so that you can always change back to the original table or view.

 Because the left portion of the Gantt Chart view contains a sheet, keep in mind that you can change the table shown at the left in the Gantt Chart view without affecting the contents of the chart side at the right.

# Using the Project Guide if You Get Stuck

Using Project is more like using a database program than a word processor. You have to do more than just type information, save, and print to get the full benefit from your effort. Because you'll be performing so many different project management tasks with Project, you might at some point need a refresher to remind you what to do next (that is, when you don't have this book handy).

Recent versions of Project, including Project 2007, include the Project Guide, a special help task pane with instructions and wizards designed to lead you through the entire process of planning and executing a project plan. If you forget how to schedule (link) tasks, for example, you can go to a Project Guide screen that enables you to create a specific type of link by clicking a button in the pane. If you forget how to specify working and non-working times for a resource, you can follow a link for help and guidance about doing that.

Because the Project Guide task pane consumes quite a bit of space onscreen, you may not want to keep it on, even if you use it often. This section explains both how to show and hide the Project Guide as needed and how to work with it to find help about next steps and procedures.

## Hiding and Redisplaying the Project Guide

The Project Guide does not appear onscreen by default. Because it is an element of the onscreen view, you use a command on the View menu to display (turn on) and close (turn off) the Project Guide as needed:

- To turn the Project Guide on, click **View** and then click **Turn On Project Guide**.
- To turn the Project Guide off, click **View** and then click **Turn Off Project Guide**.

When you turn the Project Guide on, it appears as both an added toolbar and a task pane, as shown in Figure 2.15. If you want to close (or redisplay) the Project Guide task pane but leave the Project Guide toolbar onscreen, click the Show/Hide Project Guide button at the far left end of the Project Guide toolbar.

Project Guide pane          Project Guide
 lists procedures              toolbar

![Screenshot of Microsoft Project showing the Project Guide task pane on the left and the Project Guide toolbar]

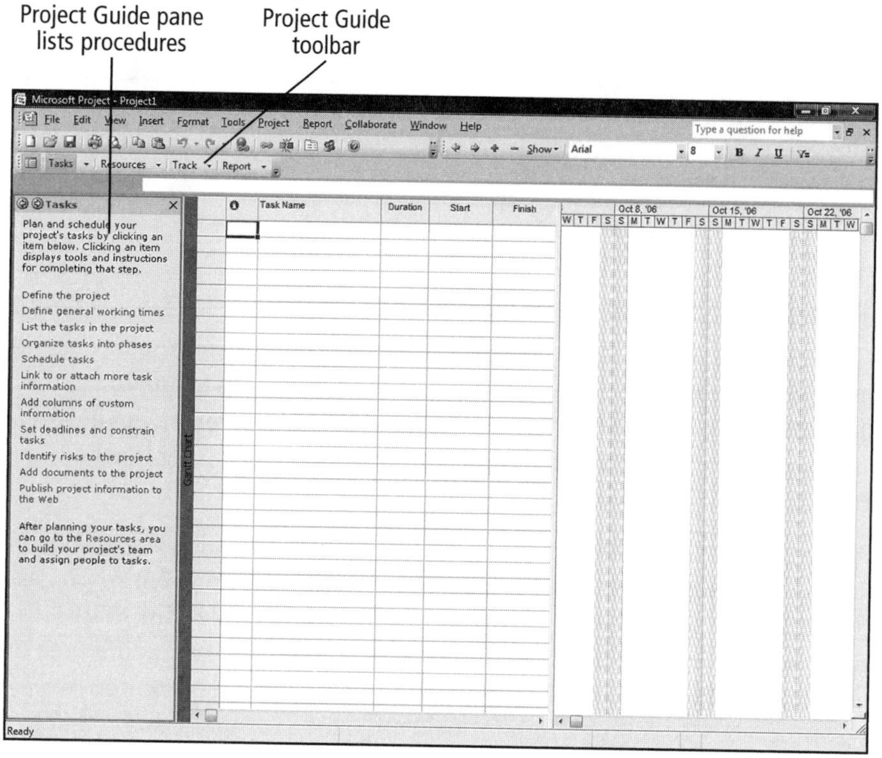

**Figure 2.15** The Project Guide includes links you can follow to get help with specific procedures.

You also can use the Options dialog box (more about it shortly) to turn the Project Guide on and off. Click the **Tools** menu and then click **Options.** Click the **Interface** tab, and check or clear the **Display Project Guide** check box as needed. Click **OK.** When the Project Guide is turned off via this method or the View menu, you cannot show and hide its toolbar because the toolbar name doesn't appear on the shortcut menu. You must first turn the Project Guide back on.

## How the Project Guide Works

The buttons on the Project Guide toolbar identify the overall functional areas about which you can get help in the Project Guide: Tasks, Resources, Track, and Report. To complete the planning, execution, and control phases of managing a project, you can complete each of the operations listed within those functional areas in the order in which they appear in the Project Guide. In other words, you can complete all the Tasks operations, complete all the Resources operations, complete all the Track operations, and then complete all the Report operations to finish your project.

Chances are you won't use the Project Guide from front to back like that but will instead dip into and out of the Project Guide when you get stuck. In that case, you can move around in the Project Guide as needed. When you click one of the four buttons on the Project Guide toolbar, the Project Guide task pane changes to list the specific help items in that category. For example, if you click the **Track** button, the task pane changes to display the list of project tracking tasks shown in Figure 2.16.

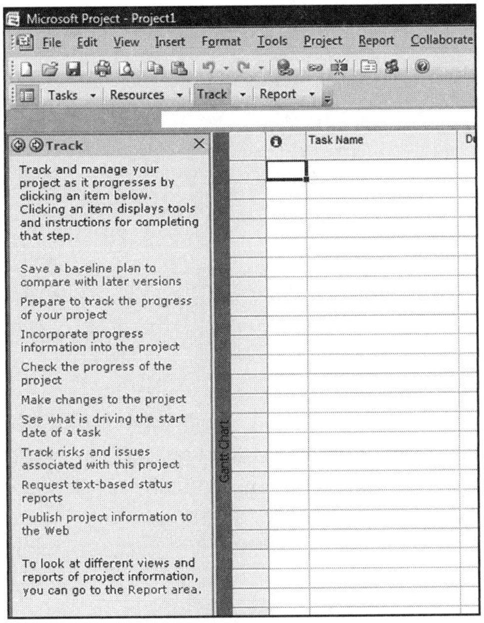

**Figure 2.16** Click a button on the Project Guide toolbar to display the items in that functional area.

When you see the specific task that you need help with in the Project Guide task pane, click the task link. The Project Guide will change to display more specific choices about how to proceed, and it might even change the Project view as needed to perform the specified operation. For example, Figure 2.17 shows what happens when you click **Resources** on the Project Guide toolbar and then click the **Specify People and Equipment for the Project**

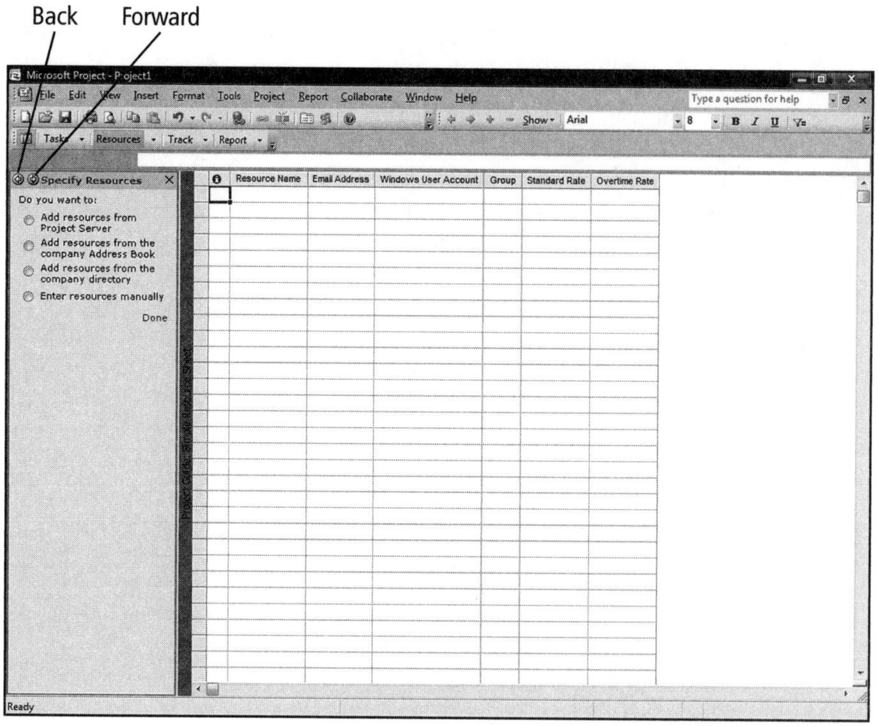

Back    Forward

Figure 2.17 The Project Guide leads you through the procedure and might even change views.

link in the Project Guide task pane. The Project Guide task pane prompts you for more information and the view changes to a variation of the Resource Sheet view, where you enter resource information.

If you've hidden the Project Guide task pane, click the drop-down list arrow beside any of the Project Guide toolbar buttons to see the procedures for that category, and then click the procedure for which you want help to unhide the task pane and display that item.

Follow the prompts as displayed in the Project Guide. For example, clicking **Enter Resources Manually**, as shown in Figure 2.17, would display additional links. Keep following along, clicking options and links until you finish the procedure at hand, and then click **Done**. You can also click the **Back** or **Forward** buttons in the upper-left corner of the Project Guide task pane to navigate through the current procedure.

## Other Help

Like other programs, Project offers a comprehensive Help system. In the case of Project 2007, the Help system automatically blends information installed with Project on your system with information from the Microsoft Office Online Web site (assuming your system has a live Internet connection) to provide you the most current, detailed help available.

The **Type a Question for Help** text box at the right end of the Project menu bar provides the fastest avenue for searching for help. Click in that text box, type a search question or topic, and then press **Enter**. Project opens the Project Help window, searches Help, and displays matching results, as you can see in the example in Figure 2.18.

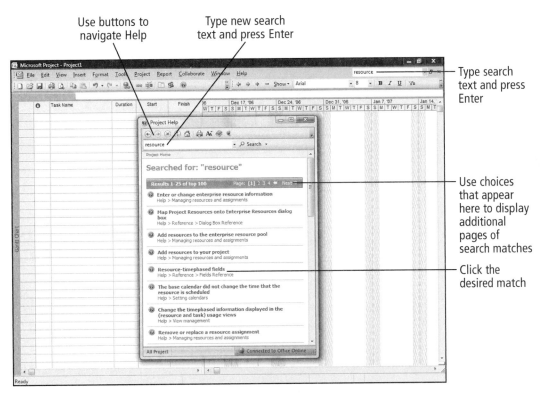

**Figure 2.18** Search for help right from the menu bar.

You can then click the matching Help topic for more detailed information. If that information doesn't answer your question, you can click the **Back** button in the Project Help window to navigate back to the search results and then click another match. If page number links and Next buttons appear above the list of search results, you can click one of those to display additional pages of matching Help topics. If you don't find the answer to your question, you can type another search question or topic in the text box in the Project Help window and press **Enter** to try another search.

If you prefer to browse for help, click **Help** and then click **Microsoft Office Project Help** or click the **Help** button on the Standard toolbar. With this method, the Project Help window displays a list of topics that you can browse, as shown in Figure 2.19. Click links in the Project Help window to review Help information, and use the navigation buttons at the top of the window to move around.

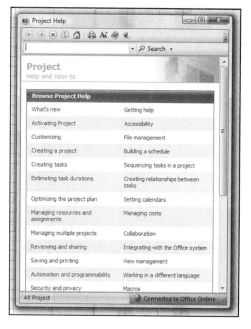

**Figure 2.19**
Browse common Help topics.

When you finish working in Help, click the Project Help window's **Close** (X) button to close the window.

 The top of the Project Help window includes buttons for printing the currently displayed information in the window and for changing the text (font) size for the text in the Project Help window, among others.

# Finding and Using Project's Options

In many computer books, the section about setting program options is buried at the end of the book, typically as a final chapter or appendix. That's because in many other programs, program options apply to the program as a whole and are items that the typical user might never need to change.

Project's Options dialog box has settings that apply to both the program as a whole and the current project plan file. Some of these settings are even important to a project plan's schedule setup or affect how particular features in Project work. For example, you can specify whether Project recalculates the schedule automatically after each change that you make, or you can choose to recalculate only when you do so manually. You can change other settings to control the default task type, which impacts scheduling, or whether a new task you insert is automatically linked to the tasks above and below it. Because options in Project have such an impact on program behavior as well as appearance, you need to know early on how to find the Options dialog box, how to determine which settings apply to the program versus the current file, and how various settings will impact your work.

To open the Options dialog box, click the **Tools** menu and then click **Options**. The Options dialog box, which has 11 tabs of settings, appears. Click a tab to display its options and make choices as needed, and then click **OK** to apply those choices and close the dialog box. Don't worry too much about specific options right now. I'll cover those as you need to know about them later in the book.

If you're using Project Professional 2007, you'll see a Local Project Cache and Enterprise Options command on the Tools menu. Unless you're connected to a server and have set up Project Professional to connect with a particular project on Project Server, you won't be able to use these commands and can disregard them.

On particular tabs, the Options dialog box groups related commands according to whether they apply to the Project program as a whole or to just the current file. Options falling under a heading reading *Tab Name* **Options for Microsoft Office Project** (see Figure 2.20) apply to the program. Options falling under a heading reading *Tab Name* **Options for '***File Name***'** apply to the current file. If neither heading appears, the options on the tab apply to the program.

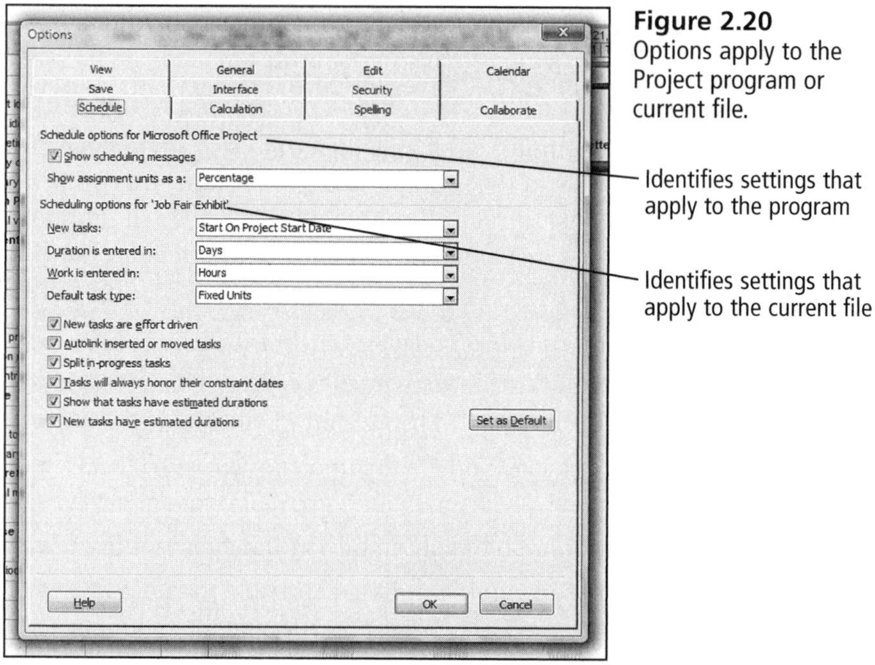

**Figure 2.20**
Options apply to the Project program or current file.

Identifies settings that apply to the program

Identifies settings that apply to the current file

# What's New in Project 2007

Even though this book was developed to appeal to brand new Project users who won't know a new feature from an existing feature, the software team that developed Project worked hard on new features that make Project an even better tool. I share the team's enthusiasm for those new features, so I'm tipping you off to them now. I'll cover many of these features in more detail as they apply later in the book:

**Multiple levels of Undo.** If you're a first-time Project user, you're lucky to be using the first version where—as in many other applications—you can undo more than just the most recent change you've made. Project 2007 now enables you to use the Undo button on the Standard toolbar to undo multiple previous changes at once. Cue "Hallelujah" Chorus.

**Change highlighting.** When you make a change that affects schedule information, Project highlights the cells with the information you changed as well as any other resulting schedule changes in the Task Sheet so that you can make sure you are comfortable with the rescheduling.

**Cell highlighting.** Project now enables you to fill any cell with a background color to call attention to the information in that cell.

| | ❶ | Task Name | Duration | Start | Fini |
|---|---|---|---|---|---|
| 0 | | ⊟ Job Fair Exhibit | .75 days | Mon 1/8/07 | Tue 4/ |
| 1 | | ⊟ Concept Phase | 1.38 days | Mon 1/8/07 | Tue 2 |
| 2 | | Develop content ide | 2 wks | Mon 1/8/07 | Fri 1 |
| 3 | | Develop design ide | 2 wks | Tue 1/9/07 | Mon 1 |
| 4 | | Idea review meeting | 3 hrs | Tue 1/23/07 | Tue 1 |
| 5 | | Write preliminary cc | 10 days | Tue 1/23/07 | Tue |
| 6 | | Create preliminary ( | 2 wks | Tue 2/6/07 | Tue 2 |
| 7 | | ⊟ Vendor Selection Ph | 8.38 days | Tue 2/20/07 | Fri 3 |
| 8 | | Identify potential ve | 3 wks | Tue 2/20/07 | Tue 3 |
| 9 | | ⊟ Vendor presenta | 1 day | Tue 3/13/07 | Wed 3 |
| 10 | | Vendor 1 | 2 hrs | Tue 3/13/07 | Tue 3 |
| 11 | | Vendor 2 | 2 hrs | Tue 3/13/07 | Tue 3 |
| 12 | | Vendor 3 | 2 hrs | Tue 3/13/07 | Wed 3 |
| 13 | | Vendor 4 | 2 hrs | Wed 3/14/07 | Wed 3 |
| 14 | | Review vendor pro | 2 days | Wed 3/14/07 | Fri 3 |
| 15 | | Vendor selection m | 2 hrs | Fri 3/16/07 | Fri 3 |
| 16 | | Sign vendor contra | 1 hr | Fri 3/16/07 | Fri 3 |
| 17 | | ⊟ Production Phase | 8.38 days | Fri 3/16/07 | Thu 4 |
| 18 | | Finalize content | 3 days | Fri 3/16/07 | Wed 3 |
| 19 | | Provide content to v | 1 hr | Wed 3/21/07 | Wed 3 |
| 20 | | Provide preliminary | 1 hr | Wed 3/21/07 | Wed 3 |
| 21 | | Vendor design refi | 1 wk | Thu 3/22/07 | Wed 3 |
| 22 | | Design approval me | 1 hr | Thu 3/29/07 | Thu 3 |
| 23 | | Fabrication | 2 wks | Thu 3/29/07 | Thu 4 |
| 24 | | ⊟ Completion Phase | 8.63 days | Thu 4/12/07 | Tue 4 |
| 25 | | Final review | 3 days | Thu 4/12/07 | Tue 4 |
| 26 | | Corrections period | 1 wk | Tue 4/17/07 | Tue 4 |
| 27 | | Delivery | 4 hrs | Tue 4/24/07 | Tue 4 |
| 28 | | Payment | 1 hr | Tue 4/24/07 | Tue 4 |

**Figure 2.21** Project highlights changes that result from a user entry.

**Task drivers.** You can display a special task pane that shows resource constraints and other factors affecting a task's schedule. This new feature can help with decision-making and project control.

**Visual reports.** If you want to chart your Project data in Excel or Visio, you can do so via this new feature.

**Cost resources.** A new type of resource called a cost resource enables you to better assign planned and actual cost settings and integrate Project data with your accounting system.

**Top-down budgeting.** View costs for the project as a whole using the project summary task.

**Enhancements to the Calendar and Gantt Chart views.** Both the Calendar and Gantt Chart views feature design changes, such as 3-D Gantt bars, to make them more attractive and readable. The Calendar view also offers easier, more flexible setup choices.

## More Project Resources

You learned about the Web site for the Project Management Institute in Chapter 1. You can go to that site to learn more about the field of project management. If you want to reach out for help and resources about using Microsoft Project that go beyond the information offered in the Project Help system, check out these online resources:

- **microsoft.public.project.** If you are familiar with Usenet newsgroups, this one in particular provides a robust exchange of information between project users from beginner to professional level. If you post a question here, you'll typically see an answer posted back within a few hours. You can access this group through any news server or news reader services.

- **www.mvps.org/project.** This is the Web site for the Microsoft Most Valuable Professionals (MVPs), a group of "power" Project professionals. This site lists answers to common questions, links to companion products and downloads, and information about higher-level topics such as Project Server.

- **www.mympa.org.** This is the Web site for the leading professional association for Microsoft Office Project users. Joining this organization enables you to take advantage of educational opportunities and chances to network with other professionals who use Project.

- **office.microsoft.com/en-us/project/default.aspx and support.microsoft.com.** These two resources enable you to search for even more detailed help about Microsoft Project, direct from Microsoft, and to download updates and files such as templates to enhance your work in Project.

Project can be modified to perform some functions for which you wouldn't normally use it by installing third-party add-in programs. However, these solutions are typically expensive and implemented on a company-wide basis. Project also can be customized via VBA programming, one of the specialties of this book's technical editor, Jack Dahlgren. You can search directory.partners.extranet.microsoft.com/project/ProjectPartners.aspx to learn more about options for expanding Microsoft Project's capabilities.

## Chapter Review

This chapter gave you your first real look at the Microsoft Office Project 2007 program. It showed you how to start and exit Project, how to find your way around in the Gantt Chart view, and how to change to another view. You also saw how to use the Project Guide and the Help system to work your way through all aspects of building a project plan and to get answers to your specific Project questions. Finally, the chapter gave you a glimpse of the new features in this version of Project and shared information about other online resources you can take advantage of to expand and enhance your use of Project. Complete the Review Questions and Projects now to reinforce what you've learned before moving on to the next chapter.

## Review Questions

Write your answers to the following questions on a sheet of paper.

1. Name one way each to start and exit Project.
2. One or more _____ appear below the menu bar and offer buttons you can click to perform actions in Project rather than having to choose menu commands.
3. To show or hide a toolbar, do this:
4. The _____ appears at the top of each column in a sheet view.
5. When you add a task, its _____ appears in the row header cell to the left of the task name.
6. Access one of the eight most-used views on the _____ menu.
7. What is a table in Project?
8. The _____ can walk you through the procedures for creating and executing your project plan file with Project.
9. The text box where you can enter a phrase or topic to search for in Help is found here:
   a. Status bar
   b. Help bar
   c. Menu bar
   d. Toolbar
10. Name one new feature in this version of Project.

## Projects

### Project 1

1. Start Microsoft Project.
2. Right-click a toolbar and then click **Tracking**. The Tracking toolbar appears.
3. Right-click a toolbar and then click **Tracking** again. The Tracking toolbar disappears.

4. Click in the first cell in the Task name field and type **Practice**. Notice how the row number (task ID number) appears to the left of the row.

5. Click **File** and then click **Exit**.

6. Click **No** when Project asks whether to save your changes to the file.

## *Project 2*

1. Open the Start menu.

2. Type **Project**. A list of matching files and applications appears.

3. Drag the **Microsoft Office Project 2007** choice from the Start menu to the desktop.

4. Press the **Esc** key to close the Start menu.

5. Double-click the new Project shortcut to start Project.

6. Click **View** and then click **Calendar**. The Calendar view appears.

7. Click **View** and then click **Resource Sheet**. The Resource Sheet view appears.

8. Right-click the **Select All** button and click **Work**. The Work table appears in the Resource Sheet view.

9. Right-click the **Select All** button again and click **Entry**. The Entry (default) table reappears in the Resource Sheet.

10. Use the View menu to redisplay the Gantt Chart view.

## *Project 3*

1. Click **View** and then click **Turn On Project Guide**.

2. Click the **Report** button on the Project Guide toolbar. Review the list of procedures that appears in the Project Guide task pane.

3. Click **Tasks** on the Project Guide toolbar.

4. Click the **List the Tasks in the Project Link**.

5. Review the information that appears in the Project Guide task pane.

6. Click **View** and then click **Turn Off Project Guide**.

7. Click in the **Type a Question for Help** text box, type **how do I print?**, and then press **Enter**.

8. Click a Help topic in the Project Help window. If a listing of additional topics appears, click a topic in that listing.

9. Review the information that appears in the Help window and then click the window's **Close** button to close Help.

10. Exit Project using the method of your choice.

# CHAPTER 3

# JUMP START: CREATE AND MANAGE A PROJECT

This Chapter Teaches You How To:

- Make a custom calendar
- Set the project start date and calendar
- Add a list of tasks
- Outline and link tasks to build the schedule
- Add and assign resources in the schedule
- Save a baseline snapshot of the plan
- Track completed work
- Use views and reports to communicate

If you really, really can't wait and work through the contents of a book to get a grasp of how to work in Microsoft Office Project 2007, then you might just like this chapter. Here you'll find a hands-on overview of how to use Project to build and track a project plan. If you take the time to sit down and follow the steps presented here, you'll have a better sense of where Project provides the greatest benefits to you as project manager and what you can expect in terms of using Project to manage a live plan in your organization.

In the example project, you will be playing the role of the leader of a team that needs to develop and implement a process change in a manufacturing environment. You will set up the project plan file, add tasks (the right way!), determine the project schedule, and identify and assign resources. You will move on to save a record of the original plan, track work against the plan, and use views and reports to access information for control and communications. So, when you've got a free hour or two to have some quality time with this book and Microsoft Project, dig in and get started!

 To see the finished solution file created by completing this chapter, go to www.courseptr.com, click the **Downloads** link in the navigation bar at the top, type **Microsoft Office Project 2007 Survival Guide** in the search text box, and then click **Search Downloads**.

## Create Your Project Calendar

Every organization has its own working hours. Many organizations follow a 40-hour work week with 8 a.m. to 5 p.m. working hours. Other companies work on a 24/7 schedule, or have shifts with various starting times. For Project to schedule work correctly in your project plan, you have to tell the program what working schedule your organization or the team involved in the project follows. This is called setting the **base calendar** for the project plan.

Project comes with three different calendars built in. However, none of these calendars have any holidays marked. So, *every* project plan file you create will require that you create a custom calendar reflecting scheduled nonworking days in your company.

You don't have to build a calendar from scratch. Because you can modify one of Project's existing calendars, creating the custom calendar usually doesn't take long. We'll assume the fictional team members working on your example project for this chapter are all on a regular 40-hour work week, so we'll simply copy the Standard calendar in Project and make our changes to the calendar copy.

So, time to start up Project and save your new file; then you'll move on and create the custom calendar:

1. Click the **Start button** on the Windows taskbar, click **All Programs**, click **Microsoft Office**, and then **Microsoft Office Project 2007** to start the Project program. It opens with a new, blank file called *Project1*.

2. Click **File** and then click **Save**. (Shortcuts: **Save** button on the Standard toolbar, **Ctrl+S**.) The Save As dialog box appears.

3. Type **Process Change** in the File Name text box, as shown in Figure 3.1. In this instance you are not changing the save location for the file. You are saving the file in the default *Documents* (Windows Vista) or *My Documents* folder on your system.

4. Click **Save**. Project displays the new file name in the title bar.

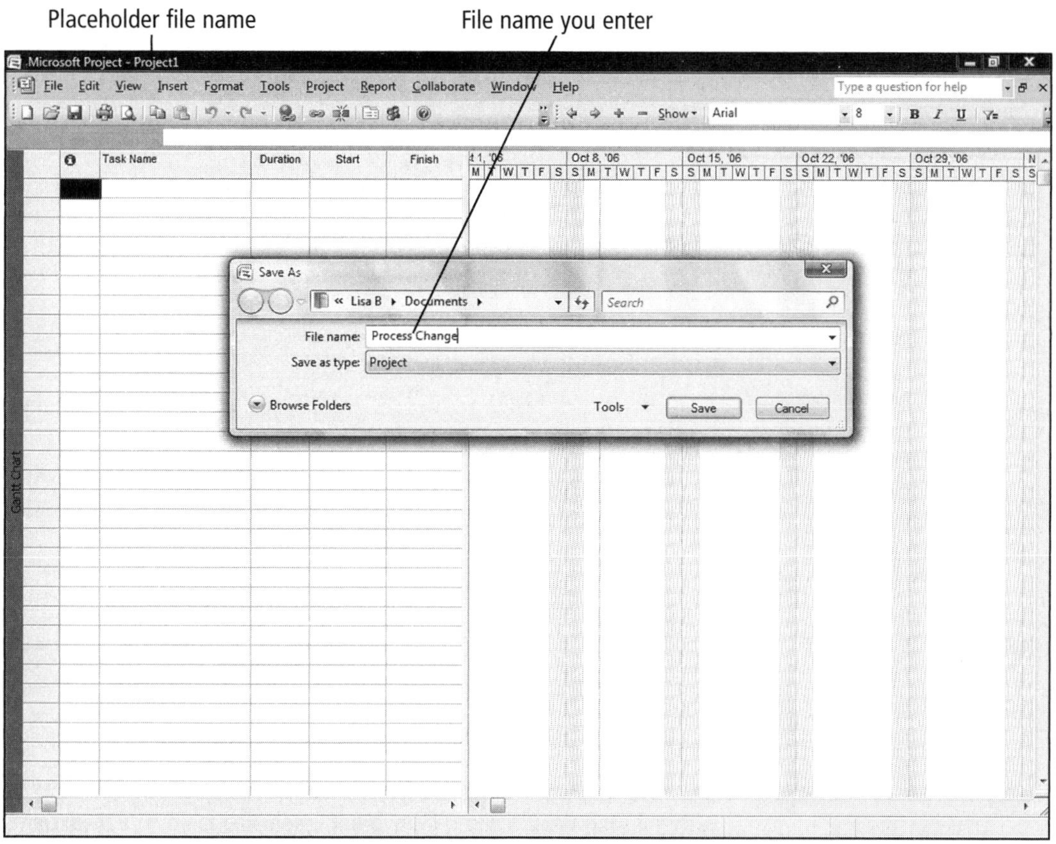

Placeholder file name          File name you enter

**Figure 3.1** Saving your new project plan in a file.

Now, make a copy of the Standard calendar in Project and make changes to the custom calendar:

1. Click **Tools** and then click **Change Working Time**.

2. Click the **Create New Calendar** button in the upper-right corner of the Change Working Time dialog box.

3. In the Create New Base Calendar dialog box that appears, first make sure that the calendar to copy is selected from the **Make a Copy of** *(name)* **Calendar** drop-down list (see Figure 3.2). If it's not, click the drop-down list and then click the calendar you want to copy.

4. Type **Process Change Calendar** into the **Name** text box. That is the name for your custom calendar.

5. Click **OK**. This takes you back to the Change Working Time dialog box. The For Calendar drop-down list now displays *Process Change Calendar*. The changes you make next will be saved into the custom *Process Change Calendar*.

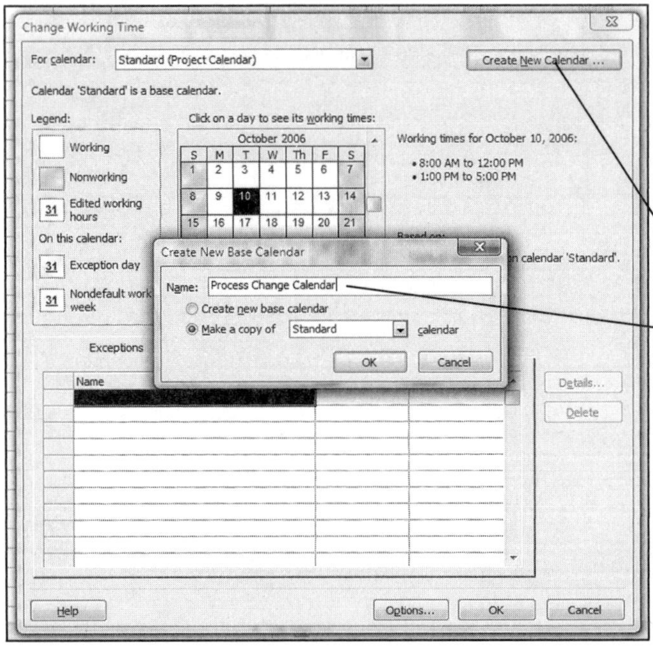

**Figure 3.2** Copying the Standard calendar to create a custom calendar named *Process Change Calendar.*

Click to create custom calendar

Enter custom calendar name

6. Use the scroll bar beside the calendar in the middle of the dialog box to scroll down (forward) to **May 2009**.

> This book assumes you are working prior to May 2009. If you are working at a later time, adjust all dates to refer to similar dates in 2010 or beyond.

7. Click the box for May 25 (**25**) on the calendar.

8. Click the first cell in the Name column on the **Exceptions** tab below the calendar, type **Memorial Day**, and press **Tab**.

9. Click the next blank cell in the Name column. This finishes marking May 25, 2009 as a nonworking day (see Figure 3.3) in the custom *Process Change Calendar* calendar.

10. Scroll the calendar to **July 2009**.

11. Click the box for July 3 (**3**) on the calendar.

12. Click the next cell in the Name column on the **Exceptions** tab below the calendar, type **July 4 Holiday**, and press **Tab**.

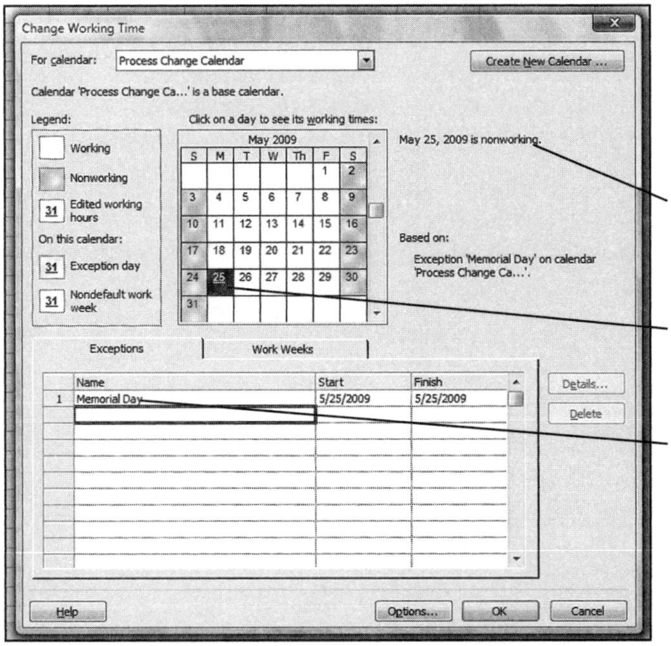

**Figure 3.3** May 25, 2009 has been marked a nonworking holiday named *Memorial Day*.

List of nonworking days

Nonworking day marked on calendar

Name of nonworking day

> If a nonworking day is an annual holiday, you can click its name on the Exceptions tab and click the **Details** button to open the Details for 'Exception Name' dialog box. Click the **Yearly** option under Recurrence Pattern, and then use the settings in the Range of Recurrence section of the dialog box to specify the number of years for which the date will be marked as a holiday. Click **OK** to return to the Change Working Time dialog box.

13. Click the next blank cell in the Name column. This finishes marking July 3, 2009 as a nonworking day (see Figure 3.4) in the custom *Process Change Calendar* calendar.

14. Click **OK**. Project finishes saving your custom *Process Change Calendar* in the *Process Change* file. The calendar isn't active in the file, yet. You'll learn to apply the calendar in the next section.

> If you choose a calendar or working hours that are different from a standard 40-hour, 8 a.m.–5 p.m. work week, you also need to change schedule options in Project to ensure tasks will be scheduled correctly. To learn more about this and techniques such as making a custom calendar available to all your project plan files so that you only need to set up your custom calendar once, see Chapter 4.

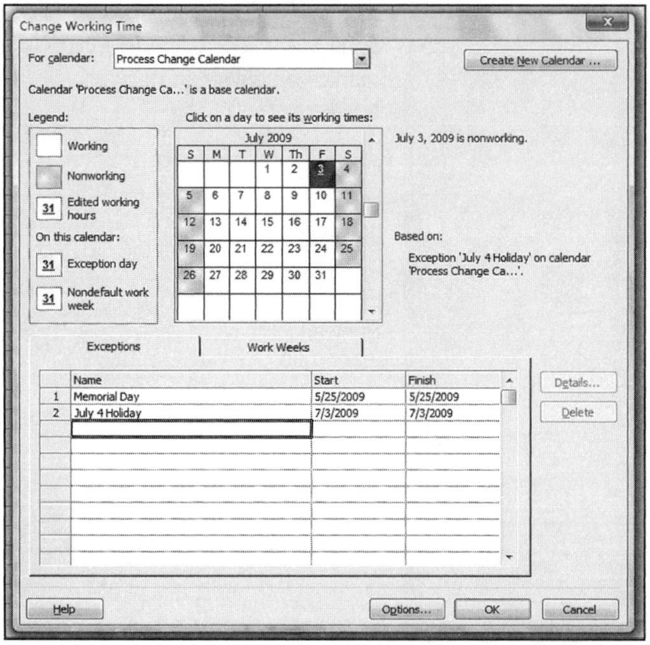

**Figure 3.4**  July 3, 2009 has been marked a nonworking holiday named *July 4 Holiday*.

## Choose Overall Project Parameters

Microsoft Project assumes that, like any good project manager, you are planning your projects well in advance of the beginning of work, so you have time to thoroughly vet your plan and seek and receive the needed approvals for the schedule and budget.

Because you're planning in advance, you need to specify in a project file when the work will begin on the project—the project **start date**. Doing so enables Project to build the schedule from the designated starting date automatically so that you don't have to enter later starting dates manually. You specify the starting date for every project plan file by using the Project Information dialog box. You also use this dialog box to specify the calendar that the project will follow.

The example process change project that you're creating will begin on May 1, 2009, the date that your imaginary boss specified. The project also needs to follow the *Process Change Calendar* custom calendar that you created earlier so that Project takes into account the holidays that you marked when you created that custom calendar. Choose both of those settings for your project now:

1. Still working in your *Process Change* file in Project, click **Project** and then click **Project Information**. The Project Information dialog box appears.
2. Click the drop-list arrow for the **Start Date** text box.

3. In the pop-up calendar that appears, click the right arrow button to the right of the month and year as many times as needed to display **May, 2009** at the top of the calendar (see Figure 3.5).

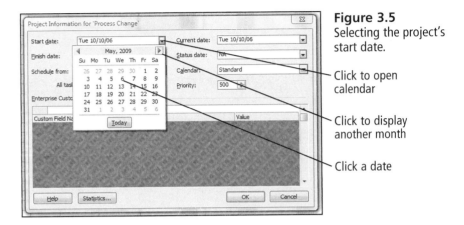

**Figure 3.5**
Selecting the project's start date.

Click to open calendar

Click to display another month

Click a date

4. Click the **1** (for May 1, 2009) on the calendar. The calendar closes and **Fri 5/1/09** appears in the Start Date text box in the dialog box.

Although you can type dates directly into text boxes, using the pop-up calendar ensures that you won't specify a weekend date accidentally.

5. Click the **Calendar** drop-down list arrow and then click **Process Change Calendar** (see Figure 3.6). This selects the custom calendar to be the calendar used by the project file.

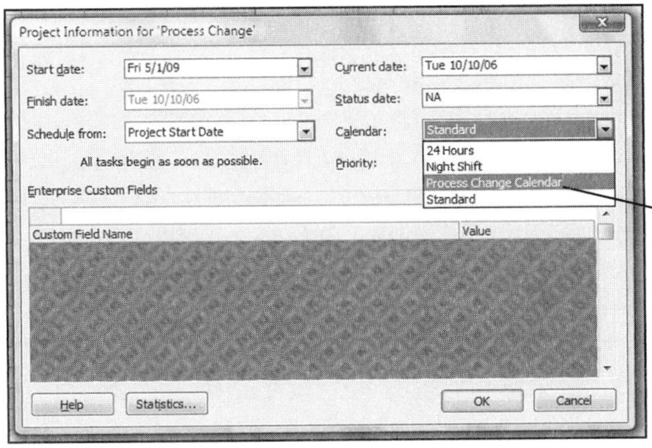

**Figure 3.6**
Assigning the custom calendar to the project file.

Choose the project calendar

6. Click **OK**. Project applies the specified start date and your custom calendar to the project file. You can verify that this happens because the timescale in the right pane of the Gantt Chart view scrolls to display the week including May 1, 2009, as shown in Figure 3.7.

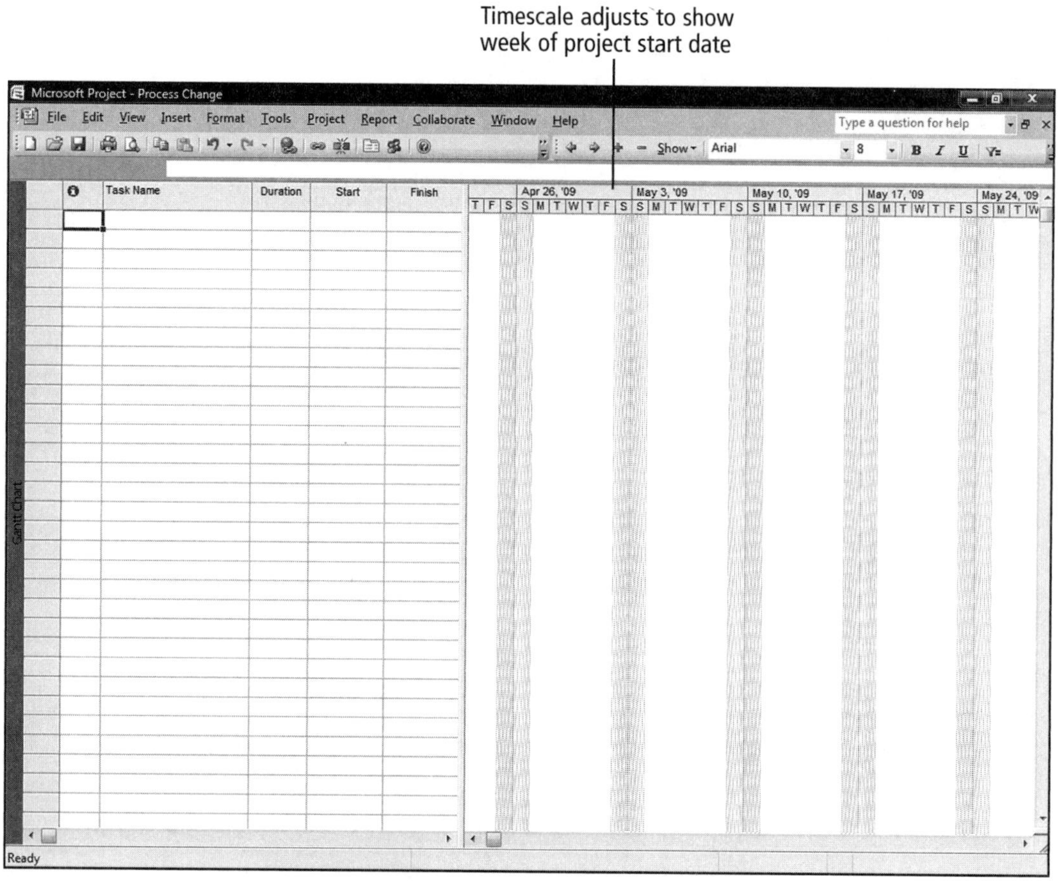

Timescale adjusts to show
week of project start date

**Figure 3.7** The view changes to display the week including May 1, 2009.

You now have established the fundamental information that Project needs to schedule your project plan correctly. You've told Project that the *Process Change* project should be scheduled to begin on May 1, 2009, and that the project will follow the *Process Change Calendar* custom calendar that you created. Save your work, and then move on to start listing what will be done during the course of your project.

# Add Tasks

After you establish the project start date and calendar, you can begin to identify the specific work that will be completed in order to produce the goals and deliverables for the project. If the deliverable for our example project is "Implement a process change," then it's your job as project manager to determine whether it will take 10, 20, or 200 tasks to complete the job and what each of those steps will consist of.

Each task should be as discrete as possible so that you can accurately track work against that completed task. For example, say part of a project involves writing a newsletter. If the newsletter consists of five articles and each is being written by a different person, then listing the individual articles as tasks gives you a clearer picture of the work than simply listing a single "Write Newsletter" task.

When you're trying to break tasks down to an appropriate level, think ahead to how you might assign the work on that task. If your gut is telling you that several people will need to work on something you're thinking of as a "task," then look at that activity again to see if it needs to be broken down further so that one or two people can handle each smaller part.

You will build the list of tasks for the project in the Task Sheet in the left pane of the Gantt Chart view. Even though the default table in the sheet portion of the Gantt Chart view contains multiple fields (columns), you will only make entries for each task in the *Task Name* and *Duration* fields.

Repeat: ONLY make entries in the *Task Name* and *Duration* fields.

While Chapter 5 provides more details about entering tasks, trust me for now that you'll be taking better advantage of Project's capabilities if you avoid typing in dates for tasks. The *Task Name* field identifies the name of each task, and the *Duration* field indicates how much time you think each task will take to complete in hours, days, or weeks, for example.

The example *Process Change* project requires that you enter a number of tasks into the Task Sheet pane at the left side of the Gantt Chart view. Table 3.1 lists the entries you should make for each task in the *Task Name* and *Duration* columns, starting from the first row of the sheet. Type the *Duration* entries exactly as shown. Note that some of the tasks will not have *Duration* field entries. You'll see why that is in the next section.

For now, make the entries listed in Table 3.1 into the *Process Change* file. You can press **Enter** or **Tab** after you make each cell entry, and use the arrow keys to move around between cells, as well. If the table shows no *Duration* field entry for a task, leave that field blank.

**Table 3.1**  Task Entries for *Process Change* File

| Task Name Field | Duration Field |
| --- | --- |
| *Preliminaries* | |
| Identify affected departments | 1w |
| Identify department representatives | 1d |
| Planning meeting to discuss process change | 4h |
| *Development* | |
| Review existing process | 2w |
| Develop list of proposed process changes | 2w |
| Send proposal to department representatives | 2h |
| Incorporate feedback | 1w |
| *Implementation Planning* | |
| White board new process | 1d |
| Role play new process | 3d |
| Refine new process adding role play changes | 2d |
| Develop implementation schedule | 1w |
| Provide implementation plan to department representatives | 2h |
| Resolve open issues or questions | 3d |
| *Document new process* | |
| ISO procedures | 2w |
| Work instructions | 3w |
| Establish training schedule | 2d |
| Perform employee training | 2w |
| Launch new process | 2d |
| Adjust documentation | 1w |
| Retrain | 1w |
| Quality Dept. audit | 1w |
| Completion | 0 |

When you finish, your file should look like Figure 3.8. After you verify that it does, save your work and move on to the next section.

**NOTE!**  If you're struggling with breaking down tasks and ending up with durations that seem out of scale (multi-week tasks versus tasks that take only a few hours), perhaps some of the detail work needs to be broken out into a separate project file. This will keep the management of the main project from becoming burdensome, while having the details covered by a second project. Chapter 15 explains how you can view information from multiple project files in a central, consolidated way.

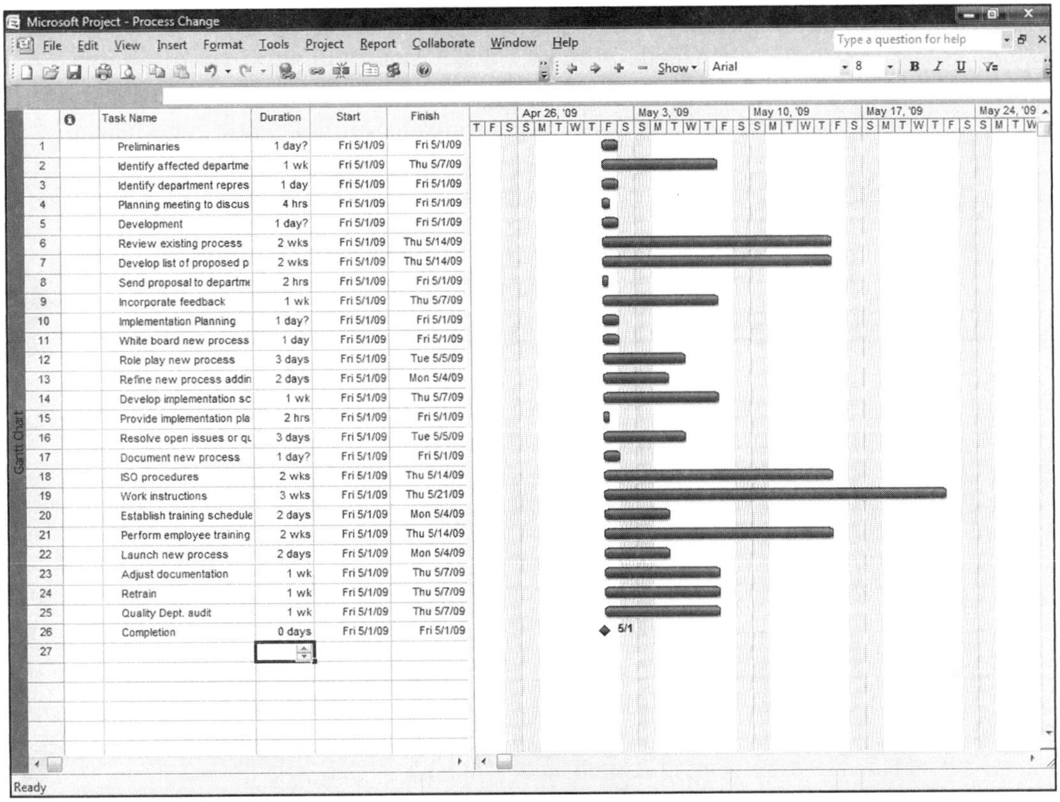

**Figure 3.8**  Tasks typed in to the *Process Change* project plan.

# Organize and Schedule Tasks

If you looked closely at your project plan (or Figure 3.8), you might have noticed two key points:

- All the tasks start on the same date.
- That date is the project start date you specified earlier—May 1, 2009.

That's exactly right. By default, Project schedules every new task you add to begin on the project start date specified in the Project Information dialog box. Project will then reschedule tasks to build out the actual schedule based on the relationships you establish between tasks.

But first, you should organize tasks in the plan into logical groups of related tasks. This process creates a type of task called a ***summary task***. The summary task summarizes (adds up) the information about all the tasks in a summary group. The tasks where you left the

*Duration* field blank will become summary tasks when you complete the steps in this section. Their estimated *Duration* field entries will be replaced with the summed *Duration* entries for the tasks (called **subtasks** or **detail tasks**) in each group.

A question mark in a *Duration* field entry—as in 1 day?—indicates an *estimated* duration. The question mark reminds you that you may need to revisit and finalize that *Duration* entry at a later time. If you enter a duration that you're not confident about, type a question mark in with your entry to remind yourself to update it when you have better information.

When you organize your list of tasks, you use techniques resembling outlining in other programs. You will *indent* (demote) tasks to make them subtasks using the Indent button on the Formatting toolbar.

In addition, you can improve your list of tasks by adding any tasks you might have forgotten, such as a summary task, or by moving other tasks around.

It's generally a better practice to organize tasks before scheduling them. Because scheduling involves creating relationships between tasks, you need those tasks in place before defining the relationships.

## Organize the Project Outline

So, pick up where you left off with the *Process Change* file. Use these steps to organize (or outline) and complete the list of tasks:

1. Drag over the task name cells for **tasks 2 through 4** to select those task names. (Remember, the row numbers that appear at the left are also the task ID numbers.) A selection highlight appears over the cells with the three task names.

2. Click the **Indent** button on the Formatting toolbar. (Shortcut: **Alt+Shift+Right Arrow**.) The button looks like a right arrow button. As shown in Figure 3.9, Project immediately indents the tasks and identifies task 1, *Preliminaries*, above as a summary task. You can tell that it's a summary task because its name now appears in bold and has a minus icon (for collapsing the group), and the task's Gantt bar changes to a black, summary task Gantt bar. Finally, the task's duration has changed from 1 day?, an estimated duration entered by Project because you did not make a *Duration* entry for task 1, to **5 days**, the current total duration for the indented subtasks: from the Start date of the earliest subtasks to the Finish date of the latest subtask.

3. Select and indent **tasks 6 through 9**.

4. Select and indent **tasks 11 through 20**.

5. Click any *Task Name* cell to deselect tasks 11 through 20.

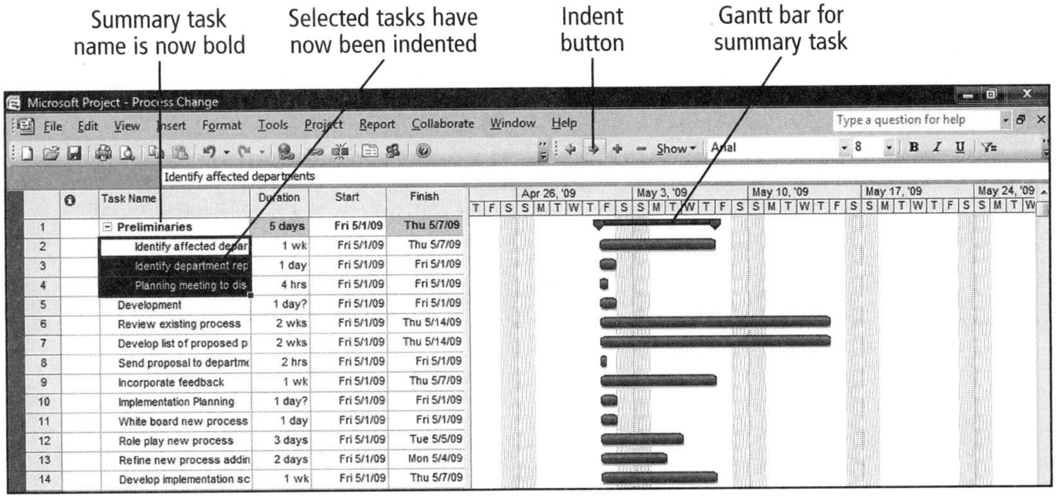

Labels on figure: Summary task name is now bold; Selected tasks have now been indented; Indent button; Gantt bar for summary task

**Figure 3.9** Indenting tasks establishes the summary tasks and project outlining.

6. Select **tasks 18 and 19** and indent them again. You can have multiple levels of tasks within the outline for a project. Use as many as needed to reflect the task organization.

7. Click **task 21**. You realize that you need a new summary task to head the last several tasks, so add it now.

8. Press the **Insert** key on the keyboard. (You also can click **Insert**, and then click **New Task**.) You can find this key somewhere in the upper-right area of your keyboard. A blank, new task appears.

9. Type **Implementation** as the task name for the new task and press **Enter**.

10. Project automatically indents the new task (task 21) to the level of the task above it. Because you want the new task to be a summary task, click **task 21** and then the **Outdent** button on the Formatting toolbar. (Shortcut: **Alt+Shift+Left Arrow**.) The task moves to the highest level, as shown in Figure 3.10.

11. Select and indent **tasks 22 through 27**.

12. Click on any *Task Name* cell to remove the selection.

13. Taking one last look at the list of tasks, you realize that task 26, *Quality Dept. audit*, should appear earlier, before task 24, *Adjust documentation*. To fix the problem, click the row header (the gray row 26 row number) for task 26. This selects the entire task. Then, move the mouse pointer to the border of the cell selection so that a four-headed arrow pointer appears with the mouse pointer. Then, drag the task up. When you drag, a gray hatched bar identifies where the task will move to when you release the mouse button. In this case, drag up until the gray bar appears above task 24, *Adjust documentation* (see Figure 3.11), and then release the mouse button.

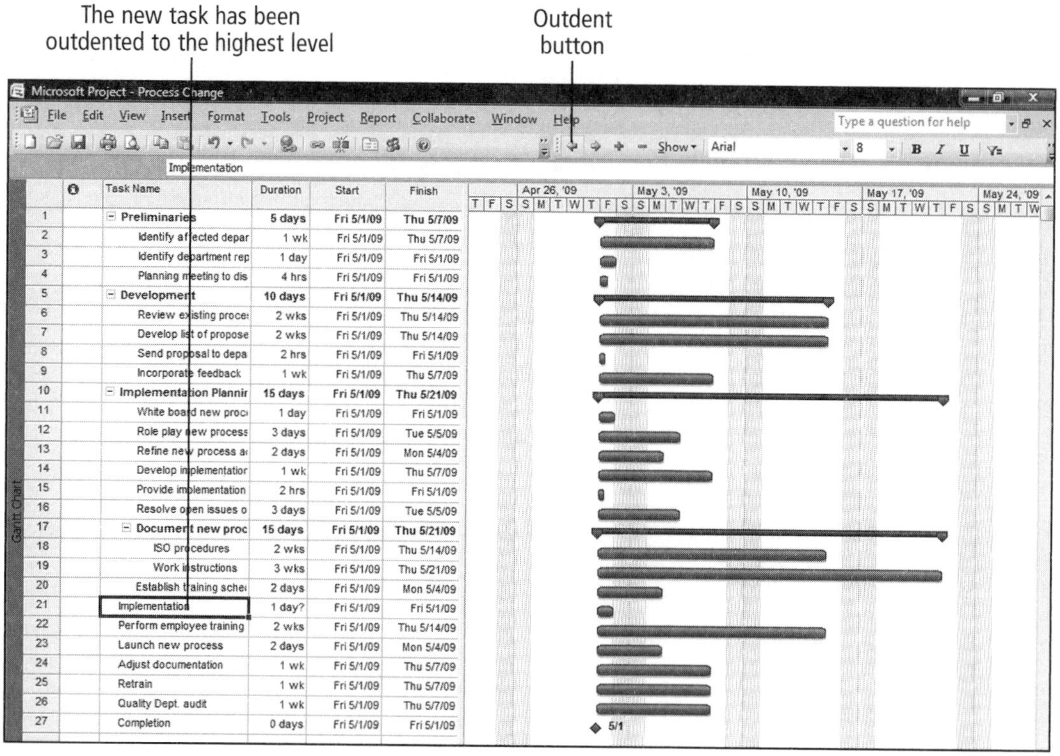

The new task has been
outdented to the highest level

Outdent
button

| | ❶ | Task Name | Duration | Start | Finish |
|---|---|---|---|---|---|
| 1 | | − Preliminaries | 5 days | Fri 5/1/09 | Thu 5/7/09 |
| 2 | | Identify affected depar | 1 wk | Fri 5/1/09 | Thu 5/7/09 |
| 3 | | Identify department rep | 1 day | Fri 5/1/09 | Fri 5/1/09 |
| 4 | | Planning meeting to dis | 4 hrs | Fri 5/1/09 | Fri 5/1/09 |
| 5 | | − Development | 10 days | Fri 5/1/09 | Thu 5/14/09 |
| 6 | | Review existing process | 2 wks | Fri 5/1/09 | Thu 5/14/09 |
| 7 | | Develop list of propose | 2 wks | Fri 5/1/09 | Thu 5/14/09 |
| 8 | | Send proposal to depa | 2 hrs | Fri 5/1/09 | Fri 5/1/09 |
| 9 | | Incorporate feedback | 1 wk | Fri 5/1/09 | Thu 5/7/09 |
| 10 | | − Implementation Plannir | 15 days | Fri 5/1/09 | Thu 5/21/09 |
| 11 | | White board new proce | 1 day | Fri 5/1/09 | Fri 5/1/09 |
| 12 | | Role play new process | 3 days | Fri 5/1/09 | Tue 5/5/09 |
| 13 | | Refine new process a | 2 days | Fri 5/1/09 | Mon 5/4/09 |
| 14 | | Develop implementatior | 1 wk | Fri 5/1/09 | Thu 5/7/09 |
| 15 | | Provide implementation | 2 hrs | Fri 5/1/09 | Fri 5/1/09 |
| 16 | | Resolve open issues o | 3 days | Fri 5/1/09 | Tue 5/5/09 |
| 17 | | − Document new proc | 15 days | Fri 5/1/09 | Thu 5/21/09 |
| 18 | | ISO procedures | 2 wks | Fri 5/1/09 | Thu 5/14/09 |
| 19 | | Work instructions | 3 wks | Fri 5/1/09 | Thu 5/21/09 |
| 20 | | Establish training sche | 2 days | Fri 5/1/09 | Mon 5/4/09 |
| 21 | | Implementatio | 1 day? | Fri 5/1/09 | Fri 5/1/09 |
| 22 | | Perform employee training | 2 wks | Fri 5/1/09 | Thu 5/14/09 |
| 23 | | Launch new process | 2 days | Fri 5/1/09 | Mon 5/4/09 |
| 24 | | Adjust documentation | 1 wk | Fri 5/1/09 | Thu 5/7/09 |
| 25 | | Retrain | 1 wk | Fri 5/1/09 | Thu 5/7/09 |
| 26 | | Quality Dept. audit | 1 wk | Fri 5/1/09 | Thu 5/7/09 |
| 27 | | Completion | 0 days | Fri 5/1/09 | Fri 5/1/09 |

**Figure 3.10** Outdenting tasks moves them to a higher outline level.

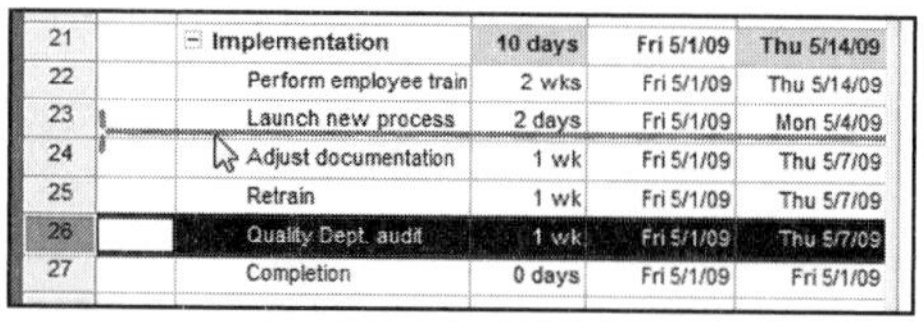

**Figure 3.11** Drag and drop a selected task into a new position.

Figure 3.12 shows how your project plan looks now that you've organized it by outlining, adding a missing task, and moving a task to the proper location in the list. There are now four tasks identified as top-level summary tasks and one additional task that summarizes at a lower level. The problem is that all the tasks still start on May 1, 2009.

The last task, for which you entered a 0 duration, is a *milestone*. The Gantt Chart shows a milestone as a black diamond.

| | ❶ | Task Name | Duration | Start | Finish |
|---|---|---|---|---|---|
| 1 | | − Preliminaries | 5 days | Fri 5/1/09 | Thu 5/7/09 |
| 2 | | Identify affected depar | 1 wk | Fri 5/1/09 | Thu 5/7/09 |
| 3 | | Identify department rep | 1 day | Fri 5/1/09 | Fri 5/1/09 |
| 4 | | Planning meeting to dis | 4 hrs | Fri 5/1/09 | Fri 5/1/09 |
| 5 | | − Development | 10 days | Fri 5/1/09 | Thu 5/14/09 |
| 6 | | Review existing proce: | 2 wks | Fri 5/1/09 | Thu 5/14/09 |
| 7 | | Develop list of propose | 2 wks | Fri 5/1/09 | Thu 5/14/09 |
| 8 | | Send proposal to depa | 2 hrs | Fri 5/1/09 | Fri 5/1/09 |
| 9 | | Incorporate feedback | 1 wk | Fri 5/1/09 | Thu 5/7/09 |
| 10 | | − Implementation Plannir | 15 days | Fri 5/1/09 | Thu 5/21/09 |
| 11 | | White board new proc: | 1 day | Fri 5/1/09 | Fri 5/1/09 |
| 12 | | Role play new process | 3 days | Fri 5/1/09 | Tue 5/5/09 |
| 13 | | Refine new process a: | 2 days | Fri 5/1/09 | Mon 5/4/09 |
| 14 | | Develop implementatior | 1 wk | Fri 5/1/09 | Thu 5/7/09 |
| 15 | | Provide implementation | 2 hrs | Fri 5/1/09 | Fri 5/1/09 |
| 16 | | Resolve open issues o | 3 days | Fri 5/1/09 | Tue 5/5/09 |
| 17 | | − Document new proc | 15 days | Fri 5/1/09 | Thu 5/21/09 |
| 18 | | ISO procedures | 2 wks | Fri 5/1/09 | Thu 5/14/09 |
| 19 | | Work instructions | 3 wks | Fri 5/1/09 | Thu 5/21/09 |
| 20 | | Establish training sche: | 2 days | Fri 5/1/09 | Mon 5/4/09 |
| 21 | | − Implementation | 10 days | Fri 5/1/09 | Thu 5/14/09 |
| 22 | | Perform employee train | 2 wks | Fri 5/1/09 | Thu 5/14/09 |
| 23 | | Launch new process | 2 days | Fri 5/1/09 | Mon 5/4/09 |
| 24 | | Quality Dept. audit | 1 wk | Fri 5/1/09 | Thu 5/7/09 |
| 25 | | Adjust documentation | 1 wk | Fri 5/1/09 | Thu 5/7/09 |
| 26 | | Retrain | 1 wk | Fri 5/1/09 | Thu 5/7/09 |
| 27 | | Completion | 0 days | Fri 5/1/09 | Fri 5/1/09 |

**Figure 3.12** Drag and drop a selected task to a new position.

> **NOTE!** After you've created a task with more than 0 duration and assigned a resource to it, you can convert the task to a milestone. This preserves the duration, schedule, and work information associated with the task but displays it as a milestone on the Gantt Chart. To make this change, double-click the task's name in the task sheet side of the view, click the **Advanced** tab, click the **Mark Task as Milestone** check box to check it, and then click **OK**.

## Use Links to Schedule the Project

To enable Project to calculate the full project schedule, you need to establish the relationship between tasks. Tasks in a project occur in a particular order and are normally related. One task must finish so that the next task can begin, for example. To establish these relationships between tasks, you *link* the tasks in the project plan. By default, Project creates Finish-to-Start links, which schedule tasks one after the other. (Chapter 6 covers links and link types in more detail.) Add links into the *Process Change* file now to have Project calculate the project schedule:

1. Drag over the task name cells for **tasks 2 through 4** to select those task names.

2. Click the **Link Tasks** button on the Standard toolbar. (Shortcut: **Ctrl+F2.**) The button looks like a chain link. As shown in Figure 3.13, Project links the tasks and changes the *Start* and *Finish* dates for tasks 3 and 4 to reflect the new sequence in the schedule.

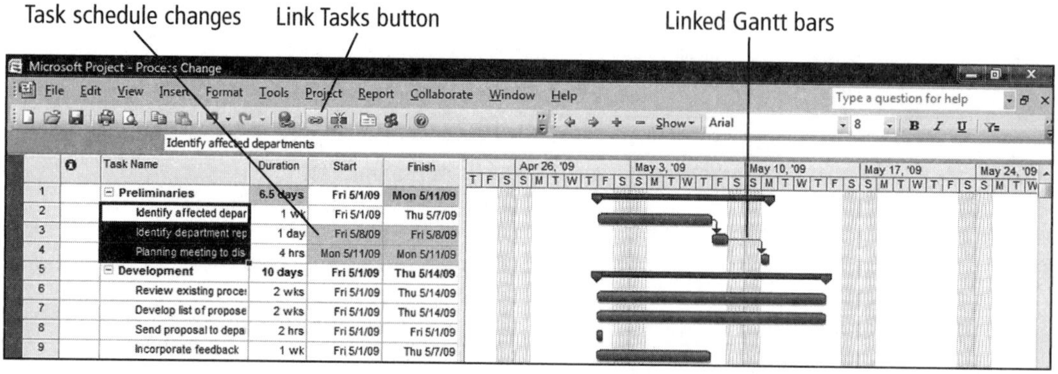

**Figure 3.13**  Linking tasks builds the schedule.

3. Click the task name for **task 4**, press and hold the **Ctrl** key, click the task name for **task 6**, and then release the Ctrl key. Now click the **Link Tasks** button. As shown in Figure 3.14, Project reschedules task 6 accordingly, but it also adjusts the *Development* summary task to reflect the change to task 6. You should not link summary tasks because they don't reflect specific work. Generally speaking, only link the detail or subtasks so that Project can accurately recalculate the schedule when individual task schedules change.

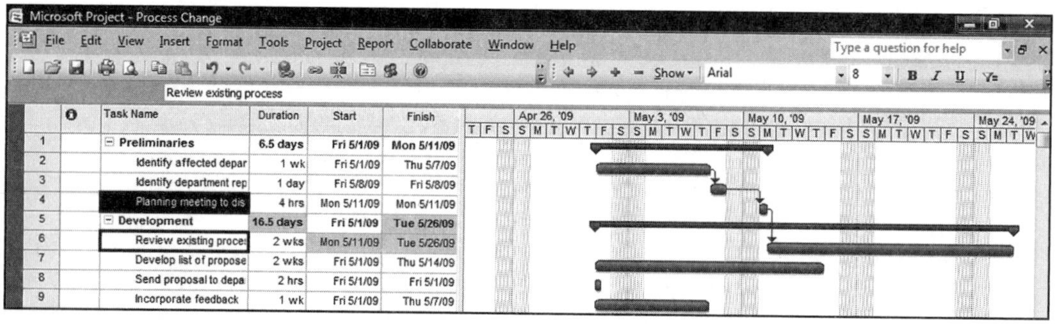

**Figure 3.14**  Don't link the summary tasks.

4. Select and link **tasks 6 through 9**.

5. Use the Ctrl+click method you learned in Step 3 to select **tasks 9 and 11** and then link them.

6. Select and link **tasks 11 through 16**.

7. Use Ctrl+click to select **tasks 16 and 18** and then link them.

8. Select and link **tasks 18 and 19**.

9. Use Ctrl+click to select **tasks 16 and 20** and then link them. This step illustrates that linked tasks don't necessarily follow one after the other in the task sheet. You may need to link tasks that are relatively far apart in the list if their work and schedules are related.

10. Use Ctrl+click to select **tasks 20 and 22** and then link them.

11. Finally, select and link **tasks 22 through 27**.

12. Look at the *Finish* field entry for task 27, the last task. Based on the links you've created, Project has calculated a finish date of Monday, 8/17/09.

13. Now scroll the chart pane to the right until you can see the Gantt bars for tasks 18 and 22. Looking at your schedule, you realize that some of the links don't make sense because the new procedures need to be documented before employee training can begin.

14. Use the Ctrl+click method to select **tasks 16 and 20**. Click the **Toolbar Options** button at the right end of the Standard toolbar and then click the **Unlink Tasks** button, which looks like a broken chain link. (Shortcut: **Ctrl+Shift+F2**.) Project moves the Gantt bars for the later tasks to reflect the fact that task 20 no longer has a task linked in before it, so it is rescheduled back to the project start date.

15. Select and link **tasks 19 and 20**. Project reschedules the last several tasks based on the new link. The *Finish* field entry for task 27 now shows a recalculated finish date of Monday, 9/21/09.

16. Press **F5**, type a **1** in the ID text box, and then click **OK**. Project moves the cell selector to task 1 and scrolls the Gantt bars for the early tasks back into view.

17. Click **Tools** and then click **Options**. Click the **View** tab, if needed, and then click the **Show Project Summary Task** check box. Click **OK**. Project now displays a special task and Gantt bar that summarize the whole project. If you move the mouse pointer over the project summary task Gantt bar, a pop-up tip shows you the start and finish dates for the whole project, as well as the total project duration, as shown in Figure 3.15.

18. Now say that you are concerned that 9/21/09 is too late as the project finish date. Let's move the project start date earlier to see the impact on the finish date. Click **Project** and then click **Project Information**. Use the **Start Date** calendar to choose a date of **April 20, 2009** and then click **OK**.

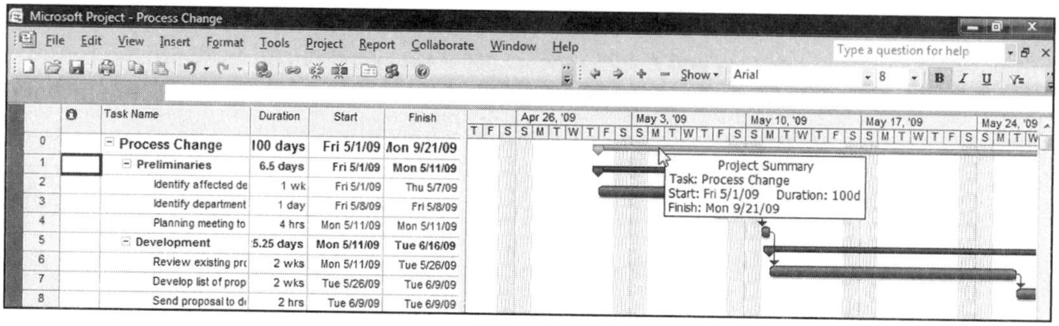

**Figure 3.15** Display the project summary task and point to it with the mouse to see a summary of the project's schedule.

19. Point to the project summary task, and note that the newly calculated finish date is Tuesday, 9/8/09.

20. Click the **Undo** button on the Standard toolbar. (Shortcut: **Ctrl+Z.**) This returns the project to the previous May 1 start date, with a finish date of 9/21/09.

> The last three steps illustrate why you don't want to type start and finish dates for tasks. Allowing Project to calculate dates based on links means that Project retains the ability to recalculate linked tasks based on earlier changes like changing the project start date. Typing in dates removes that flexibility, which would force you to have to retype dates to change the schedule. When you later mark work as complete on a task, Project will stop recalculating the task start, because the completed work set an actual start date.

21. Save the *Process Change* file.

## List Resources

So, the *Process Change* project will take nearly four months to complete, as currently scheduled. You now have mapped out what needs to be done. The next question is who will do the work and what materials will they need? In other words, what resources will you need to accomplish the project tasks? You'll use a Project view called the Resource Sheet to enter resource information. The Resource Sheet offers a number of different fields of information. You can make entries in all of or some of the fields, depending on your project planning and tracking requirements. (See Chapter 7 to learn about the Resource Sheet fields in more detail.)

For now, follow these steps to list the resources for the example project:

1. Working in the *Process Change* file, click **View** and then click **Resource Sheet**. The Resource Sheet view, which looks like a spreadsheet, appears.

2. Type the resource information listed in Table 3.2. You can press **Tab** to move between the cells, and simply skip any field not mentioned in the table.

**Table 3.2** Resource Entries for *Process Change* File

| Resource Name Field | Std. Rate Field |
| --- | --- |
| Jim Maxwell | 45 |
| Jane Riggs | 45 |
| Sandy Paulson | 40 |
| Len Wilkins | 40 |
| Jane France | 35 |
| Alan Lewis | 30 |

3. Now you need to add a last resource of a different type. This is a *material resource*—an item or consumable that will be used in some quantity during the course of the project. In the next blank cell in the *Resource Name* field, type **Binder** and press **Tab**. To set the Binder resource up as a material resource, type an **m** (material will then appear) in the *Type* field and then press **Tab**. Type **dozen** in the *Material Label* field, press **Tab** four times, type **36** in the *Std. Rate* field, and then press **Enter** or **Tab** to finish. (The *Material Label* and *Std. Rate* entries correlate, in this instance meaning binders cost $36 per dozen.) Your finished Resource Sheet entries should look like Figure 3.16.

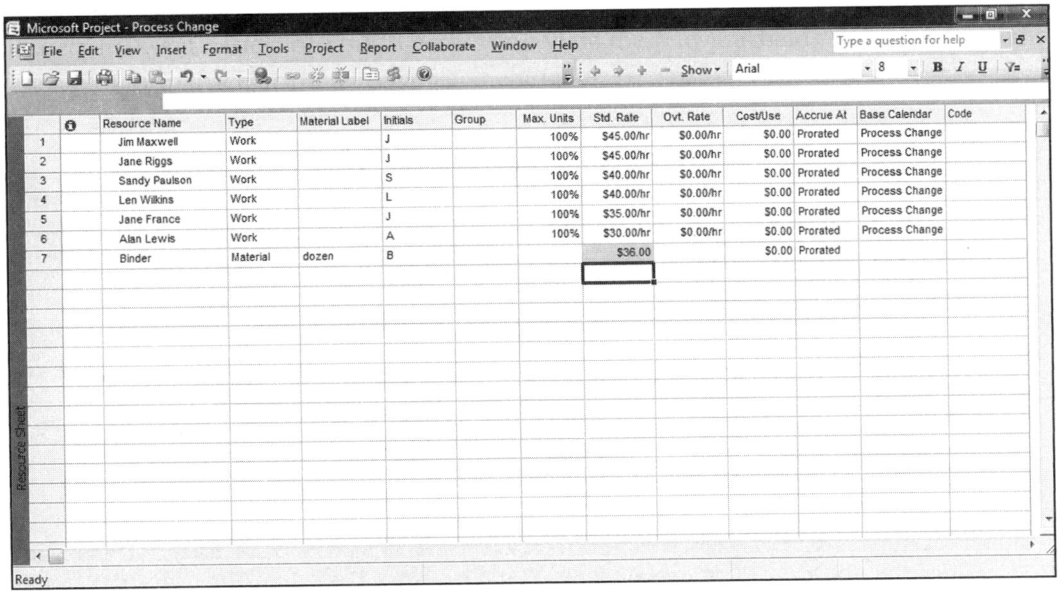

**Figure 3.16** Enter information about resources in the Resource Sheet.

> **NOTE** Notice the *Base Calendar* field in Figure 3.16. Project automatically sets up the resources to use the same calendar assigned to the project as a whole. If a resource follows a different calendar—such as when a person has vacation days—you should choose the other calendar or identify the resource's time off before proceeding with your planning. Chapter 7 explains how to adjust the calendar for an individual resource.

## Assign Resources

In the next phase of planning the project, you get specific about exactly who will be performing each particular task. You will *assign* resources to tasks.

When you assign the first resource(s) to a task, Project leaves the *Duration* field entry you made for the task the same. So, if you assign one resource to each task, the schedule will stay the same. However, Project uses a method called ***effort driven scheduling***; the program assumes that if you add more resources to a task, the task's duration should decrease because more resources can get the work done faster. (I'll go into the math behind how Project changes durations later in Chapter 8.) So, the assignments you make—how you as project manager choose to deploy resources—can dramatically affect the schedule in your project.

So, assign resources in the example *Process Change* file now. You'll start by changing back to the default Gantt Chart view because you need to be working in a view where you can see the tasks in order to make assignments.

1. Click **View** and then click **Gantt Chart**.
2. Click **task 2**, *Identify affected departments*. Notice that the task has a 1wk (1 week) duration.

 As with linking, assign resources only to detail tasks (the level at which the work actually occurs), not summary tasks. Rare exceptions exist when you might assign a resource to a summary task to account for administrative work, but remember that that is the exception, not the norm.

3. Click the **Assign Resources** button on the Standard toolbar. (Shortcut: **Alt+F10**.) The button has a picture of two people. The Assign Resources dialog box appears.
4. Click **Jim Maxwell** in the Resource Name list of the Assign Resources dialog box and then click **Assign**. Jim Maxwell's name appears beside the Gantt bar for task 2 and a check appears beside his name in the dialog box. Notice that the task retains its original duration of 1 wk (see Figure 3.17).

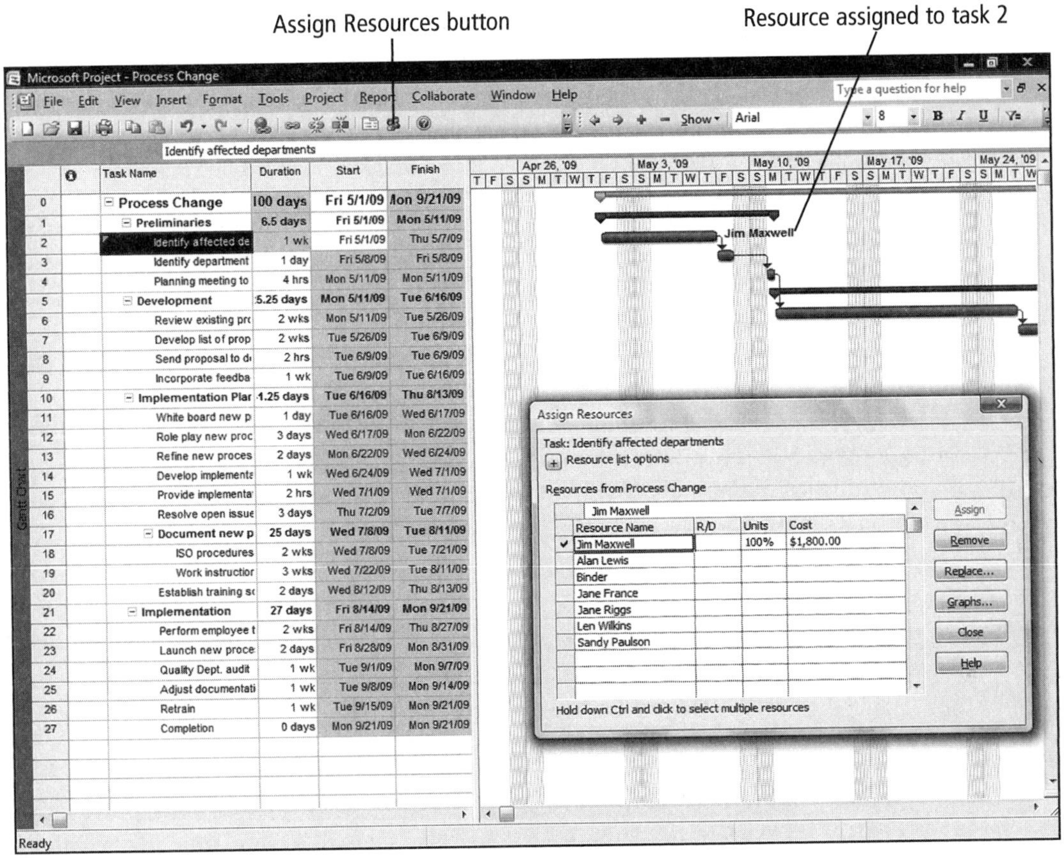

Assign Resources button                                    Resource assigned to task 2

**Figure 3.17** Add resources to tasks with the Assign Resources dialog box.

5. Leaving task 2 selected, click **Jane France** in the Assign Resources dialog box and then click **Assign**. Now both resource names appear beside the task bar in the Gantt Chart and the task's duration has decreased to .5 wks. This is effort driven scheduling in action.

6. Assume in this case that you do not want the task duration to decrease. With Jane's name still selected in the Assign Resources dialog box, click **Remove**. The task duration returns to 1 wk. However, you want to assign both Jim and Jane to the task without affecting its duration. To do so, you need to remove Jim from the task, too, so click **Jim Maxwell** in the Assign Resources dialog box and click **Remove**.

7. Now use Ctrl+click to select both **Jane France** and **Jim Maxwell** in the Assign Resources dialog box and then click **Assign**. This time, both their names appear beside the task but the task retains its 1 wk duration.

8. Click **task 3** in the task sheet and then assign **Alan Lewis** to the task using the Assign Resources dialog box. Notice that you can leave the Assign Resources dialog box open and move between using it and the task sheet.

9. Click **task 4** in the task sheet, use Ctrl+click to select all resources except the Binder resource, and click **Assign**. This assigns all the resources to the meeting task without changing the task duration. Notice that Project calculates the budgeted amount for each resource to attend the meeting based on the *Std. Rate* entry you made for each resource on the Resource Sheet.

10. Click **task 6**, *Review existing process*. Say that you want to assign Len Wilkins to the task; you want to allow him the full two-week duration to complete the task, but you know he'll only be working on the task about 25% of the time. So, you don't want Project to calculate his costs and working hours as if he were working full time on the task. To get this right, click the Resource Name cell for **Len Wilkins** in the Assign Resources dialog box, click the **Units** cell to the right of the selected resource name, and type **25**. Then click **Assign**. Figure 3.18 illustrates that Len is now assigned to work on that task 25% of his time over two weeks. If he had been assigned full time (100%), the Cost calculated by the Assign Resources dialog box would have been $3,200 rather than $800.

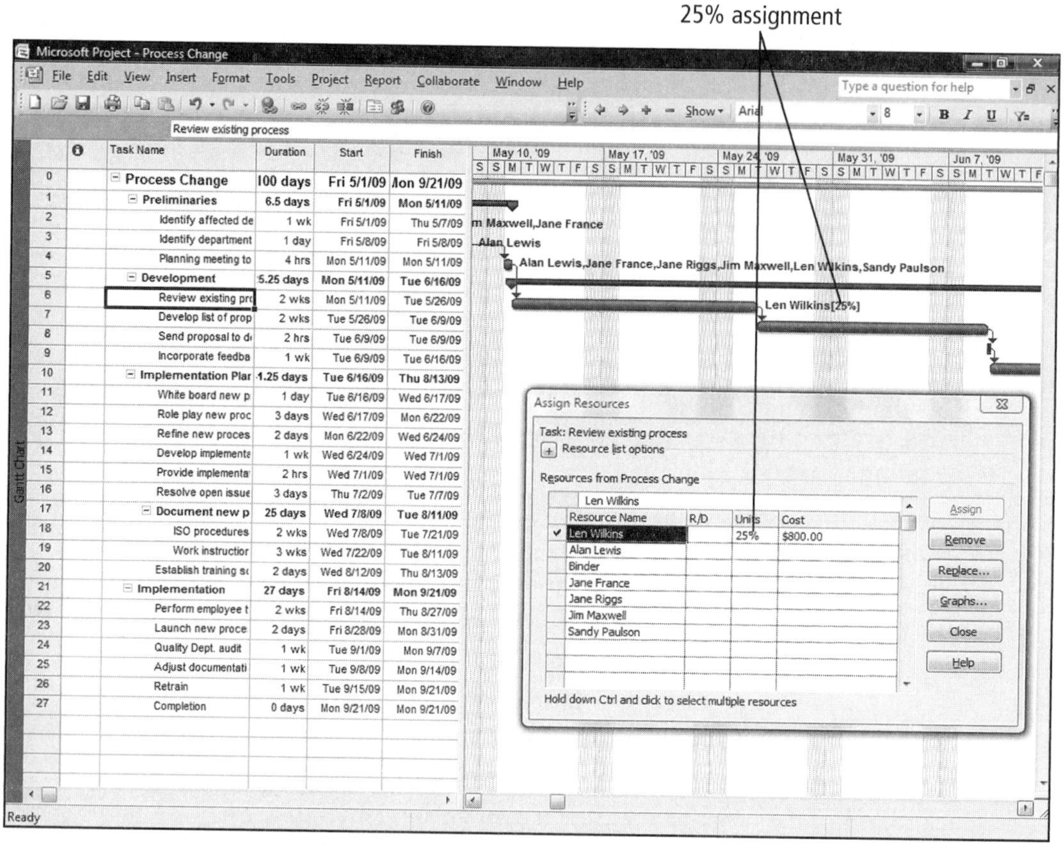

**Figure 3.18** Assigning a resource to work part time on a task.

11. Assign the resources as listed in Table 3.3 to the remaining tasks. Where the table lists multiple resources, use the Ctrl+click method to select all the resources and assign them at the same time. All of the assignments are full time.

**Table 3.3** Remaining Resource Assignments for *Process Change* File

| Task ID | Task Name | Resource(s) |
| --- | --- | --- |
| 7 | Develop list of proposed process changes | Jane France<br>Jim Maxwell |
| 8 | Send proposal to department representatives | Len Wilkins |
| 9 | Incorporate feedback | Jane France<br>Jim Maxwell<br>Len Wilkins |
| 11 | White board new process | All except Binder |
| 12 | Role play new process | Alan Lewis<br>Jane Riggs<br>Sandy Paulson |
| 13 | Refine new process adding role play changes | Jane Riggs<br>Sandy Paulson |
| 14 | Develop implementation schedule | Alan Lewis |
| 15 | Provide implementation plan to department representatives | Alan Lewis |
| 16 | Resolve open issues or questions | Jane Riggs |
| 18 | ISO procedures | Jane France |
| 19 | Work instructions | Jim Maxwell |
| 20 | Establish training schedule | Sandy Paulson |
| 22 | Perform employee training | Jim Maxwell |
| 23 | Launch new process | All except Binder |
| 24 | Quality Dept. audit | Jane France |
| 25 | Adjust documentation | Jim Maxwell |
| 26 | Retrain | Jim Maxwell |

12. Assume that you've reviewed the plan and you want to accomplish task 22, *Perform employee training*, more quickly and to help Jim Maxwell with his workload near the end of the project. Click **task 22** and assign **Sandy Paulson** to the task, too. Adding the second resource reduces the task's duration to 1 wk.

13. You also realize that the training will require a binder for each employee trained, and 48 (4 dozen) employees will be trained. With task 22 still selected, click the *Binder* resource in the Assign Resources dialog box, click the **Units** cell to the right of the selected resource, type a **4**, and then click **Assign**. As shown in Figure 3.19, Project calculates a budgeted cost for the binders based on the Std. Rate per dozen ($36) that you specified in the Resource Sheet.

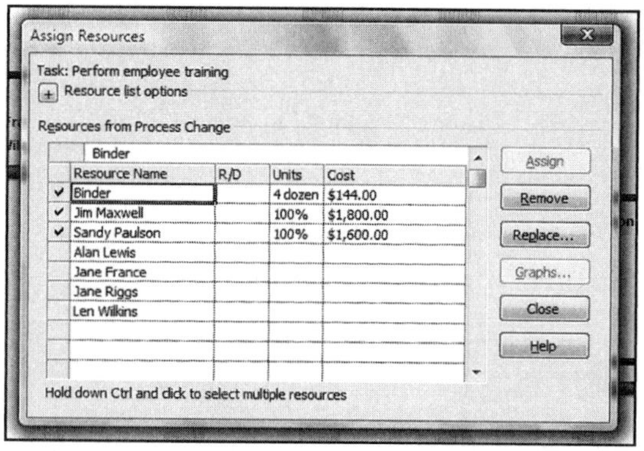

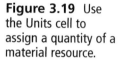

**Figure 3.19** Use the Units cell to assign a quantity of a material resource.

14. Click the **Close** button to close the Assign Resources dialog box.

15. Save your changes to the *Process Change* file.

## Save the Baseline

At this point in the real world, you would perform a thorough review of your project plan to make sure that it is complete, accurate, and realistic. You would check assignments to ensure that the resources have the bandwidth to handle the tasks assigned, and you would circulate the plan and budget to secure the necessary sign-offs. After you and other stakeholders have given the plan the "thumbs up," you can consider it final and ready for kick off.

To manage any plan, you need to see your progress versus that original plan. In Project, you can save your original plan as a *baseline*, or snapshot of the original schedule and budget. Later, as task schedules change based on actual work, you'll be able to see how the actual schedule varies from the original schedule.

Follow these steps to set and view the baseline:

1. Press **F5**, type a **1** in the ID text box, and then click **OK** to move back to the beginning of the *Process Change* file.

2. Click **View** and then click **Tracking Gantt**. The Tracking Gantt view enables you to see work completed and schedule progress in a graphical format. Each of its Gantt bars includes a completion percentage, which is initially 0%. The view initially shows one thin Gantt bar per detail task.

3. Press **F5**, type a **1** in the ID text box of the Go To dialog box, and then click OK. This scrolls the right side of the view so that you can see the task Gantt bars.

4. Click **Tools**, point to the **Tracking** choice, and click **Set Baseline** in the submenu that appears.

5. In the Set Baseline dialog box (see Figure 3.20), make sure that the Set Baseline and Entire Project options are selected and then click **OK** to save the baseline.

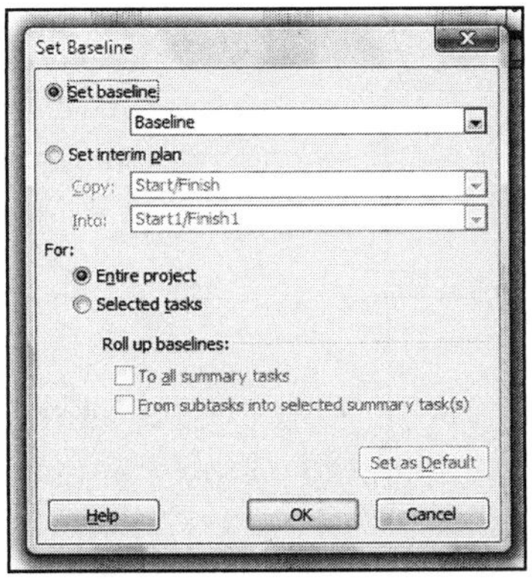

**Figure 3.20** These settings save the baseline for the entire project plan.

6. Save the *Process Change* file. In this case, saving also preserves the baseline information in the file.

Right away, you should see that the Tracking Gantt chart changes slightly. As Figure 3.21 illustrates, a second thin Gantt bar appears for each of the detail tasks. The top thin bar, which is a shaded red color, represents the current schedule for the task. The bottom thin bar, which is gray, represents the baseline (original) schedule for the task. As you mark work as complete and adjust task schedules in the next section, you'll see how the bars compare progress to the original plan.

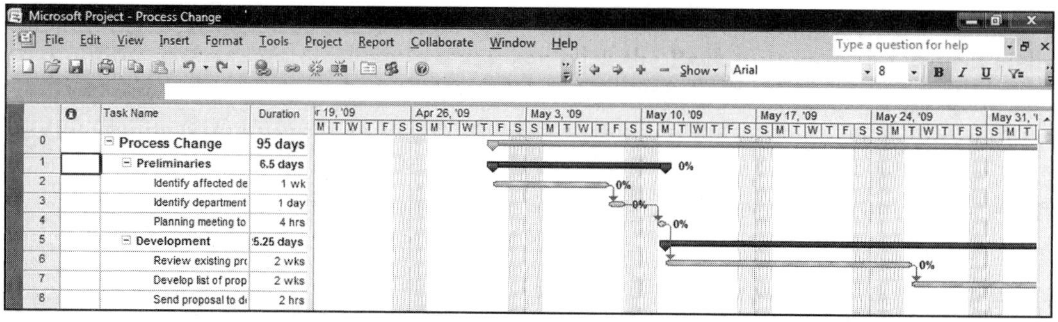

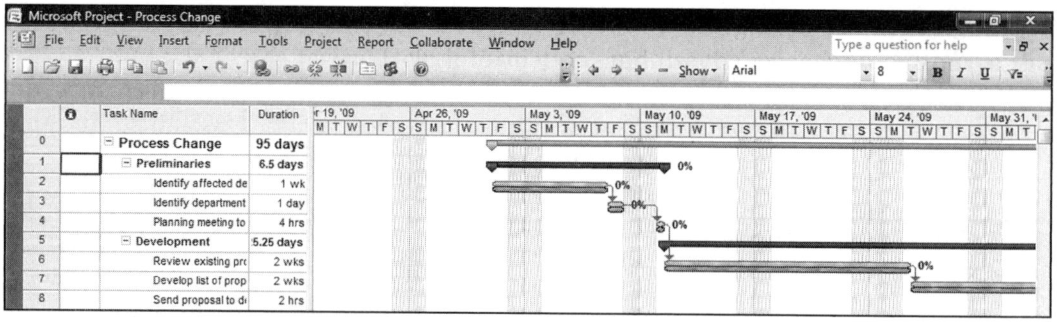

**Figure 3.21**  The Tracking Gantt bars before saving the baseline (top) and after (bottom).

## Track Completed Work

After setting your plan and saving the baseline, it's off to the races! Work begins on the project, and you establish regular communications between yourself and all the resources to gather information about the amount of work completed on each task. You will need to enter the information about work completed into the project plan so that Project can calculate data such as the percentage of work completed for the project as a whole and the portion of the budget now expended. You also will need to make adjustments to task schedules as needed so that Project can recalculate the schedules for linked tasks accordingly.

The Tracking Gantt view provides an excellent location to track progress, given that it shows completion percentages and baseline information. To access Project's convenient tracking tools, you'll also need to display the Tracking toolbar. Follow these steps to display the toolbar and track part of the work completed for the *Process Change* project:

1. Right-click one of the toolbars and then click **Tracking**. The Tracking toolbar appears. It includes percentage buttons for marking various task completion percentages, as well as some other tracking tools.

2. Click **task 2**, *Identify affected departments*, and then click the **100%** button on the Tracking toolbar. As shown in Figure 3.22, a few dramatic changes occur in the Tracking Gantt chart. A check mark appears in the indicators column to show that the task is complete. The top Gantt Bar for the task changes to solid blue and its completion percentage changes to 100%. Plus, the first summary task shows a calculated completion percentage for the group of tasks and a hatched *progress bar*.

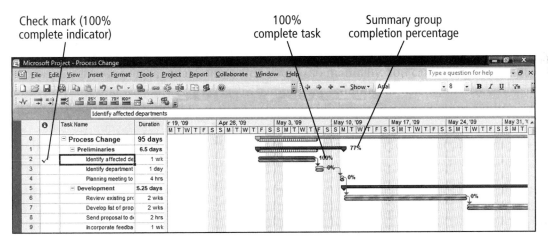

**Figure 3.22**  The Tracking Gantt illustrates progress when you mark work as complete.

3. Click **task 3**, *Identify department representatives*. This task is finished, but it started and finished a day later than scheduled, so you need to enter the actual start and finish dates that occurred. To do so, click the **Update Tasks** button on the Tracking toolbar (see Figure 3.23). In the Actual area of the dialog box, type **5/11/09** into both the Start and Finish text boxes. (You also could use the text box drop-down calendars to specify the dates, if desired.) Click **OK**. As shown in Figure 3.24, the Tracking Gantt changes even more dramatically this time. The top Gantt bar for task 3 and the one for each subsequent linked task move to reflect the fact that task 3 occurred later than originally scheduled. The gray baseline bars remain in their original positions, giving you a graphic indication of the schedule change.

---

Project keeps three sets of dates for you: the saved *baseline* dates, the evolving *current* dates, and the *actual* dates based on when work was completed. Marking some work as complete on a task sets the Actual Start date, and marking the task as 100% complete sets the Actual Finish date. Once an actual date has been set, Project will no longer reschedule the corresponding current date, because it then must match the actual date.

---

4. Click **task 4** and mark it as **100%** complete.

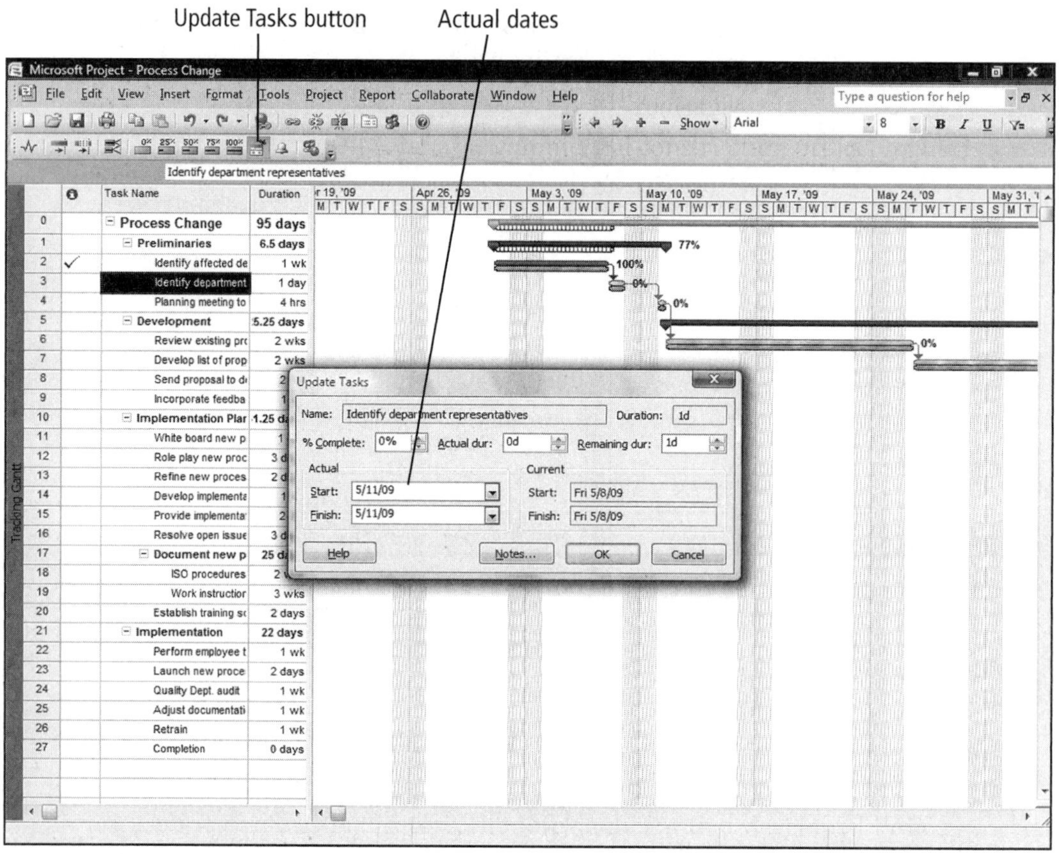

Update Tasks button          Actual dates

**Figure 3.23** Enter actual dates in the Update Tasks dialog box.

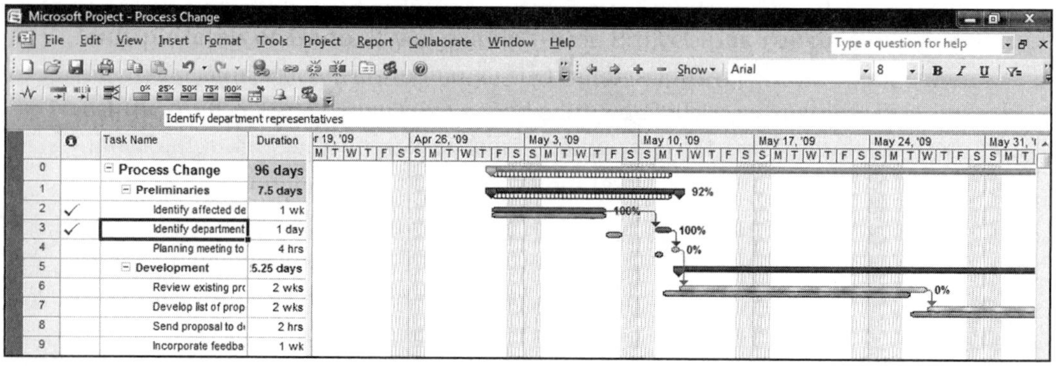

**Figure 3.24** Here's how the actual dates entered in Figure 3.23 affect the Tracking Gantt bars.

5. Click **task 6**, *Review existing process*. Click the **25%** button on the Tracking toolbar to mark that task as 25% complete. Notice that its top Gantt bar remains red, only a quarter of it is now solid red rather than shaded.

6. Let's assume that that's all the work you need to track for now. So, right-click one of the toolbars and then click **Tracking** to hide (toggle) the Tracking toolbar. (You also can use the **View, Toolbars** submenu to toggle a toolbar on and off.)

7. Save the *Process Change* file.

 As is the case for many Project features, you can use a number of different techniques and get much more detailed about tracking completed work. Chapter 11 gets into the nitty-gritty about that.

## Share the Results Through Views and Reports

Chapter 2 explained how to use the More Views dialog box to select any of the many views available in Project. To share the information onscreen in a view, you can print the view. Project prints whatever view currently appears onscreen.

Print your file now, for example:

1. With the *Process Change* file still onscreen, click **File** and then click **Print Preview**. A preview view of the file appears onscreen, as shown in Figure 3.25.

2. Click the **Page Setup** button. In the Page Setup dialog box, click the **Fit To** options button on the page tab and change the printout dimensions to **2** *Pages Wide by 1 Tall*. Click **OK**.

3. Click the **Print** button and then click **OK** to print the view and close the print preview. (Note that you could click **File** and then **Print** to print without displaying the Print Preview.)

That's it. In a few mouse clicks, you can have a hard copy of any view to distribute to any stakeholder.

Project also offers a number of reports that present the information from your project in nicely formatted layouts. Here's how to find and print a report of the information in your *Process Change* file:

1. Click **Report** and then click **Reports**.

2. Double-click **Costs** in the Reports dialog box (see Figure 3.26).

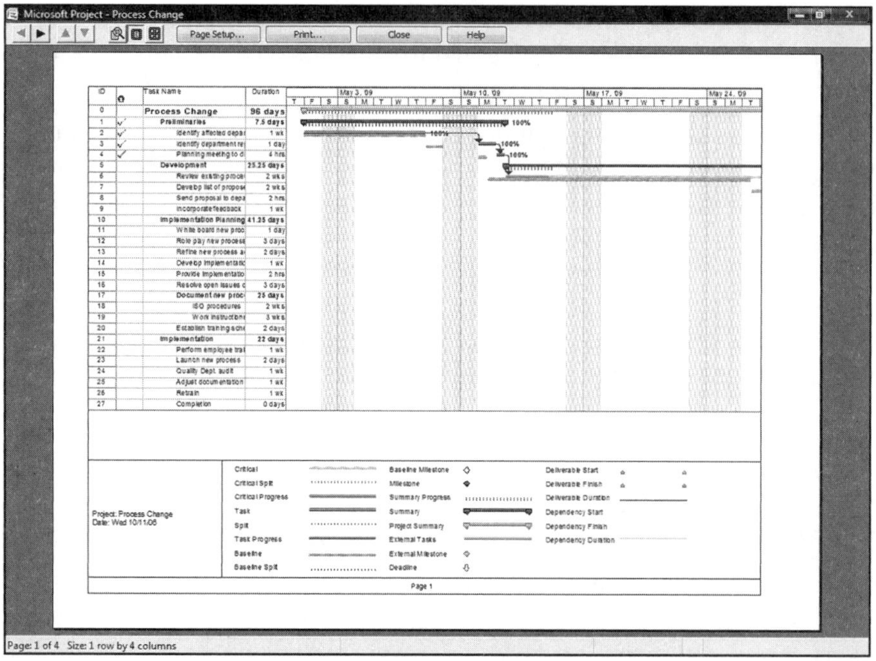

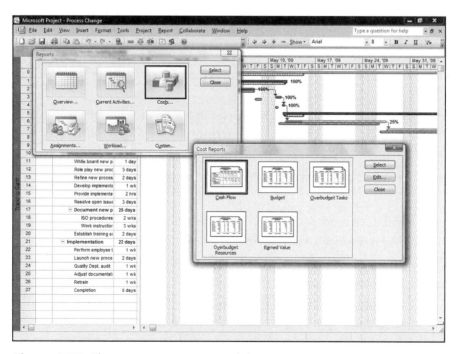

**Figure 3.25**  A print preview of the *Process Change* file in Tracking Gantt view.

**Figure 3.26**  Choose a report category and then a report.

3. Double-click **Budget** in the Cost Reports dialog box.

4. To print the Budget report that appears (see Figure 3.27), click **Print** and then **OK**.

Microsoft Project - Process Change

Page Setup...   Print...   Close   Help

Budget Report as of Wed 10/11/06
Process Change

| ID | Task Name | Fixed Cost | Fixed Cost Accrual | Total Cost | Baseline | Variance |
|----|-----------|-----------|--------------------|-----------|----------|----------|
| 7 | Develop list of proposed process change | $0.00 | Prorated | $6,400.00 | $0.00 | $6,400.00 |
| 19 | Work Instructions | $0.00 | Prorated | $5,400.00 | $0.00 | $5,400.00 |
| 9 | Incorporate feedback | $0.00 | Prorated | $4,800.00 | $0.00 | $4,800.00 |
| 23 | Launch new process | $0.00 | Prorated | $3,796.00 | $0.00 | $3,796.00 |
| 22 | Perform employee training | $0.00 | Prorated | $3,544.00 | $0.00 | $3,544.00 |
| 2 | Identify affected departments | $0.00 | Prorated | $3,200.00 | $0.00 | $3,200.00 |
| 18 | ISO procedures | $0.00 | Prorated | $2,800.00 | $0.00 | $2,800.00 |
| 12 | Role play new process | $0.00 | Prorated | $2,760.00 | $0.00 | $2,760.00 |
| 11 | White board new process | $0.00 | Prorated | $1,880.00 | $0.00 | $1,880.00 |
| 26 | Adjust documentation | $0.00 | Prorated | $1,800.00 | $0.00 | $1,800.00 |
| 25 | Retrain | $0.00 | Prorated | $1,800.00 | $0.00 | $1,800.00 |
| 24 | Quality Dept. audit | $0.00 | Prorated | $1,400.00 | $0.00 | $1,400.00 |
| 13 | Refine new process adding role play cha | $0.00 | Prorated | $1,360.00 | $0.00 | $1,360.00 |
| 14 | Develop implementation schedule | $0.00 | Prorated | $1,200.00 | $0.00 | $1,200.00 |
| 16 | Resolve open issues or questions | $0.00 | Prorated | $1,080.00 | $0.00 | $1,080.00 |
| 4 | Planning meeting to discuss process cha | $0.00 | Prorated | $940.00 | $0.00 | $940.00 |
| 6 | Review existing process | $0.00 | Prorated | $800.00 | $0.00 | $800.00 |
| 20 | Establish training schedule | $0.00 | Prorated | $640.00 | $0.00 | $640.00 |
| 3 | Identify department representatives | $0.00 | Prorated | $240.00 | $0.00 | $240.00 |
| 8 | Send proposal to department representat | $0.00 | Prorated | $580.00 | $0.00 | $580.00 |
| 15 | Provide implementation plan to departme | $0.00 | Prorated | $60.00 | $0.00 | $60.00 |
| 27 | Completion | $0.00 | Prorated | $0.00 | $0.00 | $0.00 |
|  |  | $0.00 |  | $45,580.00 | $0.00 | $45,580.00 |

Page 1

Page: 1 of 2   Size: 1 row by 2 columns

**Figure 3.27** All reports appear as a print preview.

5. Click **Close** to close the Reports dialog box.

6. Save and close the *Process Change* file.

# Chapter Review

If you've followed the steps in this chapter, you've now created and managed your first project plan in Microsoft Project. You've now seen how to set up and choose a project calendar, specify a project start date, list tasks, outline and link tasks, list resources, assign resources, save the baseline, track work, and print a view or report. And you survived the experience! Reinforce your new skills now by answering the review questions and handling the practice projects.

## Review Questions

Write your answers to the following questions on a sheet of paper.

1. True or False: The calendars that come with Project have holidays marked.

2. The information you specify to define overall project parameters include the _____ and the _____ .

3. To define each task, enter its _____ and _____ .

4. To enable Project to calculate task schedules, _____ the tasks.

5. Change to the _____ view to enter resources.

6. What is a material resource?

7. What is effort-driven scheduling?

8. Use the _____ dialog box to add resources to tasks.

9. Save the _____ so that you can track work against the original schedule.

10. For each task, the Tracking Gantt view shows:

   a. A thin bar for the current or actual task schedule.

   b. A thin bar for the baseline task schedule.

   c. Neither of the above.

   d. Both a and b.

## Projects

 To see example solution files created by completing the projects in this chapter, go to www.courseptr.com, click the **Downloads** link in the navigation bar at the top, type **Microsoft Office Project 2007 Survival Guide** in the search text box, and then click **Search Downloads**.

### Project 1

1. Click the **New** button on the Standard toolbar to create a new, blank file.

2. Click **Tools** and then click **Change Working Time**.

3. Click the **Create New Calendar** button.

4. Type **35 Hour Week** in the Name text box and then click **OK**.

5. Click the **Work Weeks** tab and then click **Details**.

6. Drag over **Monday** through **Friday** in the Select Day(s) list, and then click the **Set Day(s) to These Specific Working Times** option button.

7. Click **5:00 PM** in the To column, type **4 PM**, and press **Enter**. Click **OK** to apply the change and then click **OK** to close the Change Working Time dialog box.

8. Click **Project** and then click **Project Information**.

9. Specify a Start Date of **January 1** of the next calendar year.

10. Open the **Calendar** drop-down list and click **35 Hour Week**.

11. Click **OK**.

12. Click the **Save** button on the Standard toolbar, and save the file as *Market Opportunity Report*.

 You may want to create a folder named *PSG Exercises* in your *Documents* or *My Documents* folder and save your exercise practice files there.

## Project 2

1. Enter the following tasks into the *Market Opportunity Report* file:

| Name | Duration |
| --- | --- |
| Research | - |
| Market size | 2 |
| Competing companies | 2 |
| Competing products | 3 |
| Ideas | - |
| Test competing products | 2w |
| Develop prototype ideas | 3w |
| Secure manufacturing quotes | 2w |
| Business plan | - |
| Write business case | 1w |
| Develop financials | 2w |
| Finalize | 2 |
| Deliver | 0 |

If you enter only a number in the *Duration* field, Project assumes you are entering the duration in *days*.

2. Use the **Indent** button on the Formatting toolbar to indent these tasks:

   2 through 4

   6 through 8

   10 through 13

3. Use the **Link** tasks button on the Standard toolbar (and Ctrl+click if needed) to link these tasks:

   2 through 4

   4 and 6

   6 through 8

   8 and 10

   10 through 13

4. Click **View** and then click **Resource Sheet**.

5. Enter **Craig** and **Janet** in the first two Resource Name cells.

6. Click **View** and then click **Gantt Chart**.

7. Click the **Assign Resources** button, and then use the Assign Resources dialog box to make the following assignments (assign both resources simultaneously when instructed to add both):

| Task ID | Resource |
|---|---|
| 2 | Janet |
| 3 | Craig |
| 4 | Both |
| 6 | Craig |
| 7 | Both |
| 8 | Janet |
| 10 | Craig |
| 11 | Janet |
| 12 | Both |

8. Click **Close** to close the Assign Resources dialog box.

9. Save your changes to the *Market Opportunity Report* file.

## *Project 3*

1. Click **Tools**, point to **Tracking**, and then click **Set Baseline**.

2. Click **OK** to save the baseline for the entire project.

3. Click **View** and then click **Tracking Gantt**.

4. Right-click a toolbar, and then click **Tracking**.

5. Press **F5**, type a **1**, and then click **OK** to ensure that you can see the Gantt bars.

6. Mark **task 2** as **50%** complete.

7. Right-click a toolbar and then click **Tracking**.

8. Click **View** and then click **Gantt Chart**.

9. Click **File** and then click **Print**. Click **OK** to print the file.

10. Save and close the *Market Opportunity Report* file.

# PART TWO

# Building a
# Project Plan

# CHAPTER 4

## CREATING A PROJECT PLAN FILE AND CALENDAR

This Chapter Teaches You How To:

- Create a blank project file or use a template to create a file
- Save a file, as well as save a file as a template
- Switch to another file window
- Close a file
- Understand the project calendar, as well as calendars for tasks and resources
- Set up your own calendar that reflects holidays and a custom work schedule
- Share a calendar with other projects
- Apply a calendar and set the project start date
- Match the calendar options to the calendar

Common sense dictates the first steps of planning any project: establishing the overall schedule the project will follow and when the work on the project will actually start.

After you create your new project plan file, you need to take those two steps to ensure that Microsoft Project will calculate accurate schedule information, including an actual finish date for the project. This chapter shows you how to create a project file, establish and assign a calendar, and set the start date to ensure your planning will be accurate from the get-go.

# Making a New File for Your Project Plan

In introducing you to projects and project management, Chapter 1 explained how every project must have discrete tasks, specific deliverables, and a distinct starting and ending time for the project as a whole. Based on those facts, it makes sense to place the information about each project plan in a separate file in Project. Doing so ensures that Project can calculate accurate schedule, completion, and budget information about each specific project.

Project enables you to start from scratch with a blank file or to use a ***template*** that already includes some basic information to help you build your project plan. This section explains how to use one of those methods to create a file, how to save a file, and even how to save your own custom project templates.

 Yep, the real world will typically require you to manage more than one project at a time, and your projects might typically overlap in time and use some of the same resources. Project can show you how multiple project plans compare in schedule, as well as whether you've over-booked resources between projects. See Chapter 15 to learn more.

## Creating a Blank File

When you start Project, it opens by default a blank file named *Project1*. You can by all means enter the information for your latest project into that *Project1* file and then save it. If, for some reason, you no longer have a blank project file open but want to use one for a new project, you can create a new blank file at any time using one of the following methods:

- Click the **New** button (which looks like a sheet of paper) at the left end of the Standard toolbar or press **Ctrl+N**.

- Click **File** and then click **New**. Click the **Blank Project** link (see Figure 4.1) at the top of the New Project task pane that appears.

No matter which of those methods you choose, Project immediately opens a new file and assigns it a temporary numbered name, such as *Project2*, *Project3*, and so on. You can then establish the calendar and start date for the file, remembering to save your work, at any time.

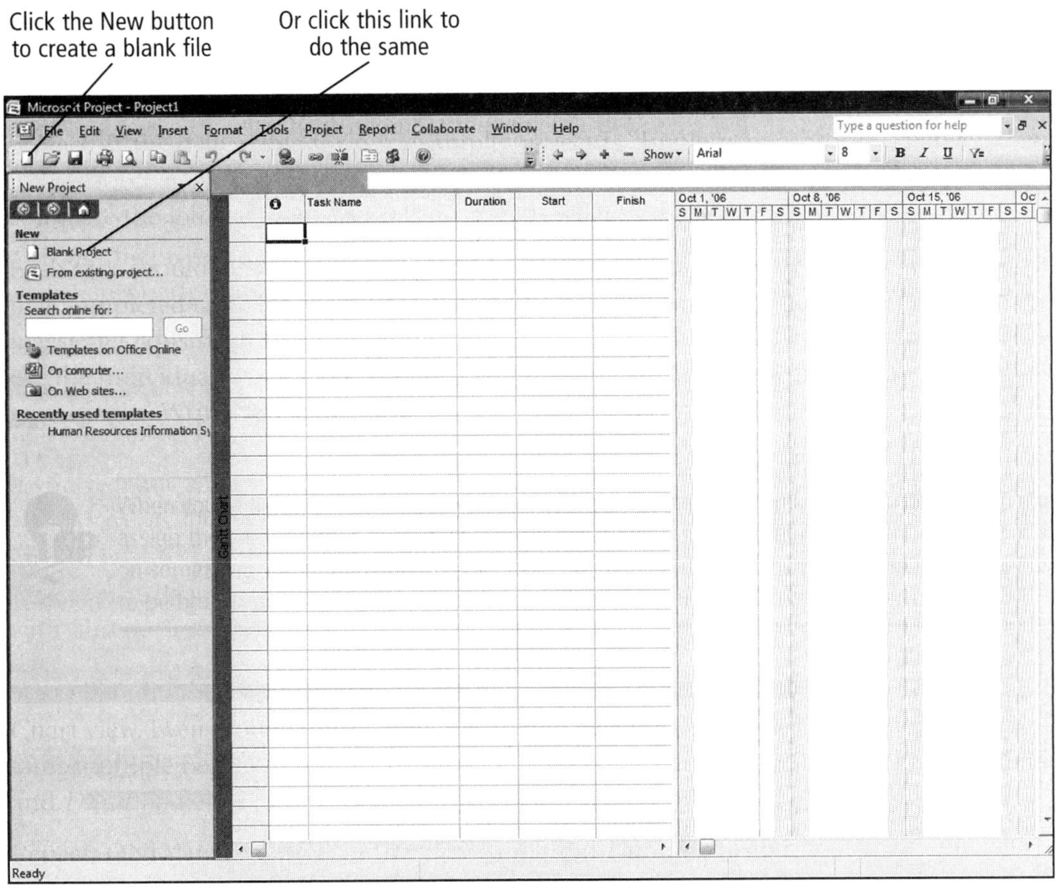

Click the New button
to create a blank file

Or click this link to
do the same

**Figure 4.1** Open a new file from the New Project task pane.

## Using a Template as the Basis for Your Project

A project template file establishes a basic framework for a project plan. When you use a template, you not only save some data entry work but also benefit from the prior planning experience of the person who created the template. The template might include tasks you may have forgotten to include that, if omitted, would lead to some unfortunate surprises when your project gets under way.

Project includes a set of more than 40 templates that install on your computer's hard disk. Most of these templates help you plan for business scenarios such as developing a product or holding a special event. But other templates work well for personal situations such as moving to or constructing a new home. Figure 4.2 shows one of the templates included with Project; this is how the template looks when first opened.

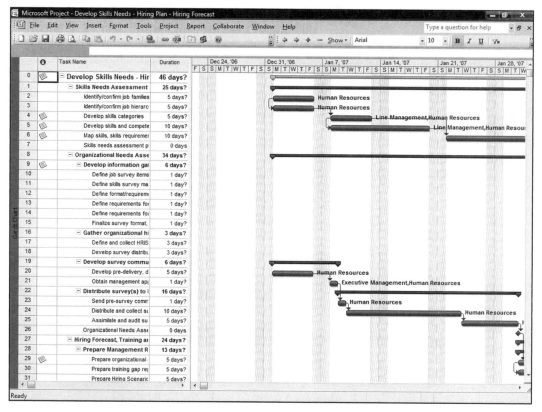

**Figure 4.2** Use a template to accelerate project planning and enhance accuracy.

As in the other Office applications, Microsoft Project doesn't limit you to installed templates. Office Online offers a variety of additional templates that you can download and use to launch your planning process. Finally, you can create your own template if you often manage projects of a similar nature.

When you use a template, Project creates a copy of the template's contents and places those contents in a new file that you can then save under a new name and modify to suit your needs. Different templates might hold different types of information. The template in Figure 4.2 includes task names, outlining, estimated durations and links to provide a basic schedule, and even generic resource names. A simpler template might include only task name and duration estimates. A template that you create on your own can include more information, such as any actual information that you've tracked.

The process for using a template to create a new file starts off like one of the methods for creating a blank file:

1. Click **File** and then click **New**.

2. Click one of these links in the New Project task pane (refer to Figure 4.1) to view and select a template:

   ■ **Templates on Office Online.** Clicking this link opens your Web browser and displays the Office Online Web site, where you can browse available templates and select a template to download. Follow the onscreen instructions for downloading the template you want to use.

   ■ **On Computer...** After you click this link, click the **Project Templates** tab in the Templates dialog box that appears. Click the icon for the template that you want to use (see Figure 4.3) and then click **OK** to open the template.

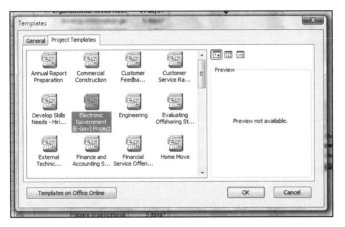

**Figure 4.3** You can use one of the dozens of templates installed with Project.

   ■ **On Web Sites...** Clicking this link opens a dialog box that you can use to navigate to a Web site that you've previously identified as a frequently visited location. You can then search for templates at the destination Web site and select and open one to use.

A template file typically includes custom elements you created or assigned—such as a custom calendar—before saving the template. However, some settings will need to be updated, such as the project start date. Also be sure to double-check the settings on the Calendar and Schedule tabs in the Options dialog box (**Tools, Options**).

## Saving a File

If you've ever had a power surge or some other incident cause you to lose your work in a computer file, then you've learned the hard way that, in most instances, none of your work can be retrieved unless you saved it to a disk. Better to play it safe by saving early and often.

The first time you save a file, you assign it a descriptive name to replace the placeholder name created by Project. Obviously, the file's name should reflect the nature of the project that you're planning. Given that you can use more than 200 characters in the name, you can be quite descriptive. Just keep in mind that in most cases, folder windows can only display the first several words in a file name. If it's possible that you will be creating multiple versions of the file over time, consider including the date you save the file in the file name. For example, if you first save a file as *Brochure Plan 2006-05-01*, saving the file later as *Brochure Plan 2006-06-01* creates a copy of the file that you can instantly identify as the most recent version.

Windows Vista includes a version tracking feature that periodically saves versions of files and folders. Don't rely on this feature to be able to backtrack to an older version of a project plan, as you may not be able to retrieve the information from the precise date or time you want. If you need older versions of a file for backup and record keeping, use Save As to create and date multiple versions of a project plan file, as advised above.

To save a project plan file for the first time and give it a file name, use the process below, which is probably familiar to you from your experience with other programs:

1. Click **File** and then click **Save**. (Shortcuts: **Save** button on the Standard toolbar, **Ctrl+S**.) The Save As dialog box appears.

2. If you're using Windows Vista, click the **Browse Folders** button to expand the dialog box and then use the Folders list to browse to and select the disk and folder where you'd like to save your file (see Figure 4.4). (Click the up arrow beside Folders to open the Folders list, if needed.) In previous Windows versions, use the **Save In** drop-down list and the list of available folders to select the save location.

Resist the temptation to save your project files to removable media like a USB flash drive (thumb drive) only. Hard disks are still the more stable storage location, and if you lose the removable media, then (ouch!) your project plan file will be gone for good. Always save to a hard disk first and then copy the file to a removable disk such as a CD-R or USB flash drive.

3. Type the name for the file in the **File Name** text box.

4. Click **Save**. Project displays the new file name in the title bar.

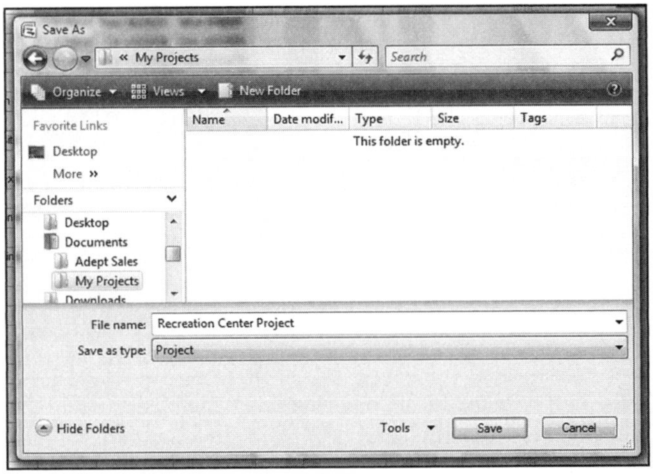

**Figure 4.4** Specify the name and location where you'd like to save a file.

 The figures in this book show Project being used with the new Windows Vista operating system. If you're running Project under Windows XP, some features, such as the Save As and Open dialog boxes, look a little different. Refer to Appendix A, "Slight Differences Between Windows Versions," for help in navigating these dialog boxes.

From that point on, to save your further changes to a file, click the **Save** button or press **Ctrl+S**. If you need to save a copy of the current file and give another name to the copy, click **File** and then click **Save As**. Then repeat the process from Step 2, above, to indicate the save location and new file name.

## Saving a File as a Template

You learned in the first chapter that detailed project tracking in Project provides a means of record keeping and preserving "tribal knowledge" about how previous plans progressed. You can put your own tribal knowledge directly to work by saving the project plan file as a template.

Say you created a project plan file for a recent project and anticipate that you'll be managing many similar projects in the future. You can save the project plan file as a template and then use the template as a basis for future projects, saving you the effort of starting from scratch.

Saving a template works much like saving an updated copy of a project plan file:

1. After you've added all the information you want to the template, click **File** and then click **Save As**.
2. Click the **Save As Type** drop-down list and then click **Template** (Figure 4.5).

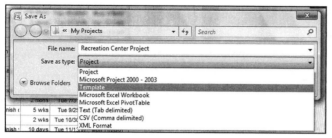

**Figure 4.5** Choose the template file type.

3. Type a name for the template in the **File Name** text box.

For easier access, don't change the disk or folder location when saving a template. Using the default location ensures that you'll be able to access your new template from the Templates dialog box.

4. Click **Save**.

5. If the template includes existing cost or actual data that you do not want to save with the template, click the check box beside the applicable data type in the Save As Template dialog box, shown in Figure 4.6. Otherwise, the data will be included in the template and every file you create based on the template.

6. Click **Save** to finish saving the template.

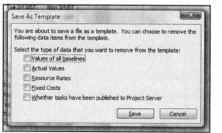

**Figure 4.6** Click the check box beside any type of data that you do not want to save in the template.

If you use the straightforward process for saving a template as described above, you can access your template in the same dialog box as the other templates installed with Project. Click **File** and then click **New**. Click the **On Computer...** link in the New Project task pane. Your custom template will appear on the General tab in the Templates dialog box, just like the *Recreation Center Project* template shown in Figure 4.7.

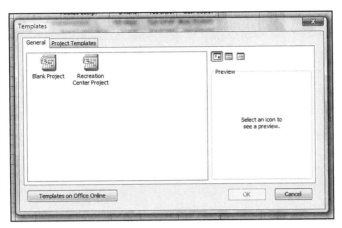

**Figure 4.7**
Templates saved in the default location appear on the General tab of the Templates dialog box.

## Other File Skills

Because Project has not adopted the new user interface presented in the other Office 2007 applications, you should be able to get up to speed quickly moving around, choosing commands, and so on. Here's just a brief reminder of two other skills for working with open project files:

- **Switching between windows.** If you have more than one project plan file open, you can use the Window menu to move between the open files. Click **Window** and then click the name of the file that you want to view and use. You also can click the button for the file to use on the Windows taskbar.

- **Closing a file.** If you've finished working with a file, click **File** and then click **Close** to close it. Or, you can click the **Close (X)** button at the far right end of the menu bar (not the title bar above it). You also can right-click the taskbar button of a file and click **Close**, or press **Alt+F4**. In either case, Project will prompt you to save any changes that you made to the file, so click **Yes** to do so.

Throughout the book, you may see command selections abbreviated. For example, rather than saying "Click **File**, and then click **Close**," a step might say "Choose **File, Close**."

# Making the Project Calendar

Although project management involves many subtle and intangible factors and skills, realizing project goals and deliverables on time serves as one of the most visible and tangible ways to measure success. An unrealistic plan is likely unachievable and can leave you looking like a less-than-competent project manager in the end.

Using Project for accurate planning requires that you first choose and likely even customize the calendar that Project will use to schedule tasks. This section discusses calendars and how they impact Project's calculations.

## Understanding the Project Calendar

Every project plan file you create in Project follows a *project calendar* or *base calendar*. Project schedules the work for each task during the working hours specified by the assigned base calendar. For example, if the calendar calls for eight-hour work days, Project will schedule a 12-hour task over the span of two days: eight hours on the first day and four hours on the second day.

Project offers three default calendars, any one of which you can assign to be the project calendar as described in the later section "Choosing the Project Calendar and Start Date." The default calendars are:

- **Standard.** This calendar specifies a typical (U.S.) office work calendar: a Monday through Friday work week with eight hours of work per day (8 a.m. to 5 p.m., with a one-hour lunch break starting at noon).

- **24 Hours.** This calendar specifies a 24/7 schedule like that followed in three-shift manufacturing environments. It schedules work from 12 a.m. to 12 a.m.

- **Night Shift.** This calendar schedules an eight-hour night schedule six days a week (Monday through Saturday). The shift runs from 11 p.m. in the evening to 8 a.m. the following morning, with a break for lunch from 3 a.m. to 4 a.m. Because by default Project assumes that each new day begins at 12 a.m., it actually lists the working hours for each shift in this calendar in three segments: 12 a.m. to 3 a.m., 4 a.m. to 8 a.m., and then 11 p.m. to 12 a.m. (the beginning of the next shift on the next day).

*None* of the default calendars include holidays! So, unless your employer offers zero holidays, at the very least you need to identify holidays in the base calendar, even if you choose to use one of the default calendars. If you're managing multiple projects over time, it makes the most sense to create a custom calendar as described next and to make it available to other files as described later in the section "Making a Custom Calendar Available for Other Files." Otherwise, you have to add the changes to the default calendar you're planning to use in every project file.

## Setting Up a New Calendar

Creating a custom base calendar in Project requires three activities: copying an existing calendar, marking holidays and other days off (called nonworking days), and making any necessary changes to the daily working hours. If you want to edit one of the default calendars, skip this first activity and move on to the next two subsections.

To create a new, custom calendar by copying an existing calendar, start here:

1. Click **Tools** and then click **Change Working Time**.
2. Click the **Create New Calendar** button in the upper-right corner of the Change Working Time dialog box.
3. In the Create New Base Calendar dialog box that appears, first make sure that the calendar to copy is selected from the **Make a Copy of** *(name)* **Calendar** drop-down list (see Figure 4.8). If it's not, click the drop-down list and then click the calendar to copy.

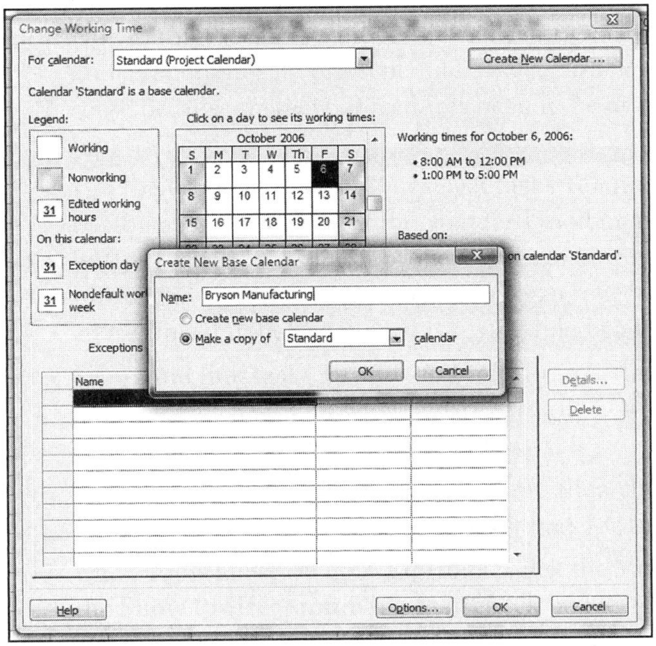

**Figure 4.8** Copying a default calendar gives you a head start when you create a custom calendar.

4. Type the desired calendar name into the **Name** text box.
5. Click **OK**. This takes you back to the Change Working Time dialog box, where you can modify the calendar, as described next.
6. After you've made the desired modifications, click **OK** to close the Change Working Time dialog box.

### Naming and Marking a Holiday

Project considers any day without working hours to be a nonworking day. Nonworking days include holidays or other days during which no work occurs, such as a scheduled plant closing. To customize a calendar, you must mark the nonworking days for your company or project. (You even can mark partial nonworking days.) Then, Microsoft Project will not schedule any hours of work to occur on the nonworking days.

In prior versions of Project, you customized a calendar by working with dates and days of the week alone. So, you didn't necessarily know at a glance that the Monday off in late May was Memorial Day. In this version of Project, you can assign names to the schedule changes that you make so that you can see at a glance why a day is marked as nonworking.

To mark a nonworking day in a calendar, follow these steps:

1. If the Change Working Time dialog box isn't open, click **Tools** and then click **Change Working Time**.

2. If the calendar you want to edit doesn't appear as the **For Calendar** choice (see Figure 4.9), open the drop-down list and click the calendar to edit.

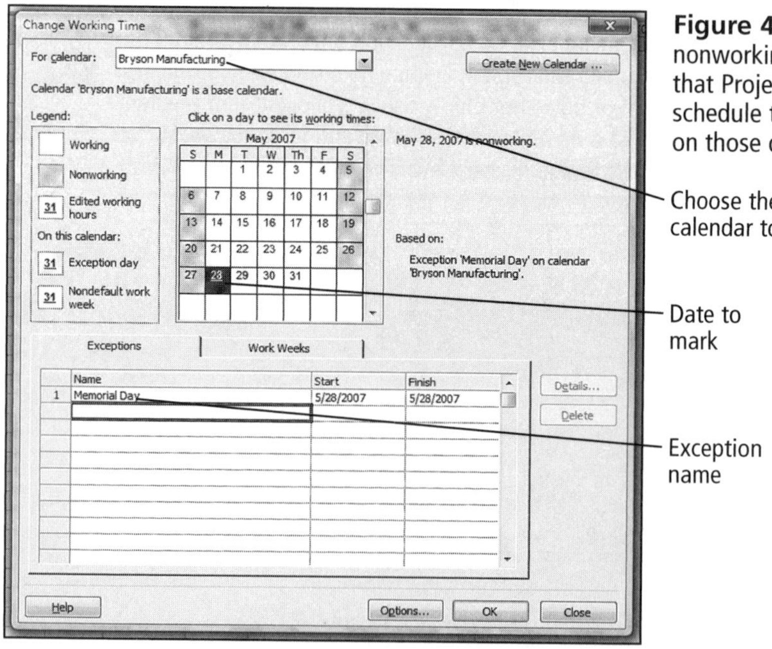

**Figure 4.9** Mark nonworking days so that Project won't schedule task activity on those days.

— Choose the calendar to edit

— Date to mark

— Exception name

3. Scroll the calendar in the middle of the dialog box until you see the date to mark and then click the date.

Drag on the calendar to select multiple days. Or, click the column heading for a day to select that day of the week throughout the entire calendar (all months and years).

4. Click the first blank **Name** cell on the Exceptions tab, type a name for the non-working day, and press **Tab**. This names and marks the date for the exception (nonworking day), as shown in Figure 4.9.
5. Click the next blank row on the **Exceptions** tab. This finishes marking the date for the exception. If you click another date on the calendar, you will see the nonworking day's box has been shaded and its date underlined and boldfaced.
6. Repeat Steps 3 through 5 to mark additional nonworking days.
7. Click **OK** to close the Change Working Time dialog box and save your calendar changes.

If you want to mark a date that's only partially nonworking, you could double-click the exception on the Exceptions tab or click it and then click the **Details** button. To change the working hours per day, click the **Working Times** option button in the Details for *(Exception Name)* dialog box and then enter the desired working times (see Figure 4.10). To delete both of the entries on a working times row listing, click the row number and then press **Delete**; Project won't let you delete individual cell entries. If the nonworking exception repeats, use the settings in the **Recurrence pattern** area to mark the frequency of occur-

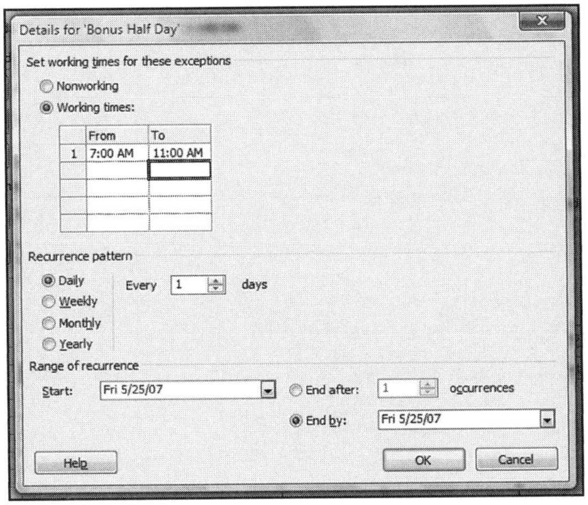

**Figure 4.10** You can change the exception's working hours and even repeat the exception.

rence. The options change based on the overall recurrence frequency you select, but figure 4.10 shows the recurrence set to happen on the fourth Friday of every third month, for four recurrences.

 When you enter times, be sure to type **am** or **pm** along with the time, as in **7 am**. Noon is **12 pm**, and midnight is **12 am**.

### Changing the Work Week Schedule

If your project follows a special schedule, such as having a 7 a.m. to 4 p.m. schedule, you can change the default work week settings in the Change Working Time dialog box, as follows:

1. If the Change Working Time dialog box isn't open, click **Tools** and then click **Change Working Time**.
2. If the calendar you want to edit doesn't appear as the **For Calendar** choice, open the drop-down list and click the calendar to edit.
3. Click the **Work Weeks** tab.
4. Double-click the [**Default**] entry, or click it and then click the **Details** button.
5. Drag over the day(s) to change in the **Select day(s)** list at the left side of the Details for *(work week name)* dialog box (see Figure 4.11).

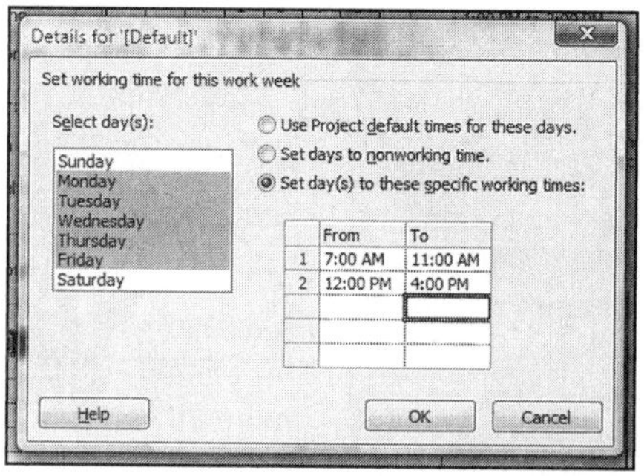

| Details for '[Default]' | |
|---|---|
| Set working time for this work week | |

Select day(s):
- Sunday
- Monday
- Tuesday
- Wednesday
- Thursday
- Friday
- Saturday

○ Use Project default times for these days.
○ Set days to nonworking time.
◉ Set day(s) to these specific working times:

|   | From | To |
|---|------|-----|
| 1 | 7:00 AM | 11:00 AM |
| 2 | 12:00 PM | 4:00 PM |

Help    OK    Cancel

**Figure 4.11** The days selected at the left will be set to the working hours entered at the right.

6. Click the **Set Day(s) to These Specific Working Times** option button.
7. Enter the adjusted working hours in the cells in the Working times area. Click each cell to edit, type the new time, and then press **Enter**.
8. Click **OK** to close the dialog box.
9. Click **OK** to close the Change Working Time dialog box and save your calendar changes.

Note that you can add additional entries on the Work Weeks tab if the project calendar needs to adjust over time. For example, if the bulk of the calendar will follow an 8 a.m. to 5 p.m. schedule but a two-week period will instead follow a 7 a.m. to 4 p.m. schedule, add another work week. To do so, click the next blank **Name** cell on the **Work Weeks** tab of the Change Working Time dialog box. Type a name for the work week and then specify the **Start** and **Finish** dates for the adjusted work week schedule. Click another row to finish the naming process, and then double-click the work week name or click it and click the **Details** button. From there, you can adjust the schedule for the alternate work week as described in Steps 5 through 8 above. Adding such an alternate work week ensures that Project will schedule work only during the adjusted schedule hours during the period specified by the custom work week.

For any field or cell where you need to enter a date in Project, click the cell. You then can type a date or click the drop-down arrow that appears to use a calendar to choose a date.

## Making a Custom Calendar Available for Other Files

Any custom element that you create in Project—such as a custom calendar or view—at first exists only in the current project file. Rather than reinventing the wheel in every project file, however, you can make any custom element such as a calendar available for use in all your project files. This not only saves work but also ensures greater accuracy and consistency in your planning.

Just as every new word processing file comes from a template that specifies default page and text sizes, every new file in Microsoft Project uses the settings stored in the *Global.MPT* file. You can use a tool called the ***Organizer*** to copy any custom item you create from the current file into *Global.MPT*. When an element like a custom calendar has been saved to *Global.MPT*, that element becomes available for use in all of your Project files.

Copying a custom calendar or another item into *Global.MPT* takes a few easy steps:

1. Click **Tools** and then click **Organizer**.
2. Click the **Calendars** tab. (Of course, you would click another tab to copy another type of item.)
3. Click the **calendar to copy** in the list at the right side of the dialog box (see Figure 4.12).

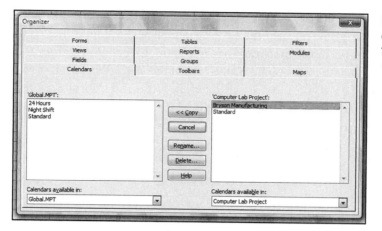

**Figure 4.12** Copy a custom calendar from the current file to *Global.MPT*.

4. Click the <<**Copy** button. The custom calendar will now also appear in the 'Global.MPT' list at the left.

5. Click **Close**.

In some cases, when you subsequently exit Project, you'll be asked whether to save changes to *Global.MPT*. Click **Yes** to do so.

## Reviewing Other Calendars

If you've jumped ahead and poked around in Project on your own, you might have noticed text boxes or fields for a *task calendar* and/or *resource calendar*. Indeed, in addition to assigning a calendar to the overall project, you can assign alternate calendars for resources and tasks.

For example, every resource probably has a scheduled vacation in addition to the company holidays. Adjusting the resource's calendar tells Project not to schedule the resource to work during the vacation period. Chapter 7 explains how to adjust a resource calendar. Likewise, a task might follow a different schedule than the rest of a project. Your project might, for the most part, follow an eight-hour work day but might include a testing task that runs continuously for 24 hours. Chapter 9 shows you where to change a task's calendar, if needed.

In general, both task and resource calendars override the project base calendar. Whenever both the task and the assigned resource have a specific calendar, Project schedules work only during the periods allowed by both the task and resource calendars. The only exception is if you specify that a task should ignore the calendars for assigned resources, another choice you'll learn about in Chapter 9.

# Choosing the Project Calendar and Start Date

You've already learned how to create a custom calendar, but that process doesn't apply the calendar to the current file. (Yes, even though the calendar is saved in the file.) So, now, you must not only assign the desired calendar to your project plan file but also specify the *project start date.*

What's the deal with the start date? This is another instance where Project assumes that you are following professional project management practices. In that case, you're planning your projects well in advance to allow ample time to have the plan and budget approved, as well as to ensure that the resources you need will be available. The specific approval process and timing varies widely from organization to organization. One company might approve plans within weeks, while a larger company or government agency might have a lengthy, strict vetting process. At any rate, be sure you're planning far enough in advance to secure any needed planning, budgetary, and resource approvals and to get buy-in from all the stakeholders for your project.

You MUST select the project calendar and change the calendar options as described next BEFORE you add tasks into the project plan. Otherwise, Project will schedule those tasks according to its defaults, which may not reflect your needs. You have to delete those tasks, apply the right calendar, and then add the tasks back in to reschedule them.

Follow these steps to assign the project start date and calendar in the current (open) project file:

1. Click **Project** and then click **Project Information**.
2. Enter the desired project start date in the **Start Date** text box (see Figure 4.13).
3. Leave **Project Start Date** selected in the **Schedule From** drop-down list.

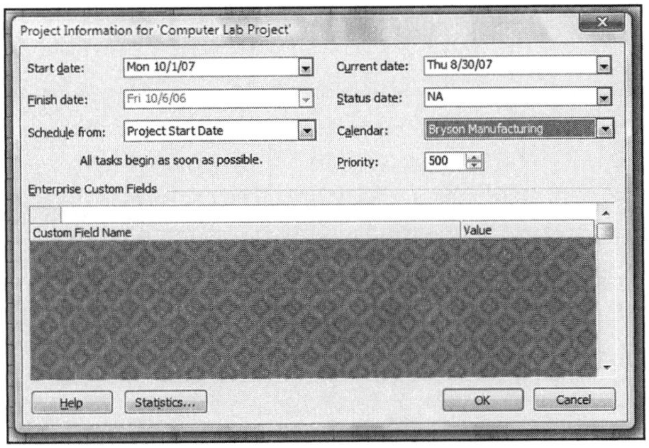

**Figure 4.13** Enter the project start date and select the project base calendar here.

4. Open the **Calendar** drop-down list and click the desired project base calendar.

5. Click **OK** to close the dialog box.

6. Save your file.

## Help! I need to schedule backward from a finish date.

So, the organization muckety-mucks have dictated that your project has to be completed by a particular date, and you want to work backward from that date. To do so, choose **Project Finish Date** from the Schedule From drop-down list in the Project Information dialog box. Then enter the desired project finish date in the **Finish Date** text box. After you click **OK**, Project will schedule all tasks you enter to end on the specified finish date, and linking (see Chapter 6) will schedule the tasks back into the present, as needed.

 If you used a template to create your project plan, change the start date to snap the first task and any linked tasks out to the desired schedule.

## Synching Calendar Options with the Calendar

One last step will ensure that Project schedules the tasks correctly in your new project plan file. You need to change settings on the Calendar tab of the Options dialog box to ensure that they match the calendar assigned to the project. This is particularly important if each work day begins at a specific time of day, such as 5 a.m., and you want to view task starting times in the various views in Project. It also applies if your company schedules and tracks more than 20 days of work per month.

For *every* project file to which you assign a calendar with custom working hours (or the Night Shift or 24 Hours default calendars), follow these steps to set calendar options that match the assigned base calendar:

1. Click **Tools** and then click **Options**.

2. Click the **Calendar** tab in the Options dialog box.

3. Change settings on the tab as needed to match the base calendar assigned to the current project file. For example, Figure 4.14 shows the **Default Start Time** and **Default End Time** entries (which specify the scheduled working hours per day) edited to match the work week schedule shown in Figure 4.11.

4. Click **OK** to close the dialog box.

5. Save your file.

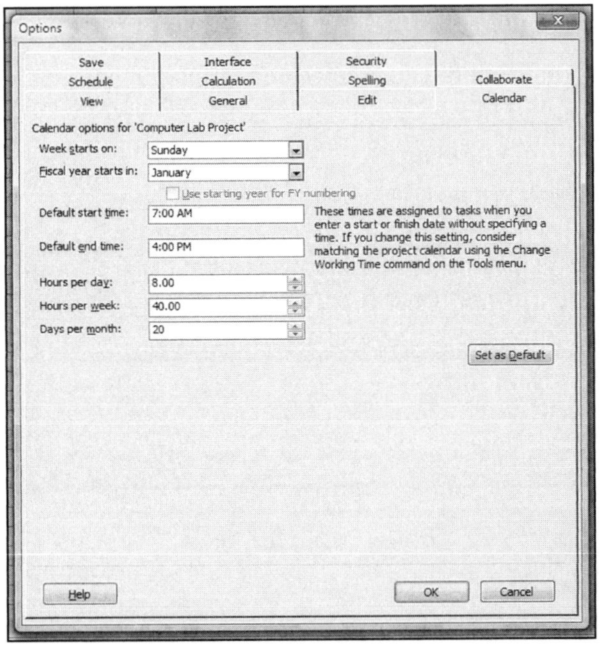

Figure 4.14 Edit
the Default Start Time
and Default End Time
entries to match the
project base calendar.

 Appendix B presents some special situations that real-world Project users encounter, such as setting up an unusual work schedule or fixing the schedule for tasks. Review that appendix to see specific examples of working with the calendar and more.

# Chapter Review

This chapter taught you the key skills you need to establish a project plan: creating a file to hold project information, setting up a calendar for work scheduling, and assigning that calendar and a start date to the project plan file. Review that information in more detail and get some hands-on practice before moving on to the next chapter.

## Review Questions

Write your answers to the following questions on a sheet of paper.

1. Why do you store each project plan in a separate file?

2. Do I have to start every new project from scratch?

3. My employer doesn't follow an 8 a.m. to 5 p.m. schedule. How do I match my project schedule to the real work schedule?

4. Why do I enter a project start date?

5. True or False: Calendar options must match the custom calendar applied.

## Projects

To see the solutions file created by completing the projects in this chapter, go to www.courseptr.com, click the **Downloads** link in the navigation bar at the top, type **Microsoft Office Project 2007 Survival Guide** in the search text box, and then click **Search Downloads**.

### Project 1

1. Create a new file based on the *New Product Launch* template installed with Project.

2. Change the project start date to the date two months in the future.

3. Save the file as *Bryson New Product Launch*.

Create a folder named *PSG Exercises* in your *Documents* or *My Documents* folder and save your exercise practice files there.

### Project 2

1. Create a new, blank project file.

2. Use the Change Working Time dialog box to create a new calendar named *Afternoon Job Share*. Change its default work week to have working hours of 1 p.m. to 5 p.m., Monday through Friday. Also use the Exceptions tab to name and mark at least two holidays.

3. Assign the *Afternoon Job Share* calendar to the file and set a project start date a few months in the future.

4. Change the Calendar options to match the *Afternoon Job Share* schedule.

5. Save the file as *Bryson File Reorganization*.

### Project 3

1. Switch to the Bryson New Product Launch file.

2. Close the file.

3. Close the *Bryson File Reorganization* file.

# CHAPTER 5

# ADDING AND
# ORGANIZING TASKS

This Chapter Teaches You How To:

- Break down the work for a project into task-sized chunks
- Enter task information the right way
- Understand and use task durations
- Create milestones
- Move, add, and delete tasks
- Import tasks from Microsoft Outlook
- Undo one or more changes
- Schedule a recurring task
- Organize the schedule with outlining
- Collapse and expand the outline
- Display a task that summarizes the project schedule

You can be a more successful project planner if you have the discipline to consider all the details. In building your project plan, you need to map out what activities need to happen and when. This chapter teaches you how to build a list of project tasks in Microsoft Project, thereby yielding a more complete and well-developed project plan. You'll learn what task information to enter, how to re-order and identify tasks, how to import tasks from Outlook, and how to add a task that repeats over time. You will learn to further develop your plan by undoing changes, applying outlining, and using the outlining to hide and redisplay schedule information.

## Understanding the WBS

If you've ever felt stuck in the face of a complex challenge, you might have gotten this good advice from a friend or colleague: "Take it one step at a time." Breaking a large undertaking down into deliverable parts enables you to focus on and complete activities, contributing to overall completion.

As a project manager, you need to take the same approach toward planning any project. You need to break the project down into a list of deliverables or outputs that fall into groups and organize those items in the order in which they need to be done. This is called creating the **Work Breakdown Structure** (or hierarchy of outcomes) for the project. The Work Breakdown Structure, also called the **WBS**, should organize the scope for the project — project goals, outcomes, and deliverables.

You might diagram the WBS on paper using a flowchart or an organization chart structure or create an outline of the planned outcomes in the WBS. The WBS can then serve as a starting point for identifying and entering specific activities in a project plan file.

After creating the WBS, you can use it for reference as you break the project down into tasks that have the right level of granularity for your tracking purposes. If a "task" is too general and really encompasses several activities, you won't really be able to track the completion of the individual activities. If you go too far in the other direction and break the schedule down into components that are too small, you risk putting yourself in a situation where you spend too much time tracking and maintaining tiny parts of the schedule.

 Like the project as a whole, each task should have a specific starting point and ending point. Generally, each task also represents a fairly discrete action (*research article*, *write article*, and so on), rather than a more general undertaking or outcome from the WBS (for example, *newsletter*). Identifying activities with specific starting and ending points can help you distinguish between what's a task and what's an overall phase or part of a project plan.

Consider the three examples shown in Figure 5.1. In the example on the left, the tasks lack enough detail to allow for useful tracking. The far right example goes to the other extreme, breaking down the activity into an unnecessary and cumbersome level of detail. Goldilocks in the middle is "just right," giving the project manager enough information to know which specific activities to check on, while not breaking the schedule down into tiny activities. The construction manager needs to know when the electrical work will be completed on each level of the house but doesn't need to know exactly when electrical outlets versus lighting fixtures will be installed.

**Figure 5.1** The left task breakdown is too general and the right one too detailed, but the center example breaks the project down to the right level.

> You can display a field of WBS codes that identify where each task falls in the hierarchy of the project. The section called "Creating a Table" in Chapter 12 illustrates how to add this field to a custom table.

If you want to use Project to lay out even small details for a project or to manage a project plan from the "10,000 feet" level, that's okay, too. Create the level of detail that suits your planning needs. The maintenance engineers at a manufacturing company might need to break a machine maintenance schedule into lots of small tasks and track them on an hour-by-hour basis, while the COO of a company might just want to track overall phases for a project. However, most projects are managed at a level somewhere in between.

People have different working styles when it comes to getting thoughts and ideas in order. The method that you use to build a list of project tasks doesn't really matter, as long as you've first carefully determined the scope, so that you can make sure you include all the needed activities and no unneeded ones. Microsoft Project can accommodate any style you use to build the list of tasks from there:

- **Top-down planning.** You like to map out overall phases or parts of a plan and then break those phases down level by level.
- **Bottom-up planning.** You like to list all the tasks or activities that need to happen in order to meet an overall goal or deliverable and then identify what phase or group the individual activities fit into.
- **Brain dump.** You like to list everything that needs to take place in a project and then go back and rearrange it into a logical or chronological order.

# Entering Basic Task Information

In Project, you enter and organize a list of tasks to create the WBS. As you learned in Chapter 1, *tasks* are the discrete actions or activities that need to be completed to meet the goals and deliverables of your project plan. Building the list of tasks is one of most essential parts of the planning process.

You type task information in the task sheet in the left pane of the Gantt Chart view. Even though that sheet holds a number of fields or columns, you only need to make entries into two of them:

- **Task Name.** Type in the name or label that you want to use to identify the task. As a rule you should stick with names that are as brief and descriptive as possible. Your organization might prefer to use a special convention for task names, such as including both subject and verb, as in "Program Module 1" rather than simply "Module 1."
- **Duration.** Enter the span of time between the start and finish for the task. If you type a number such as **3**, Project assumes you are entering the duration in days and adds *days* beside the value, as shown in Figure 5.2. ("Working with Durations," next in the chapter, explains how to work with other duration entries.) If you enter no duration, Project assumes a default duration of one day (*1 day?*, where the question mark indicates that the duration is estimated). If you are entering a task that's the name for a phase or group of other tasks, you don't need to enter the duration. Project will calculate that duration for you when you later outline and schedule the tasks.

---

I can't emphasize enough that you should ONLY enter information into *Task Name* and *Duration*. If you type a date into the *Start* or *Finish* field for a task, Project adds a **constraint** to the task, which limits Project's ability to reschedule the task and recalculate the schedule. "Using a Task Constraint," in Chapter 9, describes what constraints are, when to use them, and how to apply the right type of constraint.

---

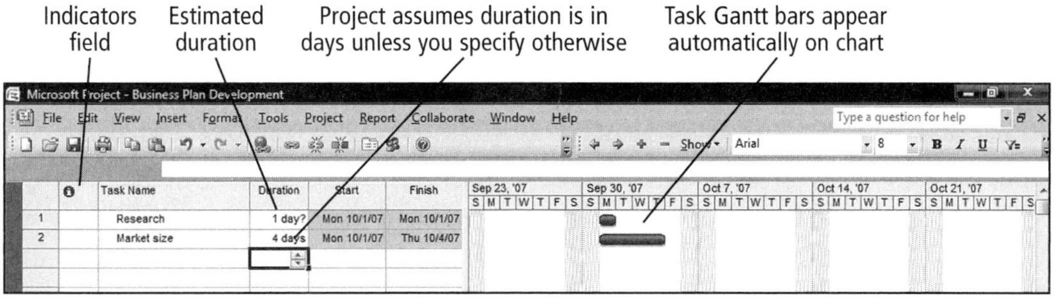
Indicators field
Estimated duration
Project assumes duration is in days unless you specify otherwise
Task Gantt bars appear automatically on chart
Microsoft Project - Business Plan Development

**Figure 5.2** Enter the task's name and duration only.

If you've ever used a spreadsheet program, entering tasks in the task sheet will come naturally. Follow these steps to create the list of tasks in your project plan:

1. Click on the first empty cell in the Task Name column.
2. Type the name for the task.
3. Press **Tab** to move to the Duration column.
4. Type the task duration value, such as **3** for 3 days (see Figure 5.3).

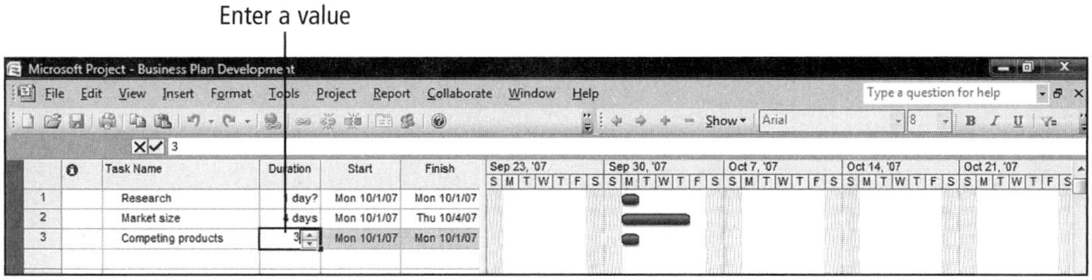
Enter a value
Microsoft Project - Business Plan Development

**Figure 5.3** Typing the Duration field entry to finish a task.

5. Press **Enter** and then press **Shift+Tab** to move the cell selector to the Task Name cell.
6. Repeat Steps 2 through 5 to add more tasks as needed.

---

TIP: You can change the formatting for the task sheet to make text smaller, add shading to cells, and so on. You'll learn more about these possibilities in Chapter 9.

---

After you enter each new task name, a number for the task appears in the gray row heading area at the left side of the task sheet. This row number is also the **task ID** number that Project uses to identify the task when you link it or perform some other activities. So, remember to check the row header area to find the task ID number for a task when needed.

Although you won't use it to enter basic task information, you should be aware that the Task Information dialog box provides another location where you can work with task values such as the *Task Name* and *Duration* field entries. If you double-click a task in the task sheet portion of the Gantt Chart view, the Task Information dialog box (see Figure 5.4) opens. You can use the tabs in this dialog box to view and change task information. (Later chapters will cover specific instances when you use the settings here.) After you make the desired changes, click **OK** to close the dialog box.

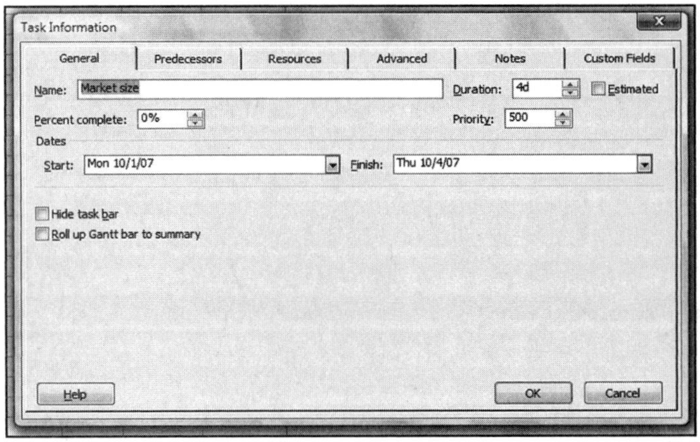

**Figure 5.4** You also can use the Task Information dialog box to work with task settings.

At one manufacturing company where I've taught Microsoft Project classes, many of the users make Task Name entries in ALL CAPITAL LETTERS for purposes of matching output from another planning system used in the company. While you might think that typing in all caps makes the tasks more readable, in reality the opposite tends to be true because the capital letters all have the same height. Lowercase letters vary more in shape and are thus easier for the brain to recognize. If you want to make text more readable, try changing the font or the text size. Chapter 9 will teach you how to make these changes and others.

## Working with Durations

You've already learned that when you type a number into the *Duration* field for a task, Project assumes the entry is in *days*. But the definition of a day depends on the calendar you've assigned to the project and the Default Start Time, Default End Time, and Hours Per Day settings on the Calendar tab of the Options dialog box. (The project start date can also play a role, but that will be described in more detail in an example in Appendix B.)

In real life and under the Standard calendar in Project, a day means a typical eight-hour work day. So, a one-day task will have a schedule of eight hours from 8 a.m. to 5 p.m., not counting an hour for lunch. However, if you've chosen the 24 Hours calendar and changed the settings on the Calendar tab to reflect a 24-hour working schedule, then a one-day task will have a 24-hour schedule.

Not every task lasts a full day (no matter what the calendar), such as a two-hour planning meeting, and some tasks last longer and might even exceed the daily working hours. For example, running your company's booth at a trade show or running a software test are tasks that might take 16 hours on a single day during a project that otherwise has eight-hour working days.

Project enables you to schedule the exact amount of time a task will take to finish based on the abbreviation or ***duration label*** that you include with the numeric value in the Duration column of the task sheet. Some duration abbreviations are for ***elapsed durations***, where you specify that the duration should be continuous, as if under a 24/7 calendar rather than the calendar applied to the project. For example, if you are entering a task that represents a 48-hour (two continuous days) curing time for a concrete slab, you would want to enter the value as an elapsed duration; otherwise, Project would break the task over six days according to a calendar with a standard eight-hour work day.

Table 5.1 lists the abbreviations or duration labels. The far right column of the table includes an example entry and what it means in terms of how Project schedules the task.

If you enter a number only in the *Duration* field, Project assumes you are entering the duration in days.

You can change how Project interprets *Duration* field entries. Click **Tools**, and then click **Options**. Click the **Schedule** tab, open the **Duration Is Entered In** drop-down list, and click the alternate type of time unit to use, such as Hours. Click **OK** to apply your change.

**Table 5.1**  Duration Labels (Abbreviations)

| Time Unit | Abbreviations | Example |
|---|---|---|
| Minutes | M<br>Min<br>Mins | **30m** means 30 working minutes |
| Hours | H<br>Hr<br>Hrs<br>Hour | **30h** means 30 working hours |
| Days | D<br>Dy<br>Day | **30d** means 30 working days |
| Weeks | W<br>Wk<br>Week | **30w** means 30 working weeks |
| Months | Mo<br>Mons<br>Months | **2mo** means 2 working months |
| Elapsed minutes | Em<br>Emin<br>Emins | **30em** means 30 consecutive elapsed minutes |
| Elapsed hours | Eh<br>Ehr<br>Ehrs<br>Ehour | **30eh** means 30 consecutive elapsed hours |
| Elapsed days | Ed<br>Edy<br>Eday | **30ed** means 30 consecutive elapsed days |
| Elapsed weeks | Ew<br>Ewk<br>Eweek | **30ew** means 30 consecutive elapsed weeks |
| Elapsed months | Emo<br>Emons<br>Emonths | **2emo** means 40 consecutive elapsed days* |

*Assumes that you've specified each month to be 20 working days using the Calendar tab of the Options dialog box in Project.

To use one of the duration labels:

1. Click the **Duration** cell for the task.
2. Type the **numeric value** for the duration.
3. Type the desired **duration label**, as in the top example in Figure 5.5.

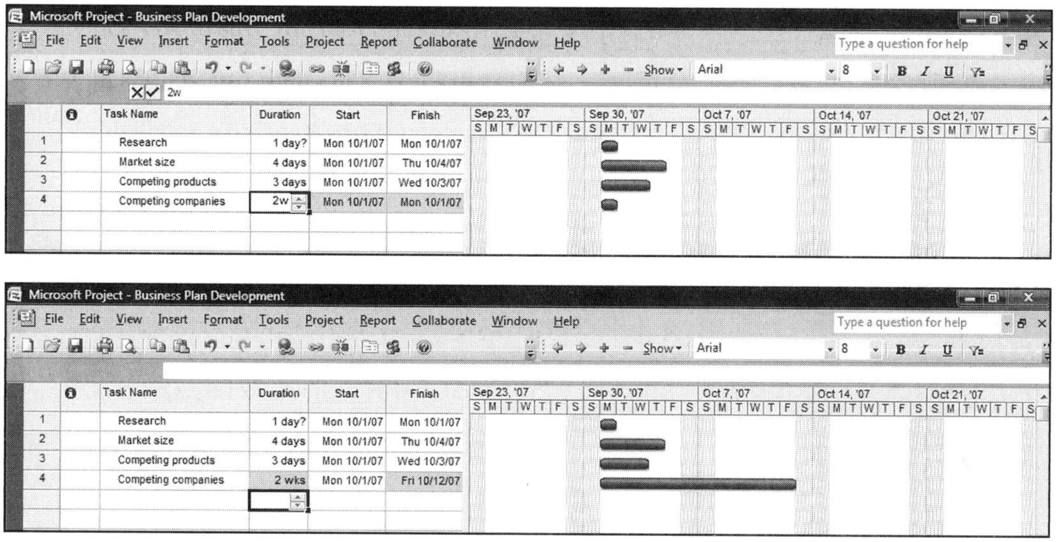

**Figure 5.5** Use a duration label to express durations in time periods other than days.

4. Press **Enter**. The Gantt bar for the task adjusts to reflect the new duration, as in the bottom portion of Figure 5.5.

> **NOTE** You do not have to type a space between the duration value and label. Project automatically inserts the space and may adjust the duration label displayed—for example, changing a *16h* duration entry to *16 hrs*. Throughout the book, I'll refer to durations using the shortest label and omitting the space, as in *16h*.

When you enter an elapsed duration, the Gantt Chart bars at the right reflect how the task runs in continuous time rather than being broken up according to a calendar. For example, Figure 5.6 compares how the schedule looks when a task is entered as a 16 hour (16h or 2d) task versus a 16 elapsed hours (16eh) task in a project using the Standard (eight hour) calendar. Project schedules the 16h task to span over two eight-hour work days, while the 16eh is scheduled to complete during a single day, exceeding the eight-hour work day. So, using duration labels not only enables you to schedule with precision but also provides you with a way to override a calendar with a standard work day to schedule all of a longer task on the day that it needs to occur.

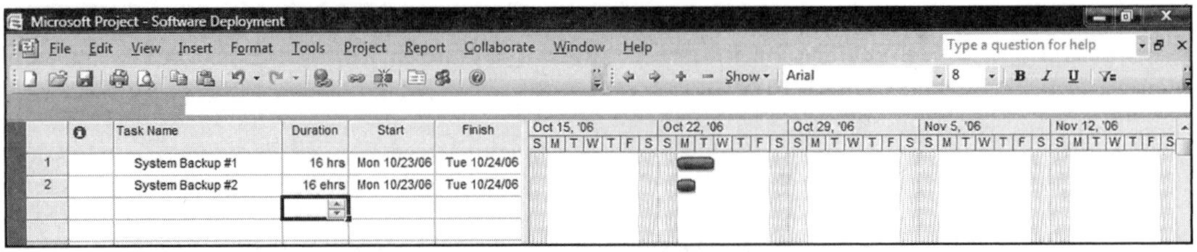

**Figure 5.6** The elapsed duration for task 2 schedules the work during consecutive hours on a single day.

## But How Do I Know What the Duration Should Be?

Even though the tools in Microsoft Project automate your ability to build and track the project plan, they aren't a substitute for the human expertise of yourself and your team. Generally speaking, use your experience to judge what the duration of each task in the plan should be. If you don't have enough expertise, you can use these methods to better identify a task's likely duration:

- Ask a team member or someone from another department who has more expertise with a particular type of task or has managed a similar project to help you develop the task estimate.

- If the task will be handled by an outside vendor and you have multiple vendors bidding for the work, be sure to have the competing vendors supply duration estimates, and then base your duration on that information.

- Think through the task requirements and develop optimistic (O), pessimistic (P), and most likely (M) durations. (Use consistent units such as hours or days.) Then, plug the estimates into the following PERT analysis formula: (O+4M+P)/6=Estimated duration. This analysis gives more weight to the most likely duration, while still considering the extremes, in producing an estimate.

- If you've used Project to track a similar task or project, refer back to your previous project plan file. The valuable history recorded in any Project file, including whether a task happened on or off schedule and notes about why that was the case, can help you identify more accurate durations the next time around.

## Adding a Milestone

When you've got a few years of life or career experience under your belt, you may look back at a particular occurrence and think, "Wow, that was really a milestone for me." While you may have invested a lot of time and sweat in pursuit of your milestone, the achievement itself—receiving the diploma or contract, for example—flies by in an instant.

Project enables you to add a ***milestone*** task to your project plan to mark a significant point or event. To mark a task as a milestone, simply enter **0** (zero) in the *Duration* field for the task. As shown in Figure 5.7, Project charts a milestone task with a diamond marker rather than a Gantt bar.

Any task for which you enter 0 (zero) duration is a ***milestone*** task.

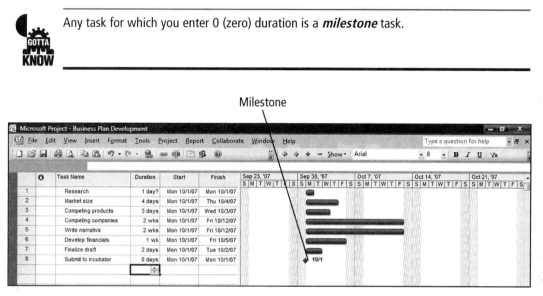

**Figure 5.7**  Use a milestone task (with a 0 duration) to mark an important point in the project schedule.

You enter milestones with a 0 duration because they have no actual work associated with them. For example, you may not be able to initiate work on a project until you receive a signed copy of the contract from the client. Although the contract receipt doesn't require any work on your part, it does trigger work on other tasks when it actually occurs. So, the milestone task enables you to track that event and use it to trigger the other work in your project plan. Some project managers use milestones to mark particular dates when they want to status the project or particular dates that might be significant checkpoints in the project, such as the day when 50% of the overall project duration has passed. You can even use a milestone to tell Project to give you a warning if a schedule change delays the project finish date. You'll learn that trick in Chapter 9.

You also can mark a task with a longer duration as a milestone after entering the task duration; just double-click the task, click the **Advanced** tab of the Task Information dialog box, click the **Mark Task as Milestone** check box to check it, and then click **OK**. This changes the task's appearance on the Gantt Chart to that of a milestone bar (diamond), but it does not reduce the duration or amount of work assigned. Because that might cause confusion when reviewing the plan, it may be a better practice to stick with milestones that have a 0 duration.

## Moving Tasks Around

If you tend to use a "brain dump" style of planning where you type all the tasks that come to mind and then rearrange them later, you need to know how to move the tasks into the proper order when the time comes.

You can use one of two methods to move a task, and both methods begin with selecting the task. To select the whole task, click the **task row number** (task ID number) in the gray row heading area at the left. As shown in Figure 5.8, Project highlights the entire task.

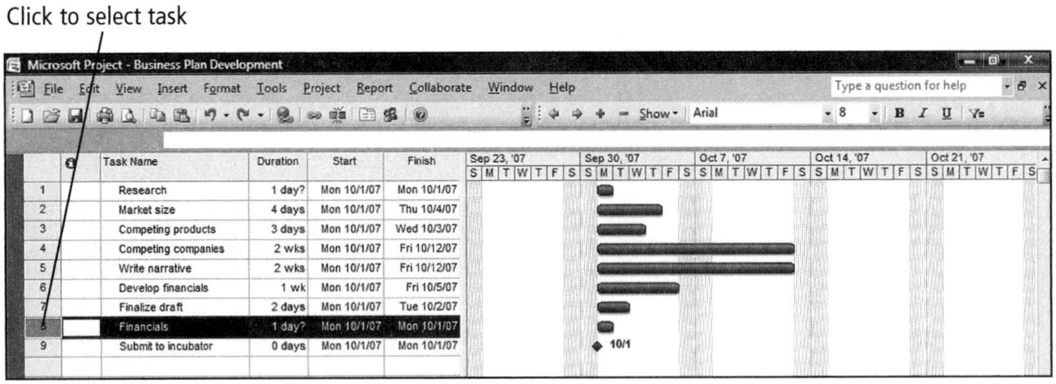

Click to select task

**Figure 5.8** Click the task row number to select the whole task.

Clicking the task name does *not* select the whole task. If you click the task name and then try to drag or cut and paste, you will move the Task Name entry only, not the task.

After you select a task, you can use one of these two methods to move it:

- Move the mouse pointer over the top or bottom border of the selected task until a four-headed arrow appears with the mouse pointer. Drag the task up or down in the list, and when the gray horizontal bar reaches the desired position (see Figure 5.9), release the mouse button to drop the task into its new position.
- Click **Edit** and then click **Cut Task** (Shortcut: **Ctrl+X**). Click a cell in the task above which you want to move the task you just cut. Click **Edit** and then click **Paste** (Shortcut: **Ctrl+V**). The task appears in the new location.

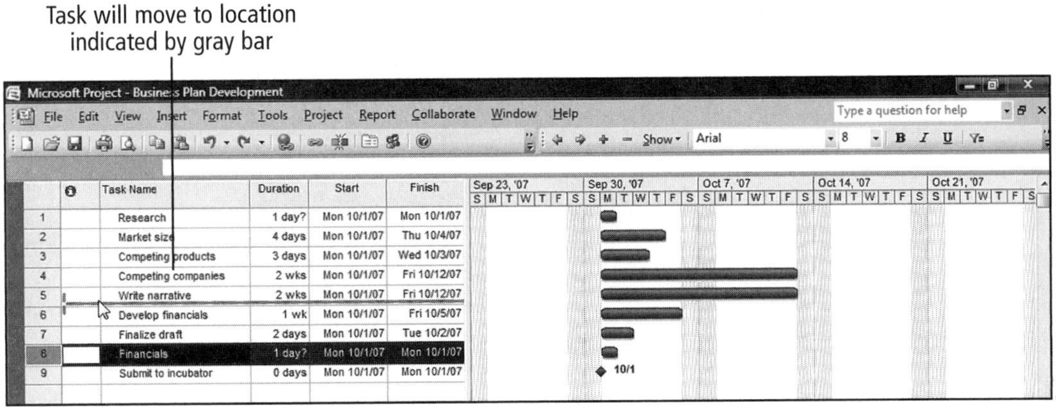

Task will move to location
indicated by gray bar

Figure 5.9  Drag a selected task to move it.

The Standard toolbar includes buttons for copying, cutting, and pasting tasks (or cells). By default, the Cut button may not appear on the Standard toolbar, so you can click the **Toolbar Options** button and then click the button in the menu that appears.

Just keep in mind that you need to be careful about moving tasks later in the process, after you've linked tasks to establish the Project schedule. (Chapter 6 describes that process.) Moving tasks around at that point can disrupt or even remove links, which can undo a significant portion of your planning. Also keep in mind that moving tasks permanently changes task ID (row) numbers to reflect the new order.

## Adding and Deleting Tasks

A thorough project manager typically calls on colleagues and team members to help build the project plan and ensure that the plan includes all the activities required to produce the project deliverables. After receiving some input, the project manager will typically need to add more tasks to the project plan or possibly delete unneeded tasks.

To add a task to the project plan:

1. Click a cell in the task above which you want to insert a new task.
2. Click **Insert** and then click **New Task** (Shortcut: **Insert**). The new, blank task row appears, as shown in Figure 5.10.
3. Add the Task Name and Duration entries as you normally would.

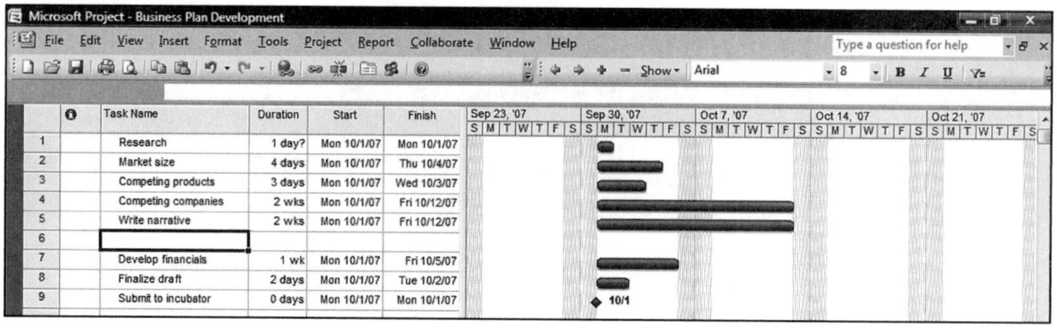

**Figure 5.10** A new, blank task 6 has been inserted.

In previous versions of Microsoft Project, pressing the Delete key on the keyboard immediately deleted the task holding the cell selector. As you might guess, this caused more than one project manager to wreak havoc on a schedule by pressing a commonly used editing key. Project 2007 still lets you delete tasks, but each of the available methods requires at least two actions to force you, basically, to confirm that you *really* want to delete the task:

- Click the **task ID** number (row header) and then press **Delete**.
- Click a cell in the task, click **Edit**, and then click **Delete Task**.
- Click the **Task Name cell** for the task and then press **Delete**. A button appears to the left of the Task Name cell. Click the button and then click **Delete the Entire Task** in the menu that appears (see Figure 5.11).

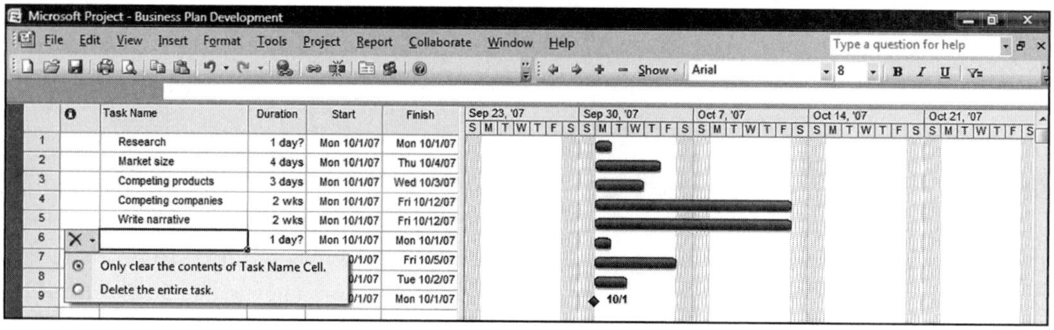

**Figure 5.11** Click the button that appears after you press Delete and then specify whether to delete the whole task or the contents of the selected cell.

If you delete a task accidentally in spite of the new safeguards, you can press **Ctrl+Z** immediately to undo the deletion. The section called "Using the New Multi-Level Undo" later in this chapter provides more information about undoing changes you make to the project plan file. In addition, keep in mind that when you add and delete tasks, Project permanently changes the task ID numbers, so if a task addition or deletion has unwanted renumbering consequences, make sure you undo the change.

Although you can add and delete tasks even after you've started tracking work on a project, it's best to take the time to build a thorough list of tasks at this point, before you've outlined or linked any tasks. That's because Project can't produce an accurate calculation of the project's duration without all the tasks being present. In such a scenario, missing tasks will mean that you've underestimated the schedule and work involved in your project, making the project plan unrealistic.

## Importing Tasks from Outlook

If you already built a list of tasks for a particular project in Microsoft Outlook, you can import them directly into Project for more robust tracking. Project can import the task name (called the Subject in Outlook), Notes, and duration. However, be aware that the duration is not based on the task Start Date or Due Date entered in Outlook. Instead, Project uses the *Total Work* field entry in the Details area for the task. To make an entry there, click the **Tasks** button in the Navigation pane at the left side of the Outlook window and then double-click the **task** in the To-Do List. In the task window, click the **Details button** in the Show group on the Ribbon (Outlook 2007) or the **Details tab** in older Outlook versions. Enter work in hours (for example, **2h**), days (for example, **2d**), or weeks (for example, **2w**) in the **Total Work** field (see Figure 5.12), and then click **Save & Close** or **Save and Close** in older Outlook versions.

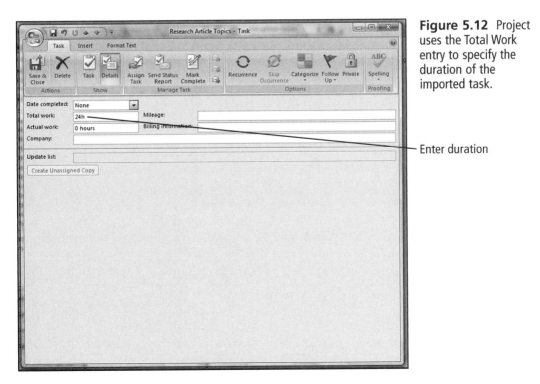

**Figure 5.12** Project uses the Total Work entry to specify the duration of the imported task.

Enter duration

Follow these steps to import a list of tasks directly from Outlook into Project:

1. Working in Project, open the Project file into which you want to add the imported tasks, or start a new, blank file.

2. Click **Tools** and then click **Import Outlook Tasks**.

 Depending on the Outlook version installed on your system, a message box may warn you that a program is trying to access your e-mail information. Click **Yes** as many times as needed to continue the import operation. You also may be prompted to choose a user profile if more than one profile has been set up in Outlook.

3. In the message box that warns you that a program is trying to access information in Outlook, click **Allow**. (You may have to click Allow repeatedly.)

4. In the Import Outlook Tasks dialog box, click the **check box for any task** that you want to import. A check mark should appear in the check box for each selected task, as illustrated in Figure 5.13. Alternately, you can click the **Select All** button to check all the tasks to specify them for import.

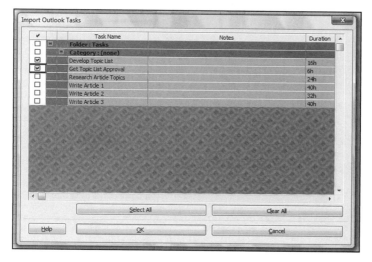

**Figure 5.13** Click to check the check box for each task to import.

5. Click **OK**. Project imports the tasks into the project file, adding them at the bottom of the list of any tasks already in the task sheet. Figure 5.14 shows an example of imported tasks. The imported tasks appear in alphabetical order by task name.

6. Rearrange and schedule the tasks as needed.

Indicator (icon) tells you the task had
note information entered in Outlook

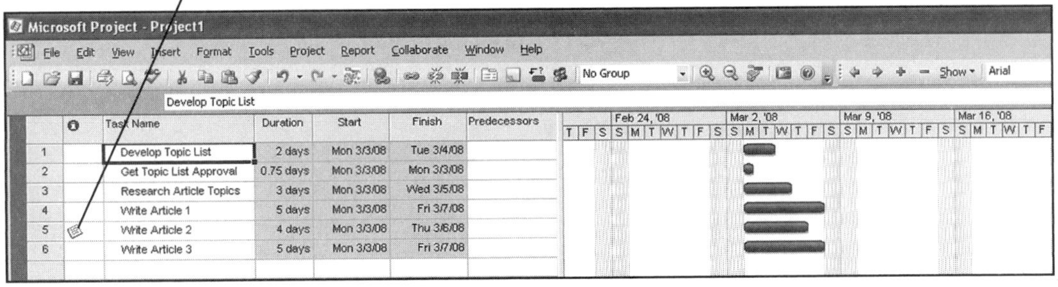

**Figure 5.14**  A list of tasks imported from Outlook.

As shown in Figure 5.14, the *Task Name* and *Duration* field information automatically imports from Outlook. Project schedules the imported tasks from the project start date, as identified in the Project Information dialog box. If a task had note information entered in Outlook, a note icon appears in the *Indicators* field beside the task's name. You can move the mouse pointer over the note icon to display a pop-up tip with the note information.

The tasks imported into Project do not remain linked to the original Outlook tasks. The import operation works more like a copy operation. So, if you want to work with the list of tasks in both Project and Outlook, you'll need to enter changes and tracking information about the tasks in both programs.

> **NOTE** If the Import Outlook Tasks command doesn't work for you or you don't use Outlook, you can still import any list of data that's saved as a .csv (comma-separated values) or delimited .txt (plain text) file. Outlook (and many other programs) can export to these formats. Chapter 14 explains how to export task information from Outlook and then import it into Project.

## Editing a Task

As you refine your project plan, you may need to make changes to task information that you've previously entered. For example, when touching base with a vendor you might learn that you overestimated the duration for a particular task, so you need to change the *Duration* field entry for the task. Or, you might want to get more specific about the names you've assigned to tasks or even replace temporary "code names" with live names for tasks.

Just like working in a spreadsheet program, you can change the entry in any cell in the task sheet portion of the Gantt Chart view. Start by clicking the cell to edit in the task, and then use one of the following methods to make the required changes:

- **Replace the entry.** Simply begin typing to replace the entire entry in a selected cell. Press **Enter** to finish the change.

- **Change part of the entry.** To edit in the cell, click again within the cell text to position the insertion point in it or press **F2**. You can use editing keys such as Backspace and the arrow keys to make changes, drag over text and then type to replace the text, and so on. When you finish your changes, press **Enter**. You also can click in the Entry bar below the toolbars, make your edits there, and click the enter (check) button when you finish.

- **Change a numerical entry.** When you click a cell in some fields, such as the *Duration* field, spinner buttons or a drop-down list arrow appears. You can use the spinner buttons or drop-down list to specify the new entry for the cell.

 If you start editing a cell but realize that you no longer want to make the change, press **Esc** on the keyboard to cancel the edit.

## Using the New Multi-Level Undo

If this is the first time you've used Microsoft Project, consider yourself lucky for starting off with Project 2007 rather than an earlier version. That's because this is the first version of Project to offer multiple undo (and redo) levels, a feature that other applications have offered for years now.

The calculations that occur behind the scenes in Project are highly complex. A duration change to a single task can ripple all the way through a lengthy project, making it difficult to reverse all the calculations resulting from even more changes. Well, the Project gurus at Microsoft have finally cracked this nut, enabling Project by default to let you undo the 20 most recent changes that you made to your project file.

 If your system has a lot of memory, you can increase the number of Undo levels up to 99. Click **Tools**, and then click **Options**. Click the **General** tab, increase the **Undo Levels** text box entry to the desired value, and click **OK**.

After you make the first change in your project plan file during the current work session, the Undo button becomes active on the Standard toolbar. Click that button to undo the most recent change that you've made.

If you want to back up in the file by undoing several changes simultaneously, click the drop-down list arrow for the Undo button and then click the name of the earliest action to undo, as in the example in Figure 5.15. When you click, Project reverses the action that you clicked, as well as any action(s) above it in the list.

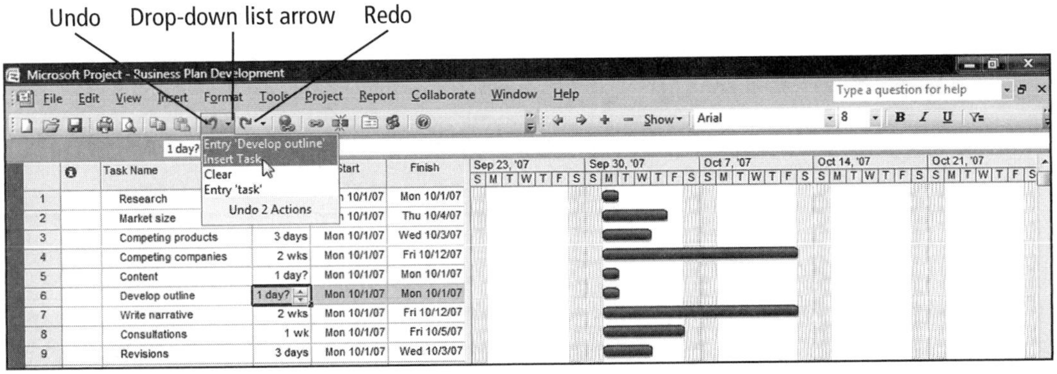

Figure 5.15 Undoing multiple changes.

After you undo one or more actions, the Redo button becomes enabled. You can click it to reinstate the change that you most recently undid, or you can click its drop-down list arrow and then click a change in the list that appears to redo that change and any changes above it.

 If you move the mouse pointer over either the Undo or Redo buttons, you'll notice that the button names change depending on the last action you performed or chose to redo.

The ability to undo and redo multiple changes in Project enhances your ability as project manager to test "what if" scenarios, seeing how a few changes might impact the project schedule. In previous versions of Project, you would have to save multiple versions of a file to get this much planning flexibility.

 Saving the file clears the stack, or history, of changes, eliminating the ability to undo. So, as you work, you'll have to balance your desire to keep undo changes available with the need to save your work from time to time to make sure that you don't lose anything should you experience a power fluctuation or other system problem.

# Adding a Task That Repeats

Sometimes, brief periods of work repeat at set intervals throughout the project. This kind of task is called a *recurring task*. Recurring tasks might include weekly team meetings, bi-weekly scheduling updates, or monthly reports to stakeholders. You also might want to schedule some general administrative time for the project as a recurring task.

 You might wonder why you wouldn't just add one big task spanning the entire length of the project schedule to account for administrative and meeting time and other intermittent tasks. Well, there's a strong reason not to. In planning your project, you want Microsoft Project to be able to calculate accurate totals for the amount of work done (and the associated costs) for the project. Using one long task to account for activities that really consume a more limited amount of time will *overstate* the real work and time required, making your project plan inaccurate. So, the best practice is to create a *recurring task* that repeats at the interval you specify.

Project can automatically calculate and schedule the repeating tasks for your project plan. This saves you the effort of identifying the date when each task instance should occur and creating that task instance manually. Project can create tasks that recur on a daily, weekly, monthly, or yearly basis. You also can schedule tasks at multiple intervals within those spans, such as creating a task that occurs weekly every Monday and Wednesday.

Use these steps to add a recurring task into your project plan.

1. Working in the task sheet of the Gantt Chart view, click the **Task Name cell** for the row where you'd like to insert the recurring task, such as the task 1 row. Other tasks will move down when you insert the task.

 You will want to insert recurring tasks at the top of the schedule for a few reasons. First, recurring tasks generally don't drive the schedules for other tasks, so it makes the project plan a bit tidier to have them located at the top. Second, because recurring tasks tend to be brief in duration, placing them at the top of the plan makes them easier to find. Finally, if you've already linked tasks, you don't want the recurring tasks to be linked in an unwanted way.

2. Click **Insert** and then click **Recurring Task**. The Recurring Task Information dialog box appears.

3. Type a name for the recurring task in the **Task Name** text box.

4  Press **Tab**, and then type an entry in the **Duration** field. Just as in the task sheet's *Duration* field, use a duration label to make your entry specific, as in **1h**.

5. Under Recurrence Pattern, click the appropriate option button: **Daily**, **Weekly**, **Monthly**, or **Yearly**.

6. Using the options that appear based on your choice in Step 5, specify the interval between recurrences in the Recurrence Pattern area:

   ■ **Daily.** Click the **Days** or **Workdays** options button and then change the **Every** text box entry to set the interval.

   ■ **Weekly.** Change the **Recur Every ___ Week(s) On** value to specify the recurrence interval, and then check the day(s) of the week on which Project should schedule the task. For example, Figure 5.16 shows a task set to repeat every Thursday.

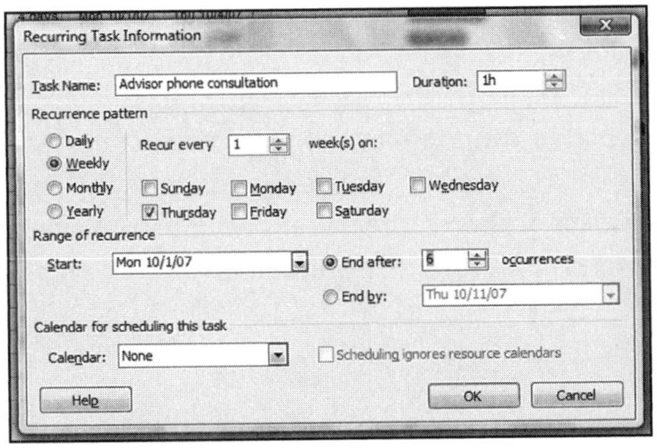

**Figure 5.16** Setting up a recurring task.

   ■ **Monthly.** To specify the task to recur on a particular numeric day of the month, leave the **Day ___ of Every ___ Month(s)** option button selected and change the text box entries to specify the particular day and number of months between instances. If you instead want to schedule the task to recur on a particular day of the week, click the **The ___ ___ of Every ___ Months** option button and use the drop-down lists and text box to specify the day of the week settings and the interval.

   ■ **Yearly.** To set the task on a particular date during the year, leave the **On** option button selected and type the desired date into the text box. To schedule by day of the week during a particular month, click the **The** option button and then use the drop-down lists to specify the desired day and month.

7. Use the settings in the Range of Recurrence area to specify the number of recurrences by date (change the **Start** and **End By** entries as desired), or click the **End After ___ Recurrences** option button and use the text box to specify how many times the task should repeat. This step is critical, if you haven't linked and scheduled tasks yet, to ensure Project schedules an adequate number of recurrences of the task. For example, Figure 5.16 also shows that the task will repeat 6 times from the project start date.

8. Choose the calendar to use from the **Calendar** drop-down list. This ensures that Project will not schedule a recurrence on a date that you've designated as a non-working day.

9. Click **OK**. Project inserts the recurring task.

> If an instance of a recurring task would occur during nonworking time based on Project's calculations, a warning appears. Click **Yes** to have Project adjust the recurrence to fall during working time.

The recurring task appears as a summary task in the task sheet. If you click the plus beside the task name, the group expands to show each of the individual task instances, like the example in Figure 5.17. (The next section explains more about working with summary tasks like this.) The *Indicator* field shows a special indicator for the recurring task summary task, as well as a constraint indicator for each of the occurrences. The constraint tells Project the task is scheduled for a particular date so that Project won't move the task unless you edit the recurring task.

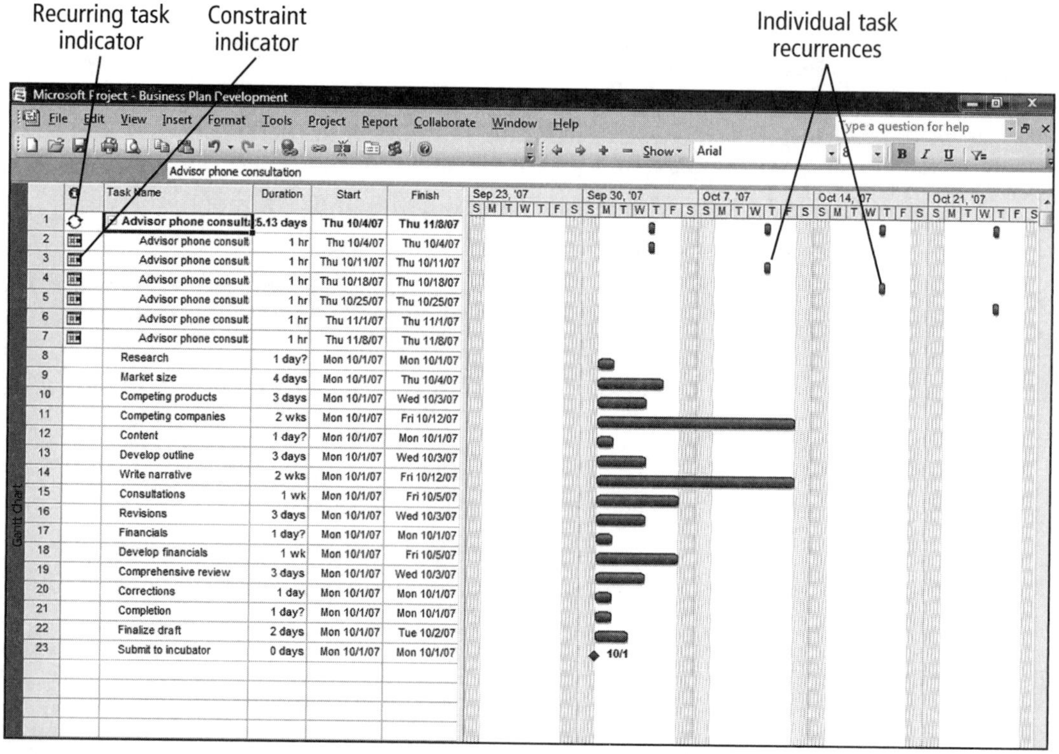

**Figure 5.17** Project schedules the multiple instances of the recurring task.

When you need to edit a recurring task, double-click the recurring task summary task to redisplay the Recurring Task Information dialog box. Make the desired changes and then click **OK**. To remove the recurring task from the schedule, select the recurring task's summary task and delete it as you would any other task.

## Using Outlining to Structure the Work

*Outlining* in Microsoft Project helps you organize tasks related by function or chronology. For example, many projects fall into logical phases or stages of activity, so outlining the tasks by phase or stage makes the project easier to follow. Project actually enables you to apply multiple levels of outlining within a project plan, but as a practical matter, you'll want to limit the outline to two or three levels for smaller project plans.

Outlining also enables you to hide and redisplay tasks by collapsing and expanding the outline. This enables you, in your role as project manager, to view project overview information when needed or to focus on specific tasks at other times.

Finally, outlining enables Project to summarize information. Outlining creates **summary tasks** and **subtasks** (or **detail tasks**). You indent subtasks to convert the task above to a summary task that calculates information about the indented subtasks. For example, as you track work in the project plan, the summary task can calculate an overall completion percentage for the tasks in the group, which gives you as project manager a better idea of overall areas where the project is on track or off track.

Indent **subtasks** (**detail tasks**) to make the task above them into a **summary task**. The summary task calculates information about all the subtasks within the summary group, such as the overall duration for the group. Use the Outdent, Indent, Show Subtasks, Hide Subtasks, and Show buttons on the Formatting toolbar to apply outlining and work with the outlined tasks.

If you applied outlining to a list in Word or Excel and copy that information into the Project task sheet, the pasted information doesn't retain its outlining. You need to reapply the outlining in Project.

### Creating Subtasks

Project's Formatting toolbar provides the tools you need to apply outlining in the project plan: the Outdent and Indent buttons at the far left end of the toolbar. You select the tasks to which you want to make an outlining change and then click one of the buttons. Clicking the *Outdent* button *promotes* the selected tasks to the next higher outline level, while clicking the *Indent* button *demotes* the selected tasks to the next lower outline level, making them into subtasks.

Even though Project offers two buttons, most novice users have an easier time outlining the project plan by working from the top down and thus only use the Indent button to demote tasks into subtasks. So, here's the easiest way to outline your project plan:

1. Identify the first task that you want to be a summary task and drag over the Task Name cells for the tasks below that you want to demote into subtasks.

2. Click the **Indent** button on the Formatting toolbar (shortcut: **Alt+Shift+Right Arrow**). The selected tasks become subtasks and the task above them becomes a summary task, as illustrated in Figure 5.18. The summary task's cells in the task sheet appear in bold, and the Gantt bar for the summary task changes to a summary taskbar.

The Outline submenu of the Project menu also offers commands for indenting and outdenting tasks.

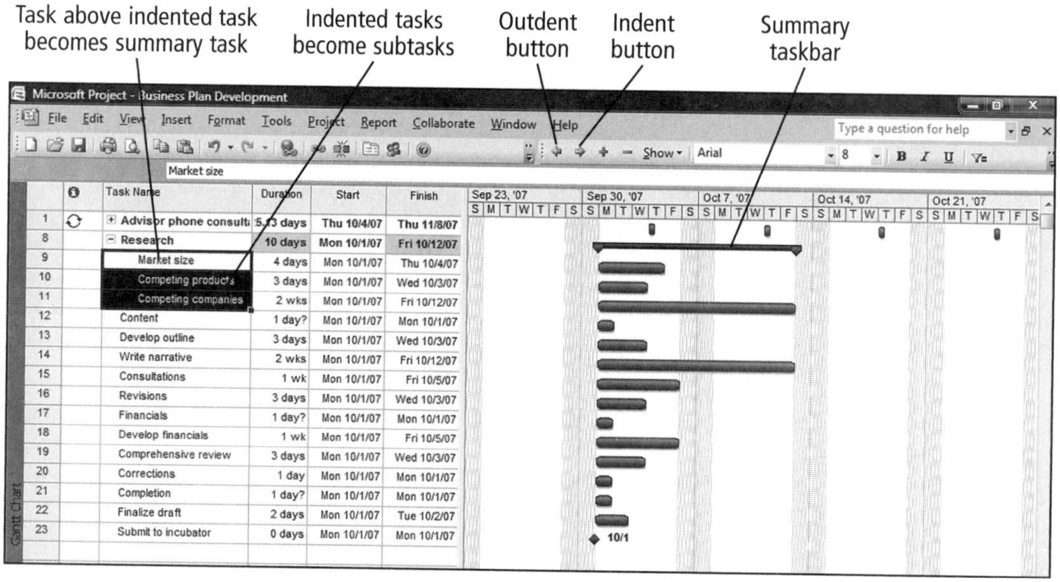

Task above indented task becomes summary task    Indented tasks become subtasks    Outdent button    Indent button    Summary taskbar

**Figure 5.18** Demote tasks to make them into subtasks and promote the task above into a summary task.

3. Repeat Steps 1 and 2 to demote other groups of tasks and thus finish creating all the top-level summary tasks, as shown in Figure 5.19.

| | ● | Task Name | Duration | Start | Finish |
|---|---|---|---|---|---|
| 1 | ◯ | ⊞ Advisor phone consult | 5.13 days | Thu 10/4/07 | Thu 11/8/07 |
| 8 | | ⊟ Research | 10 days | Mon 10/1/07 | Fri 10/12/07 |
| 9 | | Market size | 4 days | Mon 10/1/07 | Thu 10/4/07 |
| 10 | | Competing products | 3 days | Mon 10/1/07 | Wed 10/3/07 |
| 11 | | Competing companies | 2 wks | Mon 10/1/07 | Fri 10/12/07 |
| 12 | | ⊟ Content | 10 days | Mon 10/1/07 | Fri 10/12/07 |
| 13 | | Develop outline | 3 days | Mon 10/1/07 | Wed 10/3/07 |
| 14 | | Write narrative | 2 wks | Mon 10/1/07 | Fri 10/12/07 |
| 15 | | Consultations | 1 wk | Mon 10/1/07 | Fri 10/5/07 |
| 16 | | Revisions | 3 days | Mon 10/1/07 | Wed 10/3/07 |
| 17 | | ⊟ Financials | 5 days | Mon 10/1/07 | Fri 10/5/07 |
| 18 | | Develop financials | 1 wk | Mon 10/1/07 | Fri 10/5/07 |
| 19 | | Comprehensive review | 3 days | Mon 10/1/07 | Wed 10/3/07 |
| 20 | | Corrections | 1 day | Mon 10/1/07 | Mon 10/1/07 |
| 21 | | ⊟ Completion | 2 days | Mon 10/1/07 | Tue 10/2/07 |
| 22 | | Finalize draft | 2 days | Mon 10/1/07 | Tue 10/2/07 |
| 23 | | Submit to incubator | 0 days | Mon 10/1/07 | Mon 10/1/07 |

**Figure 5.19**  All the top-level summary tasks created in a project plan.

4. Create subsequent lower outline levels by selecting and demoting subtasks as needed.

If you do need to outdent (promote) one or more tasks to a higher level, select the task and click the **Outdent** button (shortcut: **Alt+Shift+Left Arrow**) on the Formatting toolbar.

Keep in mind that you can still insert new tasks into the project plan after applying outlining. An inserted task typically takes on the subtask outline level of the nearest tasks, rather than the summary task outline level. For that reason, look carefully at how Project treats the inserted task (as well as any tasks you move) and promote or demote it as needed.

---

**MIN-STEP**

Indenting a summary task typically also indents its subtasks. So, if you realize that a summary task needs to be at the same level as its subtasks, select and *demote* the summary task and then select and *promote* the subtasks.

Also, if you've already applied linking to schedule the project as described in Chapter 6, promoting a task and then demoting the tasks beneath it can break the link between the new summary and subtasks, creating unwanted scheduling changes. So you should, as much as possible, try to build and organize a thorough task list before linking. If that's not possible, be sure to examine the impact of every outline change on task links and scheduling.

---

## Hiding and Redisplaying Subtasks

If you have a project plan that includes hundreds of subtasks—and believe me, many project managers do—you may neither need nor want to see all of the subtasks onscreen at all times. Outlining enables you to *collapse* (hide) subtasks when you don't need to see them and then *expand* (redisplay) the subtasks at any later time. Examples of when you may want to collapse one or more summary groups of tasks include:

- **When you want to zero in on the activity in a single phase of the project.** You can collapse all the other summary groups and view only the subtasks for the phase under discussion.

- **When you need to discuss the "10,000 feet" level with stakeholders.** Stakeholders outside your project team often don't need to see information about every task in the project plan. Collapsing the outline to top-level summary tasks provides a framework for review while hiding details not presently needed.

- **When you want a schedule printout that includes some subtasks but not others.** Project prints the current view as it appears onscreen. If you've collapsed one or more summary groups onscreen, the same summary groups will be collapsed in the printout. This can save paper and help you deliver only the information needed by particular team members or stakeholders.

You can use either buttons on the Formatting toolbar or the outline symbols (buttons) beside the task name for each summary task to collapse or expand subtasks. Figure 5.20 shows how these various controls and a collapsed summary group look.

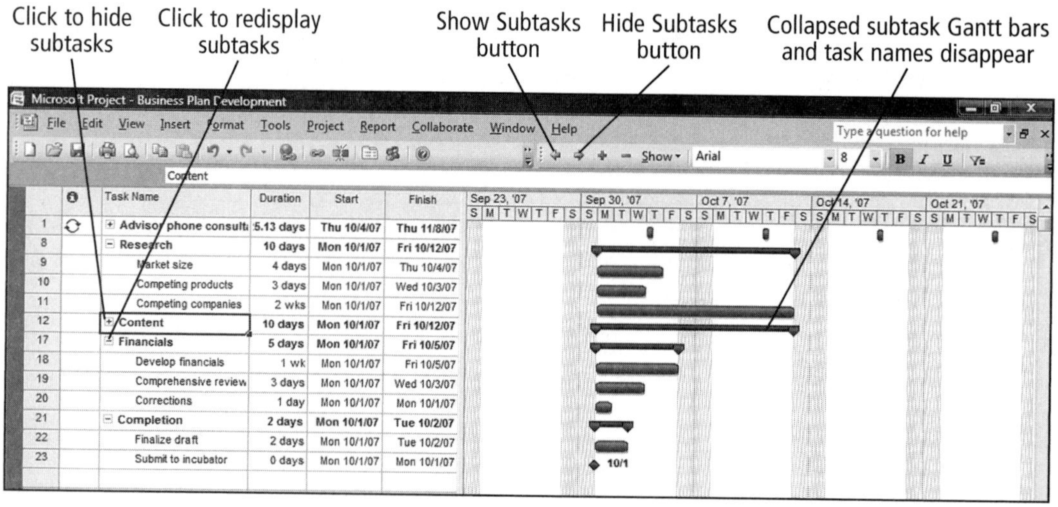

**Figure 5.20** Collapsing a summary task hides its subtasks.

Use one of these techniques to collapse or expand subtasks:

- **Collapse (hide) tasks in a summary group.** Click the **minus (-) outline symbol** to the left of the summary task name, or click the summary task and then click the **Hide Subtasks** (shortcut: **Alt+Shift+Minus**) button on the Formatting toolbar. The subtasks for the summary group collapse, hiding both the task names and the Gantt bars.
- **Expand (redisplay) tasks in a summary group.** Click the **plus (+) outline symbol** to the left of the summary task name, or click the summary task and then click the **Show Subtasks** (shortcut: **Alt+Shift+Plus**) button on the Formatting toolbar. The subtasks for the summary group expand, redisplaying both the task names and the Gantt bars.
- **Collapse or expand all the subtasks.** In a lengthy project plan, it could be quite time-consuming to collapse and expand summary groups one by one. To collapse or expand all of the subtasks in the plan, click the gray **Task Name** column heading, which selects the whole *Task Name* field. Then click either the **Hide Subtasks** button on the Formatting toolbar to hide all the subtasks (see Figure 5.21) or the **Show Subtasks** button to redisplay all the subtasks.

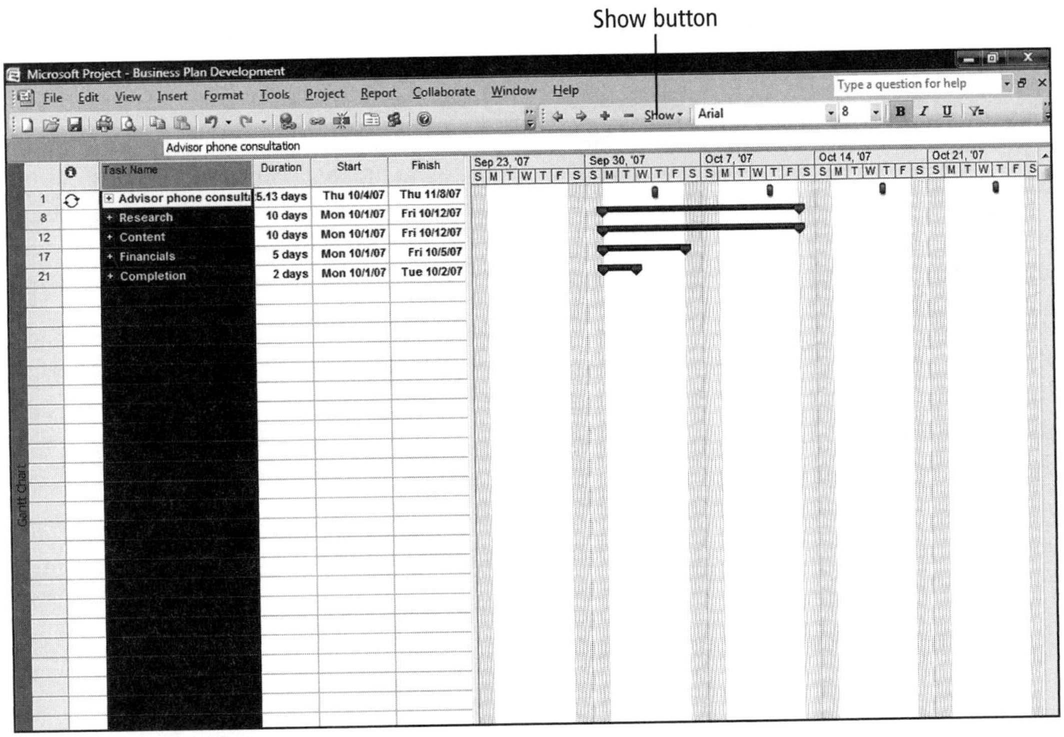

**Figure 5.21** Select the Task Name column and then use the Hide Subtasks or Show Subtasks button to hide (shown here) all subtasks or redisplay them.

■ **Display tasks down to a certain outline level.** If your project plan has numerous outline levels and you only need to show tasks down to a particular level, click the **Show** button on the Formatting toolbar (see Figure 5.21) and then click the desired outline level. You also can click the **All Subtasks** choice on the menu that appears to redisplay all the subtasks.

Note that the outlining you apply appears in other views such as Tracking Gantt view, too, and you can collapse and expand information in those views using the same techniques. The Task Usage and Resource Usage views also use similar outline symbols for assignments, which you can collapse and expand, too.

If you want to hide the outline symbols to give the task outline a cleaner look for a printout, click **Project**, click **Outline**, and then click **Hide Outline Symbols**. However, because you need the outline symbols to work effectively with the outline, choose **Project, Outline, Show Outline Symbols** to redisplay the symbols when needed. Note that you also can turn outline indenting on and off, as well as turn the display of outline numbers on and off. Choose **Tools, Options**, and use the **Indent Name** and **Show Outline Number** check boxes on the View tab to control these outline display features.

## Displaying the Project Summary Task

The *project summary task* summarizes the total duration, work, and other information for all the tasks in the project file. Although displaying the project summary task isn't a necessity, it does provide the convenience of enabling you to move the mouse pointer over the project summary task to see a pop-up tip with information about the project's overall Start, Finish, and Duration (see Figure 5.22).

Like other summary tasks, the project summary task recalculates to reflect changes you make to the project schedule. So, for example, even though all the individual tasks haven't yet been scheduled in the example shown in Figure 5.22, the project summary task will adjust to reflect the later scheduling. You also can expand and collapse the project summary task just like any other task in the project file.

Follow these steps when you want to display the project summary task in your project plan file:

1. Click **Tools** and then click **Options**.
2. If needed, click the **View** tab in the Options dialog box.
3. Click the **Show Project Summary Task** check box to check it, as shown in Figure 5.23.
4. Click **OK**. The project summary task appears as task 0 at the top of the task sheet.

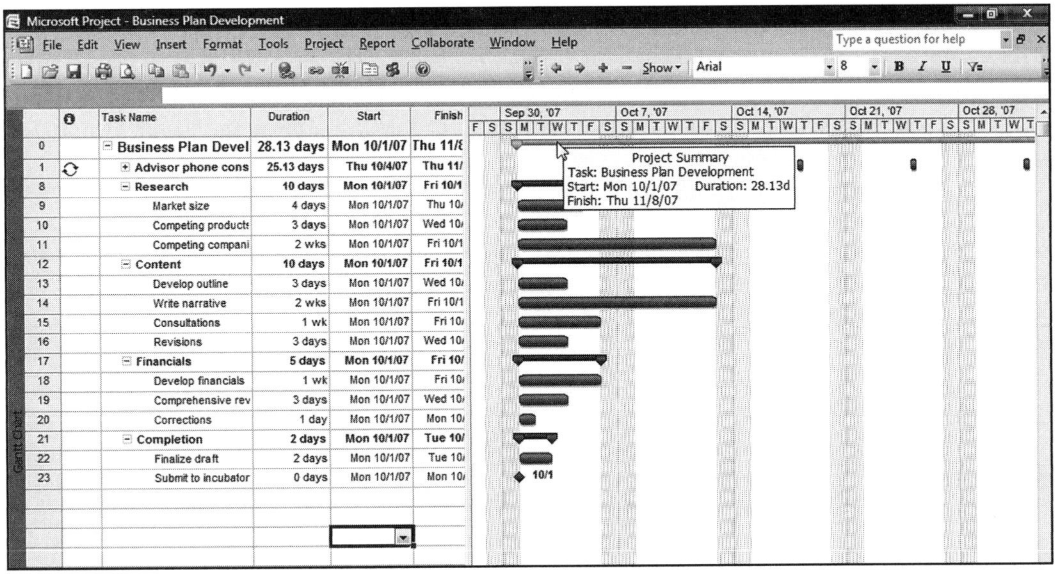

**Figure 5.22** Move the mouse pointer over the project summary task Gantt bar to see project summary information.

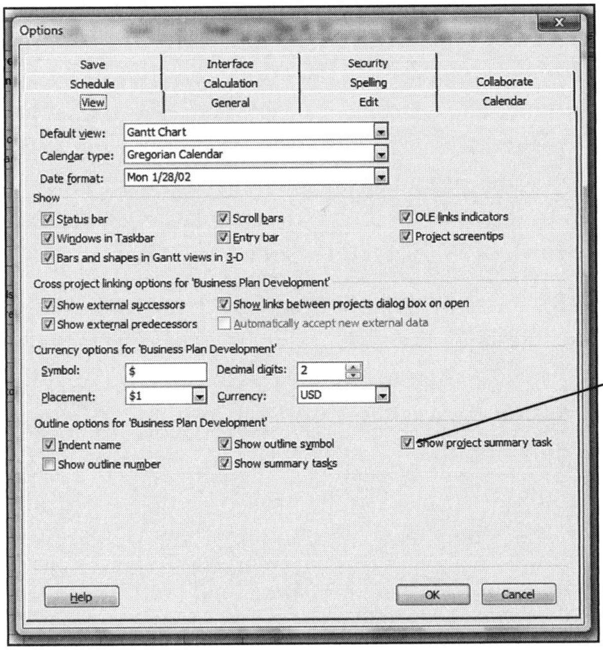

**Figure 5.23** Use the Options dialog box to display the project summary task, among other changes.

Click (check) to display project summary task

If entries such as the Duration and Start entries for the project summary task are too wide to display fully in the column, move the mouse pointer over the right column heading border until you see a resize pointer with a vertical bar and double arrows, and then either drag or double-click the border to change its size.

If you want to turn off the project summary task at any time, repeat the preceding steps. Clicking the **Show Project Summary Task** check box this time clears the check box to turn off the task display.

The Show Project Summary Task choice in the Options dialog box applies to the current file only, so you need to use the steps above to turn on the project summary task for every project file in which you require it.

## Displaying the WBS Codes

One of the "behind the scenes" data calculations that Project tracks for you are the actual WBS codes for the tasks in the outlined task list. The WBS code numbering system by default resembles an outline numbering scheme you may have seen used in an academic paper, report, or technical white paper. For example, if the project plan has five top-level summary tasks, they are numbered 1 through 5. The next level of subtasks below use a decimal followed by the subtask number. So, if summary task 2 has three subtasks, their WBS codes are 2.1, 2.2, and 2.3. In this way, WBS codes can give you a better sense than the task ID number of how a particular task fits in to the overall scheme for the project.(Note that you can define your own codes using the **Project, WBS, Define Code** command.)

The most-used views do not show the WBS codes by default. One way that you can view the WBS code for a particular task is to **double-click the task** in the task sheet to open the Task Information dialog box for the task. Click the **Advanced** tab and then view the **WBS Code** text box, which will show the task's code, as you can see in the example in Figure 5.24. Click **OK** to close the dialog box when you finish.

If, however, you need to see the WBS codes for all the tasks in the project plan, you can add a WBS code field to the task sheet in the Gantt Chart view by following these steps:

1. Right-click a gray field column heading, such as the *Task Name* field column heading, and click **Insert Column** in the shortcut menu that appears.

2. Open the **Field Name** drop-down list in the Column Definition dialog box, press **W** on the keyboard to scroll down, and then click **WBS** to select it and close the drop-down list (see Figure 5.25).

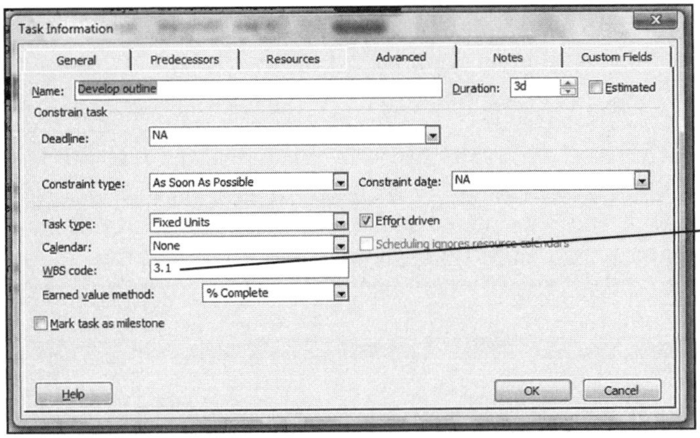

**Figure 5.24**
Viewing the WBS code for a task.

WBS code

Right-click field column header and then click Insert Column

Field to add

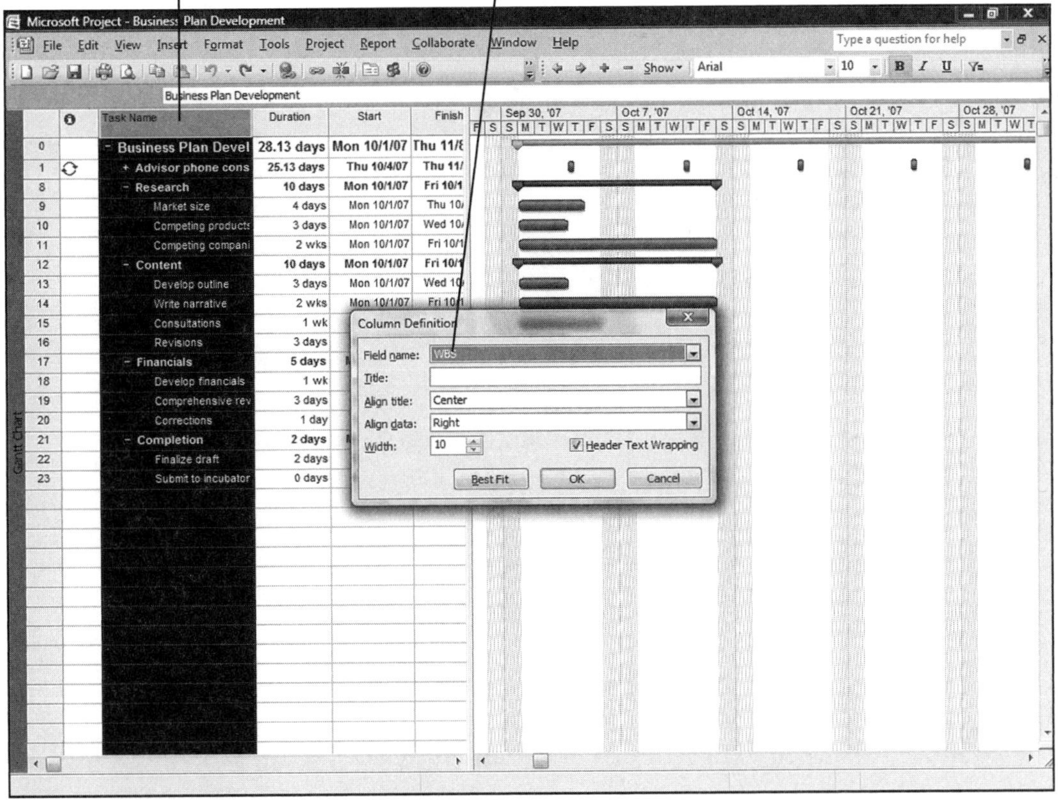

**Figure 5.25**  Adding the WBS code field.

3. Click **OK** to close the dialog box and add the field. As shown in Figure 5.26, the field shows the WBS number Project calculates for each task.

 The changes made to the task sheet of the Gantt Chart view using the steps in this section apply to the current file only. If you want to be able to see the WBS code field in all your files, you need to create a custom table and view that include it. Chapters 9 and 12 provide more details about working with fields, tables, and views.

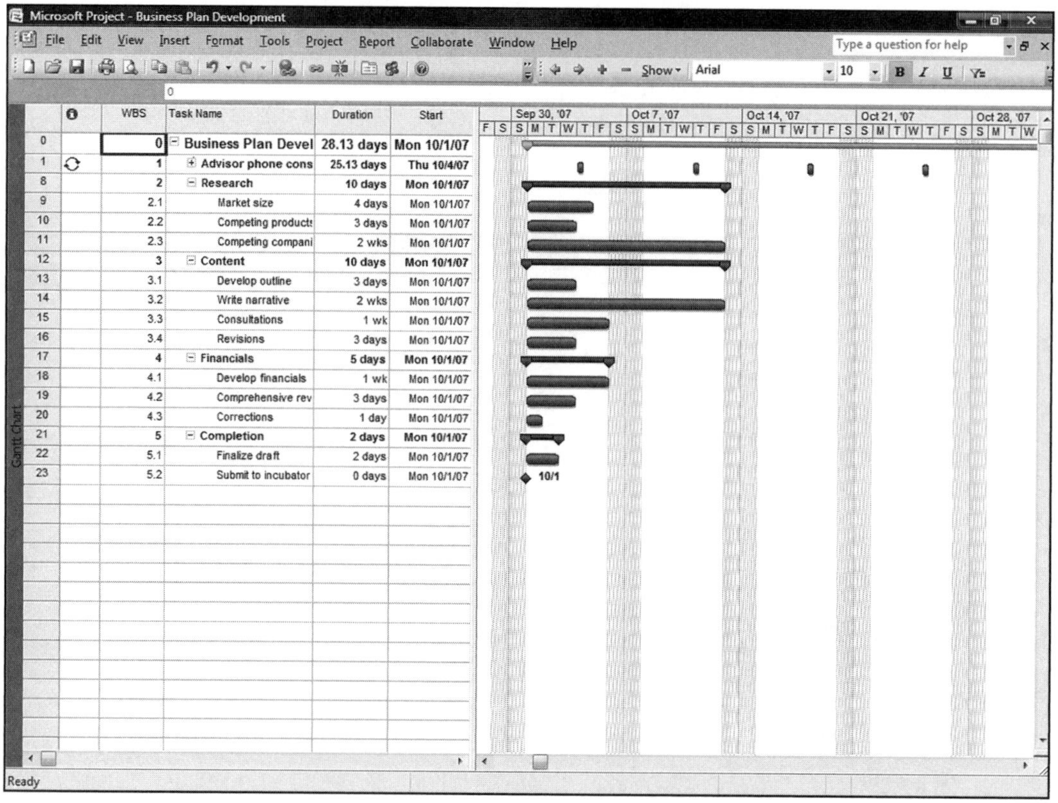

| | ⓘ | WBS | Task Name | Duration | Start |
|---|---|---|---|---|---|
| 0 | | 0 | ⊟ Business Plan Devel | 28.13 days | Mon 10/1/07 |
| 1 | ↻ | 1 | ⊞ Advisor phone cons | 25.13 days | Thu 10/4/07 |
| 8 | | 2 | ⊟ Research | 10 days | Mon 10/1/07 |
| 9 | | 2.1 | Market size | 4 days | Mon 10/1/07 |
| 10 | | 2.2 | Competing products | 3 days | Mon 10/1/07 |
| 11 | | 2.3 | Competing compani | 2 wks | Mon 10/1/07 |
| 12 | | 3 | ⊟ Content | 10 days | Mon 10/1/07 |
| 13 | | 3.1 | Develop outline | 3 days | Mon 10/1/07 |
| 14 | | 3.2 | Write narrative | 2 wks | Mon 10/1/07 |
| 15 | | 3.3 | Consultations | 1 wk | Mon 10/1/07 |
| 16 | | 3.4 | Revisions | 3 days | Mon 10/1/07 |
| 17 | | 4 | ⊟ Financials | 5 days | Mon 10/1/07 |
| 18 | | 4.1 | Develop financials | 1 wk | Mon 10/1/07 |
| 19 | | 4.2 | Comprehensive rev | 3 days | Mon 10/1/07 |
| 20 | | 4.3 | Corrections | 1 day | Mon 10/1/07 |
| 21 | | 5 | ⊟ Completion | 2 days | Mon 10/1/07 |
| 22 | | 5.1 | Finalize draft | 2 days | Mon 10/1/07 |
| 23 | | 5.2 | Submit to incubator | 0 days | Mon 10/1/07 |

**Figure 5.26**  The WBS code field appears where inserted on the task sheet.

# Chapter Review

In Chapter 5, you have covered some crucial skills for building any project plan. You learned the right way to create a task without compromising Project's ability to recalculate the task's schedule at a later time. You learned how to use duration labels to gain precision in task scheduling and to create a special-purpose task called a milestone. Because planning itself is a process, you saw how to refine your schedule by moving, adding, deleting, importing, and editing tasks, as well as how to undo changes that you decide you don't need. You learned the ins and outs of using outlining to organize the schedule, show and hide information, and identify tasks by WBS code rather than task number. Try the Review Questions and Projects now to ensure you've got a handle on the "need to know" stuff that you've just taken in.

## Review Questions

Write your answers to the following questions on a sheet of paper.

1. Where do you enter the list of tasks?

2. What two pieces of information should you enter to create each new task?

3. Why should you not type dates for a task in the *Start* or *Finish* fields?

4. What's the duration you enter to have Project mark a task as a milestone, and when would you use a milestone?

5. What is the task ID number for the task named *Competing products* in Figure 5.8?

6. Insert a _____ for any task that repeats over the duration of the project.

7. In an outline, _____ tasks summarize the data for the _____ tasks under them.

8. Use the _____ button on the Formatting toolbar to demote tasks to the next lower outline level.

9. _____ subtasks hides their task names and Gantt bars.

10. What is the WBS code for the task with task ID 20 in Figure 5.26?

## Projects

To see the solution file created by completing the projects in this chapter, go to www.courseptr.com, click the **Downloads** link in the navigation bar at the top, type **Microsoft Office Project 2007 Survival Guide** in the search text box, and then click **Search Downloads**.

## Project 1

1. Create a new, blank project file.

2. Use the Project Information dialog box (**Project, Project Information**) to set a project Start Date of **2/2/09**. Leave **Standard** selected as the Calendar setting and click **OK**.

3. Save the file as *Site Search*.

 Create a folder named *PSG Exercises* in your *Documents* or *My Documents* folder and save your exercise practice files there.

4. Make the following entries in the *Task Name* and *Duration* fields (leave *Duration* fields blank where indicated):

*Assess Needs*

| | |
|---|---|
| Infrastructure | 4d |
| Space | 1w |
| Parking | 3d |
| Expansion | 2w |
| Document | 1w |
| Interview Realtors | 2w |
| Hire Realtor | 2d |

*Identify Site*

| | |
|---|---|
| Review Listings | 3d |
| Visit Listings | 2w |

*Purchase Site*

| | |
|---|---|
| Write Offer Contract | 4h |
| Negotiate Contract | 6d |
| Secure Financing | 1w |
| Schedule Closing | 0 |
| Final Site Review | 2h |
| Closing | 4h |
| Possession | 0 |

5. Click **task 7**, *Interview Realtors.*

6. Press the **Insert** key, and then enter **Identify Realtor** as the name for the r

7. Click **task 13**, *Purchase Site.*

8 Press the **Insert** key, and then enter **Select Site** and **0** as the name and duration for the new task.

9. Select **task 19** and drag it above task 14.

10. Click the **Undo** button to return task 19 to the prior location.

11. Save your changes to the file.

## Project 2

1. Working in the *Site Search* file, use the **Demote** button on the Formatting toolbar to convert the following groups of tasks to subtasks:

   Tasks 2 through 6

   Tasks 8 through 13

   Tasks 15 through 16

   Tasks 18 through 21

2. Use the **Undo** button drop-down list on the Standard toolbar to undo your two most recent changes.

3. Use the Redo button drop-down list on the Standard toolbar to redo the changes you just undid.

4. Use the **Promote** button on the Formatting toolbar to promote task 18.

5. Demote tasks 17 and 18.

6. Demoting task 18 caused an unwanted demotion of tasks 19 through 21, so promote those tasks.

7. Save your changes to the file.

## Project 3

1. Click **Tools** and then click **Options**.

2. Click the **View** tab if needed, click the **Show Project Summary Task** check box to check it, and then click **OK**.

3. Use either the - **(minus)** outline symbol or the **Hide Subtasks** button on the Formatting toolbar to collapse the subtasks under the *Assess Needs* summary task.

4. Collapse the tasks under the other two summary tasks.

5. Use either the + (**plus**) outline symbol or the **Show Subtasks** button on the For-matting toolbar to expand the subtasks under the *Identify Realtor* summary task.

6. Click the **Task Name** field (column header) and then click the **Show Subtasks** button.

7. Right-click the **Task Name** field header and then click **Insert Column**.

8. Open the **Field Name** drop-down list, press **W**, and then click **WBS**.

9. Click **OK** to finish adding the WBS code field to the task sheet.

10. Save your changes to the file and then close the file.

# CHAPTER 6

# SCHEDULING THE PROJECT BY LINKING TASKS

This Chapter Teaches You How To:

- Link tasks to build the project schedule
- Link two tasks or many tasks at one time
- Understand the four different types of links
- Change the link type
- Unlink tasks
- Use lead time or lag time with a link
- Turn the Planning Wizard on and off

If you've ever watched a house being built, you've seen that the carpenters can't build the frame until after the foundation has been built. Just as construction tasks have to proceed in the proper order to ensure that the house is sound, your project's tasks have to be scheduled in the right order to ensure a successful outcome. This chapter teaches you how to use linking to specify the proper order for tasks, which in turn develops the overall schedule for the project plan. You'll learn how to create links, what link types are available and how to use them, and how to change or remove links. The chapter also teaches you about lead time and lag time, which are settings that work with links to provide greater scheduling accuracy. You will finish the chapter by learning about the Planning Wizard, which can warn you if a schedule change you're making could throw off your careful planning.

## Why Using Linking Works Best

While the tasks you list in your project represent discrete actions, each of those actions typically has some type of relationship with other activities in the project. For example, you will need to gather client specifications before designing a new backup storage system for the client. Without knowing how much backup space the client needs, you would likely create a system that's too small or too large, thus failing to meet the client's requirements even though you might have successfully completed the other steps for creating the system project. Other tasks can be related in an even more tangible way. For example, you can't install network equipment until you first purchase the equipment.

Those relationships between tasks—called **dependencies** in project management lingo—determine the order in which tasks should occur. After you place tasks in the proper sequence, the order plus the durations of the tasks result in the overall project schedule. In Project, you apply **links** to determine the dependencies between tasks, which also schedules or **sequences** the tasks. When you apply a link in Project, you indicate that on or around the time one task finishes, the next task should start.

 Apply links to schedule tasks rather than typing in dates. Typing dates automatically puts a Start No Earlier Than constraint on the task, which can interfere with schedule calculation and artificially hold a task to a date that no longer makes sense. The section called "Using a Task Constraint" in Chapter 9 explains how and when to apply constraints.

The last chapter emphasized that you should avoid typing dates for tasks when building your project plan. That's because instead of typing dates, you should apply links to determine the schedules for tasks and the project. Linking tasks rather than typing dates provides these benefits:

- **Linking saves time when you build the plan.** You don't have to work with a calendar to identify the start and finish date for each task. Project calculates those dates for you based on the links you apply.

- **Linking focuses your attention on the flow of activities, not the dates.** Really scrutinizing the relationships and sequence of the project activities puts you in a better position to identify potential pressure points and bottlenecks in the schedule.

- **Linking works with the calendar to make the plan more accurate and realistic.** Project will automatically skip nonworking days that you've specified in the custom calendar you created for your project. Your project plan won't be realistic from the start unless it adheres to the basic "ground rules" you've set up in the calendar.

- **Linking makes changing the schedule more manageable.** Rather than having to type in new dates for dozens of tasks, you simply change the schedule for one task; Project recalculates the start and finish dates for all subsequent linked tasks.

- **Linking enables you to create reusable project plan templates.** When all the tasks in a project plan are properly linked, you only need to change the Project Start Date in the Project Information dialog box to reschedule the entire project. If you often manage very similar types of projects, using templates will save you a tremendous amount of time.

## Applying a Default Link

When you apply a link, you are indicating that one task's schedule is dependent on another task's. Project calls the dependent task the ***successor***, and the linked task that drives the successor's schedule is called the ***predecessor***. Although the predecessor task usually precedes the successor task in terms of their schedules, that isn't always the case; these names identify the fact that the schedule for one task (the predecessor) *drives* or determines the schedule for another task (the successor), no matter when either task occurs.

By default, Project assumes that the finish date of a predecessor task drives the start date of the successor task, making the default link type a ***finish-to-start (FS)*** link. This link by default schedules the successor task to start immediately after the predecessor task finishes. On the Gantt chart, the linked tasks look like Figure 6.1.

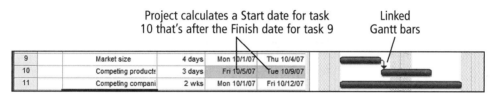

**Figure 6.1** The default finish-to-start link schedules tasks sequentially.

As you can see in Figure 6.1, Project calculates the Start date for task 10, scheduling it to start immediately after task 9 finishes. If you changed the *Duration* for task 9, Project would reschedule task 10 accordingly. Linking (rather than typing dates) preserves Project's ability to recalculate the schedule as individual tasks change.

### Linking Two Tasks

When you link tasks, you select them first and then apply the link. The links you create should reflect the reality of how tasks must proceed in the schedule. If you have a list of six tasks, for example, task 1 might be linked to task 2, but it also might be linked to task 6. Create additional links as needed to reflect the schedule of work between dependent tasks.

On the other hand, don't created links that imply dependencies where none exist, because doing so creates a needlessly complex project plan that will be harder to manage and track later. Before you add each link, make sure you take a minute to think about whether a schedule dependency really exists between the tasks or whether you're just tempted to add the link for cosmetic reasons (to make tasks look a certain way in the Gantt chart).

The steps for linking two tasks are simple:

1. Select the two tasks that you want to link. If the tasks are listed one after the other in the Task Sheet, you can drag over the task names. If the tasks are not on consecutive rows, click the first task and then **Ctrl+click** the second task.

 Project makes the task you select first the predecessor. So, if you drag up instead of down when selecting tasks, Project schedules the lower task earlier, which may be the opposite of your intent. Be sure to select tasks in the right order before linking them.

2. Click the **Link Tasks** button on the Standard toolbar. (Shortcut: **Ctrl+F2**.) The button has a picture of a linked chain on it. Project applies the link and schedules the tasks, as shown in Figure 6.2. (If automatic calculation has been turned off on the Calculation tab of the Options dialog box, you'll need to press **F9** to calculate the schedule.) The Edit menu has a Link Tasks command that you can use to apply a default finish-to-start link.

Link Tasks button

| | | Task Name | Duration | Start | Finish |
|---|---|---|---|---|---|
| 0 | | Business Plan Devel | 28.13 days | Mon 10/1/07 | Thu 11/8/07 |
| 1 | ↻ | Advisor phone cons | 25.13 days | Thu 10/4/07 | Thu 11/8/07 |
| 8 | | Research | 17 days | Mon 10/1/07 | Tue 10/23/07 |
| 9 | | Market size | 4 days | Mon 10/1/07 | Thu 10/4/07 |
| 10 | | Competing products | 3 days | Fri 10/5/07 | Tue 10/9/07 |
| 11 | | Competing compani | 2 wks | Wed 10/10/07 | Tue 10/23/07 |
| 12 | | Content | 10 days | Mon 10/1/07 | Fri 10/12/07 |
| 13 | | Develop outline | 3 days | Mon 10/1/07 | Wed 10/3/07 |
| 14 | | Write narrative | 2 wks | Mon 10/1/07 | Fri 10/12/07 |
| 15 | | Consultations | 1 wk | Mon 10/1/07 | Fri 10/5/07 |
| 16 | | Revisions | 3 days | Mon 10/1/07 | Wed 10/3/07 |
| 17 | | Financials | 5 days | Mon 10/1/07 | Fri 10/5/07 |
| 18 | | Develop financials | 1 wk | Mon 10/1/07 | Fri 10/5/07 |
| 19 | | Comprehensive rev | 3 days | Mon 10/1/07 | Wed 10/3/07 |
| 20 | | Corrections | 1 day | Mon 10/1/07 | Mon 10/1/07 |
| 21 | | Completion | 2 days | Mon 10/1/07 | Tue 10/2/07 |
| 22 | | Finalize draft | 2 days | Mon 10/1/07 | Tue 10/2/07 |
| 23 | | Submit to incubator | 0 days | Mon 10/1/07 | Mon 10/1/07 |

**Figure 6.2** Tasks 10 and 11 also have been linked with a finish-to-start link.

As you apply links in this way, Project builds the schedule for the project plan. Each Gantt bar illustrates the schedule for a particular task, laying it out along the timeline defined in the timescale along the top of the Gantt chart.

Select the tasks to link and then click the **Link Tasks** button on the Standard toolbar to apply the default link type, a ***finish-to-start (FS)*** link.

## Understanding Timephased Information

Any schedule or Project view like the Gantt Chart that plots work over time is called a ***timephased diagram or view***. Any view or pane that has a timescale above it is presenting timephased information. You also can link tasks in some other views such as the Network Diagram view, but keep in mind that those views don't necessarily give you a representation of how the linking builds each task's schedule, as you would see in a timephased view like the Gantt Chart view.

## Linking Multiple Tasks

If linking two tasks saves you some time, just think how much time you'll save when you link even more tasks at one shot. By selecting and linking multiple tasks, you can build out a lengthy schedule in a matter of minutes.

To link multiple tasks, drag over the task names (or use Ctrl+click) to make your selections and then click the **Link Tasks** button. For example, Figure 6.3 shows that finish-to-start links have been applied to tasks 11 and 13 through 16. Using Ctrl+click to select all of the tasks enabled me to skip the summary task, 12, which should not be linked.

Unless you have specialized reasons for doing so, do not link summary tasks. You want to link the detail tasks that represent work and dates in the schedule, not the summary information. Recurring tasks also often do not drive any specific subsequent tasks, so they may not need to be linked to other tasks.

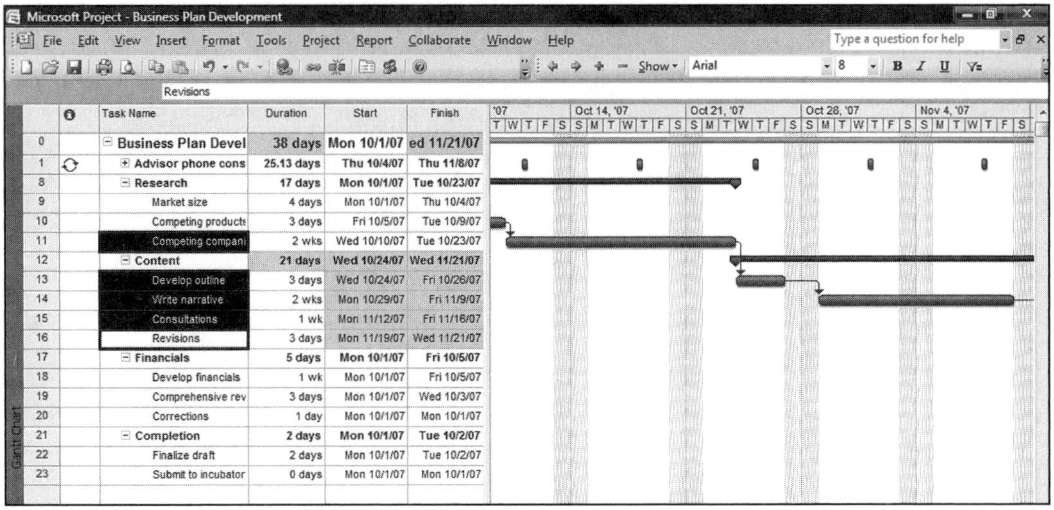

**Figure 6.3** Save even more time by selecting and linking multiple tasks.

# Understanding and Using Other Link Types

You already know from life that events don't flow one after the other in a neat, convenient sequence. Nor will the tasks in the projects you manage. Some tasks kick off at the same time but finish at different times. Others need to finish at roughly the same time. Project enables you to map out the reality of how your tasks will flow by using three additional link types in a project plan:

- **Start-to-Start (SS).** In this type of link, the successor task can start any time after the predecessor starts. By default, Project schedules the predecessor and successor to start at the same time. You should use this type of link for tasks that run concurrently. For example, say you have three newsletter tasks named *Writing*, *Editing*, and *Design*. Workflow in your organization requires that a project design cannot start until the editing starts. So, you can apply a start-to-start link between the *Editing* and *Design* tasks to reflect the stipulation that design may not begin until editing begins, but the tasks can run concurrently. Figure 6.4 shows example start-to-start links.

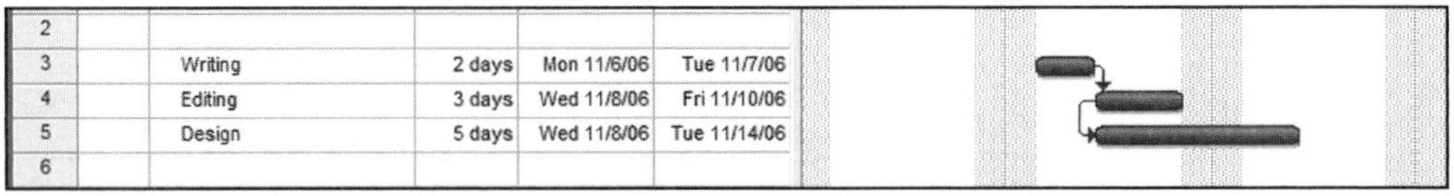

**Figure 6.4** Start-to-start (SS) links enable Project to schedule tasks to run concurrently, which means a successor can start after the predecessor starts.

- **Finish-to-Finish (FF).** When you apply this type of link, the successor task can finish any time after the predecessor finishes. By default, Project schedules the predecessor and successor to finish at the same time. As with a start-to-start link, the tasks joined by a finish-to-finish link run roughly at the same time. Going back to the newsletter example, *Proofreading* and *Page Layout* tasks can run roughly concurrently, but the last round of proofreading must finish before final page layout corrections are made, as illustrated in Figure 6.5. (In the example in Figure 6.5, I made an additional scheduling adjustment—adding some lag time— because in the real world the example successor would have to finish after the predecessor. You'll learn about lag time shortly.)

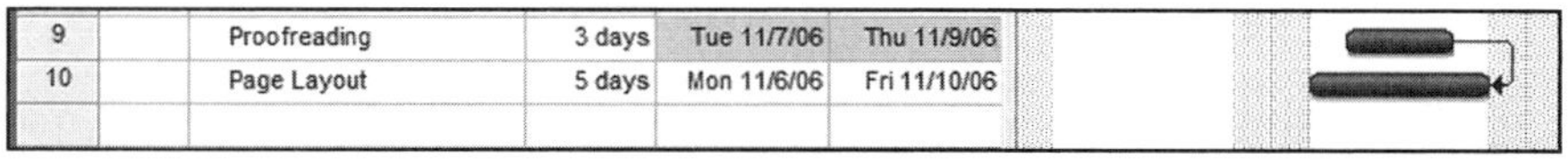

| 9 | | Proofreading | 3 days | Tue 11/7/06 | Thu 11/9/06 | |
| 10 | | Page Layout | 5 days | Mon 11/6/06 | Fri 11/10/06 | |

**Figure 6.5** A finish-to-finish (FF) link means that the successor can finish after the predecessor finishes.

- **Start-to-Finish (SF).** This type of link tells Project that the successor task can finish after the predecessor task begins. By default, Project schedules the successor task to finish just before the predecessor starts, although in the example in Figure 6.6, adjustments again have been made to show how two tasks will overlap in the real world. For example, if you're scheduling the next issue of your newsletter, the successor task *Topic List* can finish any time after the *Next Issue Plan* task begins. As you might guess, this is an unusual link type that isn't used as often as the other link types. But other examples include situations where you need to order an item or materials in advance of the completion of a successor task. For example, if you need to order a kitchen sink two weeks ahead of finishing the install for the sink, you can create a SF link between the *Order Sink* task and the *Install Sink* task and add two weeks of delay (lag time, discussed later) between them.

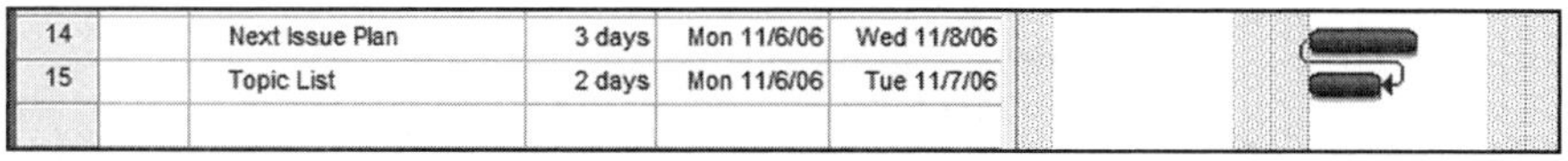

| 14 | | Next Issue Plan | 3 days | Mon 11/6/06 | Wed 11/8/06 | |
| 15 | | Topic List | 2 days | Mon 11/6/06 | Tue 11/7/06 | |

**Figure 6.6** A start-to-finish (SF) link means that the successor can finish after the predecessor starts.

The *link lines* between the Gantt bars illustrate the link type. An FS link line joins the right end of the predecessor bar to the left end of the successor bar. An SS link line joins the left ends of both bars (Figure 6.4). An FF link line joins the right ends of both bars (Figure 6.5). And an SF link line joints the left end of the predecessor bar to the right end of the successor bar (Figure 6.6).

## Changing a Link Type

When you want a task to use a link type that's not a default FS link, you have to change the link type after you apply the FS link. Changing the link type is a manual process, but it should be. As part of your diligent planning process, you need to consider how every two linked tasks should be scheduled and choose the link type that best reflects the desired schedule.

 Because the various link types enable you to capture a fairly realistic picture of how tasks will proceed in a project, adding the links is sometimes thought of as *mapping* or *modeling work-flow*.

When you work with links, you'll often work with the successor task to view or change link information. The predecessor task's Task ID number is used to identify the link. So, if tasks 9 and 10 are linked, the successor task 10 lists task 9 as a predecessor.

You can change the link type in one of three ways:

- Double-click the **link line** between the tasks. Open the **Type** drop-down list in the Task Dependency dialog box that appears (see Figure 6.7), click the desired link type, and then click **OK**.

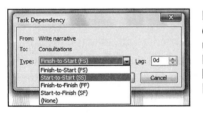

**Figure 6.7** Double-click the link line to use the Task Dependency dialog box to change the link type.

- Double-click **any cell in the task** in the Task Sheet to open its Task Information dialog box. (You also can click the task and click the **Task Information** button on the Standard toolbar.) Click the **Predecessors** tab. Open the Type drop-down list for any listed predecessor, as shown in Figure 6.8, and click the desired link type. (If you need to work with more than one entry, press **Enter** after finishing each one.) Click **OK** to close the dialog box and apply the change.

 Double-click a task cell in the task sheet portion of the Gantt chart view to open the Task Information dialog box. This dialog box offers a number of tabs where you can examine and change task settings.

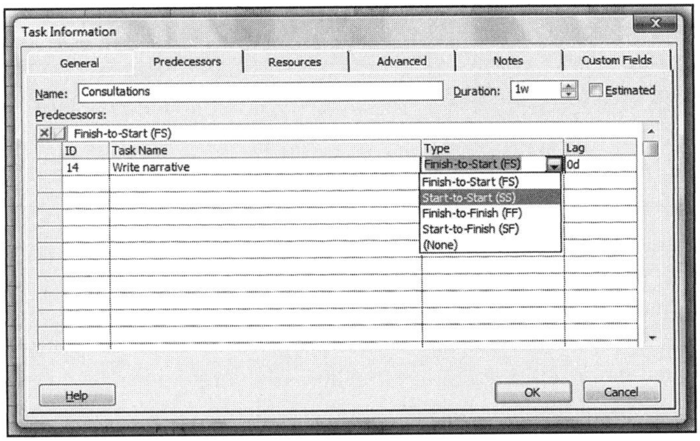


**Figure 6.8** Double-click a task cell in the Task Sheet to use this dialog box to change the link type.

- If you prefer to type rather than use the mouse, scroll the task sheet part of the view to the right so that you can see the Predecessors column. As shown in Figure 6.9, you can change the link to a type other than the default by adding the abbreviation for a start-to-start (SS), finish-to-finish (FF), or start-to-finish (SF) link. Click the **Predecessors cell**, press **F2** to place the insertion point in the cell for editing, type the desired abbreviation, and press **Enter**. Note that if a task has multiple predecessors, Project inserts a comma in between them.

Predecessor ID
and link type

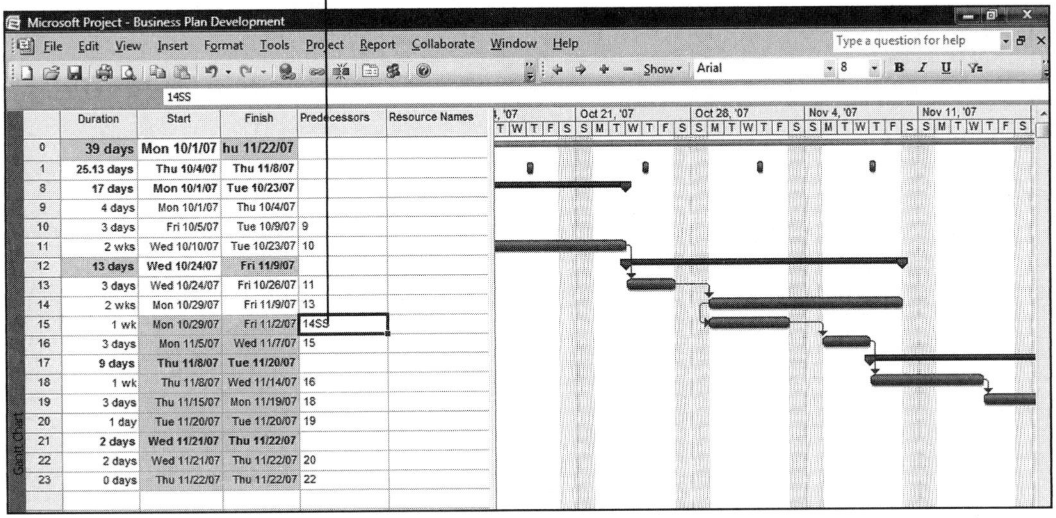


**Figure 6.9** Including the link type abbreviation with the predecessor task's ID number in the *Predecessors* field changes the link type.

After you change the link type, Project recalculates the schedule for the successor task as required. As illustrated in Figure 6.10, Project's new change highlighting feature shades any Duration, Start, or Finish cell whose entry changes as a result of a link or link type change. For example, Figure 6.10 shows the changes that were highlighted when I changed the link between tasks 9 and 10 from an FS link to an SS link. This feature reminds you, oh project manager poobah, that you need to review the impact of every change you make in your project plan to ensure that a minor change hasn't disrupted the schedule in any unexpected way.

If you want to see information about a link without opening the Task Information dialog box, point to the link line with the mouse. After you hover the mouse pointer for a moment, a pop-up box with information about the link type and predecessor, like the one in Figure 6.11, appears.

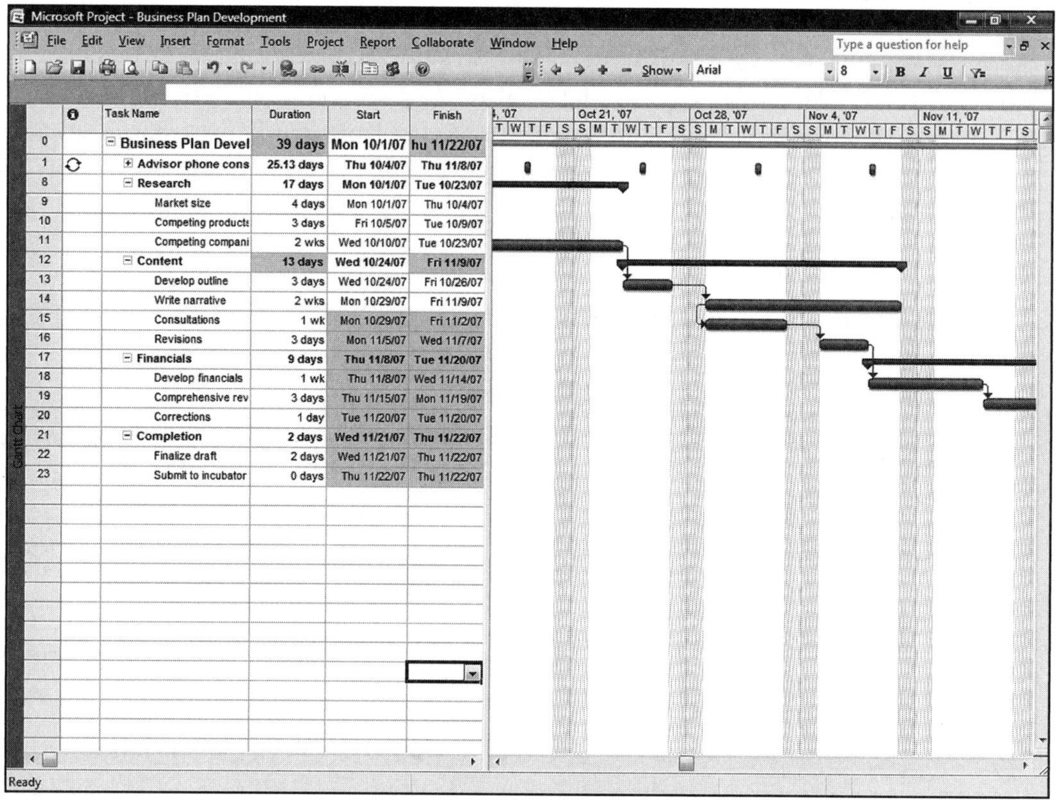

**Figure 6.10** Change highlighting helps you identify how adding or changing links impacts linked successors.

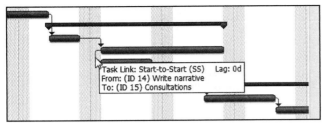

**Figure 6.11** Point to the link line for info about the link.

# Removing a Link

There will be times when you end up with a link that's unwanted or otherwise no longer needed. For example, if you've already linked a series of tasks and then you insert a new task within that series, Project by default links in the new task, as well. If you don't want those links, you need to remove them.

You can select two linked tasks and then choose **Edit, Unlink Tasks** (shortcut: **Ctrl+Shift+F2**) to remove the link. The Standard toolbar offers an Unlink Tasks button, which looks like a broken chain, that you can click to remove a link between selected tasks. To use the button if you can't see it onscreen, click the **Toolbar Options** button at the right end of the Standard toolbar and then click the **Unlink Tasks** button. The button will then appear on the toolbar.

As with applying and changing links, make sure that you examine the project plan carefully after you remove any link. You don't want any unwanted changes to come as a surprise to you later.

---

### When Links Go Bad—Turning off the Autolink Feature

By default, the *Autolink* feature in Project automatically applies a link to any new task you insert within a sequence of linked tasks, including summary tasks. It also changes links when you drag tasks around in the plan or when you cut or copy and then paste tasks.

To turn off Autolink, choose **Tools, Options**. Click the **Schedule** tab, click the **Autolink Inserted or Moved Tasks** check box to clear its check, and then click **OK**. When you're ready to use Autolink at a later time, reopen the dialog box and recheck the check box.

## Understanding Lead Time and Lag Time

Even applying the right link types doesn't go far enough in reflecting reality because time and schedules are more fluid than a basic link can allow. Although tasks might seem to follow one after another, they really flow together more loosely, overlapping or occurring after a delay. In Project, you schedule *lead time* or *lag time* along with a link to achieve more accuracy in representing how linked task schedules really compare.

 With a finish-to-start link, *lead time* overlaps the task schedules, while *lag time* inserts a delay between the tasks. You enter lead or lag time in the same dialog boxes where you change the link type.

### When to Use Lead and Lag Time

With a default finish-to-start link, *lead time* represents a period during which the tasks overlap. For example, in a new home construction project, you break down the rough electrical work into three tasks called *Basement Electrical Rough*, *Floor 1 Electrical Rough*, and *Floor 2 Electrical Rough*, you assign two days of duration to each task, and you link them in sequence with FS links. However, you know that the *Floor 1 Electrical Rough* task can really start one day before *Basement Electrical Rough* finishes, meaning that the tasks overlap in time. Likewise, *Floor 2 Electrical Rough* can start a day before *Floor 1 Electrical Rough* finishes, so those two tasks overlap, as well. In this case, you would assign lead time to the links to set up the overlap so that the series of tasks which originally added up to six days of duration compresses down to four days of duration. Figure 6.12 illustrates this scenario.

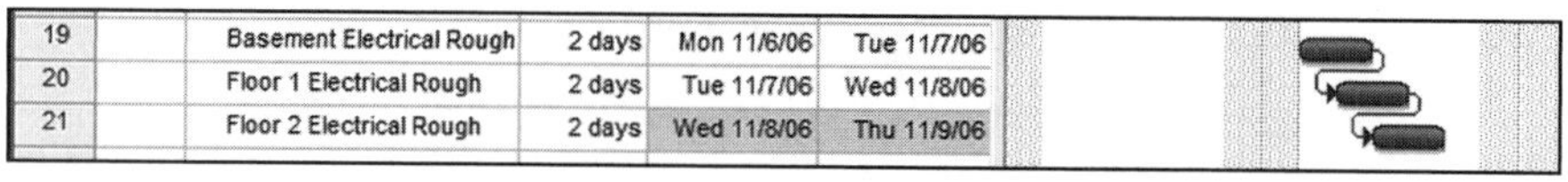

| 19 | Basement Electrical Rough | 2 days | Mon 11/6/06 | Tue 11/7/06 |
| 20 | Floor 1 Electrical Rough | 2 days | Tue 11/7/06 | Wed 11/8/06 |
| 21 | Floor 2 Electrical Rough | 2 days | Wed 11/8/06 | Thu 11/9/06 |

**Figure 6.12**  Lead time overlaps tasks linked with FS links.

*Lag time* represents the opposite of lead time—a delay or nonworking period between two tasks. Building on the example shown in Figure 6.12, say you need to add *Finish Electrical Rough* as a task, but you know it should start a week after the last of the other three tasks finishes to allow for an inspection. Adding five days (a work week) of lag time to the link between *Floor 2 Electrical Rough* and *Finish Electrical Rough* builds in the necessary break, as illustrated in Figure 6.13.

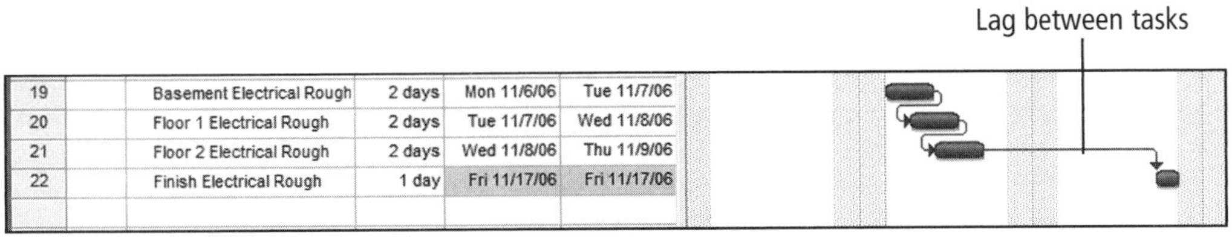

Lag between tasks

| 19 | | Basement Electrical Rough | 2 days | Mon 11/6/06 | Tue 11/7/06 |
| 20 | | Floor 1 Electrical Rough | 2 days | Tue 11/7/06 | Wed 11/8/06 |
| 21 | | Floor 2 Electrical Rough | 2 days | Wed 11/8/06 | Thu 11/9/06 |
| 22 | | Finish Electrical Rough | 1 day | Fri 11/17/06 | Fri 11/17/06 |

**Figure 6.13** Lag time inserts a delay between tasks linked with FS links.

Whether you've added lag time or lead time, keep in mind that the Lag text box entries you make remain in place even when you change task durations. You need to change the Lag entry separately, if required.

If you will be using your project plan to get accurate tracking of actual person hours of work and accumulated costs, do *not* just extend task durations rather than taking the step of adding lag times. Extending a task's duration adds hours of work plus the costs associated with using the assigned resources to plan totals calculated by Project. If no real work is occurring, the totals will be artificially high. Proper use of lag time eliminates this problem. If you will be sharing your file with other users or a version of the plan file will be reused over time, always add a task note to document how much lag or lead time you added and why you added it. Chapter 9 explains how to add a task note.

Of course, lead and lag times behave a little differently with other link types. For example, adding lag time to a start-to-start link delays the start of the successor task and impacts whether and by how much the two tasks continue to overlap. Lead time with a start-to-start link schedules the successor task to start before the predecessor.

When applying lead time and lag time to task links, always examine the impact of any change to make sure the resulting schedule reflects what you intended.

## Specifying Lead or Lag Time

Specifying lead time and lag time can be a little more cryptic than specifying a link type because you enter it as a positive or negative duration value, like this:

- **Lead times are negative values.** For example, **-2d** represents two days of lead time, and **-2h** represents two hours of lead time.
- **Lag times are positive values.** For example, **2d** (**+2d**) represents two days of lag time, while **2h** (**+2h**) represents two hours of lag time.

If you do not enter a duration abbreviation with lead or lag time, Project assumes that you mean days. Also note that you can enter lead and lag times as percentages in the task sheet, such as **+25%** to specify lag time equal to 25% of the predecessor task's duration.

You can add lead or lag time to a link in any of the same locations where you can change the link type, such as these:

- Double-click the **link line** between the tasks. Change the **Lag** entry in the Task Dependency dialog box (see Figure 6.14) by selecting and typing over the existing entry or clicking the spinner arrow buttons, and then click **OK**.

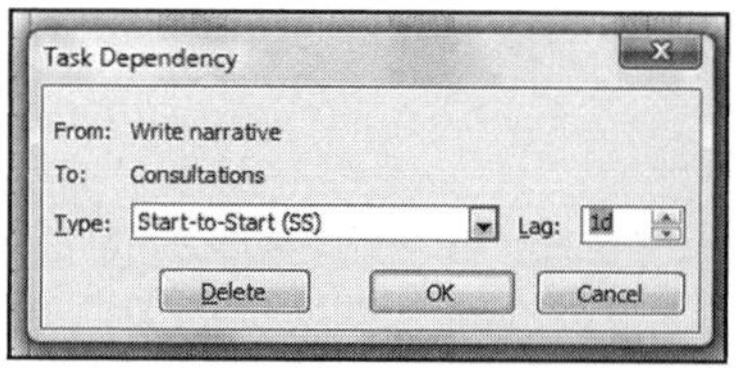

**Figure 6.14** Specify lead or lag time in the Lag text box.

- Double-click **any cell in the task's row** in the task sheet to open its Task Information dialog box. (You also can click the task row and click the **Task Information** button on the Standard toolbar.) Click the **Predecessors** tab. Click the **Lag cell entry** on the row for the predecessor task link you want to work with, and then type a new entry or use the spinner arrow buttons that appear to increment the entry. (If you need to work with more than one entry, press **Enter** after finishing each one.) Click **OK** to close the dialog box and apply the change.

You don't have to type the + (plus sign) for a lag time entry in either the Task Dependency or Task Information dialog boxes. Just enter the desired value.

- Working on the task sheet instead, scroll the Task Sheet pane to the right so that you can see the Predecessors column. As shown in Figure 6.15, you can add the lead or lag time by typing a positive or negative value, plus a duration abbreviation. Click the **Predecessors cell**, press **F2** to place the insertion point in the cell for editing, type the desired lead or lag entry to the right of the predecessor information, and press **Enter**.

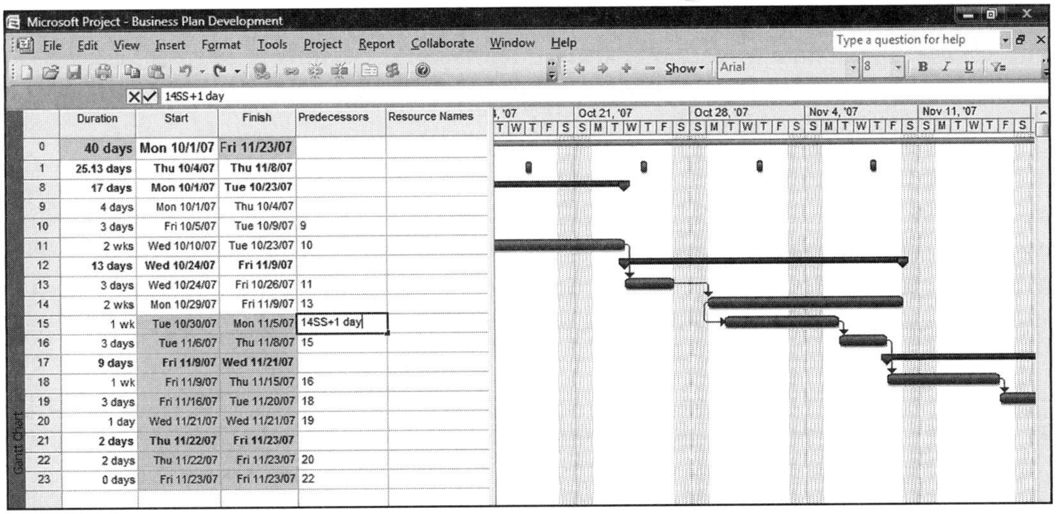

**Figure 6.15** Add the lead or lag time in with the Predecessor field entry, as for task 15 shown here.

## Lag Time and Buffers as Planning Tools

According to project management gurus, what you're about to read is not necessarily proper project planning advice. Professional project managers strive to make every project plan perfect—mapping out a schedule that will be as close to reality as possible.

However, when I've managed projects, I found it more prudent to always build in a cushion somewhere. You see, I accept the likelihood that something beyond my control might impact my project's schedule. And I also accept the reality that there is always some degree of a learning curve when planning and managing projects, so there's always the possibility that some task durations might be estimated incorrectly.

Although you can increase the length of a project plan overall by entering generous task durations, keep in mind that each duration will also represent hours of time and budgeted costs in your project plan once you assign resources. So, if you want to increase the project schedule without overly inflating the amount of work and costs scheduled, you build extra lag time in between tasks, instead.

You can add lag time by simply increasing the amount of lag time you would otherwise enter for some linked tasks. For example, if you are in the construction business and often order custom cabinetry that usually takes as little as three weeks to arrive but may take more, add four weeks of lag time rather than three between the task where you order the cabinets and the task where the cabinets are installed.

You also can add lag time between linked tasks where you wouldn't otherwise add lag time at all. For example, in a project that spans a few months, adding a day or so of lag time between two tasks per month can be a prudent way to allow for a margin of error in planning and execution.

If you need to have a cushion of extra time that's visible in the schedule and can be tracked, you can add in tasks that represent nonworking periods between tasks. As long as you don't assign resources to the tasks, Project will not add in hours or work or costs for the tasks. With this method, the buffer of extra time is explicit and perhaps more visible. However, it should be clear to everyone involved in the project that the project manager retains ownership over deciding how and when to use the buffer, if needed. Achieving a theoretical idea of perfection is a great goal, but you should do what's right for your projects and your situation. It truly is better to "under-promise and over-deliver" if you want to keep your larger career moving in the real world.

## Controlling the Planning Wizard

Project includes a tool called the Planning Wizard that monitors your activity as you build and change the project plan. If you make a change to a task's schedule by changing a link or duration and that change might cause a scheduling problem such as violating the project start date, the Planning Wizard may display a warning like the one shown in Figure 6.16.

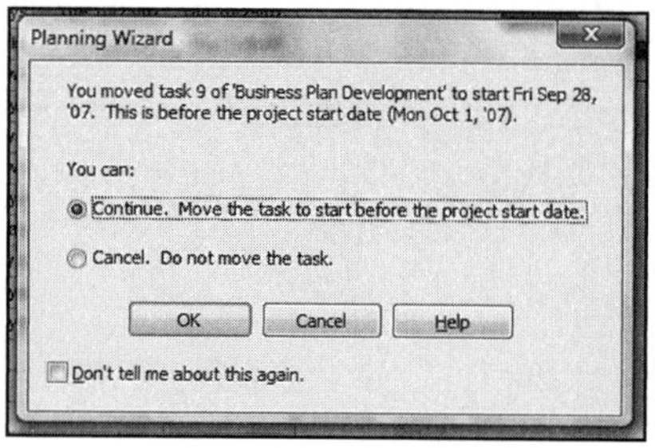

**Figure 6.16** The Planning Wizard provides alerts about how task schedule changes might impact the big picture.

It is a feature that drives some people up the wall, so in this section I will explain how to turn the Planning Wizard on and off. Before I do that, however, I want to offer a few thoughts in support of the Planning Wizard:

- If you're a newbie, the Planning Wizard makes you stop and think before you go ahead and make a change that might impact your plan. It forces you to get in the habit of thinking about how even a small change can ripple through the project, which is a good type of discipline to develop as a project manager. I recommend that new users keep the Planning Wizard on until they get comfortable with using Project.

- You don't have to turn the Planning Wizard all the way off. For example, you can turn off just the part that provides help about Project and leave on the part that checks your scheduling changes and looks for errors.

- For some types of changes, such as one that moves a task before the project start date, you will see a warning message even when the Planning Wizard is turned all the way off. However, this type of warning message requires that you close the dialog box and then undo your change, while the Planning Wizard immediately gives you the option of continuing or canceling your action.

The Planning Wizard, in conjunction with a constraint you add to the final task in a project plan, can give you a specific warning if you make a change that would push the project finish beyond a drop-dead date that you must meet. See the section "Use a Constraint to Emphasize a Finish Date" in Appendix B to learn more.

After all of that, if you still want to turn the Planning Wizard all the way or part of the way off, use these steps:

1. Click **Tools** and then **Options**.

2. Click the **General** tab.

3. Clear and check choices in the Planning Wizard section near the middle of the dialog box (see Figure 6.17) as desired. Note that the **Advice from Planning Wizard** choice turns the Planning Wizard all the way on or off. This check box must be checked (enabled) for you to work with the other choices.

4. Click OK to apply your changes.

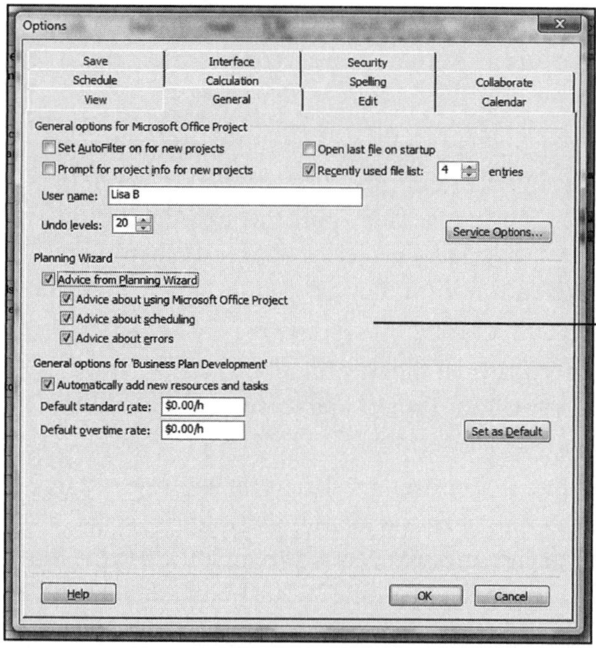

**Figure 6.17** Turn the Planning Wizard on or off here.

## Chapter Review

In Chapter 6, you saw how to move your list of tasks one step closer to a full-fledged project plan. You learned how to add basic finish-to-start links to tasks to sequence them in the schedule. You also learned about the other three link types—start-to-start, finish-to-finish, and start-to-finish—and how to change any link to another type. The chapter also taught you how to remove a link, to refine the schedule by using lead time and lag time with links, and to turn the Planning Wizard off and on to control how much warning information Project displays. Finish up by working through the Review Questions and Projects now.

### Review Questions

Write your answers to the following questions on a sheet of paper.

1. Why do you skip typing in Start and Finish dates for tasks?

2. How do you instead build the task schedules?

3. The _____ task drives the schedule of its _____ task.

4. Name the default task type and its abbreviation.

5. How do you link two tasks using the Standard toolbar?

6. How do you display the Task Information dialog box?

7. What tab in the Task Information dialog box do you use to change the link type?

8. How do you display pop-up information about a link?

9. Enter lead time as a _____ value and lag time as a _____ value.

10. Enter lead or lag time in the _____ text box in the Task Dependency dialog box.

## Projects

 To see the solution files created by completing the projects in this chapter, go to www.courseptr.com, click the **Downloads** link in the navigation bar at the top, type **Microsoft Office Project 2007 Survival Guide** in the search text box, and then click **Search Downloads**.

### Project 1

1. Create a new, blank project file.

2. Use the Project Information dialog box (**Project, Project Information**) to set a project Start Date of **6/15/09**. Leave **Standard** selected as the Calendar setting and click **OK**.

3. Save the file as *Software Project.*

 Create a folder named *PSG Exercises* in your *Documents* or *My Documents* folder and save your exercise practice files there.

4. Make the following entries in the *Task Name* and *Duration* fields:

| Gather Client Requirements | 4d |
| Write Specifications | 2w |
| Client Review and Approval | 2d |
| Launch Programming | 0 |

5. Click the Start cell for task 4 (*Launch Programming*), type **6/14/09**, and press **Enter**.

6. Review the choices in the Planning Wizard message box that appears. Leave the option for moving the task to the next working day selected and then click **OK**.

7. Click **Tools** and then click **Options**.

8. Click the **General** tab. If needed, click the **Advice from Planning Wizard** check box to clear it and then click **OK**.

9. Click the **Start cell** for task 4 (*Launch Programming*), type **6/14/09**, and press **Enter**.

10. Review the message box that Project displays in this instance and then click **OK** to close it.

11. Click the **Undo** button on the Standard toolbar or press **Ctrl+Z**.

12. Save your changes to the file and keep it open for the next project.

## *Project 2*

1. Drag over all four tasks in the *Software Project* file.

2. Click the **Link Tasks** button to link them.

3. Leaving the tasks selected, click the **Toolbar Options** button at the right end of the Standard toolbar, if needed, and then click the **Unlink Tasks** button.

4. Press **Ctrl+F2** to relink the tasks.

5. Double-click the link line for the link between tasks 3 and 4. Select **Finish-to-Finish** from the Type drop-down list in the Task Dependency dialog box, and then click **OK**.

6. Double-click any cell in task 2's row in the Task sheet.

7. Click the **Predecessors** tab, enter **-1** in the Lag cell for the task 1 predecessor, and then click **OK**.

8. Double-click any cell in task 3's row in the Task sheet.

9. Click the **Predecessors** tab, enter **2** in the Lag cell for the task 2 predecessor, and then click **OK**.

10. Save your changes to the file and then close the file.

*Project 3*

1. Open the *Site Search* file you created during the Chapter 5 projects.

2. Save the file as *Site Search with Links*.

3. Right-click the **WBS** field column header and click **Hide Column.**

4. Select the following tasks and link them with FS links by clicking the **Link Tasks** button:

   2–6

   8–13

   15–21

5. Ctrl+click and then link the following pairs of tasks:

   6 and 8

   13 and 15

6. Change the links for tasks 3–5 to Start-to-Start links by double-clicking each task, clicking the **Predecessors** tab in the Task Information dialog box, choosing **Start-to-Start** from the Type drop-down list on the predecessor's row, and then clicking **OK.**

7. Double-click the link line between tasks 5 and 6, change the Lag entry to **-2d**, and then click **OK.**

8. Use the method of your choice to change the links as indicated for the following tasks:

   17  Change to start-to-start link

   20  Add +2d lag

   21  Change to finish-to-finish link

9. Point to the project summary task to display a pop-up tip with the calculated Finish date for the project plan.

10. Save your changes to the file and close the file.

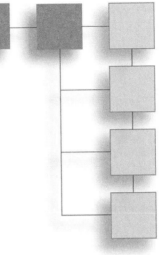

# CHAPTER 7

# LISTING THE RESOURCES YOU NEED

This Chapter Teaches You How To:

- Go to the Resource Sheet view
- Review resource information
- Add work, material, and cost resources
- Bring in resources from lists you already have
- Use generic or placeholder resources
- Understand and enter resource cost information
- Set up a resource's calendar

Each person has limited availability for getting work done. That's why most projects in organizations are tackled by teams of individuals. As the project manager, you bring the team together and guide decisions about which of the people involved will handle which tasks. You also are responsible for making sure that the team has the equipment and (in some cases) consumable materials needed to complete the assigned tasks. This chapter helps you shift your project planning in Microsoft Project from the "to do" perspective to the "who" perspective. You'll learn about the different types of resources you can use for a project and how to add different types of resources into the project plan. Most cost information also relates to resource usage, so the chapter explains how to add resource cost information. Finally, you'll see how to ensure proper scheduling by learning how to adjust a resource calendar.

## Displaying the Resource Sheet View

Until this point in your project planning, you've worked in the default Gantt Chart view to add task information, organize tasks, and link them. To add the resources that you will assign to the tasks in your project plan, you have to switch to the *Resource Sheet* view.

**Resources** are the people, equipment, and consumable items used to complete project tasks. Enter resources in the Resource Sheet view.

### Opening the Resource Sheet

Because Resource Sheet view is a view you'll need to use for virtually every project plan file that you create, Resource Sheet view is one of the choices offered directly on the View menu. To open Resource Sheet view, click the **View** menu and then click **Resource Sheet**. The Resource Sheet view immediately appears onscreen, as shown in Figure 7.1.

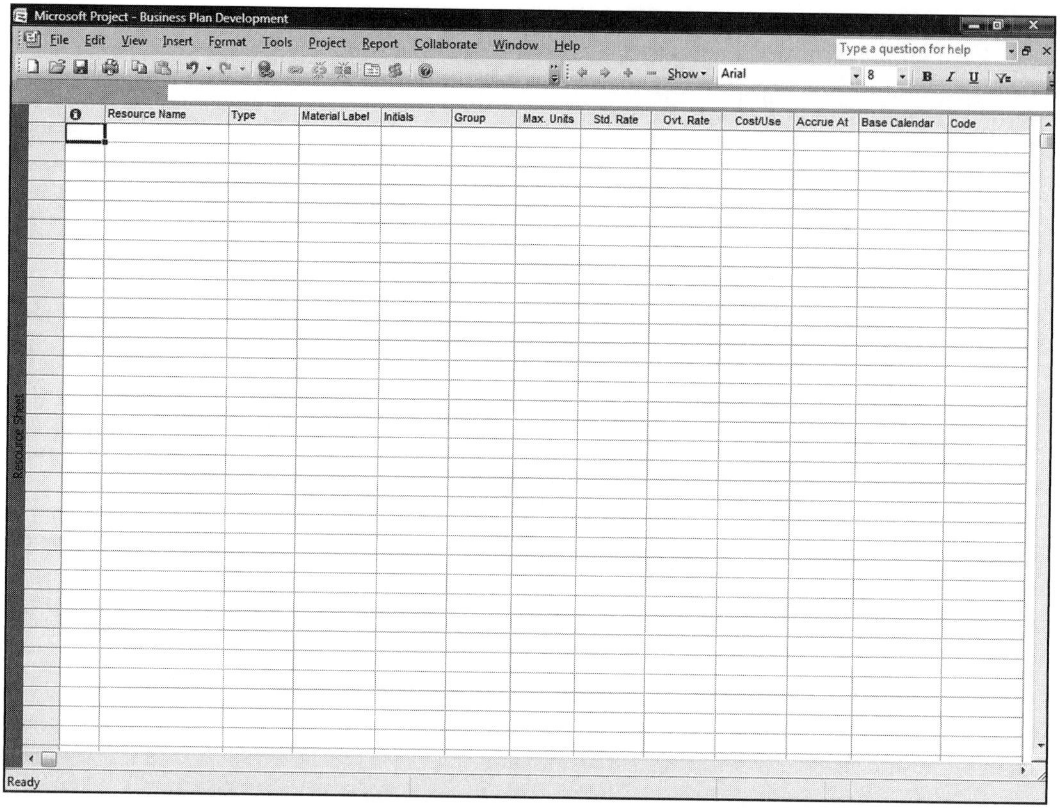

**Figure 7.1**  Use the Resource Sheet view to add resources into the project plan.

Like the Task Sheet portion of the Gantt Chart view, the Resource Sheet is a collection of rows and columns forming cells. After you make an entry in a cell, you can press the **right arrow** or **Tab** key to move to the next cell to the right, or press **Enter** to move down to the next row.

You can format and work with the Resource Sheet using the same techniques as for the Task Sheet. You'll learn about sheet formatting in Chapter 9.

## Reviewing the Resource Sheet Fields

As in the Task Sheet, each column in the Resource Sheet represents a field of information. And similarly, you don't have to use all of the fields in the Resource Sheet to set up a resource. For example, you only have to enter information into the cost-related fields if you plan to use Microsoft Project to track project cost information.

The first few fields enable you to specify some of the most essential resource information. In particular, you *must* use the *Resource Name* and *Type* fields to set up each resource. These information-oriented fields include:

- **Indicators (i).** As in the Task Sheet portion of the Gantt Chart view, this column holds special icons that make you aware of certain conditions or notes pertaining to a resource. You'll learn more about the common resource indicators that appear in this column as needed in the book.

- **Resource Name.** Enter the name that you want to use to identify the resource. You will see this name when you assign the resource to a task, and by default you will see this name beside the Gantt Chart bar for any task to which the resource is assigned.

- **Type.** This field offers a drop-down list that you use to specify the type of resource you are creating. You'll learn about the available resource types—work, material, and cost—shortly.

- **Material Label.** If you choose Material in the *Type* field, you'll make an entry in this field to identify the quantity in which the material will be consumed. See "Entering a Material Resource" later in this chapter to learn more.

- **Initials.** You don't have to make an entry in this category at all. Project will automatically fill it in for you. However, if you think you might want to display initials on the Gantt Chart, for example, you can make the entries that you want in this field.

- **Group.** You can make an entry in this field to identify whether a resource belongs to a particular department, such as *Accounting* or *Engineering*, or if a resource can be identified by another category, such as *Freelance* or *Consultant*.

The next field enables you to specify how much of the resource's time Project should allocate to your schedule:

- **Max. Units.** If you press **Tab** to move on by this field, Project will enter 100% by default. The percentage entry in this field indicates how much of the resource's daily scheduled work time will be allocated initially to each task to which you assign the resource. So, if a resource from another department can only work half-time for your project, enter 50% here. If the resource is a vendor sending three people for every assignment, enter 300%. Note that each time you assign the resource, you can either stick with the Max. Units entry you entered on the Resource Sheet or enter a new value to control the resource's units applied to that particular assignment.

If you will use Project to track cost information for your project plan, you will need to use the next four cost-related fields. Most costs in business are related to hours of work or contracted usage amounts—that's why you specify most cost information on the Resource Sheet:

- **Std. Rate.** You will make an entry in this field for most work and material resources. The amount you enter here tells Project how much cost to add to the project for each hour of work assigned for the work resource or each quantity of usage assigned for a material resource. Think of this entry as the dollars per hour or cost per amount.

- **Ovt. Rate.** You can make an entry in this field if you will need to account for overtime pay for a work resource. I have to caution you that Project doesn't automatically kick in the overtime rate for you. You have to identify hours of work manually, a topic you'll learn more about in Chapter 11.

- **Cost/Use.** You can make an entry in this field for any cost or material resource for which there is a flat charge every time you use the resource. For example, if the resource is a phone installer, it might charge a $30 fee for every installation, no matter how long it takes. That's a cost per use (Cost/Use).

 Some resources might have both a Std. Rate and Cost/Use. For example, a plumber might charge a flat service call fee of $50 (the Cost/Use), plus an hourly rate of $60 (the Std. Rate).

- **Accrue At.** The entry in this field specifies how Project accounts for the timing of resource costs in the budget for the project. The default entry, *Prorated*, means that Project adds in costs at the time when work is scheduled (or scheduled work has been marked as completed). However, with some types of resources, the costs might apply at the Start or End of the assigned task. For example, if you only have to pay an external resource after the person finishes all work on assignments, select *End* as the *Accrue At* field choice for that resource.

The last two fields enable you to specify scheduling and identification information for each resource as needed:

- **Base Calendar.** If a work resource follows a calendar that's different from the base calendar that you've assigned to the project file in the Project Information dialog box, you need to choose the correct calendar for the resource from the drop-down list here. For example, you might have set a project to use the 24 Hours calendar, but human work resources work shorter hours, so you need to choose the Standard calendar or a custom calendar with fewer work hours.

- **Code.** You can use this field for any type of alphanumeric information that you need to use to identify resources. For example, if you entered department names in the *Group* field and will need to track costs by department, you could enter the corresponding departmental accounting code in the *Code* field.

# Adding Resource Information

Now that you have a sense of the information that the fields in the Resource Sheet are set up to hold, you are ready to delve into the types of resources you can create in Project, how to use each type of resource, and how to enter the right Resource Sheet information for each type of resource. This section tells you what you need to know about creating the Resource Sheet entries for your project plan.

> If you will be using the same resources in all of your projects, you only need to build your Resource Sheet list and set up details about each resource once. You then can share the resources with other Project files. The section called "Sharing Resources from a Pool" in Chapter 15 describes how to perform the sharing.

## Understanding Resource Types

Assigning resources to tasks enables Project to track two types of information: hours of work and costs. Sometimes the costs are associated with hours of work, but sometimes costs are associated with non-work-related situations such as usage of the resource (as in a Cost/Use), the amount of something consumed, or just a fee associated with the completion of a single task. To account for all of these various cost scenarios, Project enables you to create three different types of resources.

*Work resources* have been available in Project since the earliest versions. Use this type of resource for people contributing hours of work on a project. This includes people from your company; external resources like consultants, freelancers, temps, and contract employees; and persons from vendors that you hire such as a construction company. For each hour of work assigned to a work resource, Project adds an hour's worth of cost for the resource to the project. A work resource also might include a piece of equipment for which you are charged on an hourly or daily basis, such as rented construction equipment. Any time you assign a work resource to a task, hours of work will be added to the task, even if you only added a Cost/Use entry for the resource.

*Material resources* represent items or commodities consumed to complete tasks in the project. Think reams of paper, feet of wire, units of computers, cubic yards of concrete, and so on. These material resources are used for tasks and add costs to the project, but they don't add hours of work. This type of resource was added for more recent versions of Project.

*Cost resources* are new in Project 2007. You set up a cost resource to account for something that doesn't add hours to the project and isn't consumed in quantity but does have a cost every time you use it. A courier that charges $30 per delivery or a document recording fee are examples that you would set up as cost resources.

**Work resources** typically represent people or equipment that add hours of work and have hourly costs. **Material resources** are consumables that you pay for by quantity, like quarts of oil. **Cost resources** add a single expense to the project. Neither material nor cost resources add hours of work to the project.

Project 2007 actually enables you to set up a special type of resource called a **budget resource** that you can use to enter external budget information that you want to compare with the budget information that Project calculates. Setting this up is a lengthy process that's beyond what I cover in this book, but if you want to learn more and try it out, search Project Help for **budget resource**, and then click the **Create a Budget for Your Project** topic that appears.

## Entering a Work Resource

Work resources typically require you to add information to the greatest number of fields in the Resource Sheet. You not only have to identify the resource, but you also have to enter the necessary cost and calendar information. Follow these steps to add a work resource to the list of resources on the resource sheet:

1. Click in the first blank **Resource Name** cell on the Resource Sheet.
2. Type the work resource's name and then press **Tab**.

You can sort information on the Resource Sheet. If you think you might want to sort the resources in the Resource Sheet by last name, you need to enter the resources last name first, as in *Smith Jane*. You also can add a separate last name column and sort by that, if needed. The section called "Filtering and Sorting Sheet Data" in Chapter 12 will cover sorting.

3. Leave **Work** selected in the *Type* field and press **Tab** twice to move past it and the *Material Label* field. (Project does not let you make an entry in the *Material Label* field for work or cost resources.)

4. Type the **Initials** field entry that you'd like to use for the resource and then press **Tab**.

5. Type a **Group** field entry to categorize the resource and then press **Tab**. Remember that you can create any *Group* labels that you want, but typically you might enter a department, a job description or class, or another type of identifier that your organization uses to group people.

6. Make a new percentage entry in the **Max. Units** field only if the resource is available part time for your project or if the resource represents multiple workers. Then press **Tab**.

If you leave the *Max. Units* entry set to 100%, you can override that entry when you make individual assignments. So, if a resource will be 100% available most of the time, you don't need to change the *Max. Units* field entry.

7. Type a **Std. Rate** field entry so that Project can calculate the cost for the work the resource performs. If you just enter a number, such as **25**, Project assumes you are entering the cost per hour, or $25/hr. If the costs have been provided in another way, such as an annual figure, you can use the appropriate abbreviation to make the entry. For example, 2000/w represents $2,000 per week, or 40000/y represents $40,000 per year. If you enter a figure other than an hourly figure, Project will convert to the resulting hourly rate when calculating costs for the resource's work on the project. Press **Tab** to finish the *Std. Rate* entry.

8. If you will be authorizing and tracking overtime for the resource, make the appropriate value entry in the **Ovt. Rate** field and then press **Tab**. As for the Std. Rate, you can enter this value as an hourly rate or another rate that Project will convert for you as needed when making its calculations.

9. If the resource has an associate cost per use (that is, a fee Project should add to the budget every time you assign the resource to a task), enter that amount into the **Cost/Use** field and press **Tab**.

10. If you want to choose an **Accrue At** field entry other than Prorated, click the drop-down list arrow that appears when the field is selected, click either **Start** or **End**, and then press **Tab**.

11. By default, Project assigns the Project's base calendar as the *Base Calendar* field entry for each work resource. If you need to change this entry, click the **Base Calendar** field drop-down list arrow, click the desired calendar, and press **Tab**.

12. Enter the desired value in the **Code** field, if any.

13. You can then press **Enter** to finish the last resource entry, or repeat Steps 1 through 12 to add additional work resources. Figure 7.2 shows a completed work resource entered in the Resource Sheet.

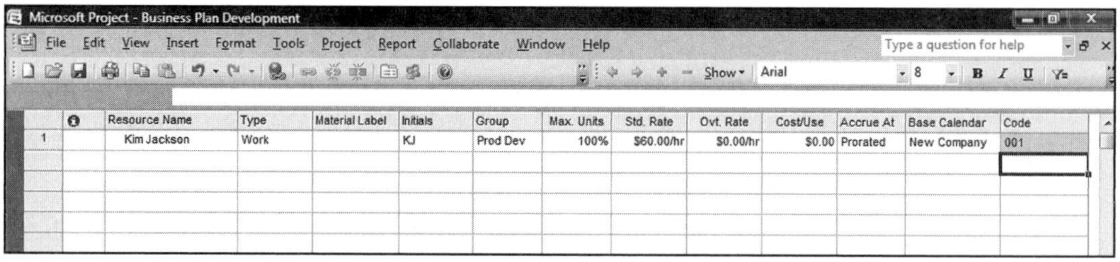

**Figure 7.2**  Row 1 of the Resource Sheet now has a work resource entered.

You may wonder what to do about making entries in the cost columns, because in many organizations salary information is confidential. In such cases, an organization might enter an average cost for each resource who falls in a particular job category. Or, resources from some departments might be assigned specific allocated cost values. You as project manager need to understand the personnel costing policies used by your organization and work within those boundaries.

Cost information for equipment resources requires your prior investigation. Consult with vendors and get a written estimate, if needed. Dramatically underestimating costs for these types of resources can come back to bite you when your project goes over budget and you don't have additional project funding to draw on.

## Entering a Material Resource

Material resources often involve fewer field entries because there are no associated hours of work and only one type of cost. However, when you create a material resource, you do have to quantify how cost will be measured and consumed by making an entry in the *Material Label* field. For example, for reams of paper, you would enter **Ream** in the *Material*

*Label* field. For cubic yards of concrete, you would enter **Cu. Yd.** or something similar. These steps walk you through material resource entry:

1. Click in the first blank **Resource Name** cell on the Resource Sheet.
2. Type the material resource's name and then press **Tab**.
3. Click the drop-down list arrow for the **Type** field, click **Material**, and press **Tab**.
4. Type the desired quantity identifier into the **Material Label** field and press **Tab**.
5. Type the **Initials** field entry that you'd like to use for the resource and then press **Tab**.
6. Type a **Group** field entry to categorize the resource and then press **Tab** twice. Project doesn't let you make an entry in the *Max. Units* field for a material resource, so you can **Tab** on past it.
7. Type a **Std. Rate** field entry. The value you enter should correspond to the entry you made in the *Material Label* field in Step 4. So, if you entered Cu. Yd. for cubic yard there, you should enter the price per cubic yard in this field. Then press **Tab** twice.
8. If the resource also has an associate cost per use, enter that amount into the **Cost/Use** field and press **Tab**.
9. If you want to choose an **Accrue At** field entry other than Prorated, click the drop-down list arrow that appears when the field is selected, click either **Start** or **End**, and then press **Tab** twice. Because material resources don't have associated hours of work to schedule, you can skip the *Base Calendar* field.
10. Enter the desired value in the **Code** field, if any.
11. You can then press **Enter** to finish the last resource entry, or repeat Steps 1 through 10 to add additional material resources. Figure 7.3 shows a completed material resource entered in the Resource Sheet.

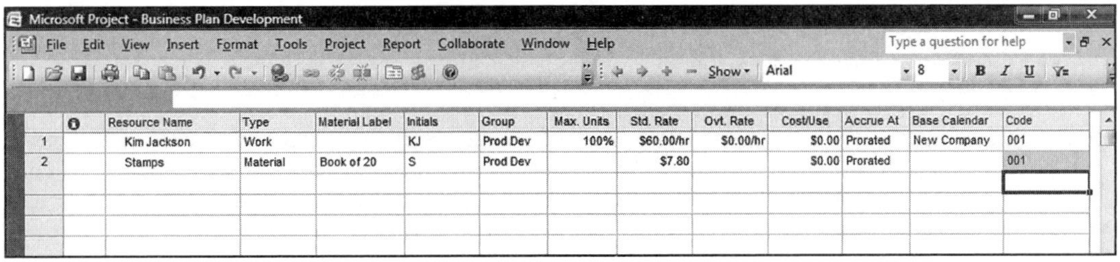

| | | Resource Name | Type | Material Label | Initials | Group | Max. Units | Std. Rate | Ovt. Rate | Cost/Use | Accrue At | Base Calendar | Code |
|---|---|---|---|---|---|---|---|---|---|---|---|---|---|
| 1 | | Kim Jackson | Work | | KJ | Prod Dev | 100% | $60.00/hr | $0.00/hr | $0.00 | Prorated | New Company | 001 |
| 2 | | Stamps | Material | Book of 20 | S | Prod Dev | | $7.80 | | $0.00 | Prorated | | 001 |

**Figure 7.3**  Row 2 of the Resource Sheet now has a material resource entered.

## Entering a Cost Resource

Cost resources, new in Project 2007, enable you to account for costs that don't involve hours of work or consumable quantities and that typically don't represent the entire cost for a task. For example, if you are managing a construction project, you might have permit fees associated with the particular tasks. Those permit fees could be entered as a cost resource. Or, if you're a special event planner and you have miscellaneous expenses associated with a particular project, such as parking fees paid during client meetings or the event itself, those fees can be set up as a cost resource.

Entering a cost resource works much like entering one of the other two types of resources, but again, the information you enter is more limited than for a work resource. Use these steps to enter a cost resource in the Resource Sheet view:

1. Click in the first blank **Resource Name** cell on the Resource Sheet.

2. Type the cost resource's name and then press **Tab**.

3. Click the drop-down list arrow for the **Type** field, click **Cost**, and press **Tab** twice to pass the *Material Label* field.

4. Type the **Initials** field entry that you'd like to use for the resource and then press **Tab**.

5. Type a **Group** field entry to categorize the resource and then press **Tab** five times. Project doesn't let you make *Max. Units* or *cost* field entries for a cost resource, so you can Tab all the way to the *Accrue At* field.

6. If you want to choose an **Accrue At** field entry other than Prorated, click the drop-down list arrow that appears when the field is selected, click either **Start** or **End**, and then press **Tab** twice. Because cost resources don't have associated hours of work to schedule, you can skip the *Base Calendar* field.

7. Enter the desired value in the **Code** field, if any.

8. You can then press **Enter** to finish the last resource entry, or repeat Steps 1 through 7 to add additional cost resources. Figure 7.4 shows a completed cost resource entered in the Resource Sheet.

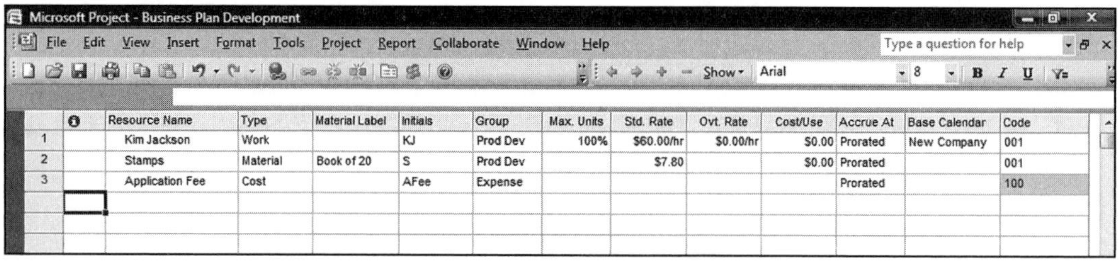

| | ⓘ | Resource Name | Type | Material Label | Initials | Group | Max. Units | Std. Rate | Ovt. Rate | Cost/Use | Accrue At | Base Calendar | Code | |
|---|---|---|---|---|---|---|---|---|---|---|---|---|---|---|
| 1 | | Kim Jackson | Work | | KJ | Prod Dev | 100% | $60.00/hr | $0.00/hr | $0.00 | Prorated | New Company | 001 | |
| 2 | | Stamps | Material | Book of 20 | S | Prod Dev | | $7.80 | | $0.00 | Prorated | | 001 | |
| 3 | | Application Fee | Cost | | AFee | Expense | | | | | Prorated | | 100 | |

**Figure 7.4** Row 3 of the Resource Sheet now has a cost resource entered.

If a task cost isn't resource-oriented at all, perhaps being a flat fee for the task charged by an outside vendor, you can enter that fixed task cost in a different location—the Cost table of the Task Sheet. You'll learn how to do this in Chapter 9.

## Copying or Importing Information

If you already have a list of resources typed into a file in another application such as an Excel worksheet or an Access database, you do not need to type the information again to add it to the Resource Sheet.

If the resources are in a table in Word or Access or in a list on an Excel worksheet, you can drag to select the cells that hold the resource names to copy; right-click the selection and click the **Copy** command or press **Ctrl+C**; switch back to Project and select the next blank cell in the *Resource Name* field; and then right-click the cell and click **Paste** or press **Ctrl+V**. If you want to copy and paste additional information such as cost information into another field, you can do so. Just keep in mind that Project requires you to paste the right type of information into each field. If you try to paste copied text into a cost field in Project, Project will display an error message.

You can copy information from another application and paste it into the Resource Sheet to save work.

When the list of resources is long and contains multiple fields of information that you want to add to the Resource Sheet, you'll likely save time by importing the resources. The process isn't complicated. It works much like opening a file, and a wizard walks you through the whole thing:

1. Switch to the Resource Sheet view for the project file to which you'd like to import resources.
2. Click **File** and then click **Open.** The Open dialog box appears.
3. Click the file type drop-down list near the lower-right corner of the dialog box (it looks like a button reading Microsoft Project Files) and then click the name of the type of file to import, such as **Microsoft Excel Workbooks**.

If you're working in Excel 2007, use the Save As command to save the file to be imported into an older file format, such as Excel 97-2003 Workbook in Excel before starting the import process. Then Project will be able to import the file directly. Word, Excel, and Access files in Microsoft Office 2007 use different file formats and file name extensions for their files than older versions of those applications. As such, Project might not display those files in the Open dialog box when you select the applicable file type. To make sure that you can see the Office file you want to import, click **All Files** in the file type drop-down list. If a message box asks whether you want to open the file as text only, click **Yes**. But be aware that the import might not work, in which case saving to a pre-2007 format is the best bet.

4. Navigate to the folder holding the file to import, click the file, and then click **Open**. The first Import Wizard dialog box appears.

5. Click **Next** to move to the next step of the wizard.

6. In the next Wizard dialog box, leave the **New Map** option button selected and then click **Next**.

7. When the next Wizard dialog box asks how you want to import the file, click the **Append the Data to the Active Project** option button and then click **Next**.

8. In the next Wizard dialog box, shown in Figure 7.5, you specify what kind of data the file to import holds. Click the **Resources** option button. Also, if the first row of the file you're importing holds field names, leave the **Import Includes Headers** check box checked so that Project does not import the information from that row. Click **Next**.

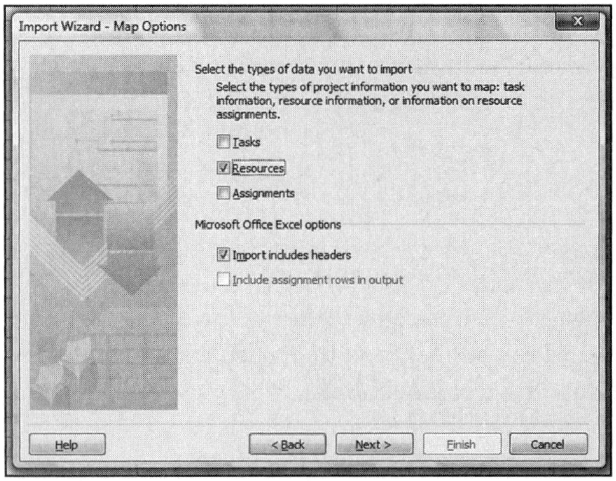

**Figure 7.5** Tell Project you are importing Resource information.

9. In the next Wizard dialog box, you ***map*** the fields, or match up information from a field in the imported file with the field where you want to place that information in Project. If you're importing an Excel file or Access table, first choose the worksheet or table holding the resource information from the drop-down list at the top. After you do so, Project will examine the information in the file being imported to match it to fields in the Resource Sheet, as shown in Figure 7.6. If you see *(not mapped)* for any field in the To: Microsoft Office Project Field column, click that cell, click the drop-down list arrow that appears, and then scroll and click the desired field name. For example, in Figure 7.6, I need to specify that the *Label* and *Rate* fields from the Excel file being imported should map to the *Material Label* and Standard Rate (*Std. Rate*) fields in Project.

10. When you have all the field mapping properly specified and the Preview area at the bottom of the dialog box shows the correct mapping, click **Finish**.

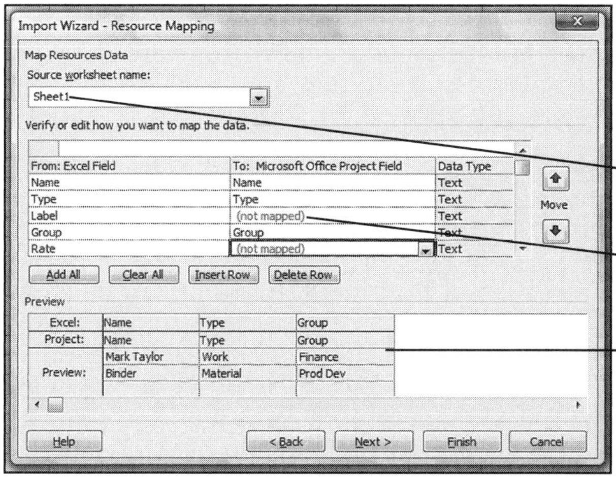

**Figure 7.6** Now tell Project which fields need to hold the imported information.

Select sheet or table

Select Project fields to map to

Mapping preview

After you paste or import resource information, always be sure to review the information in the Resource Sheet. You may need to add information that wasn't present in the original file, such as specifying an alternate *Base Calendar* or typing a *Group* or *Code* field entry. You also might need to correct information—for example, making sure to add **/y** after imported *Std. Rate* field entries that represent annual salaries rather than hourly rates.

Chapter 14 will provide more details about importing, exporting, and mapping information, including how to save any data map that you've created.

## Adding Resources from Your Address Book or Active Directory

If resources that you'll be working with already exist in your e-mail address book (for any MAPI-compliant e-mail program like Windows Mail in Vista, Outlook Express in Windows XP, or Microsoft Office Outlook), you can import them into Project and once again save yourself the trouble of typing, typing, typing.

To add a resource in this way, go to the Resource Sheet. Click **Insert**, point to the **New Resource From** command, and then click **Address Book**. The Select Resources dialog box opens. Click the name of each resource to add to the list of resources and then click the **Add** button at the bottom of the dialog box. When you've selected all the resources, click OK to close the dialog box and finish adding them to the Resource Sheet.

You also can insert resources from Active Directory if it's used by your organization. Click **Insert**, point to **New Resource From**, and then click **Active Directory**. Then select the resource to add in the dialog box that appears. Using Active Directory, in particular, ensures that all the project managers within the company enter identical resource names, which eliminates the possibility of duplicates when information is combined from multiple project plan files.

## Generic or Placeholder Resources

Because you will be building your project plan in advance of getting approval for the plan within your organization, you may not have specific information about which persons will be available to you as resources for the execution of the project. In such a case, you can enter your resources as *generic* or *placeholder resources.*

Let's say you're putting together the project plan for a software programming project. You know you will need three programmers, but you don't yet know which of the programmers in your company will be made available for your project team. In this case, you can enter the resources as *Programmer 1*, *Programmer 2*, and *Programmer 3* in the *Resource Names* field of the Resource Sheet. You can assign those resources to tasks throughout the project as you normally would.

Later, you find out the names of the three resources: Jim Smith, Angela Case, and Laird Timmons. To update the project plan to use the actual resource names, all you need to do is display the Resource Sheet, select the Resource Name cell for one of the placeholder resources (such as *Programmer 1*), and type in the actual resource name (such as Jim Smith). Project will then replace the *Programmer 1* resource throughout the project with the new resource name, Jim Smith.

This technique enables you to build your project plan completely and update every assignment for a resource simply by changing the resource's name in the Resource Sheet.

Changing a resource's name in the *Resource Name* field of the Resource Sheet updates that resource name throughout the project.

# Understanding Resource Costs

New Project users often find all the resource cost information intimidating. I always tell them not to worry. You can implement Project in stages if you wish. First, add task, outlining, and link information, and then track just that information for a project or two. For the next few projects, add resource names and types, assign the resources and track work. Then, when you're ready to use Project's cost tracking capabilities, add cost information to the Resource Sheet.

Cost tracking in Project is not always accurate to the penny like a real cost accounting system. Project rounds off values, task durations may not always match reality, and resources may do work with associated costs outside what is assigned in the project. Due to these issues, Project cost calculations and cost forecasts should always be viewed as approximate.

## Updating Costs on the Resource Sheet

You've already seen in this chapter how to enter various resource costs on the Resource Sheet. Each of these costs is used when you assign one or more resources to a task to calculate the *total cost* for the task. To find the total cost for each task, Project adds together the following values:

- *(Std. Rate x hours of work assigned)* + *(Ovt. Rate x hours of overtime authorized)* + *Cost/Use* for each work resource assigned
- *Std. Rate x quantity assigned* for each material resource assigned
- *Assigned amount* for each cost resource assigned
- *Fixed cost*, if any, assigned to the task in the Cost table of the Task Sheet

Ensuring that costs are tracked accurately means making sure you choose the right type of resource and enter the right cost information on the Resource Sheet. If you failed to enter information in a cost field previously or need to correct an earlier entry, click the desired cost field (*Std. Rate*, *Ovt. Rate*, or *Cost/Use*), type a new value, and then press **Enter**. Project displays the updated information and automatically recalculates cost information throughout the project.

If you've already saved the baseline for the project plan, Project does not recalculate baseline cost information when you change a cost value on the Resource Sheet. In such a case, you may want to clear and resave the baseline as described in the section "Working with the Baseline" in Chapter 11.

## Creating Updating Rates and a Cost Table

Resource cost rates may not necessarily remain static over the course of a project. For example, if company-wide salary increases take effect during the course of the project, the real costs for the assigned resources rise after that point in time. You need to tell the project to update the rate for a resource after an increase takes effect, in that instance.

To set up a resource so that its cost rates change at a specified date, follow these steps:

1. Double-click the **resource** in the Resource Sheet. The Resource Information dialog box for the resource opens.

Double-clicking a resource on the Resource Sheet opens the Resource Information dialog box.

2. Click the **Costs** tab. The tab appears, displaying more detailed cost information, including five Cost Rate Table tabs (A through E).

3. Click in the next blank row of the Effective Date column, type the date when the resource's rate increase becomes effective, and press **Tab** to finish the entry.

4. On the same row as the Effective Date you just entered, click in the **Standard Rate**, **Overtime Rate**, and **Per Use Cost** cells and enter new rates as needed. As shown in Figure 7.7, you can enter costs as dollar values or as a percentage increase.

5. Click **OK** to close the dialog box. For any work assigned to the resource beyond the Effective Date specified in Step 3, Project will use the new rate(s) in any cost calculations.

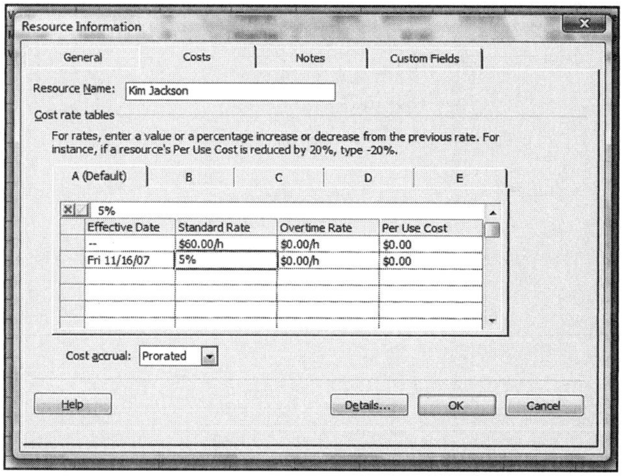

**Figure 7.7** This resource's 5 percent raise will be effective 11/16/07.

Rather than rates that change over time, other resources might have rates that vary depending on the nature of the task being performed or the specific person assigned from the external company. For example, a consulting firm might charge one rate for tasks handled by a senior consultant and another rate for tasks handled by a junior consultant. Or the consultant might charge one rate for writing a business plan for you but a lower rate for reviewing a business plan that you've already written.

When a resource works by different rates, you need to set up a *cost table* for the resource. As when specifying a rate change, use the Resource Information dialog box to create each cost table:

1. Double-click the **resource** in the Resource Sheet. The Resource Information dialog box for the resource opens.

2. Click the **Costs** tab. The tab appears, displaying more detailed cost information, including five Cost Rate Table tabs (A through E). The tab A (Default) task table is already set up based on the cost information entered for the resource in the Resource Sheet.

3. Click the next empty cost table tab. The tab should appear with zero values entered in each of the rate fields.

4. Click the *Standard Rate, Overtime Rate,* or *Per Use Cost* field, as needed, make the desired rate entry, and press **Tab**. The resource shown in Figure 7.8 normally charges a $100/h Standard Rate but for some tasks charges a lower $75/h Standard Rate, as indicated on its new cost table B.

5. Click **OK** to close the dialog box and finish creating the rate table.

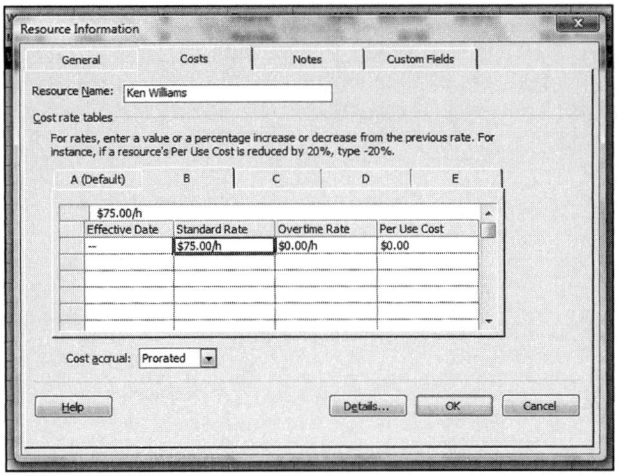

**Figure 7.8** Cost table B gives a lower Standard Rate for this resource.

In the next chapter you will learn how to select specific cost rate information when you've assigned a resource to a task.

## Adjusting a Resource's Calendar

Even if you've created a custom calendar for the project and a resource is following that calendar, not every resource has exactly the same working schedule. First, you might need to account for a resource's nonworking days like vacation days or days taken off for surgery or a maternity leave. Or, a resource might work a flexible schedule such as 7 a.m. to 2 p.m. rather than 8 a.m. to 5 p.m. In situations like these, you need to adjust the resource's calendar to reflect the resource's actual working schedule.

Whenever a resource's specific calendar differs from the project base calendar, the resource's calendar overrides the project base calendar. That is, Project schedules any task to which you've assigned a resource according to the resource's calendar rather than the project base calendar.

Follow these steps to adjust a resource's calendar:

1. Click the **resource** in the Resource Sheet.
2. Click **Tools** and then click **Change Working Time**. The Change Working Time dialog box appears, with the selected resource's name appearing as the For Calendar choice to tell you that the changes you make will apply to that resource's calendar. Figure 7.9 shows an example.

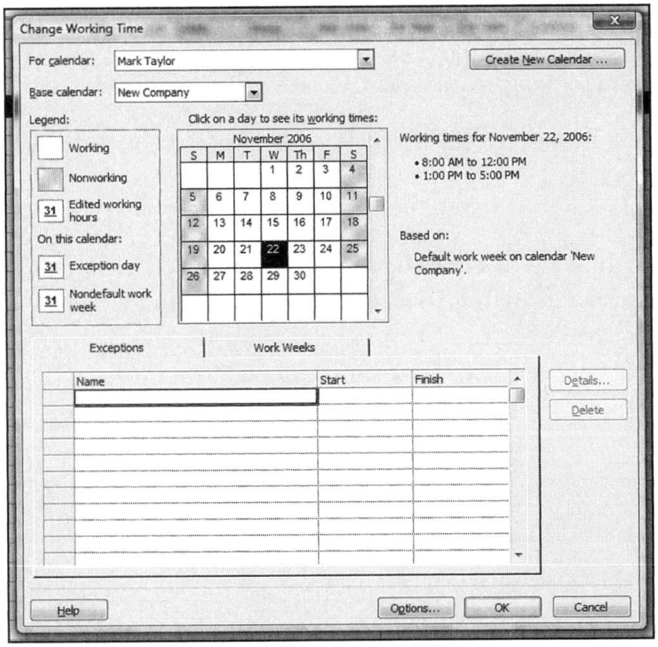

**Figure 7.9** The resource whose calendar you are changing appears as the For Calendar choice at the top of the dialog box.

3. Change the calendar settings for the resource just as you did when setting up a custom calendar. The section called "Setting Up a New Calendar" in Chapter 4 explains how to make the types of changes required, such as marking a nonworking day or changing working hours.

4. Click **OK** to close the Change Working Time dialog box and save your changes to the Resource's calendar.

## Specifying Resource Availability

Other resources may not be available to work on your project for the full duration of the project. For example, if you've "borrowed" a person from another department in your company, you might only be able to use that resource for a specific one-month period. Or, if you have limited budget available for resources from a temp service, you may only be able to hire temp workers for a week or two. In the case of outside vendors and consultants, other commitments might limit their work on your project to a very specific window of time.

In such a case, you can specify a resource's *availability*—the period or periods of time during which a resource is actually available to work on your project. Use these steps to indicate when a resource is available to work on your project:

1. Double-click the **resource** in the Resource Sheet. The Resource Information dialog box for the resource opens.

2. Click the **General** tab, if needed.

3. On a row in the Resource Availability area, click the **Available From** cell, click the drop-down list arrow, and select the availability starting date using the calendar that appears. Likewise, click the **Available To** cell and use its drop-down calendar to specify the end of the availability period. If the resource is available more or less than full time, also change the **Units** entry as needed. Figure 7.10 shows an example of these entries.

4. Repeat Step 3 to set up other availability periods for the resource as needed.

5. Click **OK** to close the dialog box and finish specifying availability.

 If you try to assign a resource with limited availability to a task scheduled during a period outside that availability, Project will reschedule the task to match the resource's available period. So, make sure you keep a close watch on the changes that Project makes when you assign a resource with limited availability specified.

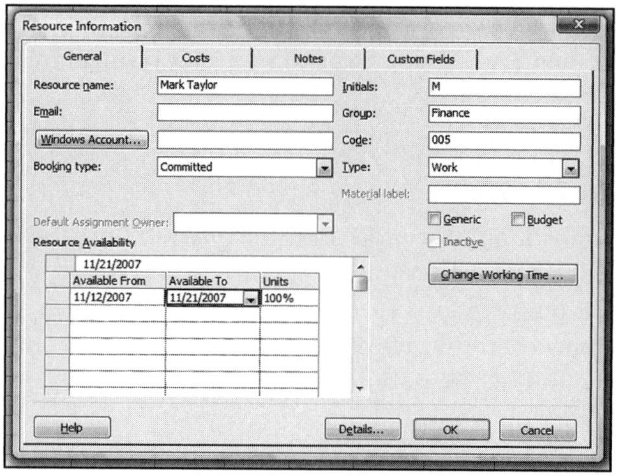

**Figure 7.10** Set up availability periods in the Resource Availability area of the General tab.

# Chapter Review

In this chapter, you shifted your emphasis to listing the people, equipment, and consumable materials you'll need to accomplish the tasks in the project, as well as the costs for using those resources and others. You learned how to display the Resource Sheet view, where you enter Resource information, and how to create work, material, and cost resources there. You learned how you could add resources from other sources and how to use a placeholder resource until you have concrete information about who will be working with you. Finally, you saw how to build in more specifics about a resource's costs and schedule, including how to set up a resource cost table, edit a resource's calendar, and identify a resource's availability for your project. Become even more familiar with these skills by completing the Review Questions and Projects now.

## Review Questions

Write your answers to the following questions on a sheet of paper.

1. What menu and command do you choose to change to the Resource Sheet view?
2. Name the three main types of resources.
3. A _____ resource has neither associated work nor consumed quantity.
4. Make an entry in the _____ field of the Resource Sheet if the resource charges a fee every time you use or assign it.
5. The entry in the _____ field of the Resource Sheet indicates whether the resource will be working full time or part time on the project or whether multiple persons will be used for each assignment.
6. How do you replace a resource throughout the project plan?
7. How do you display the Resource Information dialog box?
8. What tab in the Resource Information dialog box do you use to specify a rate increase or set up cost tables?
9. True or False: Project always follows the project's base calendar, no matter when a resource actually works.
10. When a resource can only work on your project during a fixed time period, specify that resource's _____ in the Resource Information dialog box.

## Projects

To see the solution files created by completing the projects in this chapter, go to www.courseptr.com, click the **Downloads** link in the navigation bar at the top, type **Microsoft Office Project 2007 Survival Guide** in the search text box, and then click **Search Downloads**.

### Project 1

1. Create a new, blank project file.
2. Save the file as *Resource Planning*.

Create a folder named *PSG Exercises* in your *Documents* or *My Documents* folder and save your exercise practice files there.

3. Click **Project** and then click **Project Information**. Choose 24 Hours from the Calendar drop-down list and then click **OK**.
4. Click **View** and then click **Resource Sheet** to change to the Resource Sheet view.
5. Make the following entries in the *Resource Name, Type, Material Label,* and *Group* fields, skipping other fields for now:

| John Swift | Work | blank | Accounting |
| Marc Welby | Work | blank | Engineering |
| Cat 5 Cable | Material | ft. | Expense |
| Subscription | Cost | blank | Expense |

6. Change the *Base Calendar* field entry for the two work resources to **Standard**.
7. Enter a *Std. Rate* of **50** for John Swift, a *Cost/Use* of **300** for Marc Welby, and a *Std. Rate* of **.50** for Cat 5 Cable.
8. Double-click **John Swift** and click the **Costs** tab. On the next blank row of the A cost tab, specify **1/7/08** as the Effective Date cell entry. Click the **Standard Rate** cell, type **10%,** and press **Enter**. Click **OK** to apply the rate change.
9. Save your changes to the file and keep it open for the next project.

## Project 2

1. Click the **Resource Name** cell for the **Marc Welby** resource.

2. Type **Grace Hopper** and press **Enter**.

3. Click the **Grace Hopper** resource.

4. Click **Tools** and then click **Change Working Time**. Click the **Work Weeks** tab, click the **[Default]** entry, and then click **Details**. Select **Monday through Friday** in the Select Day(s) list, click the **Set Day(s) to These Specific Working Times** option button, change 5 p.m. to **6 p.m.,** and press **Enter**. Click **OK** twice to close the dialog boxes and change Grace's calendar.

5. Enter a new work resource named **Ladder**.

6. Double-click the Ladder resource. On the General tab of the Resource Information dialog box, set its availability from **12/17/07** to **1/15/08**. Click **OK**.

7. Save your changes to the file and then close the file.

## Project 3

1. Open the *Site Search with Links* file you created during the Chapter 6 projects.

2. Save the file as *Site Search with Resource List*.

3. Click **View** and then click **Resource Sheet** to change to the Resource Sheet view.

4. Enter the following resource information in the *Resource Name*, *Type*, *Material Label*, and *Group* fields, skipping other fields for now:

| Jane Black | Work | blank | Planning |
| Smith Todd | Work | blank | Architect |
| Paper | Material | ream | Planning |
| Realtor | Work | blank | External |
| Lynnette Taylor | Work | blank | Planning |
| Attorney | Work | blank | External |
| Realtor Fee | Cost | blank | Expense |
| Closing Costs | Cost | blank | Expense |
| Loan Costs | Cost | blank | Expense |
| Land Cost | Cost | blank | Expense |

5. Enter Std. Rates of **75** for Jane Black and Lynnette Taylor and **70** for Smith Todd.

6. Enter a Std. Rate of **3.5** for the Paper resource.

7. Enter a Cost/Use of **500** for the Attorney resource.

8. Save your changes to the file and close the file.

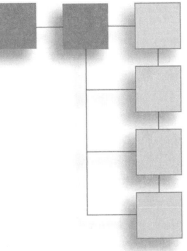

# CHAPTER 8

# ASSIGNING RESOURCES TO TASKS

This Chapter Teaches You How To:

- Understand the impact of effort-driven scheduling
- Assign single or multiple work resources to a task
- Assign a material or cost resource to a task
- Remove or replace an assigned resource
- Assign a resource part time to a task
- Review resource assignments
- Apply another cost for a resource
- Override or turn off effort-driven scheduling

After you identify the tasks and the team required for your project, you need to bring the two together to specify "who" will do "what" in the plan. Your job now as project manager is to decide which individuals and materials are needed for specific tasks and to make those connections in the project plan. This vital step enables Microsoft Office Project 2007 to give you (and your project plan) a reality check: the ability to see whether you can realistically complete all the project deliverables on time with the team, materials, equipment, and financial resources that have been allocated. This chapter shows you how to apply resources to tasks to make assignments. You'll learn more about how Project calculates task durations based on work resource assignments and how you can make those assignments. You'll see how to assign material and cost resources, as well as how to remove or replace any assigned resource. Managing resources in more detail requires other views, so the chapter explains how to view assignments and how to apply an alternate cost for a resource. The chapter concludes by explaining how you can turn off or work around effort-driven scheduling calculations.

## Understanding Effort-Driven Scheduling

When you assign a resource to a task, you make what Project calls an **assignment**. If you assign another resource to the same task, that creates a second assignment, even though it's a single task. Assign a third resource to the same task, and you've now got three assignments, but still one task.

Project uses the resource assignments you make for a task, along with the duration you initially entered for the task, to calculate the task's ultimate schedule. By default, it follows the logic that project managers intuit in the real world: If you apply more resources to a job, you can get it done more quickly. In Project lingo, this is called **effort-driven scheduling**.

So how does Project know how to recalculate the duration? It uses a simple equation for each task:

$D=W/U$

Where

$D$ = Duration (the length of time between the Start and Finish of the task)

$W$ = Work (the number of person hours required to complete the task)

$U$ = Units (the resource's assignment units for work on the task)

---

 Project uses **effort-driven scheduling** by default, meaning that when you already have at least one resource assigned to a task and then you assign more resources, Project will reduce the duration of the task to reflect the work contributed by the additional resource according to the formula $D=W/U$.

---

Until you make a first assignment for the task (assigning one or more resources at the same time), only the left side of the equation has any actual value, the duration.

As an example, consider a 1w task on a standard eight-hour per day calendar. If you assign one resource to that task on a full-time basis (100% or 1 unit), Project can then complete the formula:

$1w = 40h/100\%$

Project schedules 8h of work per day over five days (the default work week) for the resource.

It might seem that assigning the first resource part-time would cause Project to increase the duration or that assigning more than one resource right off the bat would decrease the duration, but that's not the case! Instead, Project completes the right side of the equation for the first time using the reduced or increased values indicated by the initial assignment of one or more resources. Consider the 1w task example again, but this time, assume you're assigning the first resource at 50% (half time):

$$1w = 20h/50\%$$

When Project fills in the equation in this instance, it uses the 50% unit value to calculate that it should only plug in 20h of work spread over the duration. The resource will be scheduled to work 4h per day (50% of an eight-hour work day) or each of the five days of the task's duration.

Think about the 1w task again, but this time, assume you are adding two resources to the task initially. In this case, Project plugs the following values into the right side of the equation:

$$1w = 80h/200\%$$

Project schedules a full 8h of work per resource per day, for a total of 80h of work.

These examples illustrate that the first resource assignment you make for the task completes all the values in the $D = W/U$ formula. Until that formula is complete, Project cannot recalculate the duration for the task because it does not have enough information to do so.

When you make another resource assignment for the task, however, Project can then adjust the duration by recalculating the formula result. If you add another resource to double the assigned units, the duration is recalculated to be half as long:

$$.5w = 40h/200\% \ (40/2)$$

In terms of scheduling each resource's work, Project plugs in 8h, 8h, and 4h of work over the shorter 2.5 day duration (half a default work week).

Figure 8.1 illustrates how setting the $D = W/U$ formula works and how effort-driven scheduling adjusts a task based on assignments. For Task A, I added a single full-time resource. For Task B, I added two full-time resources at the same time, setting the initial values for the task at 1w = 80h/200%. For Task C, I first added one full-time resource, setting the task values at 1w = 40h/100%; this was the first assignment made. Then I added a second resource, making a second and separate assignment that changed the Units value to 200%, Project recalculated the duration for the task accordingly (.5w = 40h/200%).

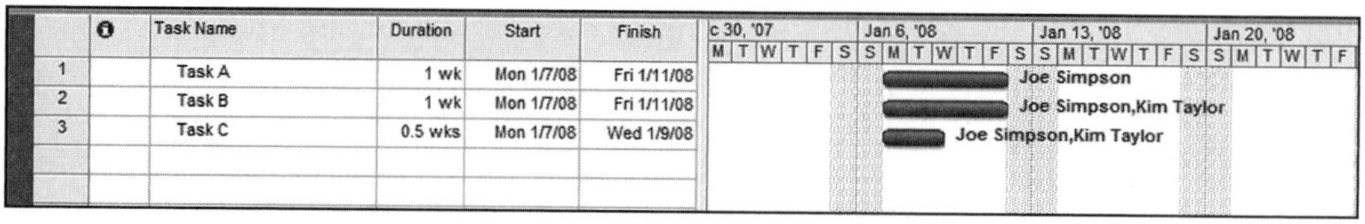

| | ❶ | Task Name | Duration | Start | Finish | c 30, '07 | Jan 6, '08 | Jan 13, '08 | Jan 20, '08 |
|---|---|---|---|---|---|---|---|---|---|
| | | | | | | M T W T F S S | M T W T F S S | M T W T F S S | M T W T F |
| 1 | | Task A | 1 wk | Mon 1/7/08 | Fri 1/11/08 | | Joe Simpson | | |
| 2 | | Task B | 1 wk | Mon 1/7/08 | Fri 1/11/08 | | Joe Simpson,Kim Taylor | | |
| 3 | | Task C | 0.5 wks | Mon 1/7/08 | Wed 1/9/08 | | Joe Simpson,Kim Taylor | | |

**Figure 8.1** Effort-driven scheduling reduced the duration when a second assignment was made for Task C.

Project adjusts the duration by default because of the default task type for tasks, the fixed units task type. See the later section called "Changing the Task Type to Override Effort-Driven Scheduling" to learn how and when you might need to change the default task type.

You don't have to remember the D = W/U formula as long as you remember these two guidelines when you assign resources in your project plan:

■ Project does not adjust the task duration when you make the initial assignment, no matter how many resources you add or how many units you specify.

■ When you add additional resources (assignment units), Project by default decreases the task duration.

Now that you understand how effort-driven scheduling works in Project, you need to consider real-world factors. For example, a substantial body of research demonstrates that two people working together don't necessarily finish a task in half the time it would take a single person, and in some cases two people may take just as long as a single person would! In practical terms, when two or more people work together, it takes time for them to communicate and coordinate their efforts. So you, as project manager, have to decide how best to account for situations where adding more resources won't reduce a task duration by as much as Project calculates. One option is to assign the additional resources and then to increase the new duration by some amount to better anticipate the actual timeframe in which the resources will create the task. Another option is to work with the task type and effort-driven scheduling settings, as described later in this chapter.

## Assigning Resources to Tasks

When you want to assign resources to tasks, you have to work in a view where you can see the tasks. Most users work in the default Gantt Chart view. The task sheet portion of the Gantt Chart view contains a Resources column where you *could* type in resource names if you want to or select them from the drop-down list that becomes available when you click any cell in the column. However, as with entering task start and finish dates, there's a better way than typing.

You can use the Assign Resources dialog box to assign resources to tasks. To open the Assign Resources dialog box, click the **Assign Resources** button on the Standard toolbar (see Figure 8.2), or click **Tools** and then click **Assign Resources** (shortcut: **Alt+F10**).

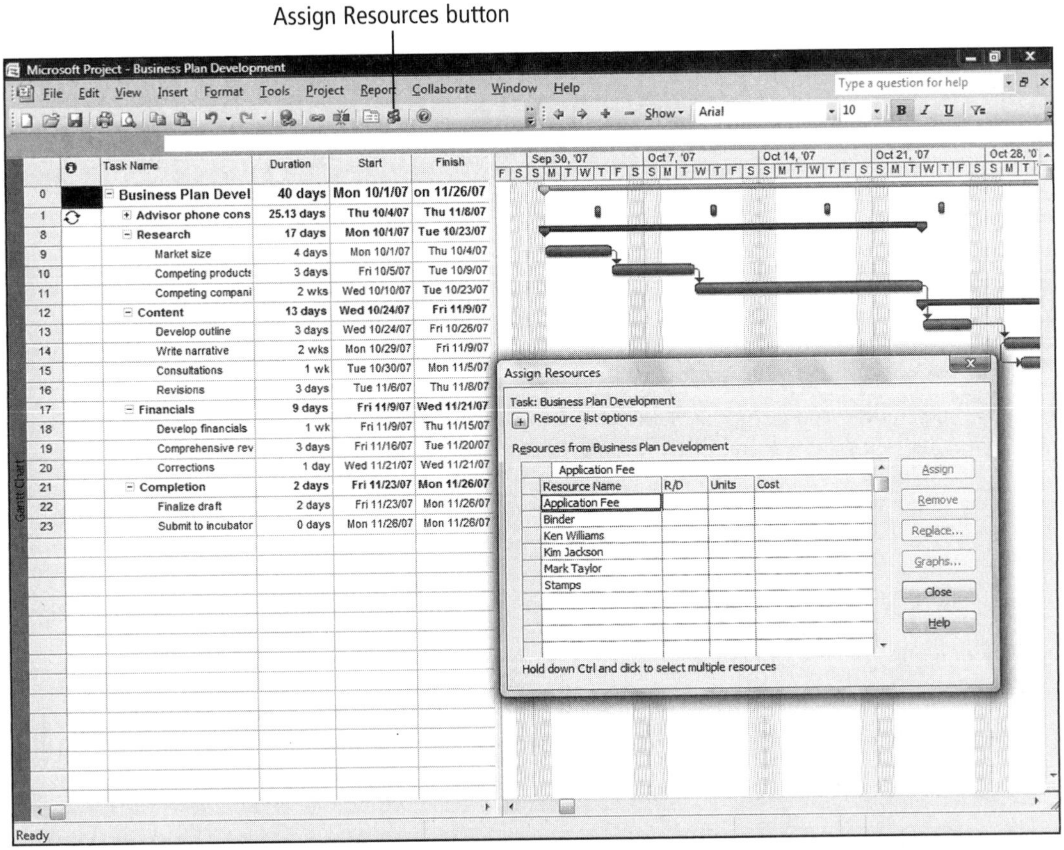

Assign Resources button

**Figure 8.2** The Assign Resources dialog box provides the most convenient method for entering resources.

Click the Assign Resources button on the Standard toolbar to open the **Assign Resources** dialog box for making assignments. The Assign Resources button has a picture of resources (people) on it. Click a task in the task sheet, click the desired resource in the Assign Resources dialog box, and then click **Assign**.

This dialog box can remain open onscreen while you work. After you make an assignment for one task, click on the task sheet to select the next task for which you want to make an assignment. This ability to keep the dialog box open and available greatly speeds the resource assignment process.

You also can use other views such as the Task Entry view to make assignments, but the Assign Resources dialog box provides the most convenient method for most users.

## Assigning the First Work Resource(s)

Assigning resources to tasks is the last major stage in building your project plan. Of course, you shouldn't make assignments for work resources randomly. As project manager, you should take a thoughtful approach toward choosing the right player to take on each position in the ballgame. If you assign a resource to a task that the person doesn't have the skills or the time to handle, your project plan will be unrealistic from the start.

Also keep in mind that the resource's calendar takes precedence over the project base calendar. If the resource has a nonworking day scheduled during the period when the task is scheduled, Project might adjust the task start, finish, and/or duration to reflect the resource's schedule. If you don't like that change, remove the resource as described later in the chapter and then apply another resource.

When you're ready to make the first work assignment for a task or tasks, follow these steps:

1. Click the **Assign Resources** button on the Standard toolbar, or click **Tools** and then **Assign Resources** (shortcut: **Alt+F10**). The Assign Resources dialog box appears.

2. Click any cell in the task to which you'd like to assign one or more resources in the task sheet.

You also can select multiple tasks and apply the assignment to all of them. To do so, Shift+click or Ctrl+click to select the Task Name cell for multiple adjacent or nonadjacent tasks.

3. Select the **resource(s)** to assign in the Assign Resources dialog box. To select multiple resources, drag over adjacent resources in the *Resource Names* column, or Ctrl+click to select resources that are non-adjacent.

Project 2007 has a quirk that you should be aware of when making assignments. When you first open the Assign Resources dialog box, *all* of the resources listed in the dialog box are selected. You must make sure you click on a specific resource to select it first, because if you click *Assign* without doing so, Project assigns *all* of the resources to the selected task.

4. Click the **Assign** button in the Assign Resources dialog box. As shown in Figure 8.3, the resource's name appears beside the Gantt bar for the task to which the resource has been assigned, and the Assign Resources dialog box both places a check mark beside the *Resource Name* and calculates a *Cost* for the assignment based on the rates for the resource that you entered in the Resource Sheet.

5. Repeat Steps 2 through 5 to make additional assignments, as needed.

6. Click **Close** in the Assign Resources dialog box to close the dialog box.

If you fail to select all the initial resource(s) that you want to assign in Step 3 and instead assign the resources one at a time, Project reduces the duration for the task. To fix this situation from the Assign Resources dialog box, first remove the resource as described later in the chapter, and then select and assign all the needed resources at the same time. Or, you can click the **Undo** button (which becomes **Undo Assign Resources** after you make the assignment) to remove the assignment and reinstate the duration.

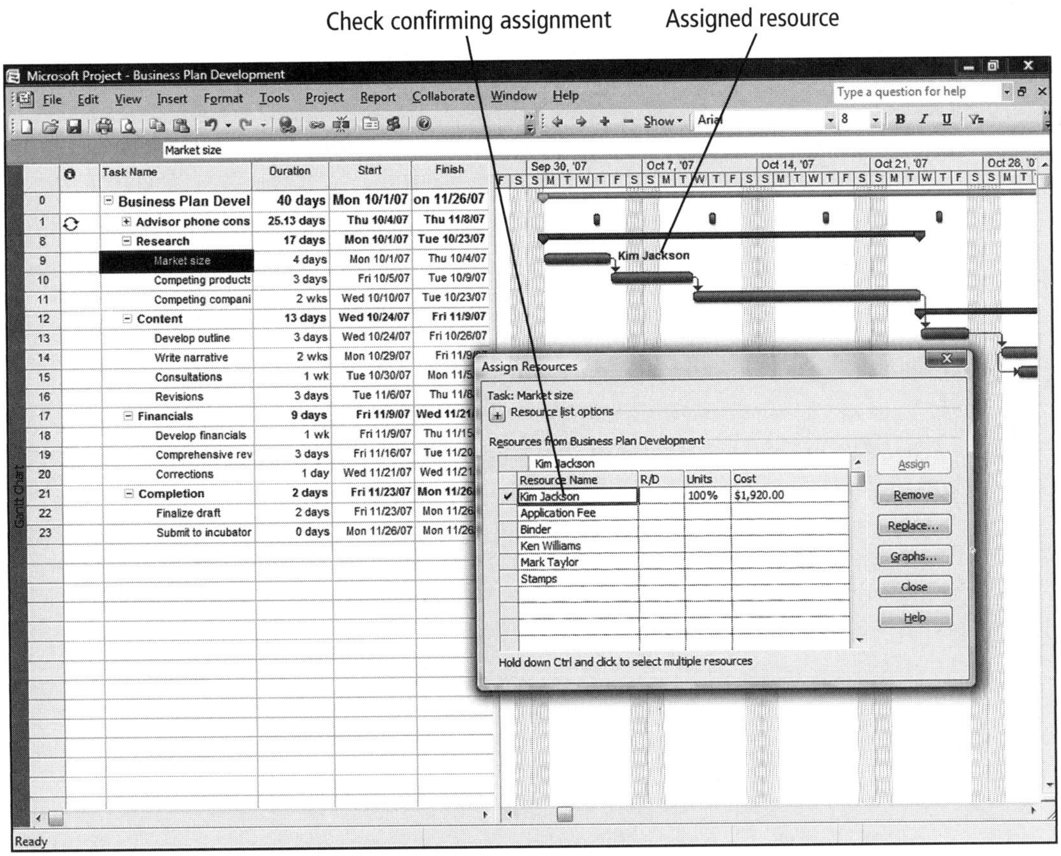

Check confirming assignment     Assigned resource

**Figure 8.3** The assigned resource's name appears by the Gantt bar.

Just as you should not link summary tasks, you also should generally not assign resources to summary tasks. That's because summary tasks are already set up to summarize the work for the resources assigned to the subtasks. Assigning work resources at the lowest outline level possible will help you get a more accurate read of project progress. You'll be able to tell which resources are up to speed on which specific subtasks, so you'll know who to ping if a task falls behind schedule. The exception to this rule of thumb might occur when you are assigning resources that reflect ongoing overhead time and costs or when you're not ready to "build out" the specific subtask detail later in a project plan. In the latter case, you can assign the resources to summary tasks until you create more detail below them.

## Adding More Work Resources

When you are reviewing your project plan to identify areas where you can improve the schedule, you will often be looking for tasks to which you can add resources to reduce the schedule. For example, if a plumbing task has a 3d duration, adding two more full-time resources will by default reduce the duration for that task down to 1d.

You can use the Assign Resources dialog box to assign additional work resources to any task so that Project recalculates the task duration based on effort-driven scheduling:

1. Click the **Assign Resources** button on the Standard toolbar, or click **Tools** and then **Assign Resources** (shortcut: **Alt+F10**). The Assign Resources dialog box appears.

2. Click any cell in the task to which you'd like to assign an additional resource in the task sheet.

3. Select the **resource(s)** to assign in the Assign Resources dialog box. To select multiple resources, drag over adjacent resources in the *Resource Names* column, or Ctrl+click to select resources that are not adjacent. (Remember, this step is not optional due to the glitch in this version of Project.)

4. Click the **Assign** button in the Assign Resources dialog box. As shown in Figure 8.4, the resource's name appears beside the Gantt bar for the task to which the resource has been assigned, and the Assign Resources dialog box now reflects the fact that multiple resources have been assigned. Because assigning the additional resources shortened the duration for task 11, Project uses change highlighting to show which task schedule was recalculated as a result of the new assignment.

5. Click **Close** in the Assign Resources dialog box to close the dialog box.

If you need to confirm more detailed information about a resource before assigning it to a task, such as the resource's group or cost information, you can double-click the resource name in the Assign Resources dialog box to open the Resource Information dialog box to review the information you need.

Highlighted schedule changes

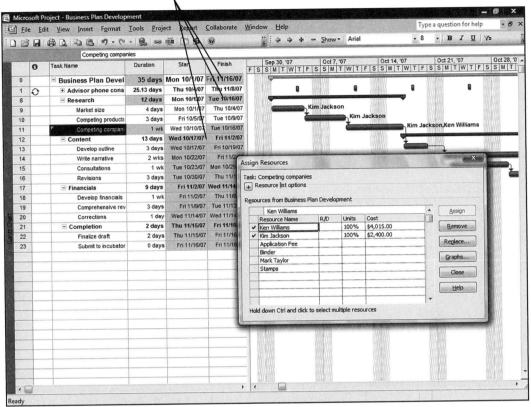

**Figure 8.4** Adding another work resource to a task reduces its duration.

If you click the Resource List Options button in the Assign Resources dialog box, you can use a filter to control which resources appear in the list or use the Available to Work option to find out which resources have time available so that you can assign them to the current task. Clicking the Graphs button in the Assign Resource dialog box shows a graphical view of resource information in the Graphs dialog box. Changing the Select Graph option to Remaining Availability makes the graph show you when resources have more hours available for assignments.

When you add another resource to a task as just described, by default a green triangle appears in the upper-left corner of the cell. If you move the mouse pointer over that green triangle and then click the option button that appears, a menu of choices for adjusting the assignment appears, as shown in Figure 8.5.

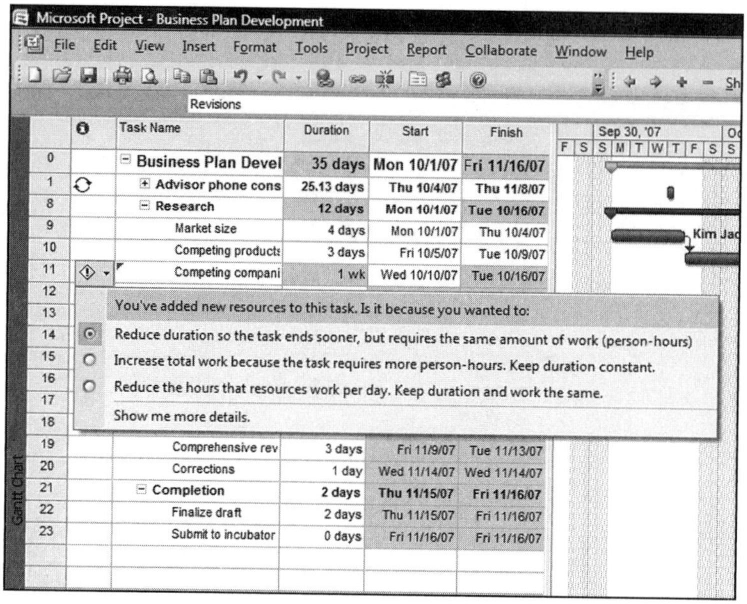

**Figure 8.5** You can choose to tell Project *not* to decrease the duration after you assign another work resource.

The first choice on the menu reflects the default behavior in Project, so you don't need to bother even opening the menu if you want to keep the effort-driven scheduling change. Clicking the second option on the menu (Increase Total Work Because the Task Requires More Person-Hours. Keep Duration Constant) undoes the duration change and adds more hours of work to the assignment. Keep in mind that this also increases the assignment expenses. Clicking the third choice on the menu (Reduce the Hours That Resources Work Per Day. Keep Duration and Work the Same.) essentially converts the assignments to part-time assignments for each assigned resource. The duration and total hours of work for the task stay the same and each resource is assigned a share of that total work.

## Assigning a Material Resource

Assigning a material resource has no impact on the schedule at all. Assigning the material resources simply indicates how much of the resource will be consumed and adds the associated cost for that quantity of the resource to the project plan. Assigning a material resource works in a similar fashion to assigning a work resource, except that you specify the quantity of the resource to be used as the units. For example, if your material resource is Binder and the material label you entered is Each, then you would enter the number of binders to be used when assigning the Binder resource. Project would then multiply the Std. Rate you entered for the Binder resource times the number of binders specified and add that cost to the budget.

To assign a material resource to a task, follow these steps:

1. Click the **Assign Resources** button on the Standard toolbar, or click **Tools** and then **Assign Resources** (shortcut: **Alt+F10**). The Assign Resources dialog box appears.

2. Click any cell in the task to which you'd like to assign the material resource in the task sheet.

3. Click the **Units** column cell for the material resource to assign in the Assign Resources dialog box and type the quantity of the material resource to be assigned.

4. Press **Enter** or click the **Assign** button in the Assign Resources dialog box. As shown in Figure 8.6, the resource's name appears beside the Gantt bar for the task along with the quantity assigned, and the Assign Resources dialog box calculates the cost for the assigned materials.

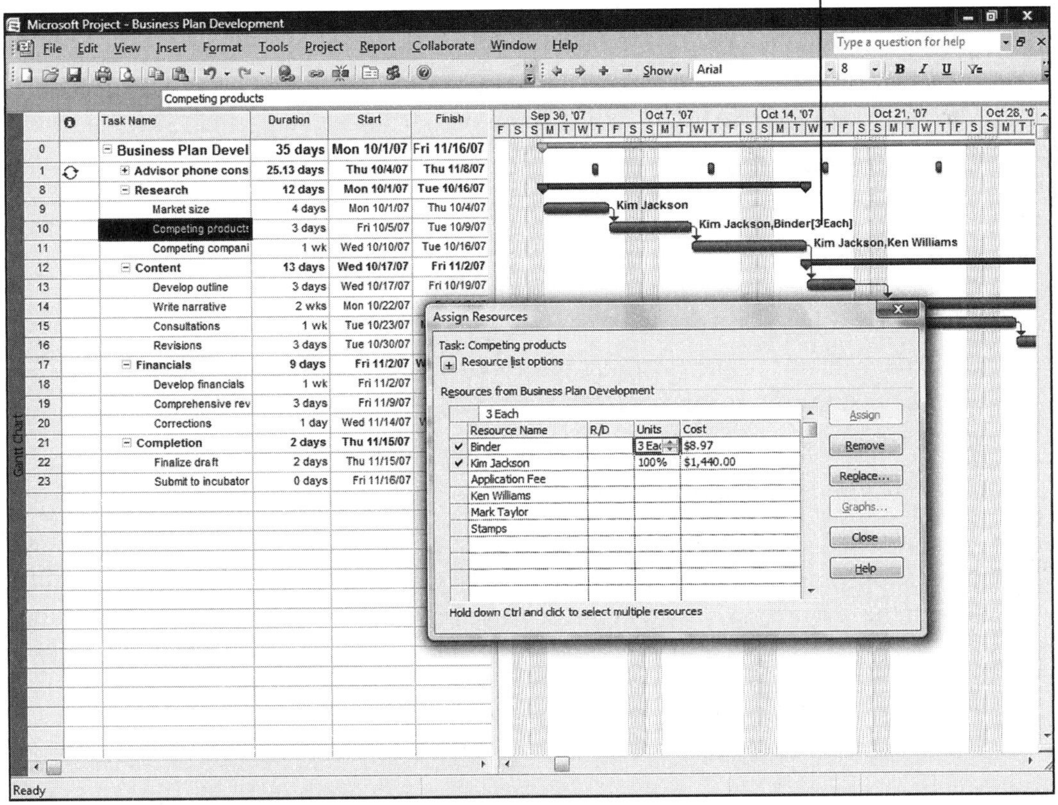

**Figure 8.6** Assigning a material resource adds cost to the plan.

5. Repeat Steps 2 through 5 to make additional material resource assignments as needed.

6. Click **Close** in the Assign Resources dialog box to close the dialog box.

## Assigning a Cost Resource

Assigning a cost resource is a bit trickier because after you make the assignment, you have to change views and enter the anticipated cost in the Assignment Information dialog box. While this means extra steps to assign a cost resource, it makes this type of resource more flexible because you can enter a different dollar amount each time you assign the resource and aren't bound by any rate entries in the Resource Sheet.

To assign a cost resource to a task, follow these steps:

1. Working in the Gantt Chart view, click the **Assign Resources** button on the Standard toolbar, or click **Tools** and then **Assign Resources** (shortcut: **Alt+F10**). The Assign Resources dialog box appears.

2. Click any cell in the task to which you'd like to assign the cost resource in the task sheet.

3. Click the **cost resource** in the Assign Resources dialog box and then click **Assign**.

4. Click **Close** in the Assign Resources dialog box to close the dialog box.

5. Click **View** and then click **Task Usage**. The Task Usage view appears.

6. Double-click the cost resource's assignment (the row with the cost resource's name) under the task to which you assigned the cost resource. The Assignment Information dialog box opens.

7. Select the contents of the **Cost** text box on the General tab (see Figure 8.7) and type the cost for the assignment.

8. Click **OK** to close the Assignment Information dialog box.

9. Click **View** and then **Gantt Chart** to return to the Gantt Chart view.

After you assign the cost resource and enter its cost using the preceding steps, the Assign Resources dialog box shows the assignment and cost whenever you select the task to which you assigned the resource, as shown in the example in Figure 8.8, which shows the cost that was shown in Figure 8.7.

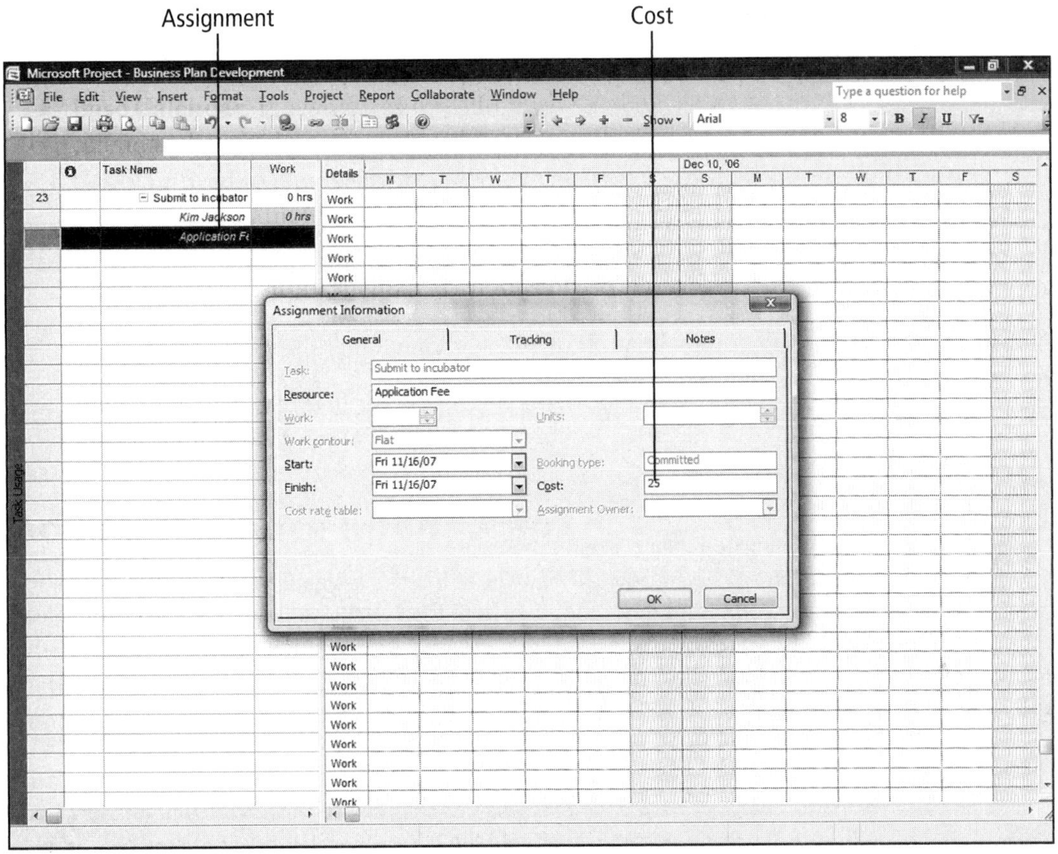

Assignment                                    Cost

**Figure 8.7** Specify the cost here each time you assign a cost resource.

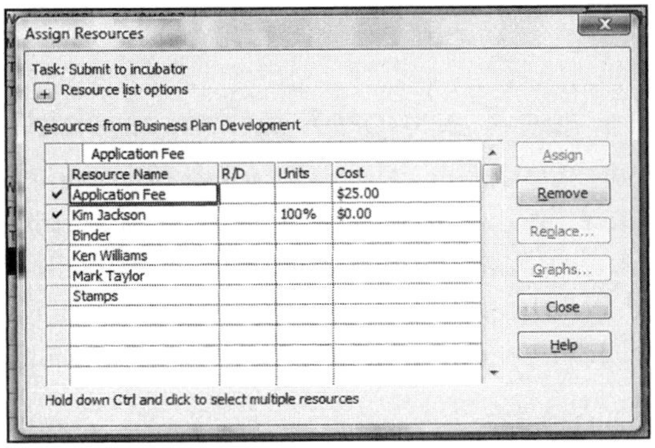

**Figure 8.8** The Assign Resources dialog box shows the cost you entered for the cost resource's assignment.

## Removing a Resource

Removing a resource takes that resource off the task. For example, you might discover that someone from another department can no longer work on your project, or you might decide that you'd like to remove a work resource from one task so that you can assign that person to another task where she will make a greater impact.

If the resource being removed was not the first resource assigned, then Project will reverse the duration change applied based on effort-driven scheduling when you assigned the resource.

To remove an assigned resource in the Gantt Chart view, click the **Assign Resources** button. Click the task from which you want to remove the resource in the task sheet and then click the **Remove** button in the Assign Resources dialog box. Click the **Close** button to close the dialog box.

Selecting a resource and then clicking the **Graphs** button in the Assign Resources dialog box opens up a dialog box where you can view the resource's assigned workload in graphical format. If you choose **Remaining Availability** from the Select Graph drop-down list, the dialog box displays a graphical representation of working days for which that resource has available hours for assignments. This can help you choose which resource to use in place of a resource that you've removed.

If you right-click the resource's row number in the Resource Sheet view and then click **Delete Resource**, keep in mind that Project removes the resource's assignments, too. So, it's a good practice to review the assignments for any resource before deleting the resource.

## Replacing a Resource

As you refine your project plan, you will be reviewing your decisions and choices to ensure you've properly staffed the project and applied persons with the right skill set to each task. But suppose you assigned a resource to a task only to have the task schedule move because the resource has nonworking time scheduled or the assignment is outside of the resource's availability for the project.

If you identify a task where you would like to change direction on an assignment or some external circumstance requires an assignment change, you can replace an assigned resource. Once again, the easiest way to do this is to use the Assign Resources dialog box. Click the

**Assign Resources** button. Click the task for which you want to replace the resource in the task sheet, and then click the **Replace** button in the Assign Resources dialog box. Select the desired new resource in the Replace Resource dialog box that appears and then click **OK** to apply the change. Click the **Close** button to close the dialog box.

| Replace Resource | | | | |
|---|---|---|---|---|
| Replace: Mark Taylor | | | OK | |
| With: | | | Cancel | |
| Mark Taylor | | | | |
| Resource Name | Units | Cost | | |
| Mark Taylor | | $4,700.00 | | |
| Application Fee | | $25.00 | | |
| Binder | | $8.97 | | |
| Ken Williams | | $10,335.00 | | |
| Kim Jackson | | $12,384.00 | | |
| Stamps | | $0.00 | | |

**Figure 8.9** The Replace Resource dialog box enables you to substitute one resource for another for a single assignment.

There may be times when you need to replace a resource throughout the entire project. For example, if the leader of another department who is making a resource available for your project decides to switch people, you will need to replace that person throughout the project plan. In other cases, if you don't know the name of a resource from another department during the planning phase, you may use a generic placeholder name (such as Analyst) and then later replace it with the person's actual name.

The fastest way to replace a resource throughout the entire project is to use the Resource Sheet view, as follows:

1. Click **View** and then click **Resource Sheet**.
2. Click on the **Resource Name** field cell for the resource to replace. For example, if you used a placeholder resource such as *Analyst*, click that resource name.
3. Type the name of the replacement resource and press **Enter**. Project immediately updates the resource assignments throughout the project.

You can choose **View**, **Gantt Chart** to change back to the Gantt Chart view after replacing the resource.

If you don't want to replace *all* of a resource's assignments in the project, you can use the Replace feature to selectively replace a resource. Choose **Edit**, **Replace** (shortcut: **Ctrl+H**). Open the **Look In Field** drop-down list and then click **Resource Names**. Enter the names of the resources to find and replace in the **Find What** and **Replace With** text boxes and then use the **Find Next** and **Replace** buttons as needed to go through the project and make replacements.

## Understanding and Using Units Percentages for Assignments

The earlier steps for assigning a resource to a task didn't call for you to make any entry in the Units column of the Assign Resources dialog box. When you leave that column blank and then click **Assign**, Project assumes that you want to use the Max. Units setting you specified for the resource on the Resource Sheet for the assignment. If you specified an accurate Units setting on the Resource Sheet, then for most assignments you won't have to enter a Units setting.

If you want to assign a resource to work part time on a task, then you have to make an entry in the Units cell for the resource in the Assign Resources dialog box when you make an assignment *before* you click the **Assign** button. If it's the first resource you assign to the task, the task duration won't change. After you've completed the assignment, however, any change to the Units setting for a single resource will cause the task duration to recalculate by default. You might change a resource to a part-time assignment after the fact, such as if a resource becomes less available for the assignment or if you believe the assignment will not require the resource's full attention. Or, if the resource is an external vendor who can provide additional staff members to help complete a task more quickly, you might want to increase the Units setting for an assignment.

To change the Units setting to reflect either scenario, open the Assign Resources dialog box by clicking **Assign Resources** on the Standard toolbar. Click the task for which you want to make the units change in the task sheet. Click the **Units** cell for the assigned resource in the Assign Resource dialog box, enter a new percentage, and press **Enter**. As shown in Figure 8.10, Project displays the new Units setting for the resource. You can then click **Close** to close the dialog box.

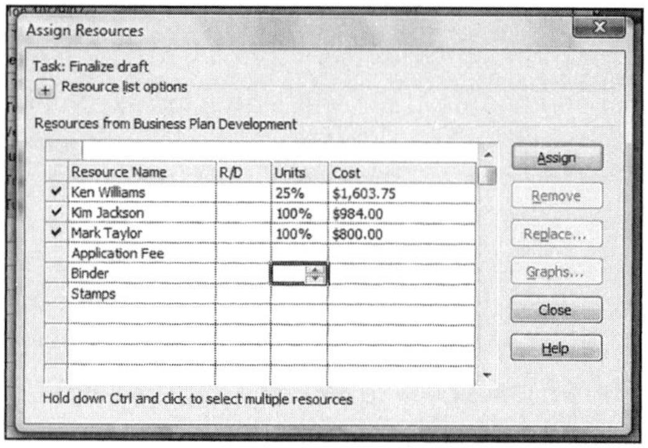

**Figure 8.10**  In this instance, Ken Williams' assignment has been reduced to 25% Units (quarter time).

When you make the entry in the Units column, type the value representing the percentage that you want. You don't need to include the percentage sign. So, for example:

- An entry of **50** would represent 50%, or an assignment where the resource can work half of her scheduled working day on the task. In other words, any percentage less than 100% is less than the resource's full working day.

- An entry of **300** would represent 300%. Change the Units entry to a value more than 100%, for example, when a vendor can send multiple staff members to work with you. 300% represents three full-time team members. In other words, any multiple of 100% represents multiple staff members handling the assignment.

What if you want to assign a part-time resource as the only person working on a task and you *do* want the task duration to increase accordingly? You can do this with little problem. When you first assign the resource, make sure you enter 100% in the Units column to override any lesser Units entry you made on the Resource Sheet. After you click the **Assign** button to assign the resource, click the Units cell again and type a new part-time percentage. Project will then recalculate the task duration.

## Viewing and Changing Resource Assignment Information

As you prepare to finalize a project plan, which is the topic of Chapter 10, you as the project manager will be looking for potential bottlenecks and problems with your schedule. As part of that process, you may need to evaluate assignments and how they play out on a day-by-day basis.

The term *timescaled* simply means that the information is broken out or charted by time period. The Task Usage and Resource Usage views by default show assigned hours on a daily basis.

Two of the views in Project provide a timescaled breakdown of each assignment that you can review when you're looking for issues or want to see what quantity of work for a task or resource is occurring during a given time period. Task Usage view (see Figure 8.11) lists the tasks in the project and then lists all the resource assignments for the task beneath it. Resource Usage view looks similar (see Figure 8.12), but it organizes assignments by resource.

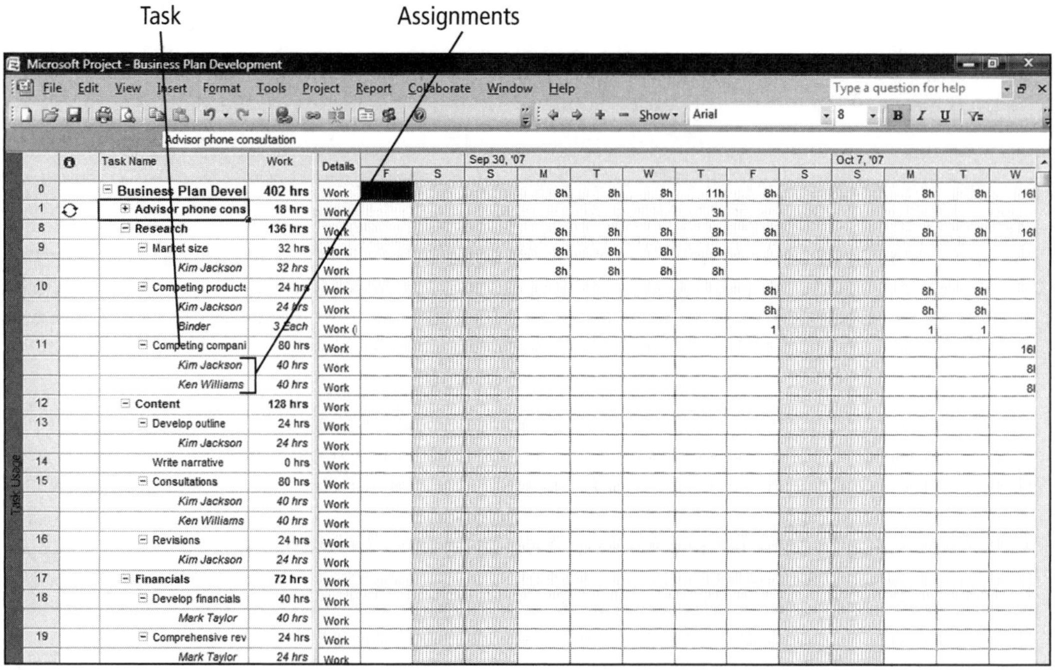

**Figure 8.11** View the assignments for each task in Task Usage view.

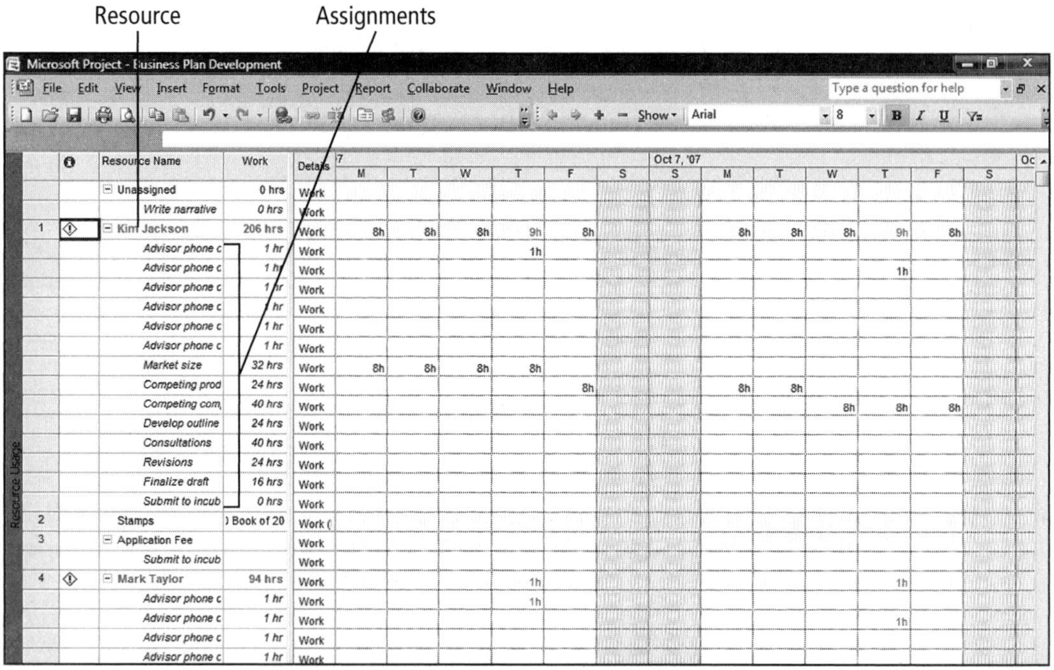

**Figure 8.12** View the assignments for each resource in Resource Usage view.

To display one of these views, click the **View** menu. Then, click either **Task Usage** or **Resource Usage**, depending on the view that you want to display. You can click the minus or plus icons that appear beside the task or resource names to collapse or expand the assignments for the task or resource.

 The exclamation point indicator that appears to the left of some of the resource names means that the resource is overbooked. You'll learn more about identifying and dealing with overbooked resources in Chapter 10.

If you need to modify the hours of work on a given day for any task or assignment, you can click the cell on the assignment row and enter a different value for the number of hours of work. Most likely, you will need to work with more overall details of the assignment, and for that you need to display the Assignment Information dialog box. To open the Assignment Information dialog box for an assignment, double-click the assignment's row in the Task Usage or Resource Usage view. Make any changes as needed in the dialog box and then click **OK**.

In addition to using the General tab of the Assignment Information dialog box to adjust such settings as the overall hours of assignment work for the resource and the Units setting, you can use the Tracking tab in the dialog box to specify the amount of work actually performed by the resource. You can use the Notes tab to document additional information about the assignment.

## Using a Different Cost Table for an Assignment

In Chapter 7, you learned how to create a cost table to indicate differing fee rates for a resource. You would typically encounter this situation when you're using an outside vendor such as a legal or consulting firm to handle work in your project. Such firms often charge different rates for different levels of service. For example, a consulting firm might charge one rate for planning and another for implementation, or an engineering firm might charge one rate for design and development and another rate for construction project management.

If you have an assignment for which you need to apply a different cost table to ensure that Project accurately calculates the planned costs for the assignment, use the Assignment Information dialog box to handle that job, as in these steps:

1. Create the cost table for the resource as described in the section "Creating Updating Rates and a Cost Table" in Chapter 7.
2. Switch to either the **Task Usage** or **Resource Usage** view by clicking the **View** menu and then clicking the View name.

3. Double-click the **assignment** to which you want to apply another cost table.

4. Click the **Cost Rate Table** drop-down list and then click the letter representing the cost rate table to apply to the assignment (see Figure 8.13).

5. Click **OK** to close the Assignment Information dialog box and apply the change. Project immediately recalculates the costs for the assignment.

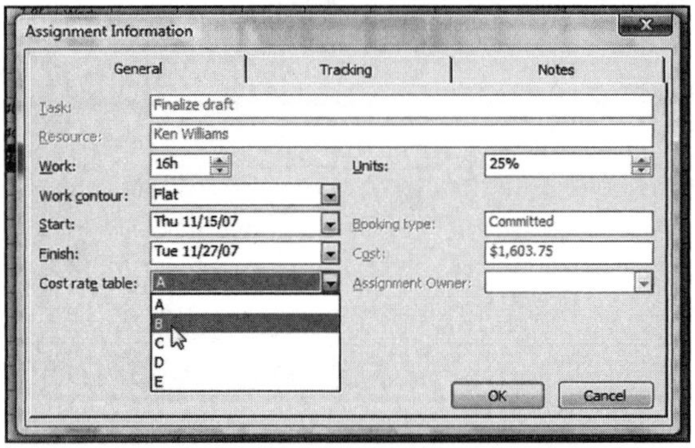

**Figure 8.13** Use the Assignment Information dialog box to apply another cost rate table.

## Communicating Assignments

If you're using Microsoft Office Project Standard 2007 or Microsoft Office Project Professional 2007 as a standalone application without Project Server 2007, then automated communication options are somewhat limited. Even so, with any standalone implementation of Project, you do have the option of e-mailing a Project file to other team members who have Project so that the recipients can review the plan and their assignments.

The process for e-mailing a project file from Project works just as it did in the 2003 versions of all the Office applications:

1. Open the Project file you want to send.

2. Click the **File** menu, point to **Send To**, and then click **Mail Recipient (As Attachment)**. Project launches your e-mail program, such as Windows Mail in Vista or Microsoft Office Outlook, and opens a new message window with the project file already inserted as an attachment, as shown in Figure 8.14.

3. Use the To: text box or button to specify the message recipient(s).

4. Enter a message Subject and body text as needed.

5. Click **Send**.

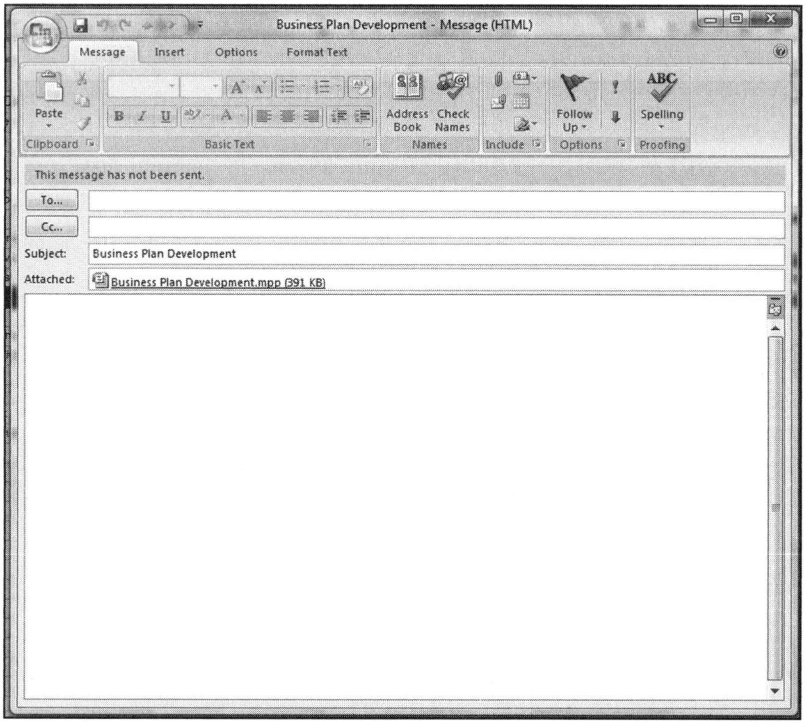

**Figure 8.14** You can communicate assignments by sending the Project file via e-mail.

Chapter 14, "Other Ways to Share and Communicate," covers how to create an HTML (Web page file) with specific project information, such as the assignments for a particular resource. It's easy to e-mail such a file to any other user, who can then view the file in his or her Web browser. That chapter also covers how to export project information into Excel format or how to paste it into Word. So, even if a team member doesn't have Microsoft Project, you still have options for communicating project information.

## Changing the Task Type to Override Effort-Driven Scheduling

This chapter has noted repeatedly that under Project's default effort-driven method of scheduling tasks, adding more work resources to a task generally causes Project to decrease the task's duration. By default, the total number of hours allocated to the task (called the work) remains constant as you add more resources (units), with Project adjusting the duration accordingly. For example, say a four-day task has the Standard eight-hour calendar. You assign the first resource, which also uses the Standard eight-hour calendar at 100% Units. Then, you assign a second full-time resource to the task (so now two people will be working full time on the task); applying that second resource to the task causes Project to recalculate the task duration and reduce its duration to two days.

You can stop Project from making duration, work, or units changes for selected tasks, if you want, by changing the Task Type setting for the task on the General tab of the Task Information dialog box:

■ **Fixed Units.** This is the default task type when effort-driven scheduling is enabled. After the initial work resource assignment has been made, adding more resources makes the duration shorter; removing resources increases the duration. Project will not adjust the assignment units for added resources, but it will adjust the duration.

■ **Fixed Work.** This task type disables effort-driven scheduling and in most cases has the same effect as working with a Fixed Units task: adding resources shortens the duration and removing resources increases the duration. Making the first resource assignment sets the hours of work for the task. So, if you have a 1w task (on a Standard calendar) but assign the initial resource at 200%, the task will have 80h of work rather than 40h. From there, adding more resources decreases the duration (by dividing the hours of work between the resources), but not the total hours of work or the units settings for the resource assignments.

■ **Fixed Duration.** This setting keeps the duration constant when you apply resources to the task. For example, if your project requires filing accounting information by a particular federal filing deadline, you'll want the duration and schedule for the task to remain fixed. With effort-driven scheduling enabled, adding resources to this task decreases the amount of work each resource contributes on each day. For example, if you apply two full-time resources to a four-day task, Project doesn't cut the duration in half; it cuts the number of hours (work) each resource supplies each day in half. If you turn off effort-driven scheduling for a Fixed Duration task, Project sets the duration for the task when you assign the initial resource(s), does not change the units setting for any resource assignments, and does change the total hours of work for the task, adding more work as you assign more work resources.

Figure 8.15 shows how Project adjusts duration, work, and units when you've made multiple assignments to various types of tasks.

You can specify the task type for a task in the Task Information dialog box. Double-click the **task** you want to change in the task sheet in the Gantt Chart view. The Task Information dialog box appears. Click the **Advanced** tab. Open the **Task Type** drop-down list (see Figure 8.16) and then click on the task type you want. Click **OK** to close the dialog box.

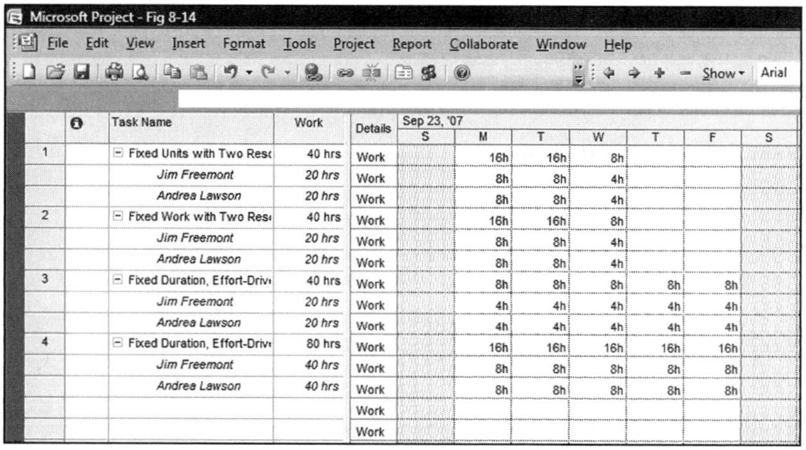

**Figure 8.15** The assignments here illustrate the impact of changing the task type and working with effort-driven scheduling.

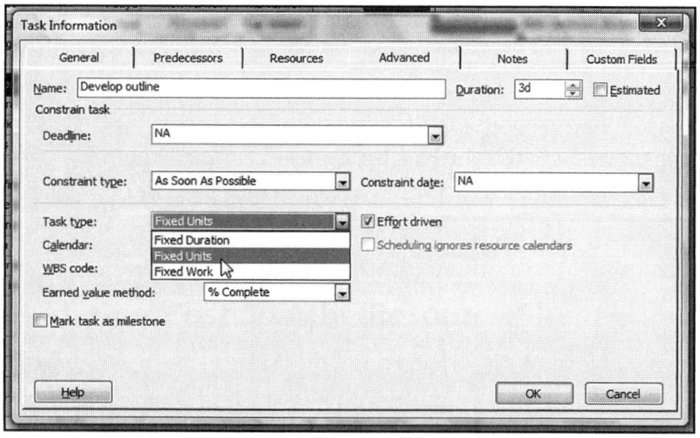

**Figure 8.16** Use the drop-down list shown in this dialog box to control whether Project adjusts the task's schedule.

You can change the default task type for a new project file by opening the Options dialog box (**Tools, Options**) and using the Default Task Type drop-down list on the Schedule tab. The section called "Setting Up a Project with Fixed Task Durations" in Appendix B covers more specifics about how to create a project plan where all tasks will have a set duration, no matter how many work resources you apply. In part, this is accomplished by changing the default task type for a new Project file.

## Turning Off Effort-Driven Scheduling for a Task

You also can turn off the effort-driven scheduling feature for a task to disable the Duration = Work/Units equation so that adding more resources doesn't automatically decrease the duration but instead adds more units and work. On the Advanced tab of the Task Information dialog box, clear the check mark beside **Effort Driven**. Then, to fix the task duration, choose Fixed Duration as the task type using the Task Type drop-down list.

## Chapter Review

You've now seen how as the project manager, you apply the resources from the Resource Sheet to the tasks in your project plan to make assignments by using the Assign Resources dialog box. The chapter taught you the impact of making the first work resource assignment on a task versus assigning additional work resources, in which case effort-driven scheduling reduces the duration of the task. You also learned how to assign material and cost resources, how to remove and replace resources, how to work with assignment units settings and cost tables, how to view more information about assignments, and how to work around effort-driven scheduling when you don't want to use that scheduling method. Stop now and review what you've learned before continuing on to Chapter 9.

### Review Questions

Write your answers to the following questions on a sheet of paper.

1. What button on which toolbar do you use to open the Assign Resources dialog box?

2. Briefly describe how to make an assignment for a work resource once the Assign Resource dialog box is open.

3. Briefly describe how to make an assignment for a material resource once the Assign Resource dialog box is open.

4. After you assign a cost resource to a task, change to the Task Usage view and double-click the assignment to open the _____ dialog box, where you can enter the expected cost for using the cost resource.

5. To take off a resource assigned to a selected task, use the _____ button in the Assign Resources dialog box.

6. To replace a resource throughout the entire project, type a new Resource Name in the _____ view.

7. True or False: An assignment with a 50% units setting is a full-time assignment.

8. If a resource such as an outside vendor or another department will be supplying two people full time for an assignment, what should the units setting for that assignment be?

9. The _____ and _____ views list project assignments.

10. If a resource charges different rates and you need to specify which rate to use, choose another _____ in the Assignment Information dialog box.

## Projects

### *Project 1*

1. Create a new, blank project file.

2. Save the file as *Quick Assignments*.

 Create a folder named *PSG Exercises* in your *Documents* or *My Documents* folder and save your exercise practice files there.

3. Click **Project** and then click **Project Information**. Set the **Start Date** to a Monday a few weeks in the future and then click **OK**.

4. Enter the following task information in the *Task Name* and *Duration* fields of the task sheet of the Gantt Chart view:

| | |
|---|---|
| Planning | 1w |
| Writing | 2w |
| Layout | 1w |
| Proof and Print | 1w |

5. Link the tasks with default finish-to-start (FS) links.

6. Click **View** and then click **Resource Sheet** to change to the Resource Sheet view.

7. Make the following entries in the *Resource Name, Type, Material Label,* and *Std. Rate* fields, skipping other fields for now:

| | | | |
|---|---|---|---|
| Lynne C | Work | blank | 45 |
| Tim L | Work | blank | 35 |
| Proof | Material | page. | 7.50 |
| Printing | Cost | blank | blank |

8. Click **View** and then click **Gantt Chart** to switch back to the Gantt Chart view in the *Quick Assignments* file.

9. Save your changes to the file and keep it open for the next project.

### Project 2

1. Click the **Assign Resources** button on the Standard toolbar, or choose **Tools**, **Assign Resources**.

2. Click the **Planning** task in the task sheet, if needed, click the **Tim L** resource in the Assign Resources dialog box, and then click **Assign**. This assigns the Tim L resource to the task.

3. Click the **Writing** task in the task sheet.

4. Click the **Tim L** resource in the Assign Resources dialog box and then click **Assign**. This assigns the Tim L resource to the task.

5. With the Writing task still selected, click the **Lynne C** resource in the Assign Resources dialog box, type **25** in the Units column, and press **Enter**. This adds Lynne C as a second part-time work resource, reducing the task duration to 1.6w.

6. Click the **Layout** task in the task sheet. Click the **Lynne C** resource Assign Resources dialog box, Ctrl+click the **Tim L** resource to select it as well, and then click **Assign**. This assigns both resources to the task. Because both were assigned simultaneously, the duration does not change.

7. Click the **Proof and Print** task in the task sheet.

8. Click the **Proof** resource in the Assign Resources dialog box, type **32** in the Units column, and press **Enter**. This adds Proof as a material resource, adding $240 in expenses (32 x the $7.50 Std. Rate for the material resource) to the project.

9. With the Proof and Print task still selected, click the **Printing** resource in the Assign Resources dialog box and click **Assign**. This adds the cost resource, and you must now specify the cost information.

10. Click **Close** to close the Assign Resources dialog box.

11. Click **View** and then **Task Usage** to change to the Task Usage view.

12. Double-click the **Printing** assignment under the Proof and Print task to open its Assignment Information dialog box.

13. Click the **General** tab, if needed, enter **1250** in the Cost text box, and click **OK**.

14. Click **View** and then click **Gantt Chart** to switch back to the Gantt Chart view.

15. Click the **Assign Resources** button on the Standard toolbar, or choose **Tools**, **Assign Resources**.

16. Click the **Proof and Print** task in the task sheet. You can see that the cost you entered in the Assignment Information dialog box for the Printing cost resource now appears in the dialog box.

17. Click **Close** to close the dialog box.

18. Save your changes to the file and then close it.

### Project 3

1. Open the *Site Search with Resources* file you created during the Chapter 7 projects.

2. Save the file as *Site Search with Assignments*.

3. Click **View** and then click **Gantt Chart** to change to the Gantt Chart view, if needed.

4. If the Gantt bars aren't visible onscreen, press **F5**, type **1** in the ID text box of the Go To dialog box, and then press **Enter** or click **OK**.

5. Click the **Assign Resources** button on the Standard toolbar to open the Assign Resources dialog box.

6. Make the following assignments. If multiple resources are listed for a task, use Ctrl+click to select them both before assigning them. If no Units are specified, you need not make a Units entry:

| Task | Resource | Units |
|------|----------|-------|
| 2 | Jane Black | |
|   | Smith Todd | |
| 3 | Jane Black | |
|   | Smith Todd | |
| 4 | Jane Black | |
|   | Smith Todd | |
| 5 | Jane Black | |
|   | Smith Todd | |
| 6 | Jane Black | |
|   | Smith Todd | |
|   | Lynnette Taylor | |
| 8 | Lynnette Taylor | 25 |
| 9 | Lynnette Taylor | 25 |
| 10 | Lynnette Taylor | |
|   | Realtor | |
| 11 | Lynnette Taylor | |
|   | Realtor | |
| 12 | Lynnette Taylor | |
|   | Realtor | |
| 13 | Jane Black | |
|   | Smith Todd | |
|   | Lynnette Taylor | |
|   | Realtor | |

| 15 | Jane Black |
|----|------------|
|    | Realtor |
| 16 | Jane Black |
|    | Realtor |
| 17 | Jane Black |
|    | Realtor |
| 18 | Jane Black |
|    | Realtor |
| 19 | Smith Todd |
| 20 | Lynnette Taylor |
|    | Realtor |
|    | Attorney |
|    | Closing Costs |
|    | Land Costs |
|    | Loan Costs |
|    | Realtor Fee |

7. Select task **6** in the task sheet, click the **Paper** resource in the Assign Resources dialog box, type **4** as the units, and press **Enter**.

8. Click **Close** to close the Assign Resources dialog box.

9. Click the **Duration** cell for task 10 (Identify Site), type **6w**, and press **Enter**.

10. Click **View** and then click **Task Usage**.

11. Scroll down and add the following cost information for each of the cost resource assignments under task 20, Closing. To enter each cost, double-click the assignment, enter the value specified in the Cost text box on the General tab of the Assignment Information dialog box, and then click **OK**.

| Realtor Fee | 25000 |
|-------------|-------|
| Closing Costs | 6500 |
| Loan Costs | 2500 |
| Land Cost | 350000 |

12. Click **View** and then click **Gantt Chart** to change to the Gantt Chart view.

13. Save your changes to the file and close it.

To see the solution file created by completing the projects in this chapter, go to www.courseptr.com, click the **Downloads** link in the navigation bar at the top, type **Microsoft Office Project 2007 Survival Guide** in the search text box, and then click **Search Downloads**.

## CHAPTER 9

# ENHANCING TASK AND RESOURCE INFORMATION

This Chapter Teaches You How To:

- Shade a cell and format and wrap its text
- View task, resource, or assignment information
- Add a task, resource, or assignment note
- Link to another document
- Apply an alternate calendar to a task
- Constrain a task
- Apply a work contour
- Add a deadline for a task
- Work with fields in the sheet
- Find and replace information

Now that you've been through the major steps for setting up a project plan in Microsoft Project 2007, you might be wondering how you can achieve a greater level of detail about your plans. Perhaps you need to track additional information about a task or resource, or you want to work with the specific schedule for an assignment or compare the scheduled finish date for a task versus an alternate deadline. Project enables you to nail down this type of information and more with regard to the tasks, resources, and assignments in your project plan. While the available settings exceed the space available to cover them in this book, this chapter will introduce you to some of the most obvious and essential changes

209

you might want to make in your project plan. You will learn how to format sheet cells and text and work with Task Information and Resource Information, including adding notes and even hyperlinks to files in other programs. You will also learn how to change a task's calendar or apply a constraint or deadline for the task, in addition to learning how to account for a fluctuating work schedule for a particular assignment. Finally, you'll learn how to change the fields in a sheet or find and replace information.

## Adding Shading to a Sheet Cell and Formatting Text

One way that you can adjust the appearance of your project plan is to change the formatting of the text in the sheet part of the Gantt Chart view. You also can change the formatting of text in any other sheet-based view such as the Resource Sheet. So, for example, if others think that the schedule is too hard to read, you can increase the size of the text or perhaps choose another font.

For the first time, Project 2007 enables you to also shade or fill the cell itself. So, you might apply shading to identify key tasks in the plan or to flag an item for further follow up. You apply both text formatting and a cell background color in the Font dialog box by using these steps:

1. Select the cell(s) to format by dragging over them. You can select an entire field (column) or row by clicking the gray field or row header.
2. Choose **Format, Font**. The Font dialog box opens.
3. Select new settings for the text, if desired, in the **Font**, **Font Style**, and **Size** lists in the dialog box. You also can use the **Underline** check box to apply underlining and the **Color** drop-down list to select a new text color.
4. To shade or fill the selected cell(s), make a choice from the **Background Color** drop-down list. If you prefer that the fill not be a solid color or if you've chosen a dark color and need to make sure that the text is more readable, also make a choice from the **Background Pattern** drop-down list. As shown in Figure 9.1, the Sample area in the dialog box previews your choices.
5. Click **OK** to apply the text and shading choices and close the dialog box.

Unlike in Excel, you can't pre-shade sheet cells before making entries in them. Cell shading only "takes" when the cell already contains an entry. Also keep in mind that Project's new change highlighting uses the Aqua color, so you probably don't want to apply that color to cells in the *Duration*, the *Start*, the *Finish*, or any other calculated field in a sheet; if you do, you won't be able to see the impact of schedule changes via change highlighting.

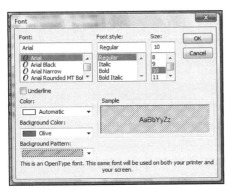

**Figure 9.1** Project now enables you to apply a cell fill by making Background Color and Background Pattern selections in this dialog box.

# Wrapping Text in a Cell

If your task or resource names are long or you've increased the size of the text, the full task name might not appear in the sheet field. One way to solve this is to drag the right border of the gray column header to the right to make the field wider. If you don't want to make the field wider—perhaps because only a limited number of entries are too long—then you can instead **wrap** the text.

As in Excel, wrapping means that the text will appear on multiple lines within the cell. In contrast with Excel, however, you can't apply a formatting command to wrap text in Project. You have to do it manually.

Move the mouse pointer to the bottom border of the row header for the row holding the cell. When the double-headed resizing pointer shown in Figure 9.2 appears, drag down until the text appears on multiple rows, as it does for the shaded *Task Name* field cell in the figure.

To wrap text in multiple rows, drag over the row headers first or click the gray **Select All** button at the upper-left corner of the sheet. Then point to the lower border of one of the row headers and drag it to size.

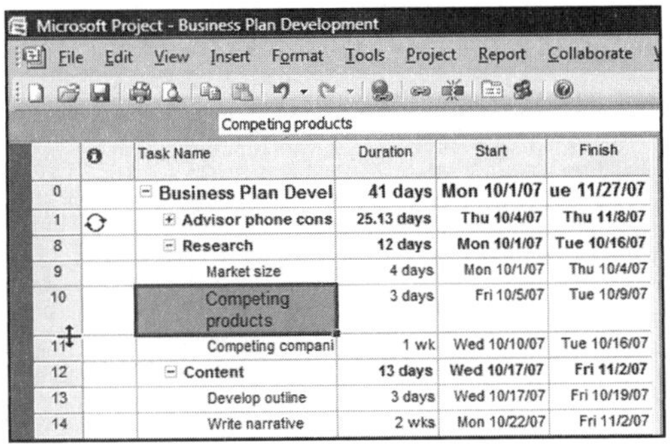

| | ⓘ | Task Name | Duration | Start | Finish |
|---|---|---|---|---|---|
| 0 | | ⊟ Business Plan Devel | 41 days | Mon 10/1/07 | ue 11/27/07 |
| 1 | ↻ | ⊞ Advisor phone cons | 25.13 days | Thu 10/4/07 | Thu 11/8/07 |
| 8 | | ⊟ Research | 12 days | Mon 10/1/07 | Tue 10/16/07 |
| 9 | | Market size | 4 days | Mon 10/1/07 | Thu 10/4/07 |
| 10 | | Competing products | 3 days | Fri 10/5/07 | Tue 10/9/07 |
| 11 | | Competing compani | 1 wk | Wed 10/10/07 | Tue 10/16/07 |
| 12 | | ⊟ Content | 13 days | Wed 10/17/07 | Fri 11/2/07 |
| 13 | | Develop outline | 3 days | Wed 10/17/07 | Fri 10/19/07 |
| 14 | | Write narrative | 2 wks | Mon 10/22/07 | Fri 11/2/07 |

Microsoft Project - Business Plan Development
File  Edit  View  Insert  Format  Tools  Project  Report  Collaborate
Competing products

**Figure 9.2** Drag the bottom row header border to wrap text.

To remove the wrapping from a row, drag the bottom row header border up until it's over the first line of text in the cell. When you release the mouse button, the row snaps back to its original size.

## Opening the Task Information, Resource Information, or Assignment Information Dialog Box

When you want to work in detail with the settings for a task, resource, or assignment, open its Task Information, Resource Information, or Assignment Information dialog box. For example, Figure 9.3 shows that the Task Information dialog box offers six different tabs of settings for working with a task.

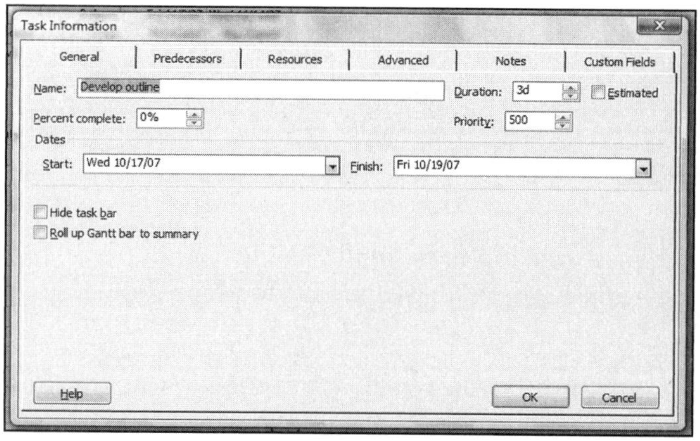

**Figure 9.3**  Get into more details in the Task Information dialog box shown here or in its counterparts for resources and assignments.

If you are looking for a setting but don't want to change views, using the applicable information dialog box is your best bet. You can display these dialog boxes in a number of different ways:

Double-click a task, resource, or assignment to open its information dialog box.

- Double-click a cell in the task or resource in the sheet or a sheet portion of a view.
- Click a cell in the task, resource, or assignment and then click the **Task Information**, **Resource Information**, or **Assignment Information** button on the Standard toolbar. These three buttons are actually the same button; its name changes depending on whether you're working with a list of tasks, resources, or assignments. This button's picture looks like a tabbed index card.

- If you're making assignments, you can double-click a resource name in the Assign Resources dialog box to open the Resource Information dialog box.

- If you're working in the Task Usage view, double-click the task name in the sheet at the left to open the Task Information dialog box. Double-click the name of a resource listed under a task to open the Assignment Information dialog box.

- If you're working in the Resource Usage view, double-click the resource name in the sheet at the left to open the Resource Information dialog box. Double-click the name of a task listed under a resource to open the Assignment Information dialog box.

## Adding a Note about a Task, Resource, or Assignment

Moving your project forward on the right course will require you to have a handle on many details surrounding tasks, resources, and assignments—why a task was scheduled at a particular time, what feedback a resource has given about how to handle a task, or why an assignment was switched from one resource to another, for example.

The Task Information, Resource Information, and Assignment Information dialog boxes each contain a Notes tab. You can click that tab and type in the note text, as shown in the example in Figure 9.4. The buttons above the text box where you enter the note text enable you to format the note or insert a picture into the note. When you finish creating the note, click **OK** to close the dialog box.

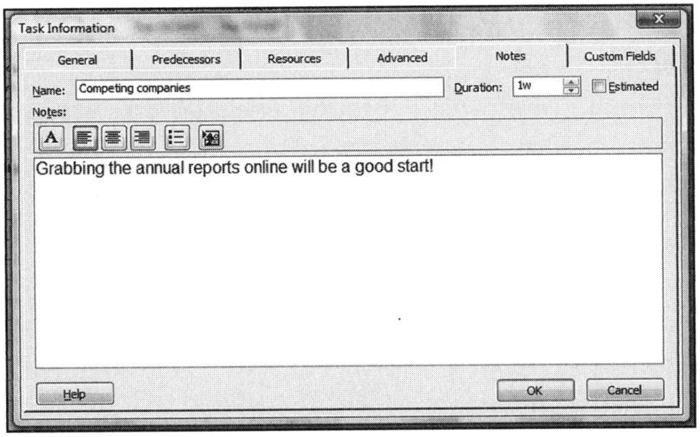

**Figure 9.4** Use the Notes tab to track details about a task, resource, or assignment.

An indicator for the note appears in the *Indicators* field to the left of the task, resource, or assignment name. To view the note, move the mouse pointer over that indicator. The note pops up, as shown in Figure 9.5.

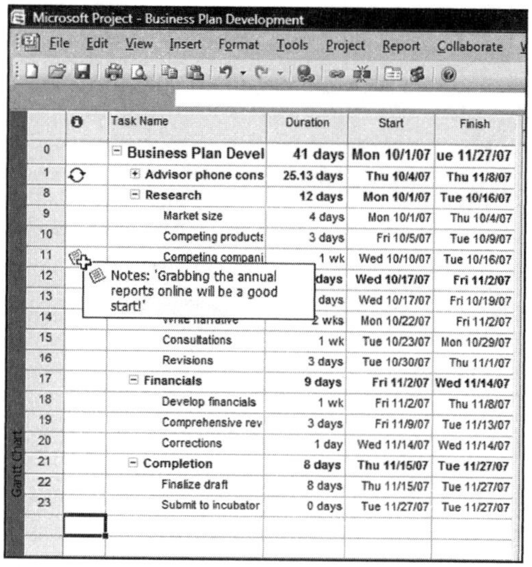

**Figure 9.5** Point to the note indicator to view the note contents.

> **NOTE!** Notes do not print by default. You specify whether or not to print notes on the View tab of the Page Setup dialog box. Chapter 12 will cover printing your project in more detail.

## Hyperlinking an External Document to a Task, Resource, or Assignment

If a document with information critical to your project already exists, there's no need to retype that information in the form of a note in Project. Instead, you can link or *hyperlink* the document to the applicable task, resource, or assignment. For example, you might hyperlink to a contract with a particular resource or to a document that contains background information about the project.

Use these steps to create a hyperlink in your project plan file:

1. Change to the view that holds the task, resource, or assignment to link to and then click a cell in the task, resource, or assignment.

2. Click **Insert** and then click **Hyperlink**. (Shortcut: **Ctrl+K**.) You also can click the **Insert Hyperlink** button on the Standard toolbar. The Insert Hyperlink dialog box appears.

3. Navigate to the folder that holds the file to link to by using the **Look In** list and the list of files.

4. Click the file name (see Figure 9.6) and click **OK**.

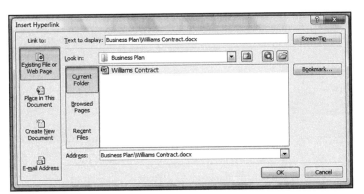

**Figure 9.6** Create a hyperlink in this dialog box.

Then, to view the linked document, click the hyperlink indicator that appears in the *Indicators* column beside the task, resource, or assignment name. Click **Yes** in the Microsoft Office Project Security Notice dialog box to continue. The document opens in the application used to create it.

You also can hyperlink to a Web page, such as a page that lists specifications for a piece of equipment or a material resource used during the project.

Keep in mind that the path to a file hyperlink is static, so if the file you link to is on your system's hard disk or a network drive that different users may map in different ways, the hyperlink will not work when the project plan file is copied to another computer. Also keep in mind that you can add only one hyperlink per task. Attempting to add a new hyperlink simply overwrites the older one.

## Assigning a Task Calendar

When you created resources in the Resource Sheet view in Chapter 7, you saw where you can assign the calendar that a resource will follow and you learned how to update a resource's calendar to reflect vacation days. When the resource's calendar differs from the project base calendar and you assign the resource, Project will move or partially reschedule the task so that it falls within the resource's allowable working times.

Similarly, you can assign an alternate calendar to a task; like a resource's calendar, a task's calendar will override the project base calendar and cause the task to be scheduled differently. For example, if your project calendar follows a calendar similar to the default Standard calendar and you have a task that you want Project to schedule after hours, such as backing up information stored on the network, you can assign a custom calendar with evening hours to the task. This forces Project to schedule the task during evening hours.

To assign a calendar to a task, use these steps:

1. Create the alternate calendar to apply to the task, if needed.
2. Change to a view that lists tasks, such as Gantt Chart view.
3. Double-click a cell in the task in the sheet to open the Task Information dialog box.
4. Click the **Advanced** tab.
5. Click the **Calendar** drop-down list arrow and then click the calendar to apply.

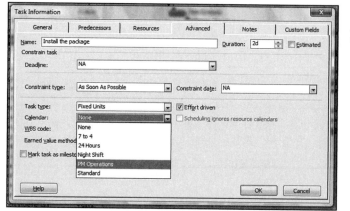

**Figure 9.7**
Applying a calendar to a task.

6. After you change the calendar, the Scheduling Ignores Resource Calendars check box becomes active. Check it if you want the task calendar to override any calendars for resources assigned to the task.
7. Click **OK**. Project applies the calendar to the task and reschedules the task if needed. An indicator appears in the *Indicators* column to let you know that the task has a special calendar applied.

## Task and Resource Calendar Conflicts

When both an assigned resource and the task itself follow calendars that are different from the project base calendar, Project attempts to schedule the task during any time period that's in common for both the task and resource calendars. If the task and resource calendars don't overlap at all, an error message appears telling you that there's Not Enough Common Working Time. The message informs you that you need to either change the task or resource calendar or check the **Scheduling Ignores Resource Calendars** check box covered in Step 6, above.

# Using a Task Constraint

Normally, Project is free to calculate and recalculate a task's schedule as needed based on the link to one or more predecessor tasks, the project base calendar, or alternate resource and task calendars, if applied. A *constraint* further limits Project's ability to recalculate a task's schedule by tying the task's schedule, either loosely or more specifically, to a particular date called the *constraint date*.

By default, all tasks in a project scheduled from the project start date have an As Soon As Possible constraint applied. With that constraint, Project will always schedule the task as early as possible given all other scheduling factors. A similar constraint, As Late As Possible, applies when scheduling from the finish date. You also can apply this constraint, for example, when you want to put off the work and expense associated with a task to the latest point possible in the schedule. These two constraints also are considered the most flexible, because they do not tie the task to a particular start or finish date.

Some constraints reduce Project's scheduling capability but still enable Project to change a task's schedule as long as the new schedule does not violate the constraint date you specify. Choose the Start No Earlier Than or Start No Later Than constraint and enter a constraint date to limit the timeframe for the task start date. Choose the Finish No Earlier Than or Finish No Later Than constraint and enter a constraint date to limit the timeframe for the task finish date.

The final two constraint types are the least flexible. When you choose Must Finish On and enter a constraint date, Project can recalculate the task start date as needed, but the finish date must match the constraint date entered. Similarly, the Must Start On constraint locks the task to the designated start date, no matter what the finish date.

 Applying a constraint to a task limits Project's ability to reschedule the task and may even tie the task to a particular constraint date. Typing a date into the *Start* field for a task always applies a Start No Earlier Than constraint (when scheduling from the project start date), which you may not want in your schedule.

As with many other task settings, use the Task Information dialog box to apply a constraint:

1. Double-click a cell in the task in the sheet portion of the view to open the Task Information dialog box.
2. Click the **Advanced** tab.
3. Click the **Constraint Type** drop-down list arrow and then click the constraint to apply.

4. If the constraint requires that you specify a constraint date (as for all constraints except As Soon As Possible or As Late As Possible), use the **Constraint Date** drop-down calendar to select the date.

5. Click **OK**. Project applies the constraint to the task. An indicator appears in the *Indicators* column to let you know that the task has a constraint applied. Move the mouse pointer over the indicator to get information about the constraint type and constraint date, like the example shown in Figure 9.8.

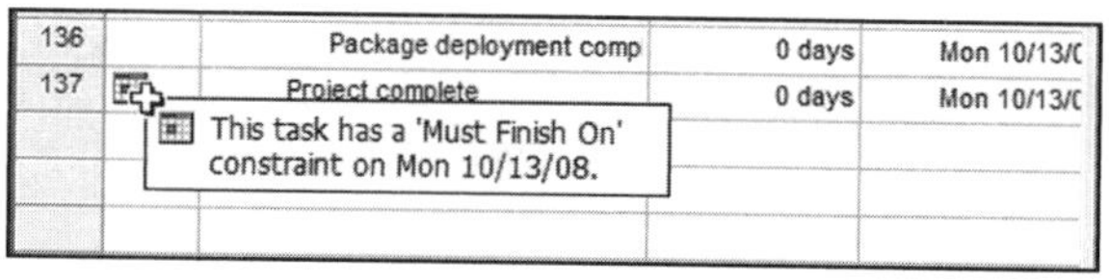

| 136 | | Package deployment comp | 0 days | Mon 10/13/0 |
| 137 | | Project complete | 0 days | Mon 10/13/0 |
| | This task has a 'Must Finish On' constraint on Mon 10/13/08. | | | |

**Figure 9.8** Move the mouse pointer over a constraint indicator to see information about the constraint type and date.

To see a warning whenever a schedule change will violate a constraint, you need to leave Project's Planning Wizard turned on. Choose **Tools, Options**, click the general **Tab**, and make sure that the **Advice from Planning Wizard**, **Advice About Scheduling**, and **Advice About Errors** check boxes are checked. Click **OK**.

You can apply a Must Finish On constraint to the final task. If you leave the Planning Wizard turned on, Project will display a warning whenever a schedule change to an earlier task might cause the project as a whole to finish late. See the section titled "Use a Constraint to Emphasize a Finish Date" in Appendix B to learn more about this technique.

In this book, I've intentionally avoided talking about another way to create and work with task schedules—by dragging on the Gantt chart to create and move Gantt bars. Dragging around Gantt bars is another inadvertent way to add unwanted constraints, so I advise against using this method until you're very proficient in Project and have a good sense of which changes will create constraints to look out for.

## Using a Work Contour

By default, Project assumes an assigned resource will put in the same number of hours of work per day for each day of an assignment. However, for lengthy tasks or part-time assignments, the number of hours per day the resource puts in may fluctuate. The resource might put in more work at the beginning or end of the task or more during the middle. This distribution of the hours of work for the assignment is called the *contour* or *work contour*.

The default work contour, which distributes hours equally through each day of the assignment, is called the Flat work contour. Project also offers these additional contour types that you can apply to any assignment:

- **Back Loaded.** Schedules most of the hours of work at the end of the assignment.
- **Front Loaded.** Schedules most of the hours of work at the beginning of the assignment.
- **Double Peak.** Schedules the hours of work to reach a maximum twice during the duration of the assignment.
- **Early Peak.** Schedules the hours of work to reach a maximum near the start date of the assignment and then decline through the end.
- **Late Peak.** Schedules the hours of work to build up to the maximum near the end of the assignment and then decline.
- **Bell.** Schedules the work to increase quickly to a maximum amount, sustain that amount for a period, and then decline.
- **Turtle.** Schedules the assignment like the Bell contour but increases and decreases the hours of work at a slower rate.

Project can't schedule more hours of work per day than the resource's calendar allows, no matter what contour you apply.

You might apply a contour to an assignment for practical reasons, such as if you know a resource has a lot of other work going on during the starting timeframe for the assignment or if you know that more work needs to be completed on another task before work can really take off on the current assignment. You also can add a constraint for financial reasons, such as to delay the accrual of costs associated with the assignment.

Follow these steps to apply a work contour to an assignment:

1. Choose **View, Task Usage** to display the Task Usage view, where you can see assignments. (You also could change to the Resource Usage view.)
2. Double-click a cell in the assignment in the sheet portion of the view at the left.
3. Click the **General** tab in the Assignment Information dialog box if needed.
4. Click the **Work Contour** drop-down list arrow and then click the desired contour. Figure 9.9 shows this drop-down list.
5. Click **OK** to apply the contour. An assignment indicator like the one shown in Figure 9.10 indicates that a contour has been applied to the assignment.

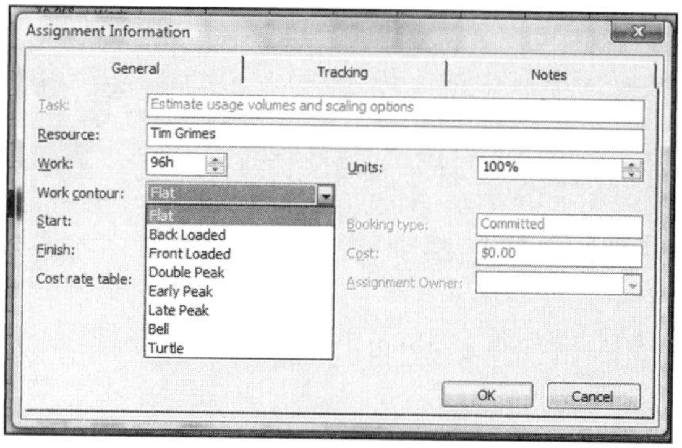

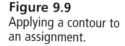

**Figure 9.9**
Applying a contour to
an assignment.

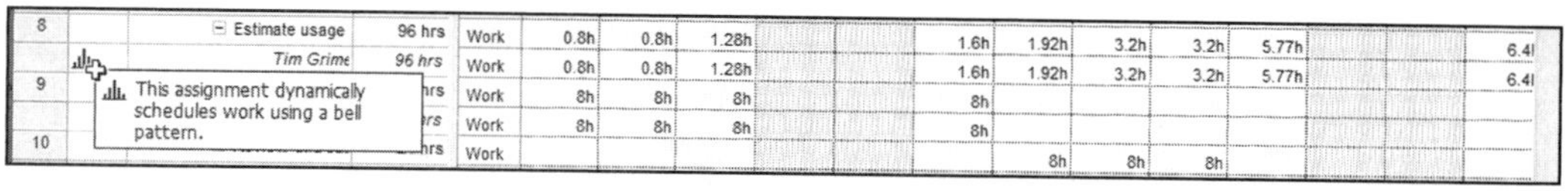

**Figure 9.10** Point to the assignment indicator to see contour information.

If you look across the assignment row shown in Figure 9.10, you'll see that the daily hours of work applied often seem like nonsensical amounts. (Does anyone track whether they worked 1.28 hours on a task versus 1.25, for example?) To some degree, you'll be able to ignore slight scheduling issues introduced by applying a contour. On the other hand, applying a contour can cause Project to reschedule the duration of the task. For example, applying the Turtle contour might change the duration of a 12-day task to 17 or so days to reflect that the 96 hours of work originally assigned to the resource handling the task now have been stretched over a longer timeframe. Make sure that you check the impact a work contour assignment has on the duration of a task to which that assignment applies.

# Adding a Task Deadline

Assigning a *deadline* to a task provides Project with another way to flag your attention if the task runs late based on work you mark as complete and other changes you make to the schedule. Figure 9.11 shows the marker for a deadline on a task's Gantt bar, as well as the indicator that appears when the task's finish date moves beyond the deadline.

Arrow marks deadline on Gantt bar

**Figure 9.11** Apply a deadline to tell Project to display additional information about when a task misses its due date.

Adding a task deadline only requires a few brief steps:

1. Double-click a cell in the task in the sheet portion of the view to open the Task Information dialog box.

2. Click the **Advanced** tab.

3. Click the **Deadline** drop-down list arrow and then use the calendar that appears to choose the deadline date.

4. Click **OK**. Project applies the deadline to the task, and an arrow for the deadline appears on the task's Gantt bar.

## Adding a Fixed Cost to a Task

Chapter 7 talked about the various types of cost information that Project tracks with regard to an assigned resource: the Std. Rate (which is multiplied by the hours of work assigned to a work resource or the quantity assigned of a material resource), as well as any Ovt. Rate or Cost/Use. In some cases, you may want to assign a cost to the task rather than the resource. For example, say you're working directly with a consulting firm that will program certain parts of an overall project for you. Your contract with the firm might specify a set fee for each completed deliverable. When you enter each deliverable into the project plan, you would then assign the contract cost to the task (and leave off cost information for the vendor's resource entry in the Resource Sheet). A cost assigned directly to a task in this way is called a *fixed cost*. If a resource is charging you both hourly or Cost/Use rates and per-task costs, then Project uses them all to calculate the *total cost* or sometimes just called the *cost* for the task.

 To find the *total cost* for a task, Project adds (hours of work or quantity consumed times Std. Rate) + (hours of authorized overtime work times Ovt. Rate) + Cost/Use + Fixed Cost (for the task).

To enter a fixed cost for a task, you need to use another *table* (collection of fields) for the task sheet portion of the Gantt Chart view. These steps explain how:

1. Choose **View, Gantt Chart** to change to the Gantt Chart view, if needed.

2. Click the **View** menu, point to the **Table:** *Table Name* command, and then click **Cost** in the submenu that appears. You also can click the gray **Select All** button where the row and column headers intersect at the upper left and then click **Cost**.

3. Click the **Fixed Cost** field cell for the task, type the cost amount, and press **Enter**. As indicated by the change highlighting shown in Figure 9.12, Project enters the new fixed cost value and adds it to the amount for the task calculated in the *Total Cost* field.

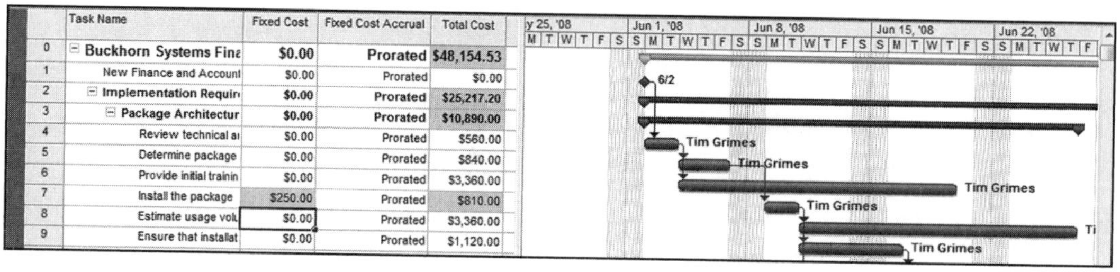

Task Name
Fixed Cost
Fixed Cost Accrual
Total Cost
y 25, '08
Jun 1, '08
Jun 8, '08
Jun 15, '08
Jun 22, '08
0 Buckhorn Systems Fina $0.00 Prorated $48,154.53
1 New Finance and Account $0.00 Prorated $0.00
2 Implementation Requir $0.00 Prorated $25,217.20
3 Package Architectur $0.00 Prorated $10,890.00
4 Review technical a $0.00 Prorated $560.00
5 Determine package $0.00 Prorated $840.00
6 Provide initial trainin $0.00 Prorated $3,360.00
7 Install the package $250.00 Prorated $810.00
8 Estimate usage vol $0.00 Prorated $3,360.00
9 Ensure that installat $0.00 Prorated $1,120.00
6/2
Tim Grimes
Tim Grimes
Tim Grimes
Tim Grimes
Tim Grimes


**Figure 9.12** The amount entered in the *Fixed Cost* field for task 7 has been added into the *Total Cost* field entry for that task.

4. To change back to the default Entry table, click the **View** menu, point to the **Table: *Table Name*** command, and then click **Entry** in the submenu that appears. You also can click the gray **Select All** button where the row and column headers intersect at the upper left and then click **Entry**.

GOTTA KNOW

A ***table*** in Project is the collection of fields shown in a sheet view or the sheet portion of a view. The default table for every sheet is called the Entry table.

## Modifying the Task or Resource Sheet

Even many novice Project users learn quickly that they need to tweak the information that appears in the common views to meet their own project planning and reporting needs. For example, why include the *Predecessors* field in the Gantt Chart view when the chart portion of the view shows the link lines? And why not change the widths of columns so that information displays properly? In this section, you'll learn about a few basic changes you can make to the table shown in any sheet view or sheet portion of a view.

MISSTEP

Be aware that any changes you make onscreen change the default table for the view within that project plan file. For example, if you hide one field and add another in the Gantt Chart view in a file, that's how the Gantt Chart view will look from that point forward. To return to the default appearance for the Gantt Chart, you have to remember all your changes and undo them. If you want to make serious changes to a view but retain the ability to easily switch back to the view's original appearance, save yourself some frustration by creating your own custom view and editing it instead. Chapter 12 leads you through creating custom views while leaving Project's views intact.

## Changing Field (Column) Width

Often, Project gives you an onscreen clue that you need to change the width for the column in a sheet. If the field holds text entries, long entries won't fully display in the column. If the field holds numbers or dates, you'll see pound signs filling the field rather than the actual field entries. You can use any of these methods—some of which have already been touched on previously in the book—to change the width for a field:

- **Dragging to an approximate width.** Drag the right border of the gray field (column) header to change the field width.

- **Getting the best fit.** Double-click the right border of the column header. Or, double-click the column header itself and click the **Best Fit** button in the Column Definition dialog box that appears.

- **Entering a precise character width.** Double-click the column header, enter the width for the field (in characters) in the **Width** text box of the Column Definition dialog box (see Figure 9.13), and then click **OK**.

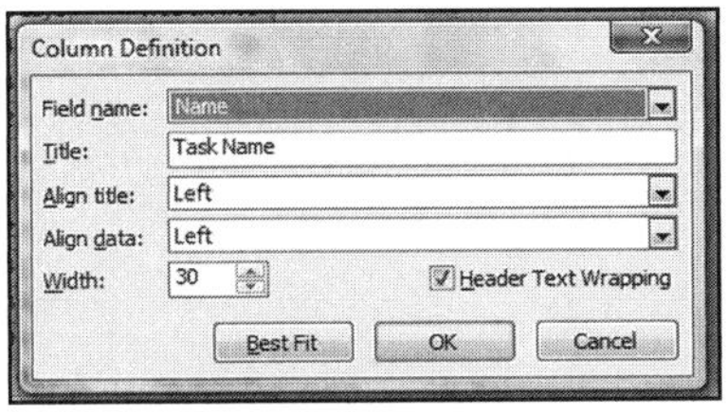

**Figure 9.13** You can use this dialog box to enter a precise width for the field in the Width text box.

## Hiding and Reinserting a Field

When you no longer want to see a field within a view, you can *hide* it. Hiding a field does not delete it or the data it holds in Project. Hiding the field merely removes the field from the current table (and therefore the current view). To hide a field in any sheet, right-click the field column header and click **Hide Column** in the shortcut menu that appears, as in the example shown in Figure 9.14.

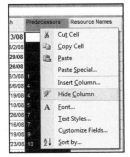

**Figure 9.14**
Right-click a column heading and click **Hide Column** to remove the column from the current table.

To redisplay the column, right-click the header of the column to the left of where you want to reinsert the field and click **Insert Column**. Choose the field to reinsert from the **Field Name** drop-down list of the Column Definition dialog box and then click **OK**.

> Clicking a column header selects the entire field (column). Clicking a row header selects the entire row (task or resource).

## Adding a Basic Custom Field

Project by default includes a number of fields that are empty placeholders for you to customize and use for your own purposes. You can use any of the numbered fields whose names start with *Text* (*Text1*, *Text2*, *Text3*, and so on) as a custom text field in your project plan. There are placeholder cost fields (*Cost1*, *Cost2*, and so on), placeholder number fields (*Number1*, *Number2*, and so on), and more. For example, you could add one of the number fields to the Resource Sheet view to hold a quality rating assigned to each resource.

The empty placeholder fields available for customization include the:

    Cost1-10 fields

    Date1-10 fields

    Duration1-10 fields

    Finish1-10 fields

    Flag1-20 fields

    Number1-20 fields

    Outline Code1-10 fields

    Start1-10 fields

    Text1-30 fields

> The method for customizing fields shown here is really a quick and dirty method that doesn't nearly show you all the possibilities in Project. Chapter 12 will introduce you to the more powerful tools for creating custom fields in Project.

Follow these steps to add a basic custom field to a sheet:

1. Right-click the column header of the field to the left of where you want to insert the custom field and then click **Insert Column**.

2. Click the **Field Name** drop-down list arrow and then scroll to and click the place-holder field to customize.

 To scroll the fields in the drop-down list more quickly, press the first letter in the field name. For example, press the **t** on the keyboard to jump down to the fields whose names begin with *T*.

3. Click in the **Title** field of the Column Definition dialog box and type the name that you want to appear for the field in its column header. Figure 9.15 shows an example.

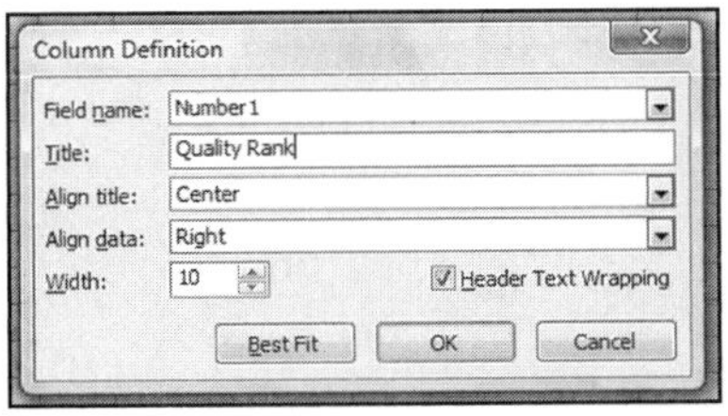

| Column Definition | |
|---|---|
| Field name: | Number1 |
| Title: | Quality Rank |
| Align title: | Center |
| Align data: | Right |
| Width: | 10    ☑ Header Text Wrapping |
| | Best Fit    OK    Cancel |

**Figure 9.15**  The **Title** text box entry will appear in the field column header.

4. (Optional) Change the **Align Title** and **Align Data** settings to specify how information will line up in the field.

5. Change the **Width** entry to specify a column width that's at least as wide as the number of characters and spaces in the **Title** entry you specified (otherwise, the field title won't display fully). (Alternately, you could leave Header Text Wrapping checked and then drag the bottom border of the header row to wrap text, but that affects all the titles.)

6. Click **OK**. The new field appears in the sheet, ready for you to type entries.

## Saving Time with Find and Replace

One last trick that can help you as you finesse all the details in your project plan is to use Find and Replace to update information in one or more tasks or to replace a resource in selected instances in the project plan. Find and Replace in Project works much as it does in Word and Excel, so the process should be familiar to you. Even so, there are a couple of small differences, which you'll see in the following steps. In most instances, you'll start these steps with the Gantt Chart view displayed, where you can see the impact of your changes:

1. Click **Edit** and then click **Replace**. (Shortcut: **Ctrl+H**.)

2. Type the words or phrases to find and replace in the **Find What** and **Replace With** text boxes, as in the example shown in Figure 9.16.

3. Click the **Look In Field** drop-down list and select the field in which you want to find and replace data.

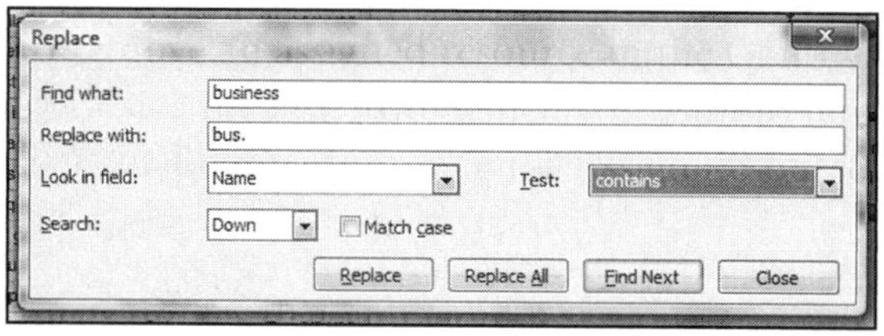

| Replace | |
|---|---|
| Find what: | business |
| Replace with: | bus. |
| Look in field: | Name      Test: contains |
| Search: | Down   ☐ Match case |
| | Replace   Replace All   Find Next   Close |

**Figure 9.16** Use Find and Replace to change entries in a specific field.

When you're working in a view that shows tasks, the *Name* field in a list of fields refers to the *Task Name* field. When you're working with a view that shows resources, the *Name* field in a list of fields refers to the *Resource Name* field.

4. (Optional) Change the **Test** setting to make the search more or less precise, choose another **Search** direction, and indicate whether the replace operation should **Match Case** of the item being replaced.

5. Conduct the replace. You can click **Find Next** and then **Replace** to review and replace individual instances of the items (such as when you want to replace some but not all of the assignments for a resource in the project) or you can click **Replace All** to replace all the instances of the Find What term specified.

6. When a final message box informs you that the search is finished and that Project has made a certain number of replacements, click **OK** and then click **Close** to close the Replace dialog box.

## Chapter Review

This chapter taught you about a wide range of skills all used for a particular purpose: making the tasks, resources, and assignments in your project plan more detailed and accurate to further flesh out the project plan. In the chapter, you learned how to format the contents of sheet cells to highlight their information. You learned how to view the information dialog boxes for tasks, resources, and assignments, as well as how to add a view note for each. You learned how to add a hyperlink to an external file created in another program so that you have important information at hand for managing the project. The chapter further showed you how to add an alternate calendar to a task, as well as how to apply a constraint or a deadline. You also learned how to contour the work on an assignment to account for a resource's real-world daily schedule or other conflicts between tasks. Finally, you learned how to work with the fields shown in a sheet and how to find and replace information. In the next chapter, you'll learn about the important items in the plan that you must review as project manager before kicking off the work on the project.

## Review Questions

Write your answers to the following questions on a sheet of paper.

1. True or False: You apply formatting to sheet text and shading to cell backgrounds in different dialog boxes.

2. Drag the _____ to wrap text in a cell.

3. To open the Information dialog box, do this to a task, resource, or assignment.

4. Type in extra information on the _____ tab of the Task Information, Resource Information, or Assignment Information dialog box.

5. Do this to see what an indicator means.

6. When a task follows a different schedule than the overall project, assign a _____ to the task.

7. A _____ reduces Project's flexibility in rescheduling a task.

8. If you add a _____ to a task, a white down arrow on the task's Gantt bar appears and an indicator appears when the task runs late.

9. Unlike other costs associated with resources, you enter a _____ for a task.

10. Do this to a column header to begin the process for hiding or inserting a field.

## Projects

 To see the solution files created by completing the projects in this chapter, go to www.courseptr.com, click the **Downloads** link in the navigation bar at the top, type **Microsoft Office Project 2007 Survival Guide** in the search text box, and then click **Search Downloads**.

## Project 1

1. Open the file named *Quick Assignments* that you created in the projects for Chapter 8.

2. Save the file as *Quick Assignments Adjustments*.

 Create a folder named *PSG Exercises* in your *Documents* or *My Documents* folder and save your exercise practice files there.

3. Select the Task Name cell for task 4, **Proof and Print**.

4. Click **Format** and then click **Font**. Select **Arial Black** as the Font and change the Size to **12**.

5. Open the **Background Color** drop-down list and click **Yellow**. Click **OK**.

6. Drag the bottom row header border for task 4 down so that the text wraps in the Task Name cell.

7. Scroll the sheet portion of the view to the right until you can see the *Predecessors* field. Right-click the **Predecessors** field column header and then click **Hide Column**. Scroll the sheet portion of the view back to the left.

8. Double-click a task sheet cell in task 4, **Proof and Print**.

9. Click the **Notes** tab, type **Check on proof type issued** in the Notes text box, and then click **OK**.

10. Move your mouse pointer over the note indicator to view its contents.

11. Save your changes to the file and keep it open for the next project.

## Project 2

1. Double-click a task sheet cell in task 2, **Writing**.

2. Click the **Advanced** tab in the Task Information dialog box, specify **8/6/08** as the task's Deadline entry, and then click **OK**.

3. Double-click a task sheet cell in task 4, **Proof and Print**.

4. Click the **Advanced** tab, choose **Finish No Later Than** from the Constraint Type drop-down list, and then enter or specify **8/20/08** as the Constraint Date. Click **OK**.

5. Click **Continue. A Finish No Later Than Constraint Will Be Set** and then click **OK** in the Planning Wizard dialog box, if it appears.

6. Click **View** and then click **Task Usage** to change to the Task Usage view.

7. Double-click a task sheet cell in the **Tim L** assignment under task 2, **Writing**.

8. On the General tab, open the Work Contour drop-down list and click **Turtle**. Click **OK**.

9. Click **Continue. Allow the Scheduling Conflict** and then click **OK** in the Planning Wizard dialog box, if it appears. This message refers to the constraint applied to the final task.

10. Observe the contour indicator beside the assignment you just edited, as well as the indicator for the missed deadline that appears beside the task name.

11. Click **View** and then **Gantt Chart** to change to Gantt Chart view.

12. Notice the white deadline down arrow on the Gantt bar for task 2.

13. Save your changes to the file and then close the file.

## *Project 3*

1. Open the *Site Search with Assignments* file you worked on during the Chapter 8 projects.

2. Save the file as *Site Search with Ratings.*

3. In the left task sheet portion of the Gantt Chart view, right-click the **Start** field column header and click **Insert Column**.

4. Open the **Field Name** drop-down list, type a **T** to scroll, and then click **Text1**. Enter **Rating** in the Title text box and then click **OK**.

5. Make the following entries in the new *Rating* field for the listed tasks only:

| Task | Rating entry |
|------|--------------|
| 2 | Top |
| 3 | Middle |
| 4 | Top |
| 5 | Middle |
| 6 | Low |

6. Press **Ctrl+Home** to go to the first cell in the task sheet.

7. Click **Edit** and then click **Replace**. Type **Middle** in the Find What text box and **Mid** in the Replace With text box. Select **Text1** as the Look In field drop-down list choice and then click **Replace All**. Click **OK** and then **Close** to finish making the replacements.

 You only specified an alternate title for the Text1 field, you didn't change the field name. You'll see how to do that in Chapter 12.

8. Double-click the right border of the **Rating** column header to make the field a bit more narrow.

9. Click **View** and then click **Resource Sheet**.

10. Right-click the **Initials** column header and then click **Hide Column**.

11. Right-click the **Group** column header and then click **Insert Column**.

12. Choose **Initials** from the Field Name drop-down list and then click **OK**.

13. Click **View** and then click **Gantt Chart** to change to the Gantt Chart view.

14. Click **View**, point to **Table: Entry**, and then click **Cost**. The Cost table appears in the sheet part of the view.

15. Click the **Fixed Cost** cell for task 15, **Write Offer Contract**.

16. Type **250** and then press **Enter** to reflect an added attorney review flat fee. Note the new value calculated in the *Total Cost* field.

17. Click **View**, point to **Table: Cost**, and then click **Entry**. The Entry table reappears in the sheet part of the view.

18. Save your changes to the file and close the file.

# PART THREE

# FINALIZING AND LAUNCHING A PROJECT

# CHAPTER 10

## REVIEWING AND ADJUSTING THE PLAN

This Chapter Teaches You How To:

- Perform a thorough review of your plan
- Review overall project statistics
- Display and use the critical path
- Review the drivers for a task schedule
- Remove negative slack
- Adjust a task duration
- Find an overbooked resource and adjust assignments
- Manually edit an assignment
- Turn change highlighting off and back on
- Split a task

Before your plan achieves lift off, a key project management step is to make one last reality check. This chapter shows you the tools in Microsoft Project 2007 that enable you to identify specific problems and pressure points in the schedule so that you can adjust the plan accordingly. You will learn how to view statistics about the project plan, how to identify tasks that are critical, and how to improve the schedule by working with critical tasks. You'll see how to uncover factors like the drivers for tasks and the amount of slack to check for and correct issues. Corrections you'll learn about include changing task durations and splitting tasks and finding overbooked resources and changing their assignments.

## The Need to Ensure a Realistic Plan

Project does a good job of scheduling a project based on the information you supply, but it cannot provide you with a judgment as to whether the plan meets the project objectives. Project also can't tell you if the plan is realistic. However, if the plan fails to meet either of those tests, then the project will not finish on time and it will not deliver what it needs to deliver. When a project demands too much work in too little time with too few resources, the plan is likely to fail.

You as the project manager need to be as objective as possible in reviewing the project to ensure that it measures up. In finalizing the project plan before work begins, you need to ask and answer the following questions using the Project tools described in this chapter to help you find the answers and take corrective action, when appropriate:

> Is the project scheduled to finish at the right time?
>
> Are the task durations accurate and based on the best information I have at this time?
>
> Does the sequence of the tasks make sense and provide the quickest route to project completion?
>
> Are there any risks that I haven't anticipated and planned for?
>
> Is the budget adequate for the planned work and deliverables?
>
> Are the resources adequate for the amount of work scheduled?
>
> Is too much work scheduled for any one resource?

## Viewing Overall Project Stats

Turning on the project summary task and then moving the mouse pointer over it displays a pop-up tip with the project start date, finish date, and overall duration. This basic information gives you a snapshot of the project timeframe, but not much more. When you want to see more information about the overall project for review and decision making purposes, you can view the project statistics through the Project Information dialog box using the following steps:

1. Choose **Project**, **Project Information**.
2. Click the **Statistics** button near the lower-left corner of the Project Information dialog box.
3. When you finish reviewing the statistics, click **Close**.

| Project Statistics for 'Business Plan Development' | | | | | ☒ |
|---|---|---|---|---|---|
| | Start | | | Finish | |
| Current | | Mon 10/1/07 | | | Tue 11/27/07 |
| Baseline | | NA | | | NA |
| Actual | | NA | | | NA |
| Variance | | 0d | | | 0d |
| | Duration | | Work | | Cost |
| Current | 41d | | 402h | | $27,037.97 |
| Baseline | 0d? | | 0h | | $0.00 |
| Actual | 0d | | 0h | | $0.00 |
| Remaining | 41d | | 402h | | $27,037.97 |
| Percent complete: | | | | | |
| Duration: 0%    Work: 0% | | | | | Close |

**Figure 10.1** The Project Statistics dialog box provides additional information about the project status.

The Project Statistics dialog box shows you overall project start, finish, and duration information just as the pop-up tip for the project summary task does. In addition, it shows the total hours of work scheduled for the project and the budgeted cost. If the duration, finish date, and budget don't meet your needs, you can change your plan before the work begins.

As you later use Project to track completed work for the project, the Project Statistics dialog box calculates even more information for you, such as actual duration, work, and cost, as well as completion percentages for duration and work. You can check this dialog box at any time to see how "on track" the project is relative to your original plan. Chapter 11 will provide more details about what the evolving project statistics mean.

Project also offers a report that conveys the overall project statistics. To learn how to view and print reports, see Chapter 13.

## Understanding and Displaying the Critical Path

Not every activity in a project has the same impact on the project's schedule and outcome. Project managers often need to focus on the tasks that are critical, but in this instance, "critical" has a specific meaning. In a project plan, the *critical path* is the sequence of tasks in the project that must finish on time for the project to finish on time.

A project might have several paths or linked sequences of tasks. The longest such path is the critical path and often runs all the way through the final tasks in the project. The critical path, therefore, defines the overall duration for the project. If the critical path becomes longer, the overall project duration increases, and vice versa.

Critical tasks have 0 *slack* time. Slack identifies the amount of time by which a task can slip or be delayed without affecting another task or the project finish. While all tasks on the critical path are critical, some tasks not on the critical path also might be marked as critical based on their calculated slack time.

The ability to see the critical path enables you to make better decisions about planning and schedule changes. Project can apply different formatting to the Gantt bars for critical tasks so that you can see the critical path. Use the Gantt Chart Wizard to format the critical path by following these steps:

1. Click the **Format** menu and then click **Gantt Chart Wizard**. You also can click the **Gantt Chart Wizard** button on the Formatting toolbar (use the Toolbar Options button to display it, if needed).

2. Click **Next** in the first Gantt Chart Wizard dialog box.

3. Click the **Critical Path** option button in the next Gantt Chart Wizard dialog box. The dialog box shows a preview of how the wizard will format the Gantt bars for critical tasks in red (see Figure 10.2).

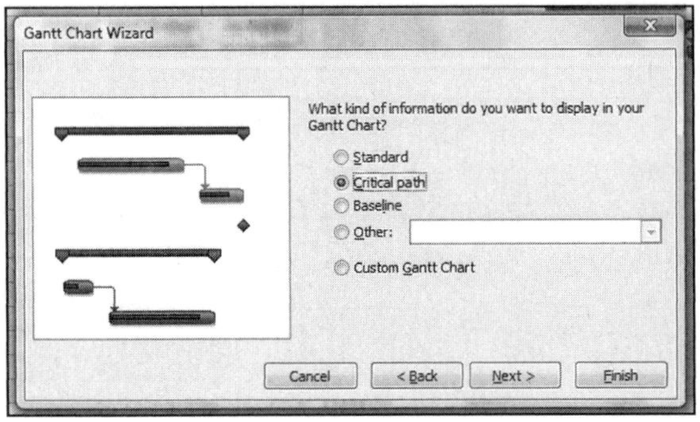

**Figure 10.2** Use the Gantt Chart Wizard to display the critical path.

4. Click **Finish**. The Gantt Chart Wizard does have steps for changing other formatting, but you can skip them when you format the critical path.

5. Click **Format It**. The Gantt Chart Wizard formats the Gantt bars for critical tasks in red and displays its final dialog box.

6. Click **Exit Wizard**. You can now see the critical path in your project plan.

 Some project plans have multiple critical paths. To get Project to calculate multiple critical paths, click **Tools**, and then click **Options**. Click the **Calculation** tab, click the Calculate Multiple Critical Paths check box to check it, and then click **OK**.

# Improving the Critical Path Schedule

Now that you can identify which tasks are critical, you can make better decisions about the project schedule. If you see that the calculated finish date for the project is too late based on the previously defined parameters for the project (such as a drop-dead project completion date handed down by your boss), then you need to make changes to the plan to improve or pull in the finish date. Or, if you've already started the project and it's running behind, you need to make adjustments to catch back up. In either case, you should focus on the tasks in the critical path, because shortening the critical path will shorten the project's overall duration.

> The *critical path* identifies tasks that need to finish on time for your project to finish on time. When you want to improve the project's overall schedule, focus on shortening the critical path. As you change the plan to improve the schedule, check to make sure your changes haven't resulted in another area of the schedule becoming the critical path, at which point you'll need to shift your attention there.

You can make one of or any combination of the following changes to the project plan to shorten the critical path and project duration:

- **Move resources from non-critical to critical tasks.** If a resource has the appropriate skill set and schedule for a task on the critical path, shifting the resource from a non-critical task to the critical one can improve the schedule.

- **Move non-critical tasks so that you can redeploy their resources.** If you can't shift a resource from one task to another without making another schedule change, see if you can move a non-critical task earlier or later in the schedule to free up an assigned resource to work on a critical task, instead.

- **Secure more resources for the project.** If budget and other factors allow, you can bring more resources to the team, with an eye toward making reassignments that shorten the critical path. For example, adding a temporary or freelance resource for a non-critical task might free up all or some of another resource's time to work on a critical task.

> Throwing more resources at a project is sometimes called *crashing* or *expediting* the project. A project manager has to balance the costs for securing and using the added resources or for paying an external resource to work more aggressively versus the time gained in the project plan.

- **Use more of a resource's time, if available, for a critical task.** If you assigned a resource to work part time (less than 100% units) on a task, you may be able to secure more of the resource's time. You can also authorize overtime for some resources assigned to critical tasks. Chapter 11 explains how to authorize overtime for a resource.

- **See if any work can be done simultaneously.** If some tasks can be rescheduled to occur at the same time, change links to adjust the schedule accordingly (that is, apply start-to-start links rather than finish-to-start links).

- **Examine critical tasks to see if they are all truly critical.** For example, you might be able to break down a task with a longer duration into multiple shorter tasks and move some of those tasks off the critical path. Or, you may have assumed that a certain task needed to be linked to a predecessor, when in reality the predecessor's schedule doesn't drive the task.

If you've done your best to bring the project plan in within the needed duration and you just can't get there, then you need to communicate about that reality with project stakeholders. If you're asked to continue with the plan, you will be doing so with full disclosure about the risk of the project being late. Otherwise, there may be an opportunity to adjust expectations by reducing the deliverables for the project, allowing more time, or completing only part of the project in the near term.

# Viewing Task Drivers

When you need to change a task's schedule, it's important to understand why Project has scheduled a task at a particular point in the schedule to begin with. Project 2007 includes a new tool called the Task Drivers pane. This pane identifies the *drivers* or other settings for the task that affect the task's start date. Task drivers include:

- Resource assignments
- Constraints and constraint dates
- Summary task constraints
- Links to predecessor tasks
- Subtask schedules (for a summary task)
- Delays applied by the resource leveling feature in Project
- Calendars for the task and assigned resources
- Actual information entered to track project progress

When you want to see task drivers, click the **Project Menu** and click **Task Drivers**. You also can click the **Task Drivers** button on the Standard toolbar (use the Toolbar Options button to display it, if needed). The Task Drivers pane appears at the left side of Project. Click on a task, and Project lists its drivers in the Task Drivers pane, as in the example shown in Figure 10.3. You can then click other tasks to view the information for them. When you finish working with the pane, click its **Close** (X) button.

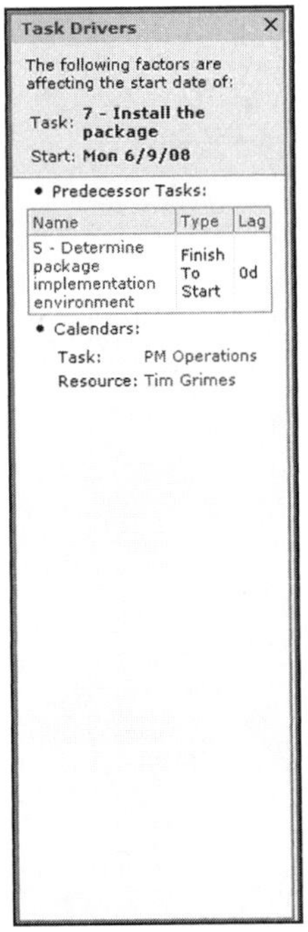

**Figure 10.3** View this Task Drivers pane to learn more about the factors surrounding a task's start date.

# Eliminating Negative Slack

Sometimes, despite your best efforts, little inconsistencies will crop up in the project plan. This can be especially true if you've turned the Planning Wizard off and thus aren't seeing its error and scheduling warning messages. One type of inconsistency or error that occurs is negative slack. If you keep in mind that slack represents time by which a task can be delayed before delaying other work, then negative slack means that the task is effectively already delaying other tasks or the project completion—even before the work begins!

There are basically two situations in which negative slack occurs: when a successor task linked via a finish-to-start link has a Must Start On constraint date earlier than the finish date for the predecessor task; and when a task's finish date is after any deadline date assigned to the task.

To view negative slack, you change to the Schedule table in the sheet portion of the Gantt Chart, Tracking Gantt, or Detail Gantt views. To display the Schedule table, choose **View, Table:** *Table Name,* **Schedule.** You also can right-click the **Select All** button and then click **Schedule.** Scroll the table portion of the view to the right to show the *Free Slack* and *Total*

*Slack* fields (as shown in Figure 10.4) that you want to check for negative values. **Free slack** is the amount of time a task can slip without delaying other tasks, while **total slack** is the amount of time it can slip without delaying the project finish date.

| | Finish | Late Start | Late Finish | Free Slack | Total Slack |
|---|---|---|---|---|---|
| 0 | on 10/13/08 | Fri 5/30/08 | on 10/13/08 | 0 days? | -0.5 days? |
| 1 | Mon 6/2/08 | Fri 5/30/08 | Fri 5/30/08 | 0 days | -0.5 days |
| 2 | Mon 7/28/08 | Fri 5/30/08 | Mon 10/13/08 | 0 days? | -0.5 days? |
| 3 | Thu 6/26/08 | Fri 5/30/08 | Mon 10/13/08 | 0 days | -0.5 days |
| 4 | Tue 6/3/08 | Fri 5/30/08 | Tue 6/3/08 | 0 days | -0.5 days |
| 5 | Fri 6/6/08 | Tue 6/3/08 | Fri 6/6/08 | 0 days | -0.5 days |
| 6 | Thu 6/19/08 | Fri 9/26/08 | Mon 10/13/08 | 82 days | 82 days |
| 7 | Tue 6/10/08 | Fri 6/6/08 | Tue 6/10/08 | 0 days | -1.38 days |
| 8 | Thu 6/26/08 | Fri 9/26/08 | Mon 10/13/08 | 77 days | 77 days |
| 9 | Mon 6/16/08 | Wed 10/1/08 | Mon 10/6/08 | 0 days | 80 days |
| 10 | Thu 6/19/08 | Tue 10/7/08 | Thu 10/9/08 | 0 days | 80 days |
| 11 | Mon 6/23/08 | Fri 10/10/08 | Mon 10/13/08 | 80 days | 80 days |
| 12 | Mon 6/23/08 | Tue 6/10/08 | Tue 6/24/08 | 0 days | -0.5 days |
| 13 | Wed 6/11/08 | Tue 6/10/08 | Tue 6/10/08 | 0 days | -0.5 days |
| 14 | Fri 6/13/08 | Wed 6/11/08 | Thu 6/12/08 | 0 days | -0.5 days |
| 15 | Wed 6/18/08 | Fri 6/13/08 | Wed 6/18/08 | 0 days | -0.5 days |
| 16 | Mon 6/23/08 | Thu 6/19/08 | Tue 6/24/08 | 0 days | 0.67 days |
| 17 | Mon 6/23/08 | Tue 6/24/08 | Tue 6/24/08 | 0 days | 0.67 days |
| 18 | Fri 7/11/08 | Tue 6/24/08 | Mon 7/14/08 | 0.67 days | 0.67 days |
| 19 | Wed 6/25/08 | Tue 6/24/08 | Thu 6/26/08 | 0 days | 0.67 days |
| 20 | Tue 7/1/08 | Thu 6/26/08 | Wed 7/2/08 | 0 days | 0.67 days |
| 21 | Mon 6/30/08 | Fri 6/27/08 | Wed 7/2/08 | 1 day | 1.67 days |
| 22 | Fri 6/27/08 | Mon 6/30/08 | Wed 7/2/08 | 2 days | 2.67 days |
| 23 | Thu 6/26/0 ▾ | Tue 7/1/08 | Wed 7/2/08 | 3 days | 3.67 days |
| 24 | Mon 7/7/08 | Wed 7/2/08 | Tue 7/8/08 | 0 days | 0.67 days |
| 25 | Wed 7/9/08 | Tue 7/8/08 | Thu 7/10/08 | 0 days | 0.67 days |
| 26 | Thu 7/10/08 | Thu 7/10/08 | Fri 7/11/08 | 0 days | 0.67 days |
| 27 | Fri 7/11/08 | Fri 7/11/08 | Mon 7/14/08 | 0 days | 0.67 days |
| 28 | Fri 7/11/08 | Mon 7/14/08 | Mon 7/14/08 | 0 days | 0.67 days |
| 29 | Wed 7/23/08 | Mon 7/14/08 | Thu 7/24/08 | 0.67 days? | 0.67 days? |
| 30 | Mon 7/14/08 | Mon 7/14/08 | Tue 7/15/08 | 0 days | 0.67 days |
| 31 | Wed 7/16/08 | Tue 7/15/08 | Thu 7/17/08 | 0 days | 0.67 days |

**Figure 10.4** The Schedule table shows slack values in the *Free Slack* and *Total Slack* fields.

Although it may seem counterintuitive, in some cases you need to look at the latest task with a negative slack entry and fix that task first. For example, to create the example in Figure 10.4, I added a Must Start On constraint to task 15. Removing that constraint removed all the negative slack entries for the tasks above it in the schedule.

When you've finished checking slack values to look for negative slack, change back to the default Entry table.

Slack can be a good thing. It gives you some wiggle room to move resources and tasks around as you execute the project plan. Although excessive amounts of slack might indicate a schedule that's too generous, in general you don't need to spend your time trying to eliminate all slack from the schedule.

## Changing Durations

One simple adjustment you can make to a project plan is to change the duration for a task. You might need to change the duration based on feedback from an assigned resource that the task will take more or less time, for example. Or, if you entered an estimated duration (by including a question mark) because you were waiting for the data needed to finalize the task schedule, you can replace the estimated duration when the data is available.

To change the duration for a task, click its *Duration* field cell in the Gantt Chart view, type a new duration (including any duration abbreviation needed), and press **Enter**. Project's change tracking feature will highlight all dates affected by the duration change. You should review those carefully, as well as reviewing Project Statistics as described earlier in the chapter, to ensure that the change doesn't have an unexpected negative impact elsewhere in the plan.

When you're later tracking actual work completed on a task, Project will automatically recalculate the duration as needed based on the actual start and actual finish information that you specify.

Avoid the temptation to just extend a task duration to pad the schedule. Remember, that will add more hours of work and costs to the project totals. If you want to build in a schedule cushion, add some lag time to linked tasks on the critical path, instead. If you don't mind adding extra hours of planned work into the schedule, then you also could add a task that represents a time contingency buffer. On the other hand, if a task's duration does need to increase and you get push back about it, call it as you see it. By presenting a well-developed, thoughtful plan in Project, you're demonstrating that you take the project and the need for it to succeed seriously.

## Finding Overbooked Resources

One planning mistake almost certainly will cause your project to run longer than expected: assigning too much work to a work resource. Such a resource is said to be ***overallocated*** or ***overbooked*** in Project lingo. A resource is considered overallocated any time the hours of work assigned on a day exceed the resource's daily working hours per the calendar assigned to the resource.

The most obvious ramification of overbooking a resource is that it can make your project plan unrealistic. If you've assigned a resource 24 hours of work on a single day, all those tasks aren't going to happen. Even if you're working with salaried resources who you assume will put in the hours needed to "Git 'er done," your organization will eventually pay the price in terms of lower productivity and lower morale, and that's assuming none of your resources burn out during the course of your project and thus slow it down.

On the other hand, very small overallocations may occur depending on how you've created assignments. Even if a resource is only overallocated by .06 hours on a particular day, Project will show the resource as overallocated. It's a valid decision to just "live with" some small overallocations in the plan rather than wasting your time making changes that aren't really meaningful in the plan.

All of the resource-oriented views in Project show you when a resource has been overallocated. The view will display the name of each overbooked resource in red. Some views, like the Resource Sheet view, also display an exclamation point indicator (see Figure 10.5). Pointing to the indicator tells you that the resource needs to be leveled (a Project feature that will adjust the resource's assignments to fix the overallocation, covered next).

| | 0 | Resource Name | Type | Material Label | Initials | Group | Max. Units | Std. Rate | Ovt. Rate | Cost/Use | Accrue At | Base Calendar | Code |
|---|---|---|---|---|---|---|---|---|---|---|---|---|
| 1 | | Kim Jackson | Work | | KJ | Prod Dev | 100% | $60.00/hr | $0.00/hr | $0.00 | Prorated | New Company | 001 |
| 2 | | This resource should be leveled based on a Day by Day setting. | | Book of 20 | S | Prod Dev | | $7.80 | | $0.00 | Prorated | | 001 |
| 3 | | | | | AFee | Expense | | | | | Prorated | | 100 |
| 4 | | Mark Taylor | Work | | M | Finance | 100% | $50.00/hr | $0.00/hr | $0.00 | Prorated | New Company | 005 |
| 5 | | Binder | Material | Each | B | Prod Dev | | $2.99 | | $0.00 | Prorated | | 001 |
| 6 | | Ken Williams | Work | | KW | Consultan | 100% | $100.00/hr | $0.00/hr | $15.00 | Prorated | New Company | 100 |

**Figure 10.5** The indicator beside resources 1, 4, and 6 tells you that the resource is overallocated.

When a resource's name appears in red in any resource-oriented view, you've **overallocated** the resource, or assigned that person too much work when compared with his calendar. Take the time to review and fix overallocations as needed before work on the project kicks off. Otherwise, you might be moving forward with a highly unrealistic plan.

Red formatting for the resource name doesn't tell you very much. You need more detailed information to understand exactly when the resource is overallocated and by how much, and which specific tasks are affected by the resource's schedule issues. Two other views can help you identify that information:

- **Resource Graph.** Choose **View, Resource Graph** to display this view, shown in Figure 10.6. To view the information about various resources, use the scroll bar below the left part of the view. The name of any resource with an overallocation appears in red. Press **Alt+F5** to display the first overallocation for the resource and then press **Alt+F5** again to view subsequent overallocations. By default, this view charts Peak Units for the resource, which you can see at the bottom of the left pane. To display other information in the view, right-click the chart portion of the view and click the information to chart. For example, if you click **Work**, you'll see the hours

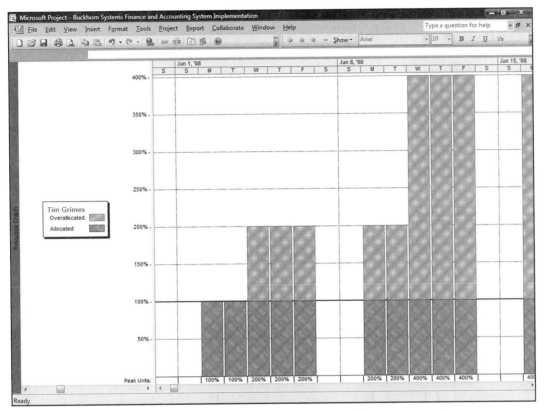

**Figure 10.6** Resource Graph view shows a column chart of overallocations.

of work assigned to the resource per day, which can help you get a better sense of the magnitude of the overallocation.

- **Resource Usage.** Choose **View, Resource Usage** to display this view, shown in Figure 10.7. Resource Usage view lists each of a resource's assignments under the resource's name in outline format. The resource name row totals the hours of work assigned per day, and any total that appears in red is an overallocation. As in Resource Graph view, press **Alt+F5** as needed to view overallocated dates. You also can right-click the right side of the view and click a shortcut menu choice to determine what information appears in this view; for example, you can click **Overallocation** to add a row for each assignment and the daily total that shows the total hours of overallocation.

The Resource Management toolbar includes a Go To Next Overallocation button that you can click to move between overallocations in some views. To display this toolbar, right-click any toolbar and click **Resource Management**, or click it in the **View, Toolbars** submenu.

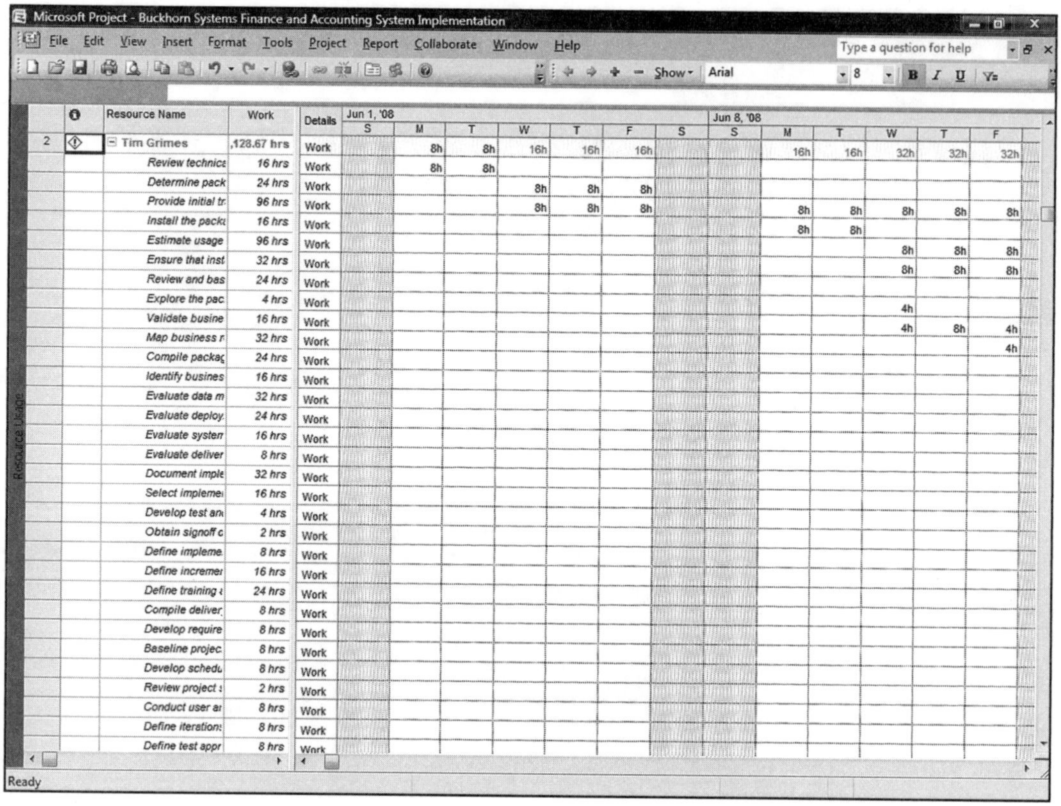

Figure 10.7 See overallocation amounts by assignment in Resource Usage view.

The rule of thumb varies, but many professional project managers never assume that a resource will give even a full 8 hours per day of task-related work. For example, I know of one project manager who only counts on 6 or 7 hours per day of actual work per person, with the remaining time being used for activities not specific to a particular project, such as e-mail, phone calls, and administrative tasks. You, too, should take a realistic look at how much actual "work time" occurs on a daily basis in your organization and adjust for it in your planning. This may mean adjusting each resource's calendar to account for a shorter work day. Or, take real conditions into account during your planning, making sure that task durations allow for the "overhead" of other ongoing activities.

# Changing Assignments

After you've taken a look at the nature of the resource overallocation(s), you can decide how to address them to make sure that your plan only calls for a realistic amount of work for each resource. Note that the proper course might mean doing *nothing*. If a resource is only overbooked a few hours over the duration of the project and that resource is a salaried person, you can probably safely assume that the resource will absorb the extra time without delaying tasks or the project.

On the other hand, if a resource has consistently been assigned multiple extra hours of work per day over the entire course of the project or if there's a single day with an unreasonable amount of work assigned (such as 18 hours), you need to take action to impose sanity on the plan.

Generally speaking, you can use one of three methods to fix an overallocation:

- Remove the overallocated resource from a task and assign a different resource.
- Apply resource leveling.
- Edit the assignment details in Resource Usage view, as described in the next section, "Editing Assignments Manually."

To substitute one resource for another, use the Assign Resources dialog box just as you learned in Chapter 8, "Assigning Resources to Tasks." In the Gantt Chart view, click the **Assign Resources** button on the Standard toolbar. Click the name of the task for which you want to change an assignment. Click the name of the resource to remove and then click the **Remove** button. Next, click the name of the replacement resource and click **Assign**. Click the **Close** button when you finish making the reassignments.

 Of course, you should make sure that the replacement resource has time available to take on the new assignment. One way to do this is to view the resource's remaining availability in hours of work per day. To see this information, choose **View, Resource Usage**. Right-click the right portion of the view and click **Remaining Availability**. You also can click the **Graphs** button in the Assign Resources dialog box and then choose **Remaining Availability** from the Select Graph drop-down list to see the resource's availability.

*Resource leveling* removes an overallocation by either delaying a task to which the resource has been assigned or by splitting the task, as described later in this chapter. You can level the entire project (all tasks and resources), or you can choose whether to level only during a certain time period or for a selected resource.

I like to advise a healthy dose of caution with regard to using this leveling feature. First of all, it can make a lot of changes, and you'll have to be ready to communicate about those changes with team members and others. Second, it can delay the finish date of your project, which again you need to review and communicate about. But I guess my biggest reservation about it is that when using leveling, you're turning over some decision making to a "dumb" program. Rather than you as project manager making the best choice about how to fix an allocation problem, you're letting Project do it. While you may find Project's calculated approach valuable, at least for previewing potential scheduling changes, don't stick with any change that contradicts your professional experience. The buck stops with you, the project manager, and so you shouldn't overly rely on Project's calculations for your planning decisions.

TIP    To prevent Project from leveling a task, change the task's Priority setting to 1000. Double-click a cell in the task in the Gantt Chart view, click the **General** tab if needed, enter **1000** in the Priority text box, and click **OK**.

Use the following steps to level resources in the project plan:

1. If you want to apply leveling to selected resources, change to the Resource Sheet view and select the resources to level.

2. Click **Tools** and then click **Level Resources**. The Resource Leveling dialog box shown in Figure 10.8 appears.

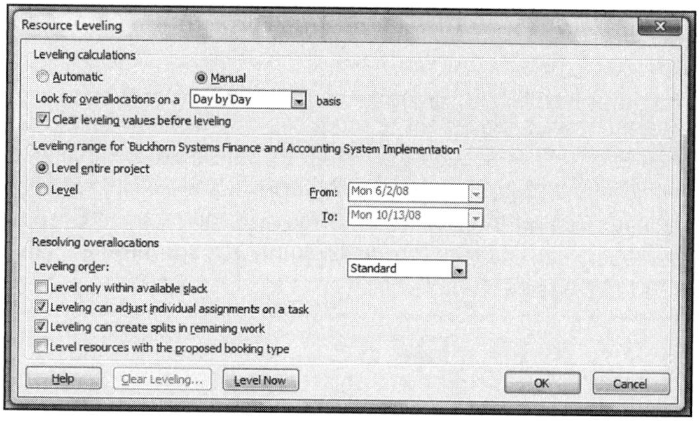

**Figure 10.8**  Level resources here.

3. (Optional) If you want to level a selected range of time, click the **Level** option button and then specify the range using the **From** and **To** drop-down calendars that become active.

Clicking the **Automatic** option button in the Resource Leveling dialog box turns leveling on all the time. If you choose this option, Project will immediately reschedule any task affected by an overallocation. Because novices or other users of your project plan file might find this disconcerting, in most instances, it's preferable to leave Manual selected.

4. Click **Level Now**.
5. In the Level Now dialog box that appears, click the **Selected Resources** option button if you selected one or more resources to level in Step 1 and then click **OK**.

Project makes changes as needed to level the resource assignments. If you want to get a better look at what changes Project made, change to the Leveling Gantt view by choosing **View, More Views**, clicking **Leveling Gantt** in the Views list of the More Views dialog box, and then clicking **Apply**. As shown in the example in Figure 10.9, this view divides each Gantt bar into two portions, with the top green portion showing the original task schedule and

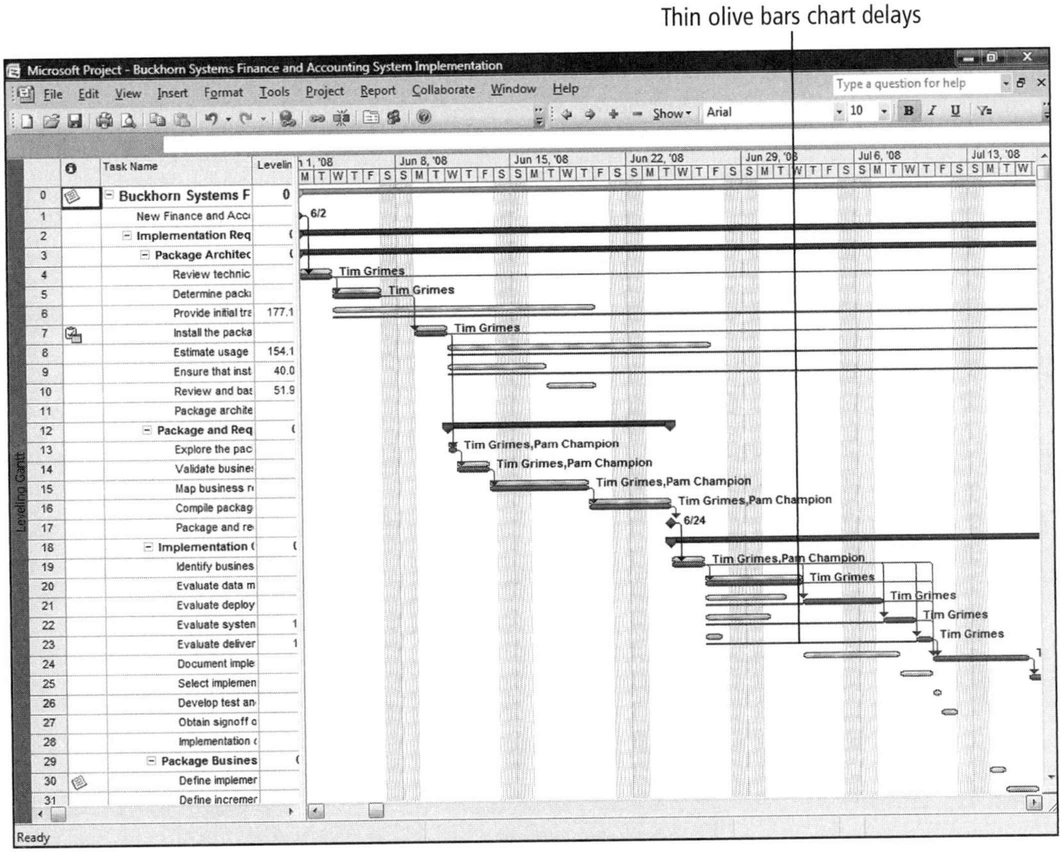

**Figure 10.9** The Leveling Gantt view shows task delays and splits.

the bottom blue portion showing the leveled schedule. A thin olive green bar to the left of each rescheduled task charts the delay for the task. You can point to the delay bar to show a pop-up tip with the task's previous Start date (Early Start) and current Start date.

To remove leveling, work from a task-oriented view and select the tasks from which to remove the leveling, if applicable. Choose **Tools, Level Resources**, and this time click the **Clear Leveling** button in the Resource Leveling dialog box. In the Clear Leveling dialog box that appears, click **Selected Tasks** if applicable and then click **OK**.

## Editing Assignments Manually

If you need to track hours of work and costs associated for resources in greater detail, you can edit assignments on a day-by-day basis as needed. While you can perform this action in the Task Usage view, using the Resource Usage view works better because you can see the resource's total daily hours of work, so you'll know whether a change you make corrects the overallocation. Even better, you can add the overallocation information to the right side of the view so that you can see how many hours of work you need to reduce or eliminate. Choose **View, Resource Usage**, right-click the right side of the view, and then click **Overallocation** (see Figure 10.10).

You can change the hours of work on any day for any assignment. You can delete the hours of work from the cell for one day and type that same amount into the cell for another day; just make sure you make the entry on the same row as the entry you deleted. You can even split an assignment between resources by deleting the hours of work for a particular date from one resource and adding those hours for another resource assigned to the task.

When you make an entry in a cell in the right side of the Resource Usage view, Project assumes you are entering hourly values, so you don't need to type the **h**. Keep in mind that if the Planning Wizard is on, you will see messages about the impact that your changes have on linked and constrained tasks. Because this process is strictly manual, you can use the **Undo** button (shortcut: **Ctrl+Z**) to back up through changes that you've made. If you want to use this method to take a "what if" look at your project plan, you should consider making a copy of the file and then editing the copy so that you can view the Gantt chart for each file to review the difference your changes made.

 When you edit an assignment manually, an indicator that looks like a contour indicator with a pencil on it appears in the indicators column.

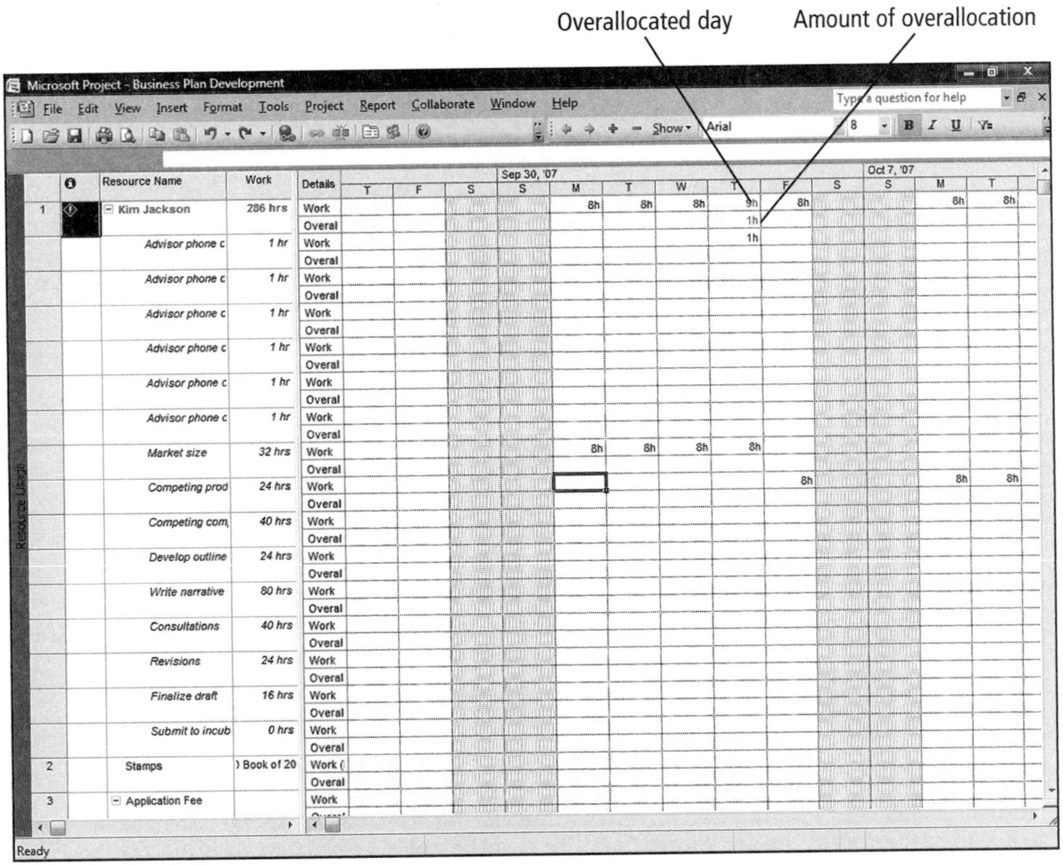

Overallocated day    Amount of overallocation

| | | Resource Name | Work | Details | Sep 30, '07 | | | | | | | | Oct 7, '07 | | | |
|---|---|---|---|---|---|---|---|---|---|---|---|---|---|---|---|---|
| | | | | | T | F | S | S | M | T | W | T | F | S | S | M | T |
| 1 | | ⊟ Kim Jackson | 286 hrs | Work | | | | | 8h | 8h | 8h | 9h | 8h | | | 8h | 8h |
| | | | | Overal | | | | | | | | 1h | | | | | |
| | | Advisor phone c | 1 hr | Work | | | | | | | | 1h | | | | | |
| | | | | Overal | | | | | | | | | | | | | |
| | | Advisor phone c | 1 hr | Work | | | | | | | | | | | | | |
| | | | | Overal | | | | | | | | | | | | | |
| | | Advisor phone c | 1 hr | Work | | | | | | | | | | | | | |
| | | | | Overal | | | | | | | | | | | | | |
| | | Advisor phone c | 1 hr | Work | | | | | | | | | | | | | |
| | | | | Overal | | | | | | | | | | | | | |
| | | Advisor phone c | 1 hr | Work | | | | | | | | | | | | | |
| | | | | Overal | | | | | | | | | | | | | |
| | | Advisor phone c | 1 hr | Work | | | | | | | | | | | | | |
| | | | | Overal | | | | | | | | | | | | | |
| | | Market size | 32 hrs | Work | | | | | 8h | 8h | 8h | 8h | | | | | |
| | | | | Overal | | | | | | | | | | | | | |
| | | Competing prod | 24 hrs | Work | | | | | | | | | 8h | | | 8h | 8h |
| | | | | Overal | | | | | | | | | | | | | |
| | | Competing com | 40 hrs | Work | | | | | | | | | | | | | |
| | | | | Overal | | | | | | | | | | | | | |
| | | Develop outline | 24 hrs | Work | | | | | | | | | | | | | |
| | | | | Overal | | | | | | | | | | | | | |
| | | Write narrative | 80 hrs | Work | | | | | | | | | | | | | |
| | | | | Overal | | | | | | | | | | | | | |
| | | Consultations | 40 hrs | Work | | | | | | | | | | | | | |
| | | | | Overal | | | | | | | | | | | | | |
| | | Revisions | 24 hrs | Work | | | | | | | | | | | | | |
| | | | | Overal | | | | | | | | | | | | | |
| | | Finalize draft | 16 hrs | Work | | | | | | | | | | | | | |
| | | | | Overal | | | | | | | | | | | | | |
| | | Submit to incub | 0 hrs | Work | | | | | | | | | | | | | |
| | | | | Overal | | | | | | | | | | | | | |
| 2 | | Stamps | ) Book of 20 | Work ( | | | | | | | | | | | | | |
| | | | | Overal | | | | | | | | | | | | | |
| 3 | | ⊟ Application Fee | | Work | | | | | | | | | | | | | |

Ready

**Figure 10.10** Edit assignments in the Resource Usage view, displaying the Overallocation row, if desired.

If you've applied a work contour to a resource, Project might assign a tiny amount of work (such as .06 hour) to a resource at the beginning or end of the contour. Even this small amount of work will cause Project to flag the resource as being overallocated. In such an instance, you might simply choose to ignore the overallocation because it's not really measurable or meaningful.

## Working with Change Highlighting

Project's new change highlighting feature, which highlights any cell whose date entry changes as a result of a change you make to the project, is turned on by default. However, you have the option of turning it off and on as needed. For example, early in the planning process, you might want to turn it off because you're making a lot of changes as you initially shape the plan. However, when you get to this point of refining the plan and move on to execution and tracking, the change tracking feature can give invaluable feedback about your scheduling decisions, so you may want to turn it back on.

To turn this feature off, click **View** and then click **Hide Change Highlighting**. To turn the feature back on, click **View** and then click **Show Change Highlighting**.

## Splitting a Task

Splitting a task inserts a non-working period within the task so that the task is scheduled to start, stop for a period of time, and then resume and finish. You can split a task manually to correct a resource overallocation rather than leveling the project plan. This means that you as project manager are evaluating which task to split and how to schedule the split.

Follow these steps to split a task:

1. Click **Edit** and then click **Split Task**. Or, click the **Split Task** button on the Standard toolbar. The button's picture looks like a broken blue Gantt bar. The mouse pointer changes to a special split pointer: double vertical lines with a right arrow.

2. Move the mouse pointer over the bar until the yellow pop-up box shows the date on which you want the split to begin.

3. Drag right with the mouse until the pop-up box displays the desired Start and Finish dates for the resumed portion of the task (see the example in Figure 10.11).

4. Release the mouse button to finish the split.

To remove the split from a task, point to the right portion of the split Gantt bar and drag back to the right until it bumps back into the left portion of the bar, as shown in Figure 10.12. When you release the mouse button, Project removes the split.

Split Task button

Preview of moved portion of task

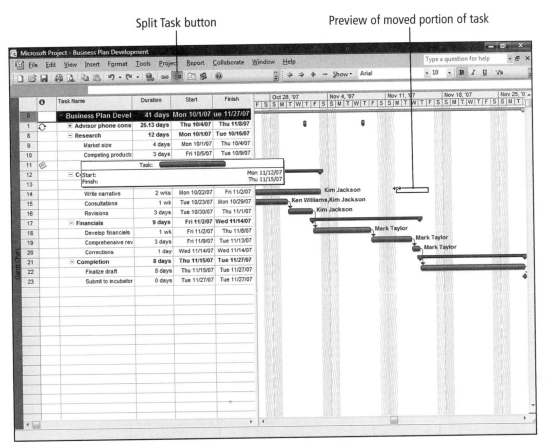

**Figure 10.11** Splitting a task inserts a nonworking period within it.

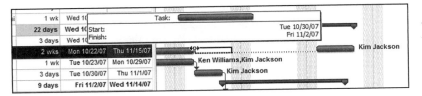

**Figure 10.12** Drag the right portion of the bar to remove the split.

# Chapter Review

In this chapter, you learned techniques for going over the project plan with a fine-toothed comb to identify and correct problems before the work begins. The chapter started by showing you how to find overall statistics about your project that you can revisit as work evolves. You learned what the critical path is, how to display it, and how to use it for planning purposes. You saw how to identify the drivers for a task, as well as how to view and eliminate negative slack, which indicates that a task has a scheduling conflict. You learned how to edit task durations and split a task, how to find and fix resource allocations, as well as how to turn the change highlighting feature off and back on as you prefer.

## Review Questions

Write your answers to the following questions on a sheet of paper.

1. True or False: You can use various views and features in Project to perform a review of your project plan.
2. Access project statistics via the _____ dialog box.
3. A task is _____ when delaying it will delay the finish of the project as a whole.
4. Taking steps to make the _____ shorter will have the greatest positive impact on the project schedule.
5. Use the _____ to format (display) the critical path in the project.
6. A resource with too much work assigned is _____.
7. The name for a resource with too much work appears in this color in resource-related views.
8. Name at least one view in which you can see more detail about resource overallocations.
9. Name at least one way to fix a resource overallocation.
10. A _____ inserts a nonworking period within a task.

## Projects

 To see the solution files created by completing the projects in this chapter, go to www.courseptr.com, click the **Downloads** link in the navigation bar at the top, type **Microsoft Office Project 2007 Survival Guide** in the search text box, and then click **Search Downloads**.

### Project 1

1. Open the file named *Quick Assignments Adjustments* that you worked with in the projects for Chapter 9.
2. Save the file as *Quick Assignments Review*.

 Create a folder named *PSG Exercises* in your *Documents* or *My Documents* folder and save your exercise practice files there.

3. Click **Project** and then click **Project Information**.

4. Click the **Statistics** button.

5. Make a note of the Current Duration, Work, and Cost information. Click **Close**.

6. Display the Schedule table by choosing **View, Table: Cost, Schedule** or by right-clicking the **Select All** button and then clicking **Schedule**.

7. Scroll the sheet portion of the view to the right until you can see the fields identifying slack. Notice that there are negative slack entries in the *Total Slack* field.

8. Double-click a task sheet cell in *task 4*, **Proof and Print**.

9. Click the **Advanced** tab, open the **Constraint Type** drop-down list, and click **As Soon As Possible**. This removes the previously applied constraint. Click **OK**.

10. Notice that some tasks still include negative *Total Slack* field entries. These are caused by the deadline assigned to task 2, because the deadline date precedes the task finish date.

11. Double-click a task sheet cell in *task 2*, **Writing**.

12. Click the **Advanced** tab, delete the **Deadline** text box entry, and click **OK**. This removes the remaining negative *Total Slack* field entries.

13. Redisplay the Entry table by choosing **View, Table: Schedule, Entry** or by right-clicking the **Select All** button and then clicking **Entry**.

14. Click **Project** and then click **Project Information**.

15. Click the **Statistics** button. Compare the Current calculated Duration, Work, and Cost values. Note that only the Duration value has changed.

16. Click **Close** to close the Project Statistics dialog box.

17. Save your changes to the file and keep it open for the next project.

## Project 2

1. Double-click a task sheet cell in *task 2*, **Writing**.

2. Click the **Predecessors** tab in the Task Information dialog box, enter **-2** in the Lag cell for the predecessor link, and then click **OK**. This enters some lead time so that tasks 1 and 2 now overlap.

3. Choose **View, Resource Sheet** to change to the Resource Sheet view. Notice that the **Tim L** resource is now overbooked.

4. Choose **View, Resource Graph** to change to that view.

5. Use the left side's scroll bar to scroll the **Tim L** resource name into view and then press **Alt+F5** to view the overallocated days.

6. Choose **View, Resource Sheet** to change to that view and then press **Alt+F5**.

7. Click **View** and then click **Task Usage** to change to the Task Usage view. Notice that because **Tim L's** assignment to the **Writing** task has been contoured, there are few hours of work for that task on the overallocated days.

8. Delete the first Friday (F) cell entry for the **Writing** task for **Tim L** and change the following Monday (M) entry to **8** (8h). This corrects the largest overallocation for that resource.

9. Choose **View, Gantt Chart**. Notice that despite the edited assignment, no change appears in the Gantt Chart layout.

10. Save your changes to the file and then close the file.

## *Project 3*

1. Open the *Site Search with Ratings* file you worked on during the Chapter 9 projects.

2. Save the file as *Site Search Review*.

3. Click **Format** and then click **Gantt Chart Wizard**. Click **Next**.

4. Click the **Critical Path** option button, click **Finish,** and then click **Format It**.

5. The wizard applies the formatting. Click **Exit Wizard** to finish.

6. Double-click a task sheet cell for *task 3*, **Space**. Click the **Predecessors** tab, click the cell with **2** in the first row of the ID column, press **Delete**, and then click **OK**. This removes the link between tasks 2 and 3 so that task 2 is no longer critical. Its Gantt bar changes from red to blue.

7. Choose **View, Resource Sheet**. Notice that three resources are overallocated.

8. Click **Tools** and then click **Level Resources**.

9. Leave the default settings as is and click **Level Now**.

10. Choose **View, More Views**. Click **Leveling Gantt** in the Views list of the More Views dialog box and then click **Apply**.

11. Scroll the right pane of the view, if needed, to review the changes that leveling applied.

12. Click **Tools** and then click **Level Resources**. Click **Clear Leveling**, leave Entire Project Selected, and then click **OK**.

13. Take a look at how the tasks look with the leveling removed, and then choose **View, Gantt Chart** to change to the Gantt Chart view.

14. Save your changes to the file and close the file.

# CHAPTER 11

# SETTING THE BASELINE AND TRACKING WORK

This Chapter Teaches You How To:

- Understand, save, and clear the baseline
- Understand interim plans and when to use them
- Mark percentage of work complete on a task
- Update and reschedule work
- View overall statistics and progress
- View costs
- Apply another cost from a cost table
- Authorize overtime
- Override a cost
- Cut the project duration

At this point, your project has arrived at a major transition point: moving from the planning phase to executing and controlling the project. Microsoft Project 2007 offers some great tools to assist you with tracking work, analyzing progress, and managing costs as the work on the project moves forward. This chapter shows you how to save a version of the starting plan for later comparison. You will learn about a number of tools and techniques for tracking work and tasks completed and making plan adjustments as circumstances evolve. You'll also see how to review overall project progress and review how specific tasks compare against the original schedule. And, because projects don't get finished for free, you'll see how to adjust cost information for specific assignments, including looking at ways to save costs or authorize overtime work.

# Working with the Baseline

When you look back on your work on a project during the closing phase of project management, you'll want to be able answer key questions like "What went wrong?," "What went right?," and "Where did we improve on the schedule (or not)?" You'll be better able to answer those questions when you have a detailed record of how the work on the project flowed and how the actual outcomes compared with your original plan.

In Project, you can put yourself in a better position to execute, control, and later evaluate and close a project if you save a *baseline* version of the plan before the work (executing) begins. Saving the baseline saves data about your original plans. Then, as you begin to track work being done on the project, you can get a data-based reading about how progress compares against the original plan.

The *baseline* saves starting data about the project for later comparisons. The saved baseline data includes planned task start and finish dates and cost information.

## The Baseline and Tracking

As you have been building your project plan, Project has been calculating task start and finish dates based on the durations and links you specified, as well as adding up cost information based primarily on the resource rates and assignments. That date and cost information, with the dates being charted in the default Gantt Chart view, is the *current* schedule and cost information.

Saving the baseline copies the original plan information from fields such as the task *Start Date, Finish Date*, and *Cost (total cost)* fields into corresponding baseline fields: *Baseline Start, Baseline Finish*, and *Baseline Cost* fields, respectively, for the three fields listed. The saved data becomes the plan's baseline data. The baseline also preserves some other values, such as duration and work values for tasks, timing and cost data about assignments, and timephased values for work and cost. Baseline dates and values do not change as the project evolves over time, whereas current dates and values might change based on the tracking information and other changes you enter.

After you start tracking work performed on the project plan, Project starts recording *actual* data. For example, once you mark any amount of work as completed on a task, the task now has an *Actual Start date* field entry.

By comparing actual data (or current data, where no actual data yet exists) to baseline data, Project can calculate **variance** amounts. A variance indicates the quantity or percentage by which an actual (or current) value falls short of or exceeds the baseline value. In general, negative variance values mean that the task or project is ahead of schedule or under budget. Positive variance values tell you that a task or project is behind schedule or over budget.

The plan's evolving values comprise the **current** data. When you mark any work as complete, Project records **actual** data. Project compares saved **baseline** data to the actual data (or current data, where no actual data yet exists) to calculate **variances** that indicate early or under budget results (negative variance values) or late or over budget results (positive variance values).

The section later in this chapter called "Viewing Project Progress" explains various ways that you can see baseline, actual, and variance data in Project.

## Saving the Baseline

When you've finished revising and fine-tuning the plan and have received the necessary approvals and buy-in from stakeholders and team members, saving the baseline marks the transition from the planning phase to executing and controlling the project.

When you save the baseline, you have the option of saving the baseline for all the tasks in the project plan or saving the baseline for only selected tasks. You might save a baseline for selected tasks, for example, if you've only completed and gotten approvals for a portion of the project plan, but you can't wait for approvals on later work before kicking off the project.

After you save the initial baseline, Project also enables you to save up to 10 additional baselines for comparison. Each additional baseline also stores start, finish, duration, work, cost, and timephased information. Typically, you would only save additional baselines for a very lengthy project. For example, for a year-long project, you might save an additional baseline at the end of each quarter. Each additional baseline is numbered, and the fields of information for that baseline have the corresponding number. For example, when you save Baseline 1 (the first additional baseline), the fields of data for that baseline include, among others, *Baseline 1 Duration* and *Baseline 1 Cost*.

When you've saved multiple baselines, use the Multiple Baselines Gantt view to see the additional baseline information.

Follow these steps to save a baseline:

1. If you want to save the baseline for selected tasks only, drag over the task names. You also can use **Ctrl+click** to select non-adjacent tasks.

2. Click **Tools**, point to the **Tracking** choice, and click **Set Baseline**. The Set Baseline dialog box opens (see Figure 11.1).

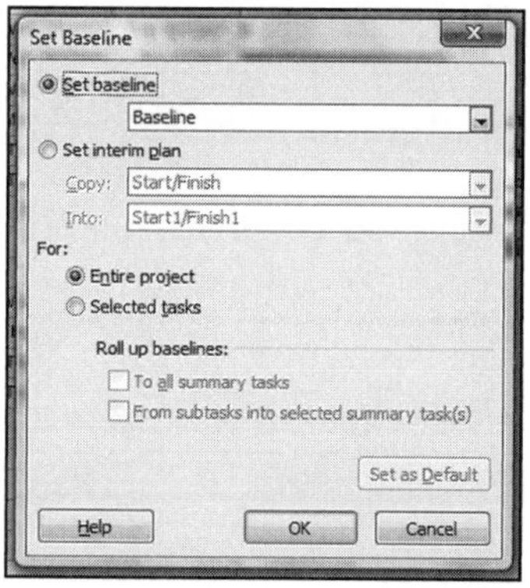

**Figure 11.1** Save the baseline for tracking purposes using this dialog box.

3. If you need to save an additional baseline after saving the initial baseline, open the drop-down list below the Set Baseline option and click on the numbered baseline (Baseline 1 through Baseline 10) to set.

4. If you selected tasks in Step 1 and want to save the baseline only for those tasks, click the **Selected Tasks** option button under For. When you select this option, the Roll Up Baselines options become active and you can check one or both of them to save summary task data and give details about how to save it:

   ▪ **To All Summary Tasks.** Check this option to roll up (add in) the baseline data for the detail task(s) to not only the immediate summary task but also any summary tasks at higher levels that encompass the selected summary task.

   ▪ **From Subtasks into Selected Summary Task(s).** Check this option to roll up the baseline data for the detail task(s) into only the immediate and selected summary task.

5. (Optional) If you chose the Select Tasks option in Step 4, you can make that setting (and your Roll Up Baselines choices) the default for all project files by clicking the **Set As Default** button.

6. Click **OK**. Project saves the baseline information.

Make sure you save the initial baseline before you track any work in the project plan. Otherwise, to get clean baseline values when work is already ahead of or behind schedule, you will need to remove the tracking changes you already made.

## Taking a Look at the Baseline Task Schedule Data

By default, the task sheet portion of the Gantt Chart view doesn't show the fields for the saved baseline data (nor do the other often used task-oriented views such as the Task Sheet and Tracking Gantt views). To see the key *Baseline Start* and *Baseline Finish* field data that was saved when you created the initial baseline, you need to display the Variance table of fields.

To view the Variance table, choose **View, Table:** *Table Name,* **Variance**. You also can right-click the **Select All** button and then click **Variance**. As shown in Figure 11.2, if you display this table immediately after saving the baseline and change highlighting is active, the newly saved values in the *Baseline Start* and *Baseline Finish* fields will be highlighted.

If you examine Figure 11.2 carefully, you can see for yourself that saving the baseline was essentially a simple copy operation. The *Start* field date for each task was copied to the *Baseline Start* field, and the *Finish* field data for each task was copied to the *Baseline Finish* field.

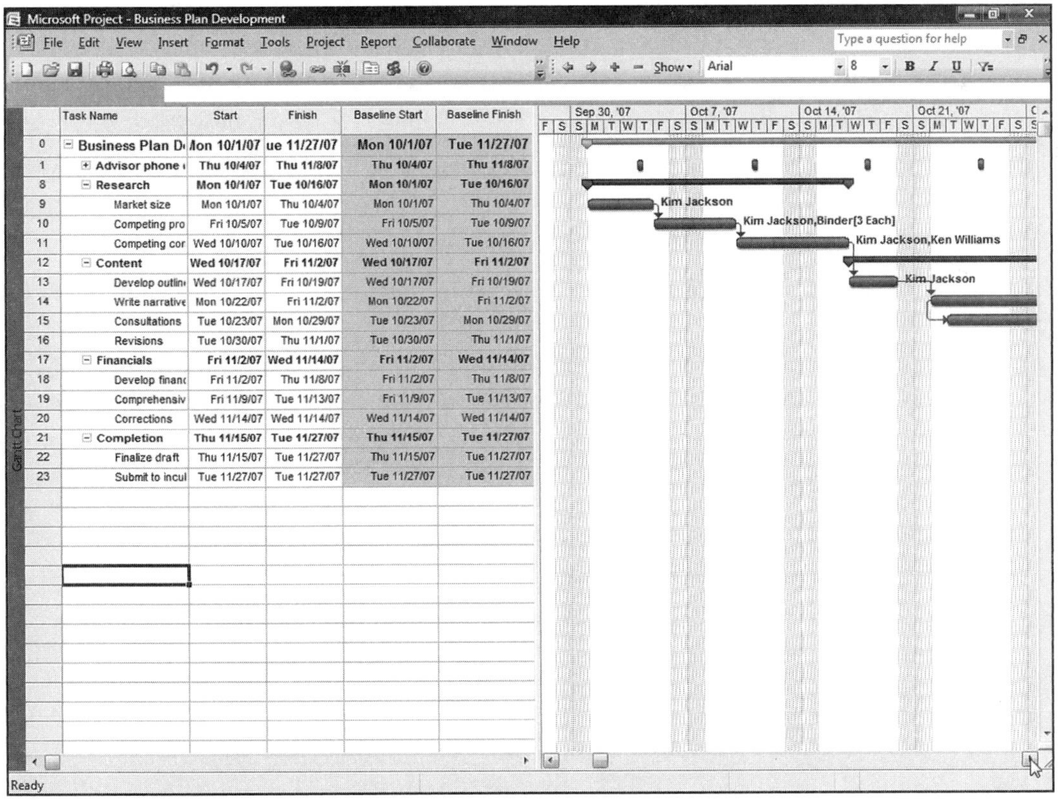

**Figure 11.2** The Variance table shows the saved baseline data.

When you finish viewing the baseline data, you can redisplay the default Entry table for the task view that you're using. Choose **View, Table:** *Table Name,* **Entry.** You also can right-click the **Select All** button and then click **Entry.**

## When and How to Clear the Baseline

In certain situations, saving an additional baseline will not be your best choice for capturing the data that you need to measure project progress accurately. For example, if relatively early during project execution the scope and deliverables undergo a major change, you may need to significantly retool the project and capture a new baseline. If you saved the baseline before you got signoff on the project and the work can't start, you may need to push out the project and start with a baseline that matches the new schedule. Or, if the project started but was subsequently placed on hold due to a change in resource and budget priorities in the organization, the original baseline won't be valid for the project when the work resumes.

In the situations just described, changes in the plan mean that the original baseline is no longer relevant. When you're measuring project progress, you want to measure against the right starting line. If you think of your project as a race, having an outdated baseline is like moving the starting line 10 meters behind the real starting line. The data will look like you're running a slow race even when you're kicking butt and taking names.

In other instances, you might want to create a new project plan by using the Save As command to copy any older plan to a new file. If that older plan contained baseline information, you will need to clear the baseline in the copied file.

To make sure Project can calculate accurate variance data for a dramatically changed or delayed project, you can clear the baseline and then resave it. As when saving the baseline, you can clear the baseline for selected tasks only. So, for example, if the first part of the project is complete and only the latter part is delayed, you can clear and reset the baseline for those latter tasks only.

Use these steps to clear a baseline:

1. If you want to clear the baseline for selected tasks only, drag over the task names. You also can use **Ctrl+click** to select non-adjacent tasks.

2. Click **Tools**, point to the **Tracking** choice, and click **Clear Baseline**. The Clear Baseline dialog box opens (see Figure 11.3).

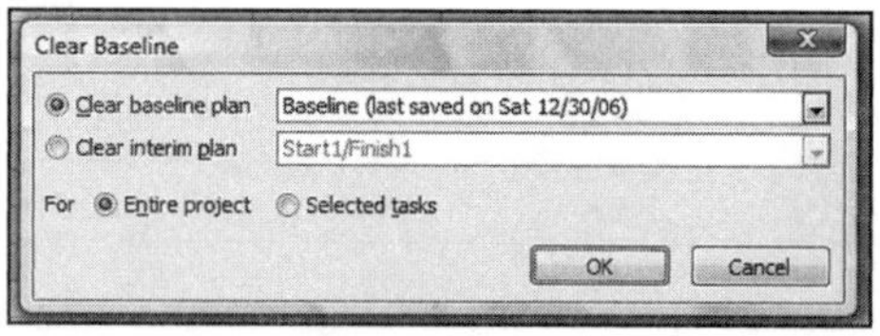

**Figure 11.3**
Clearing an outdated baseline and resaving the baseline provides a more valid basis for progress calculations.

3. If you need to clear a baseline other than the initial baseline, open the Clear Baseline Plan drop-down list and click on the numbered baseline (Baseline 1 through Baseline 10) to clear.

4. If you selected tasks in Step 1 and want to clear the baseline only for those tasks, click the **Selected Tasks** option button to the right of For.

5. Click **OK**. Project clears the baseline information. You can then make adjustments to the plan as needed and set a new baseline.

 You also can ensure your project plan has the most appropriate data by updating (resaving) the baseline rather than clearing the baseline and saving a new baseline. Or, to preserve the existing baseline data but also capture new data in a new baseline, choose another (higher numbered) baseline from the **Set Baseline** drop-down list in the Set Baseline dialog box. You might use this approach when you don't need to make significant changes to the project plan but just want to capture new baseline data. To update the baseline, use the same steps as described earlier under "Saving the Baseline."

## About Interim Plans

In addition to saving 11 baselines (the initial baseline plus baselines numbered 1 through 10), you can save up to 10 *interim plans* for a project plan file. An interim plan saves more limited information than a baseline: only task start and finish dates from the *Start* and *Finish* fields. So, for example, if you're saving the second interim plan, Project will copy the dates from the task *Start* and *Finish* fields to the *Start 2* and *Finish 2* fields.

The process for saving an interim plan is nearly identical to saving the baseline, starting with the **Tools, Tracking, Set Baseline** command. However, in the Set Baseline dialog box, click the **Set Interim Plan** option button and use the **Into** drop-down list below it to specify which pair of interim plan fields to copy data into, as shown in the example in Figure 11.4. You can then specify whether to save the interim plan for selected tasks or the entire project and click **OK**.

 To view interim plan fields, you have to add them to the current task sheet table or create a new table. To chart the interim plan versus the current data and/or the baseline, you have to create custom Gantt bars. Chapter 12 explains how to create custom tables, Gantt bars, and views so that you can generate the information you need for project decision-making and reporting.

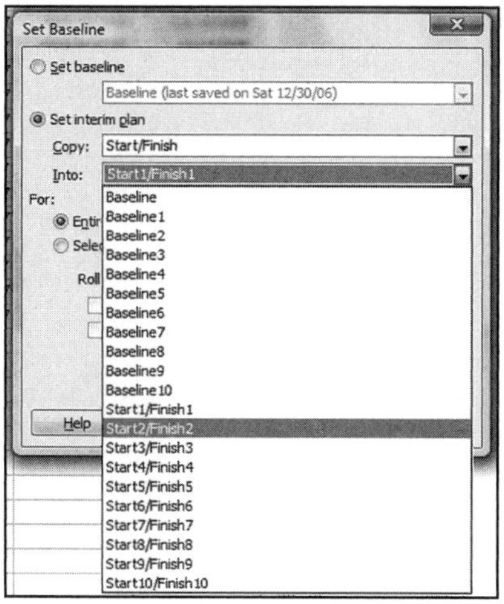

**Figure 11.4**
Choose the interim plan fields into which to copy the *Start* and *Finish* field data.

# Tracking Completed Work

As work moves forward on your project, you need to track the results of completed effort, usually on a task-by-task basis. Project 2007 provides you with a number of methods for tracking completed work. You can choose the method that works best for you based on how often you gather information and the level of tracking detail that you'd like to use.

## Maintaining a Routine for Gathering and Entering Data

When using Project as a standalone product, you as project manager must make sure that the most current task work information is gathered and that the plan is updated to reflect it. If you think that this type of data entry sounds about as fun as updating a client database, well, I don't necessarily disagree. However, just as a customer database would, over time, become less accurate as information becomes less current, so will your project plan not reflect the actual project status without an investment of time to enter tracking updates.

You should consider these factors when determining how to keep the plan as up-to-date as possible in terms of tracking completed work:

- **Update frequency.** Determine how often the updated tracking information should be entered in the project. The schedule you set will be primarily based on your needs in terms of controlling project execution. For a relatively brief project, weekly updates might give you the information you need to maintain project momentum. For a longer project, you might need less frequent updates. Stakeholder requirements also might drive update frequency. If your stakeholders require weekly progress reports, you'll need to schedule the update period in advance of the necessary reporting and at the corresponding interval.

- **Method for gathering data.** Unlike the Project Enterprise Project Management (EPM) solution, in which resources can enter information about their own progress, with the standalone Project program, you'll need to gather the data yourself. Decide whether the best method for doing so will be regular e-mail requests, phone calls, or status meetings or conference calls.

 If the project plan file is stored on a network and multiple team members have Project installed on their connected systems, then it is possible for team members to enter their own data. However, the cost of making Project available to numerous users for data entry purposes needs to be weighed against the time savings that might result.

- **Who will handle the updates.** Depending on the nature of your organization, you may have another resource available to take on the manual (data input) portion of updating the project plan file to reflect tracked work. It might be possible to make arrangements to have an administrative assistant or temp provide help with that part of the process. For example, a group of electrical utility engineers and the administrative assistant for their group attended a class I taught. They had already agreed that each engineer would be responsible for updating his project file, while the administrative assistant would be responsible for generating printed materials for reporting as well as reporting information from multiple projects.

- **What will be gathered.** Make sure that there's clear understanding about the level of detail that will be gathered about each task. If you want to just track completion percentages, you need less information than if you want to track completion percentages, actual dates, and even further details about the work completed. Both the reporting resources and anyone who's helping you track the work need to be on the same page about what will be tracked.

 You can track work in a number of Project views, but most people do so in either the Gantt Chart or Tracking Gantt views, in order to see schedule changes in both text and graphic formats.

## Marking Completion Percentages

The most straightforward way to track completed work is to specify a completion percentage. If the resource(s) assigned to the task tells you about 25% of the work has been completed, you can mark the task as 25% complete. Project will calculate that 25% of the task's duration has passed and that 25% of the hours of work for the task (based on its duration and the resource assignments) have also been completed. As shown in Figure 11.5, a progress bar appears in the center of the Gantt bar for the partially completed task to illustrate the completion percentage.

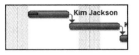

**Figure 11.5** A black completion bar graphically illustrates completion percentage in Gantt Chart view.

You can use one of two methods to mark a task completion percentage. For the first method, you specify the completion percentage in the Task Information dialog box. Double-click the task, click the **General** tab if needed, type the completion percentage in the **Percent Complete** text box, as shown in Figure 11.6, and then click **OK**. This method has an obvious drawback: You have to work with one task at a time.

 When you assign a completion percentage to a task, Project calculates the corresponding amount of Actual Work, in hours, for each assigned resource.

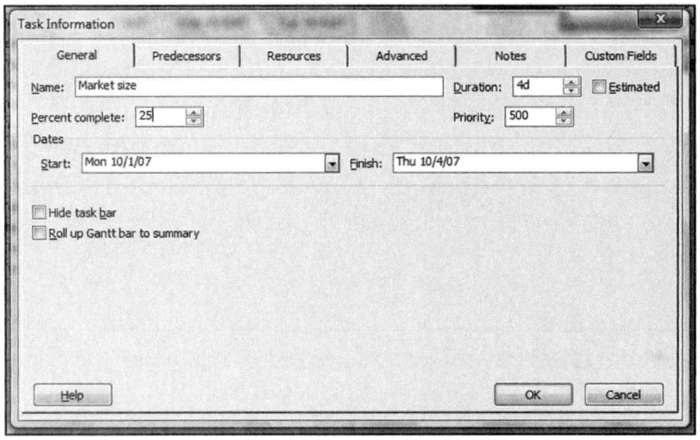

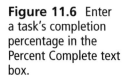

**Figure 11.6** Enter a task's completion percentage in the Percent Complete text box.

To work more quickly and have the capability of marking completion percentages for multiple tasks at one time, you can use the Tracking toolbar. To display the Tracking toolbar, right-click any other toolbar and then click **Tracking**; or click **View**, point to **Toolbars**, and then click **Tracking**. You can then select one or more tasks (drag over task names in the task sheet or use Ctrl+click) and click one of the percentage buttons on the Tracking toolbar. The toolbar offers 25% Complete, 50% Complete, 75% Complete, and 100% Complete buttons, as well as a 0% Complete button for removing previously marked work, as shown in Figure 11.7.

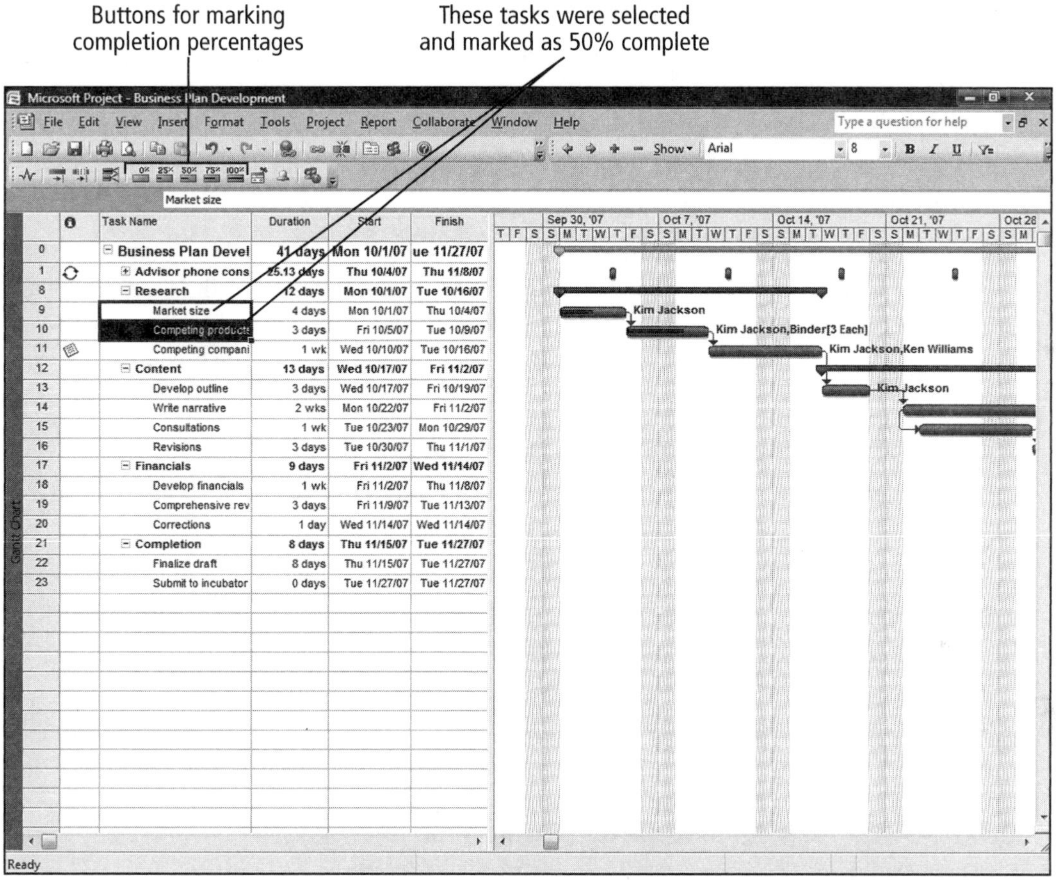

Buttons for marking
completion percentages

These tasks were selected
and marked as 50% complete

| | 0 | Task Name | Duration | Start | Finish |
|---|---|---|---|---|---|
| 0 | | ⊟ Business Plan Devel | 41 days | Mon 10/1/07 | Tue 11/27/07 |
| 1 | ↻ | ⊞ Advisor phone cons | 25.13 days | Thu 10/4/07 | Thu 11/8/07 |
| 8 | | ⊟ Research | 12 days | Mon 10/1/07 | Tue 10/16/07 |
| 9 | | Market size | 4 days | Mon 10/1/07 | Thu 10/4/07 |
| 10 | | Competing products | 3 days | Fri 10/5/07 | Tue 10/9/07 |
| 11 | 🔖 | Competing compani | 1 wk | Wed 10/10/07 | Tue 10/16/07 |
| 12 | | ⊟ Content | 13 days | Wed 10/17/07 | Fri 11/2/07 |
| 13 | | Develop outline | 3 days | Wed 10/17/07 | Fri 10/19/07 |
| 14 | | Write narrative | 2 wks | Mon 10/22/07 | Fri 11/2/07 |
| 15 | | Consultations | 1 wk | Tue 10/23/07 | Mon 10/29/07 |
| 16 | | Revisions | 3 days | Tue 10/30/07 | Thu 11/1/07 |
| 17 | | ⊟ Financials | 9 days | Fri 11/2/07 | Wed 11/14/07 |
| 18 | | Develop financials | 1 wk | Fri 11/2/07 | Thu 11/8/07 |
| 19 | | Comprehensive rev | 3 days | Fri 11/9/07 | Tue 11/13/07 |
| 20 | | Corrections | 1 day | Wed 11/14/07 | Wed 11/14/07 |
| 21 | | ⊟ Completion | 8 days | Thu 11/15/07 | Tue 11/27/07 |
| 22 | | Finalize draft | 8 days | Thu 11/15/07 | Tue 11/27/07 |
| 23 | | Submit to incubator | 0 days | Tue 11/27/07 | Tue 11/27/07 |

**Figure 11.7**  Use the Tracking toolbar to mark completion percentages, even for multiple selected tasks.

If you need to remove already-marked work from a task, click the task in the task sheet and then click the **0% Complete** button.

Right-click a toolbar and then click **Tracking** to display the Tracking toolbar, which has buttons for marking task completion percentages.

A check mark indicator appears in the *Indicators* field column for any task that you've marked as 100% complete.

## Working with Actual Start and Finish Dates

Any time you mark a task as more than 0% complete, that task begins to have actual data along with its baseline and current data. If you've marked some work on a task but haven't yet marked it as 100% complete, the task has an actual start date, among other actuals (some actual work and actual cost data). Marking a task as 100% complete means that it has both an actual start date and an actual finish date.

When you enter a completion percentage for a task using either the Task Information dialog box or the Tracking toolbar, Project assumes that the task started and finished on schedule, unless you specify otherwise by editing the actual start and/or actual finish information. You can specify that actual information by using the Update Tasks dialog box, as in the following steps:

1. Select the task to work with in the task sheet portion of the view.

2. Click **Tools**, point to **Tracking**, and then click **Update Tasks**. Or, click the **Update Tasks** button on the Tracking toolbar. The Update Tasks dialog box appears.

3. Enter or edit a completion percentage for the task in the **% Complete** text box.

4. If the completion percentage you specified is less than 100% and the task started on a different date than the Start date shown in the Current section of the dialog box, specify the real start date in the Actual section of the dialog box by typing in the date or using the drop-down calendar for the **Start** text box. See the example in Figure 11.8.

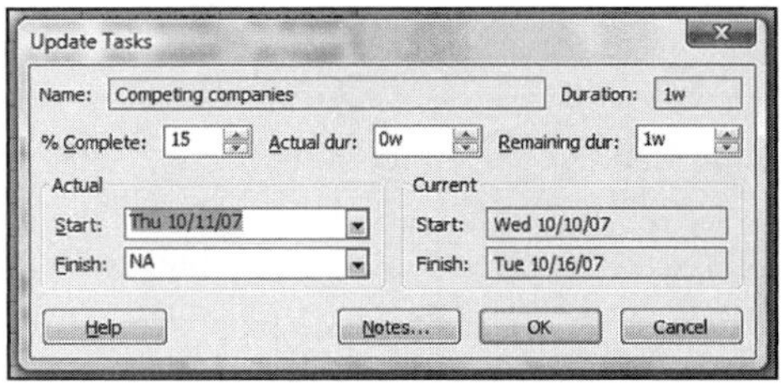

**Figure 11.8** If needed, enter Actual task Start and Finish dates in the Update Tasks dialog box.

5. If you've marked a task as 100% complete, you can specify either or both **Start** and **Finish** dates in the Actual section to reflect the task's real schedule.

6. Click **OK** to close the Update Tasks dialog box and apply the completion percentage and task schedule changes.

If the actual start or finish information you entered in the Update Tasks dialog box affects the schedule for any linked tasks, Project immediately recalculates the project schedule. The change highlighting feature shades the date changes in the task sheet portion of the Gantt Chart view. If you change to the Gantt Chart view, as described later in the chapter, you'll be able to see how the actual schedule changes affect the plan when compared with the baseline.

## Updating Work Completed by a Particular Date

If you've planned well and no surprises have yet disrupted the schedule, all your resources will give you feedback that their tasks are on schedule. In such a case, you can skip the added work of updating tasks on a one-by-one basis and instead update the tasks all at once. This method marks work as complete on all project tasks up to a date that you specify. So, if tasks 1 through 5 are scheduled to be partially complete as of a particular date, Project can mark them as complete up to that date for you, calculating the proper completion percentages as needed.

Follow these steps to update work to a given date:

1. Click **Tools**, point to **Tracking**, and then click **Update Project**. The Update Project dialog box appears.

2. Enter the date through which to update the tasks in the **Update Work As Complete Through** text box (see Figure 11.9), or use its drop-down calendar to specify the date.

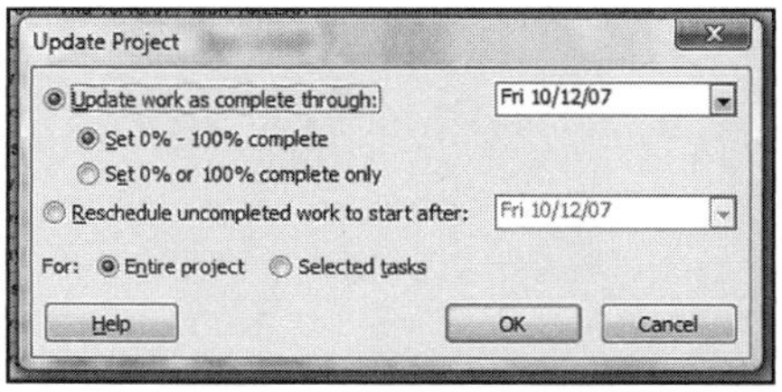

**Figure 11.9** You can update tasks through the date specified in the upper-right text box of the Update Project dialog box.

3. Under **Update Work As Complete Through Option**, click an option button to specify how Project should update tasks:

   - **Set 0% - 100% Complete.** Project marks any task that's complete before the date you specified in Step 2 as 100% complete. For any task that starts before the specified date but doesn't finish until after the date, Project calculates a completion percentage and marks the task as complete to that date.

   - **Set 0% or 100% Complete Only.** Project marks any task scheduled to complete before the date specified in Step 2 as 100% complete. For any task scheduled to start before the date but finish afterward, Project leaves the completion percentage set to 0%. In other words, this choice marks a task as 100% complete or does not change the completion percentage at all.

4. (Optional) If you selected any tasks before Step 1, you could click the **Selected Tasks** option button to have Project update only those tasks. You can do this if you have a lengthy, complicated project and only want to update a section at a time.

5. Click **OK**. Project calculates and marks task completion percentages through the specified date.

You also can use the Update Project dialog box to update a project's task to a future date, if you know that the project will be on track at that time. For example, if you have to give a status report on Friday but want to prepare your materials in advance on a Wednesday, you can specify the coming Friday's date as the Update Work As Complete Through date, finish the update, and then print the necessary reporting materials.

Alternately, you can mark tasks as complete through a particular date on a one-by-one basis, but first you have to set the *status date* to which you want Project to mark the task as complete. You specify the status date in the Project Information dialog box. Choose **Project, Project Information**. Use the **Status Date** text box or drop-down calendar to select the desired date and then click **OK**. Then, you can select a task in the task sheet and click the **Update As Scheduled** button on the Tracking toolbar (see Figure 11.10) to mark the selected task as complete through that date, with Project calculating the appropriate completion percentage.

**Figure 11.10**
Update a task to the status date using the Update As Scheduled button on the Tracking toolbar.

## Rescheduling an Uncompleted Task

Project can make another type of change when you've set a status date in the Project Information dialog box. Project can reschedule uncompleted work on a task to begin on the status date that you set. If the task is 0% complete, Project moves the whole task so that it starts on the status date. If you've marked the task as partially complete, Project leaves the part of the task that's actually complete in place, inserts a split in the task, and schedules the work to resume on the specified status date. Use these steps to reschedule the uncompleted work on a task:

1. Choose **Project, Project Information**.
2. Use the **Status Date** text box or drop-down calendar to select the desired date after which work should be rescheduled.
3. Click **OK**.

4. Click the task for which you'd like to reschedule work, or select multiple tasks by dragging over the *Task Name* cell entries or by Ctrl+clicking.

5. Click the **Reschedule Work** button on the Tracking toolbar. As shown in Figure 11.11, Project reschedules the work on the task to resume on the specified date.

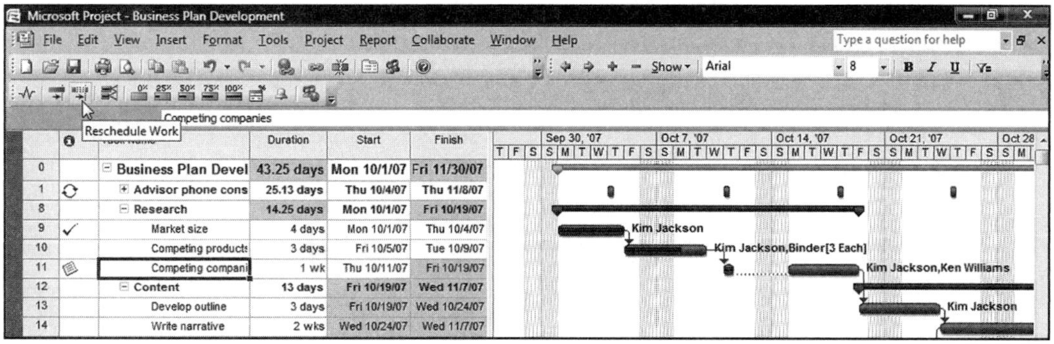

**Figure 11.11** You also can use the Tracking toolbar in conjunction with a status date to reschedule uncompleted work.

MILE STEP

If you need to reschedule all the work on a task, make sure you reset the task's completion percentage to zero (0%).

Project doesn't limit you to using the Tracking toolbar to reschedule task work. You can, of course, make specific adjustments to task durations, link types, constraints, and so on as execution continues. In fact, remaining watchful of evolving circumstances and staying flexible and creative in addressing new realities are crucial requirements for project execution and control. You retain the power to make the necessary scheduling changes. Project will show you the impact of those scheduling changes versus the saved baseline for the project in the Tracking Gantt view, shown later in the chapter.

## Tracking a Single Resource's Work on a Task

Different projects and environments require managing to different levels of detail. In many instances, tracking task completion percentages suffices because the project manager doesn't need to be concerned with the hours of work completed by each particular resource. Task and project completion and the successful achievement of deliverables carry the most weight in those situations.

However, you may find yourself in an environment or an instance where you do need to document a reading of a specific resource's performance, especially when one resource assigned to a task isn't delivering when others are. For example, if the resource comes from another department that's been unreliable in the past, you may need to have evidence to support your case if you need to ask for a different or additional resource. Or, if you're dealing with a costly outside vendor and large payments are tied to task completions, you need to track that vendor's completion despite what other assigned resources have contributed.

In Project, you can use either the Task Usage or Resource Usage views—wherein you can see assignments—to track hours of work for a resource's assignment on a particular task. The changes described in this section don't affect completed work marked for other resources; you're only working with one resource's assignment. As a reminder, you can open the **View** menu and then click either **Resource Usage** or **Task Usage** to change to the corresponding view.

Once you've displayed the desired view, double-click a cell in the assignment's row in the task sheet portion of the view. Click the **Tracking** tab in the Assignment Information dialog box (see Figure 11.12), edit the entry in the **Actual Work** text box as needed (or change the entry in the **% Work Complete** text box), and then click **OK**. This specifies how much work that resource has completed on the task, and Project will recalculate the overall task completion percentage accordingly. An indicator telling you that the assignment's work has been edited will appear.

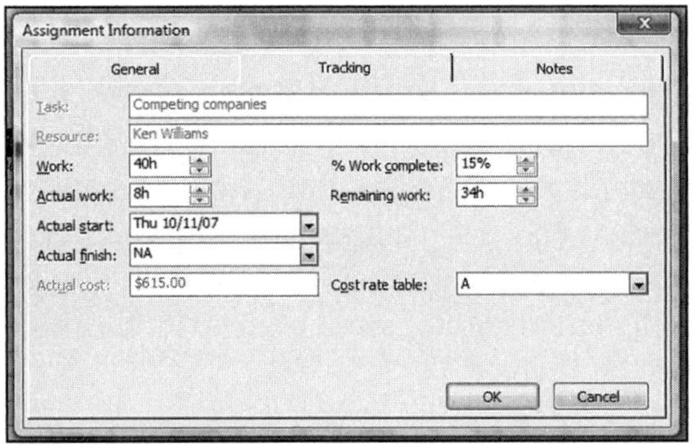

**Figure 11.12** Use the Tracking tab of the Assignment Information dialog box to change the completion percentage or actual work value for a single resource's work on a task.

If you need to nail down even more detail about the actual work performed by a resource, you can enter the actual hours of work performed by a resource on a daily basis. To do so, change to Task Usage or Resource Usage view. Right-click the right side of the view and click **Actual Work**. This adds an *Act. Work* row below each *Work* row in the timephased chart area at the right, as shown in Figure 11.13. You can then enter daily actual work values in the *Act. Work* row.

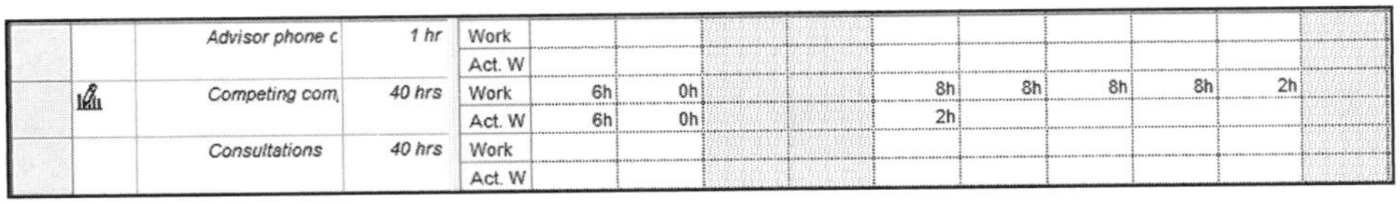

| | | | | | | | | | | | | |
|---|---|---|---|---|---|---|---|---|---|---|---|---|
| | Advisor phone c | 1 hr | Work | | | | | | | | | |
| | | | Act. W | | | | | | | | | |
| 📊 | Competing com | 40 hrs | Work | 6h | 0h | | | 8h | 8h | 8h | 8h | 2h |
| | | | Act. W | 6h | 0h | | | 2h | | | | |
| | Consultations | 40 hrs | Work | | | | | | | | | |
| | | | Act. W | | | | | | | | | |

**Figure 11.13** Display the *Act. Work* row in Task Usage or Resource Usage view if you need to specify daily hours of completed resource work.

# Viewing Project Progress

Tracking work puts you in the position to report to others, including team members and stakeholders, about the progress on your project. Project offers a variety of locations, views, and tables that show various combinations of tracking information that you might want to share with stakeholders and team members. Take some time to familiarize yourself with the choices presented in this section so that you can choose the information that's most useful and relevant to you in your continuing leadership of the project.

## It's a Numbers Game. Or Is It?

Project's ability to calculate and graphically demonstrate progress against a plan may provide you with empirical data you didn't previously have to work as an advocate for your team. But, for a project that's off course, don't be discouraged by the realities uncovered in Project's progress data. Just as Project can't take the place of your human expertise, it also can't account for less tangible indicators of project progress and team accomplishments. For example, if the project is running behind but a brand new team is coming together and turning the corner, Project can't demonstrate that. Or, deliverables and stakeholder satisfaction being provided may exceed the apparent "progress" calculated by Project in terms of tasks completed and work completion percentages. When you're managing your project, make sure that you're keeping mental or written notes about *all* the team's achievements, so you can dole out the kudos and discuss the team's success at appropriate times.

## Project Statistics

You learned in Chapter 10 how to view overall project statistics so that you can verify the project's overall finish date, scheduled work, and cost. You saw how to click the Statistics button in the Project Information dialog box to open the Project Statistics dialog box.

The Tracking toolbar also enables you to open the Project Statistics dialog box by clicking the Project Statistics button at the far left end of the toolbar (see Figure 11.14). Now that you've tracked work in the project, the Project Statistics dialog box provides more information. As shown in Figure 11.14, in addition to the Current information, the dialog box includes Baseline data and Actual and Variance data where applicable. It also calculates Remaining values for Duration, Work, and Cost.

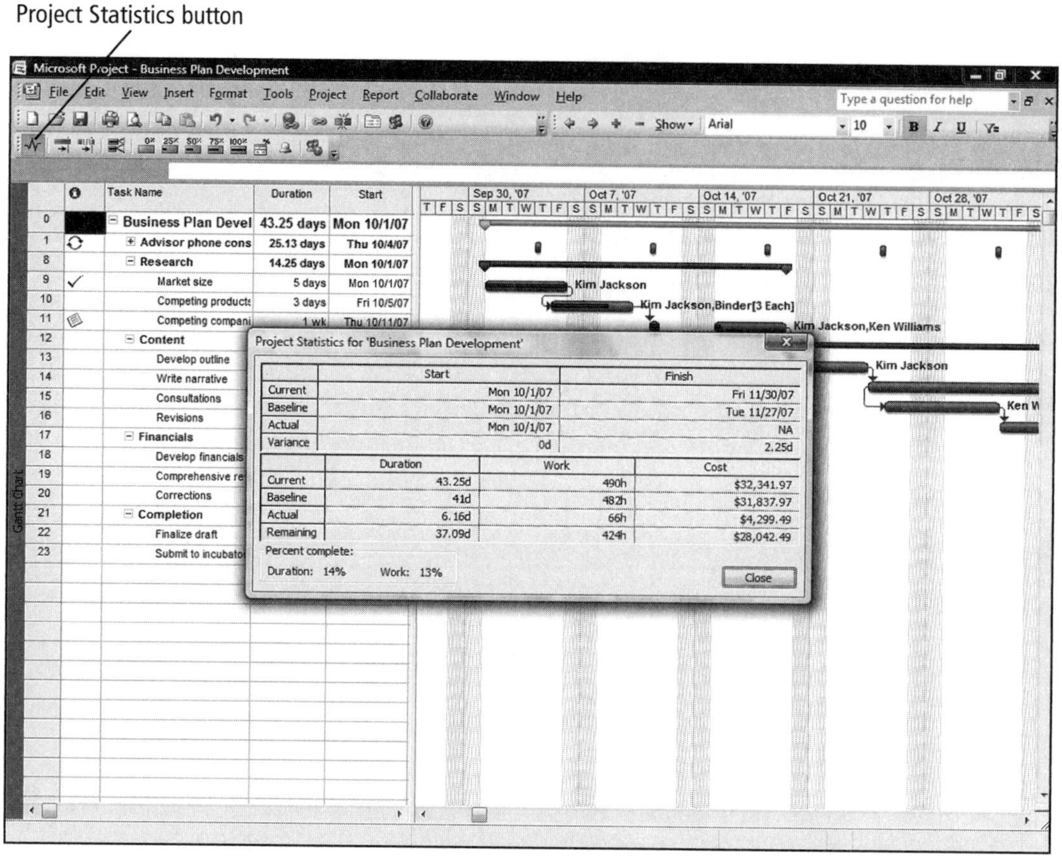

Project Statistics button

**Figure 11.14** As you track work, project statistics evolve and include actual data and variances.

In its lower-left corner, the dialog box presents completion percentages for the overall Duration and Work in the project. These values won't necessarily be as close as the ones shown in Figure 11.14 for your projects. If the project overall is front loaded, with most of the hours of work occurring at the beginning of the project, the Work completion percentage might dramatically exceed the Duration completion percentage. Conversely, when most of the work occurs near the end—a back-loaded project—the Duration completion percentage will likely exceed the Work completion percentage for much of the project.

When you finish viewing the information, click the **Close** button to close the Project Statistics dialog box. You can redisplay this dialog box as often as needed to get a read on work progress and to check how much of the project budget has been expended.

## Gantt Chart View

The default Gantt Chart view doesn't provide any information about project progress beyond the progress bars with the Gantt bars on the chart portion of the view and the check mark indicator that appears for any task marked as 100% complete. You can, however, display other tables in the task sheet portion of the view to evaluate progress information. Choose the table to view from the **View, Table: *Table Name*** submenu or by right-clicking the **Select All** button and then clicking the desired table.

These tables display valuable progress information after you begin tracking work in the project plan:

- **Summary table (see Figure 11.15).** This table includes the *Cost* and *Work* fields that show the total cost and hours of work scheduled for each task. The *% Comp.* field shows the marked completion percentage for each task.

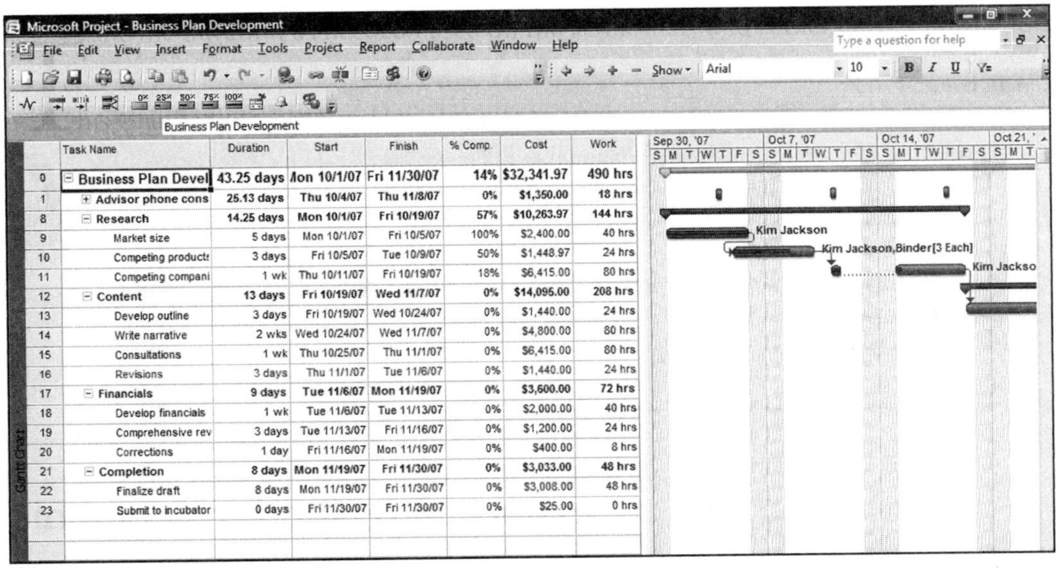


| | Task Name | Duration | Start | Finish | % Comp. | Cost | Work |
|---|---|---|---|---|---|---|---|
| 0 | Business Plan Devel | 43.25 days | Mon 10/1/07 | Fri 11/30/07 | 14% | $32,341.97 | 490 hrs |
| 1 | Advisor phone cons | 25.13 days | Thu 10/4/07 | Thu 11/8/07 | 0% | $1,350.00 | 18 hrs |
| 8 | Research | 14.25 days | Mon 10/1/07 | Fri 10/19/07 | 57% | $10,263.97 | 144 hrs |
| 9 | Market size | 5 days | Mon 10/1/07 | Fri 10/5/07 | 100% | $2,400.00 | 40 hrs |
| 10 | Competing products | 3 days | Fri 10/5/07 | Tue 10/9/07 | 50% | $1,448.97 | 24 hrs |
| 11 | Competing compani | 1 wk | Thu 10/11/07 | Fri 10/19/07 | 18% | $6,415.00 | 80 hrs |
| 12 | Content | 13 days | Fri 10/19/07 | Wed 11/7/07 | 0% | $14,095.00 | 208 hrs |
| 13 | Develop outline | 3 days | Fri 10/19/07 | Wed 10/24/07 | 0% | $1,440.00 | 24 hrs |
| 14 | Write narrative | 2 wks | Wed 10/24/07 | Wed 11/7/07 | 0% | $4,800.00 | 80 hrs |
| 15 | Consultations | 1 wk | Thu 10/25/07 | Thu 11/1/07 | 0% | $6,415.00 | 80 hrs |
| 16 | Revisions | 3 days | Thu 11/1/07 | Tue 11/6/07 | 0% | $1,440.00 | 24 hrs |
| 17 | Financials | 9 days | Tue 11/6/07 | Mon 11/19/07 | 0% | $3,600.00 | 72 hrs |
| 18 | Develop financials | 1 wk | Tue 11/6/07 | Tue 11/13/07 | 0% | $2,000.00 | 40 hrs |
| 19 | Comprehensive rev | 3 days | Tue 11/13/07 | Fri 11/16/07 | 0% | $1,200.00 | 24 hrs |
| 20 | Corrections | 1 day | Fri 11/16/07 | Mon 11/19/07 | 0% | $400.00 | 8 hrs |
| 21 | Completion | 8 days | Mon 11/19/07 | Fri 11/30/07 | 0% | $3,033.00 | 48 hrs |
| 22 | Finalize draft | 8 days | Mon 11/19/07 | Fri 11/30/07 | 0% | $3,008.00 | 48 hrs |
| 23 | Submit to incubator | 0 days | Fri 11/30/07 | Fri 11/30/07 | 0% | $25.00 | 0 hrs |

**Figure 11.15** The Summary table shows the completion percentage (*% Comp.*) for each task.

- **Tracking table (see Figure 11.16).** This table includes fields with actuals for start, finish, duration, cost, and work. You can use the *Phys. % Comp.* (Physical % Complete) field to enter an alternate completion percentage if the *% Comp.* doesn't totally reflect the actual work expended. For example, a writing task might take more hours of work earlier and fewer later, when the writer is editing the already-written work.

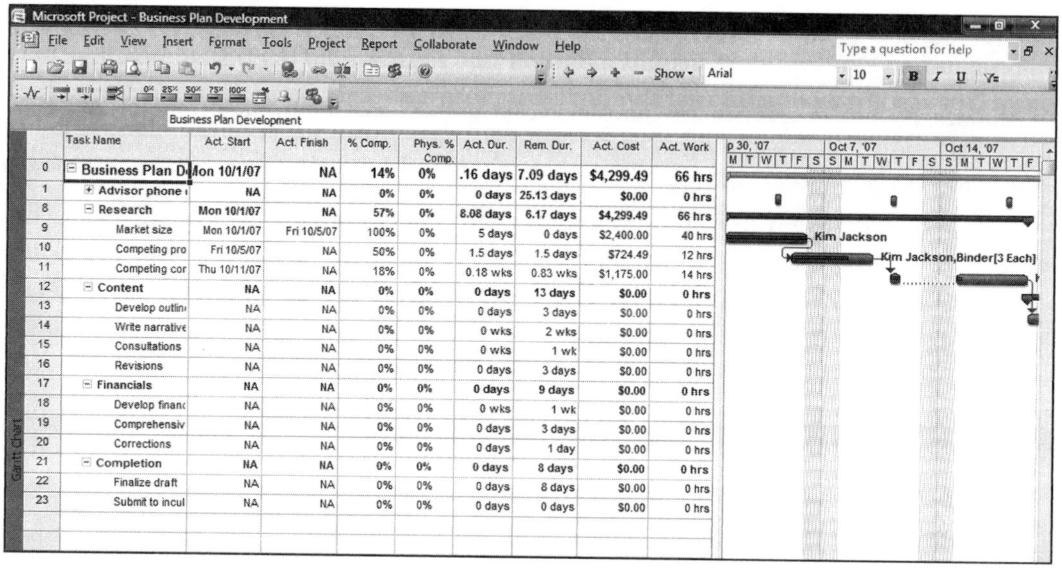


| | Task Name | Act. Start | Act. Finish | % Comp. | Phys. % Comp. | Act. Dur. | Rem. Dur. | Act. Cost | Act. Work |
|---|---|---|---|---|---|---|---|---|---|
| 0 | Business Plan D | Mon 10/1/07 | NA | 14% | 0% | .16 days | 7.09 days | $4,299.49 | 66 hrs |
| 1 | Advisor phone | NA | NA | 0% | 0% | 0 days | 25.13 days | $0.00 | 0 hrs |
| 8 | Research | Mon 10/1/07 | NA | 57% | 0% | 8.08 days | 6.17 days | $4,299.49 | 66 hrs |
| 9 | Market size | Mon 10/1/07 | Fri 10/5/07 | 100% | 0% | 5 days | 0 days | $2,400.00 | 40 hrs |
| 10 | Competing pro | Fri 10/5/07 | NA | 50% | 0% | 1.5 days | 1.5 days | $724.49 | 12 hrs |
| 11 | Competing cor | Thu 10/11/07 | NA | 18% | 0% | 0.18 wks | 0.83 wks | $1,175.00 | 14 hrs |
| 12 | Content | NA | NA | 0% | 0% | 0 days | 13 days | $0.00 | 0 hrs |
| 13 | Develop outlin | NA | NA | 0% | 0% | 0 days | 3 days | $0.00 | 0 hrs |
| 14 | Write narrative | NA | NA | 0% | 0% | 0 wks | 2 wks | $0.00 | 0 hrs |
| 15 | Consultations | NA | NA | 0% | 0% | 0 wks | 1 wk | $0.00 | 0 hrs |
| 16 | Revisions | NA | NA | 0% | 0% | 0 days | 3 days | $0.00 | 0 hrs |
| 17 | Financials | NA | NA | 0% | 0% | 0 days | 9 days | $0.00 | 0 hrs |
| 18 | Develop finan | NA | NA | 0% | 0% | 0 wks | 1 wk | $0.00 | 0 hrs |
| 19 | Comprehensiv | NA | NA | 0% | 0% | 0 days | 3 days | $0.00 | 0 hrs |
| 20 | Corrections | NA | NA | 0% | 0% | 0 days | 1 day | $0.00 | 0 hrs |
| 21 | Completion | NA | NA | 0% | 0% | 0 days | 8 days | $0.00 | 0 hrs |
| 22 | Finalize draft | NA | NA | 0% | 0% | 0 days | 8 days | $0.00 | 0 hrs |
| 23 | Submit to incul | NA | NA | 0% | 0% | 0 days | 0 days | $0.00 | 0 hrs |

**Figure 11.16** The Tracking table provides more actual information.

- **Variance table (see Figure 11.17).** This table, which you first saw in Figure 11.2, shows the calculated start date variance (*Start Var.*) and finish date variance (*Finish Var.*) for each task.

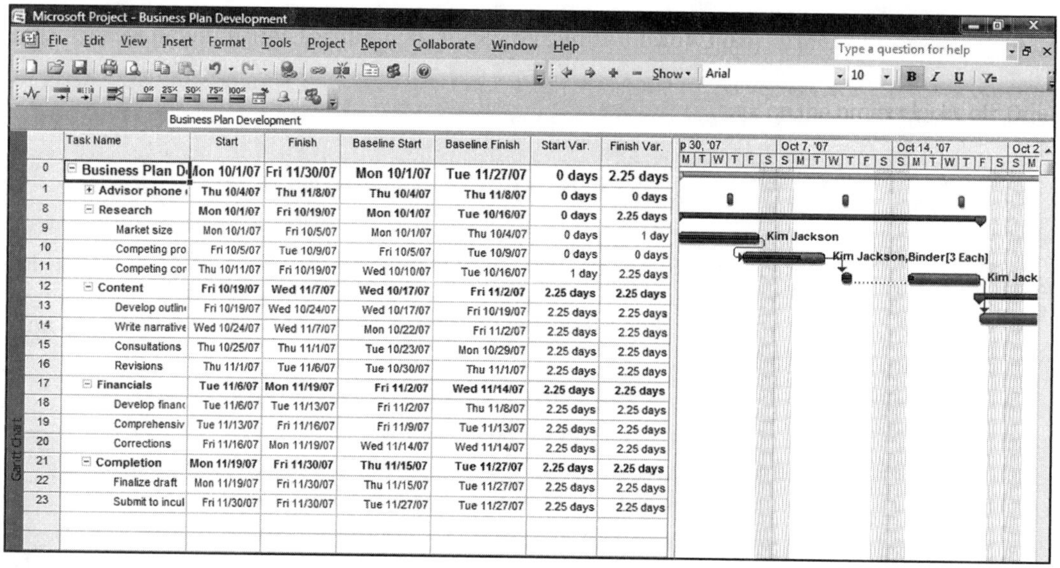


| | Task Name | Start | Finish | Baseline Start | Baseline Finish | Start Var. | Finish Var. |
|---|---|---|---|---|---|---|---|
| 0 | Business Plan D | Mon 10/1/07 | Fri 11/30/07 | Mon 10/1/07 | Tue 11/27/07 | 0 days | 2.25 days |
| 1 | Advisor phone | Thu 10/4/07 | Thu 11/8/07 | Thu 10/4/07 | Thu 11/8/07 | 0 days | 0 days |
| 8 | Research | Mon 10/1/07 | Fri 10/19/07 | Mon 10/1/07 | Tue 10/16/07 | 0 days | 2.25 days |
| 9 | Market size | Mon 10/1/07 | Fri 10/5/07 | Mon 10/1/07 | Thu 10/4/07 | 0 days | 1 day |
| 10 | Competing pro | Fri 10/5/07 | Tue 10/9/07 | Fri 10/5/07 | Tue 10/9/07 | 0 days | 0 days |
| 11 | Competing cor | Thu 10/11/07 | Fri 10/19/07 | Wed 10/10/07 | Tue 10/16/07 | 1 day | 2.25 days |
| 12 | Content | Fri 10/19/07 | Wed 11/7/07 | Wed 10/17/07 | Fri 11/2/07 | 2.25 days | 2.25 days |
| 13 | Develop outlin | Fri 10/19/07 | Wed 10/24/07 | Wed 10/17/07 | Fri 10/19/07 | 2.25 days | 2.25 days |
| 14 | Write narrative | Wed 10/24/07 | Wed 11/7/07 | Mon 10/22/07 | Fri 11/2/07 | 2.25 days | 2.25 days |
| 15 | Consultations | Thu 10/25/07 | Thu 11/1/07 | Tue 10/23/07 | Mon 10/29/07 | 2.25 days | 2.25 days |
| 16 | Revisions | Thu 11/1/07 | Tue 11/6/07 | Tue 10/30/07 | Thu 11/1/07 | 2.25 days | 2.25 days |
| 17 | Financials | Tue 11/6/07 | Mon 11/19/07 | Fri 11/2/07 | Wed 11/14/07 | 2.25 days | 2.25 days |
| 18 | Develop finan | Tue 11/6/07 | Tue 11/13/07 | Fri 11/2/07 | Thu 11/8/07 | 2.25 days | 2.25 days |
| 19 | Comprehensiv | Tue 11/13/07 | Fri 11/16/07 | Fri 11/9/07 | Tue 11/13/07 | 2.25 days | 2.25 days |
| 20 | Corrections | Fri 11/16/07 | Mon 11/19/07 | Wed 11/14/07 | Wed 11/14/07 | 2.25 days | 2.25 days |
| 21 | Completion | Mon 11/19/07 | Fri 11/30/07 | Thu 11/15/07 | Tue 11/27/07 | 2.25 days | 2.25 days |
| 22 | Finalize draft | Mon 11/19/07 | Fri 11/30/07 | Thu 11/15/07 | Tue 11/27/07 | 2.25 days | 2.25 days |
| 23 | Submit to incul | Fri 11/30/07 | Fri 11/30/07 | Tue 11/27/07 | Tue 11/27/07 | 2.25 days | 2.25 days |

**Figure 11.17** See task schedule variances in the Variance table.

- **Work table (see Figure 11.18).** The Work table zeroes in on *Baseline, Actual, Variance,* and *Remaining* hours of work. It also shows the *% W. Comp.* (% Work Complete) for each task.

| | Task Name | Work | Baseline | Variance | Actual | Remaining | % W. Comp. |
|---|---|---|---|---|---|---|---|
| 0 | ⊟ Business Plan Devel | 490 hrs | 482 hrs | 8 hrs | 66 hrs | 424 hrs | 13% |
| 1 | ⊞ Advisor phone cons | 18 hrs | 18 hrs | 0 hrs | 0 hrs | 18 hrs | 0% |
| 8 | ⊟ Research | 144 hrs | 136 hrs | 8 hrs | 66 hrs | 78 hrs | 46% |
| 9 | Market size | 40 hrs | 32 hrs | 8 hrs | 40 hrs | 0 hrs | 100% |
| 10 | Competing products | 24 hrs | 24 hrs | 0 hrs | 12 hrs | 12 hrs | 50% |
| 11 | Competing compani | 80 hrs | 80 hrs | 0 hrs | 14 hrs | 66 hrs | 18% |
| 12 | ⊟ Content | 208 hrs | 208 hrs | 0 hrs | 0 hrs | 208 hrs | 0% |
| 13 | Develop outline | 24 hrs | 24 hrs | 0 hrs | 0 hrs | 24 hrs | 0% |
| 14 | Write narrative | 80 hrs | 80 hrs | 0 hrs | 0 hrs | 80 hrs | 0% |
| 15 | Consultations | 80 hrs | 80 hrs | 0 hrs | 0 hrs | 80 hrs | 0% |
| 16 | Revisions | 24 hrs | 24 hrs | 0 hrs | 0 hrs | 24 hrs | 0% |
| 17 | ⊟ Financials | 72 hrs | 72 hrs | 0 hrs | 0 hrs | 72 hrs | 0% |
| 18 | Develop financials | 40 hrs | 40 hrs | 0 hrs | 0 hrs | 40 hrs | 0% |
| 19 | Comprehensive rev | 24 hrs | 24 hrs | 0 hrs | 0 hrs | 24 hrs | 0% |
| 20 | Corrections | 8 hrs | 8 hrs | 0 hrs | 0 hrs | 8 hrs | 0% |
| 21 | ⊟ Completion | 48 hrs | 48 hrs | 0 hrs | 0 hrs | 48 hrs | 0% |
| 22 | Finalize draft | 48 hrs | 48 hrs | 0 hrs | 0 hrs | 48 hrs | 0% |
| 23 | Submit to incubator | 0 hrs | 0 hrs | 0 hrs | 0 hrs | 0 hrs | 0% |

**Figure 11.18**  See work variances in the Work table.

The values for summary tasks are calculated based on the tracking date entered for detail tasks.

If you want to view only the field data for the tables discussed here, you can change to the Task Sheet view, which omits the right chart portion.

## Tracking Gantt View

The Tracking Gantt view provides the best graphical view of project progress. To display this view, click **View** and then click **Tracking Gantt**. As shown in Figure 11.19, the Gantt bars for the Tracking Gantt view are divided. The top portion of the bar shows the actual (when solid) or current (when shaded) schedule for the task, while the gray bottom

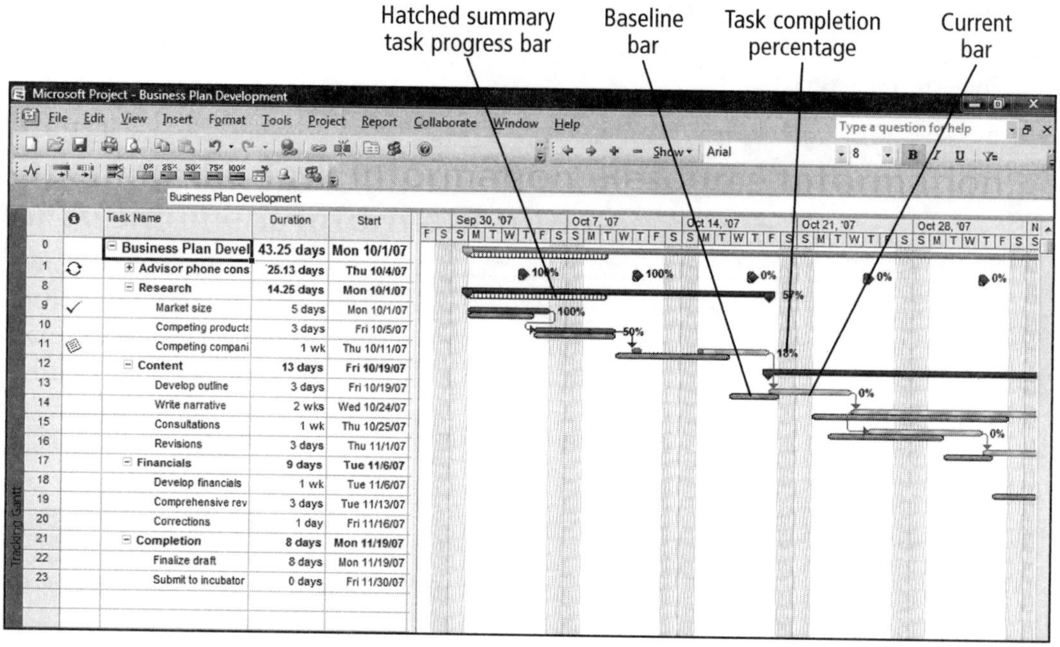

Hatched summary    Baseline    Task completion    Current
task progress bar    bar    percentage    bar

**Figure 11.19** The Tracking Gantt view provides a graphical view of progress versus the baseline plan.

portion shows the task's baseline schedule. A current or actual bar that's longer than the baseline bar means that the task took longer than scheduled. A current or actual bar that's shifted to the right of the baseline bar means that the task occurred or is now scheduled to occur later than originally planned; a left shift indicates an earlier schedule.

Hatched progress bars illustrate the calculated completion percentages for summary tasks; the completion percentage for each task appears to the right of its Gantt bar(s).

 Choose **View, Tracking Gantt** to display a view that charts current or actual task schedules versus the baseline.

# Working with Cost Information

Ensuring that resources complete work and the project deliverables arrive on time may absorb the majority of a project manager's attention, but budget management must receive attention, as well, for many projects.

Sometimes new Project users get too ambitious with regard to attempting to track everything in Project the first time around. When you initially begin to use Project to track cost information, you also should track project costs using another trusted method. If that's the case for you, you can export cost information from Project for use in another application; Chapter 14 covers how to export information. Keep in mind that because Project rounds certain values, it doesn't offer the level of precision provided by a company accounting system. Project can be used for overall budgeting and tracking purposes but not for real accounting.

## Viewing Costs in the Cost Table

Whether you're working in the Gantt Chart, Tracking Gantt, or Task Sheet view, you can display the Cost table to view actual costs versus baseline costs, as well as cost variances. Project calculates these values on a task-by-task basis based on the task completion percentages (and therefore hours of work completed) that you track.

To display this table, choose **View, Table:** *Table Name,* **Cost,** or right-click the **Select All** button and then click **Cost.**

## Cutting Back Costs

When you see that actual costs exceed the amounts you budgeted, you must evaluate whether you need to take action to reduce costs going forward. If you allowed for cost overruns by being conservative in planning the budget or if the quantity and quality of work being delivered warrants the extra expense, then action might not be required. You can consider a number of different strategies for reducing project costs, and Project can help by recalculating cost information based on changes that you make. Try these techniques when you need to reduce the project's budget:

- **Target expensive tasks.** Identify the more expensive uncompleted tasks (you can look at the *Total Cost* field in the Cost table shown in Figure 11.20, for example) and see if you can decrease the scheduled work for them or negotiate a more favorable fee or hourly rate. Then reduce the task duration in Gantt Chart view or change the resource's *Std. Rate* field entry in the Resource Sheet accordingly.

- **Substitute less expensive resources.** As when you were fine-tuning during the planning phase, you can continue to make resource substitutions as part of executing and controlling the project. If you need to remove a more expensive resource and assign a less expensive one, use the same techniques as described in the section "Changing Assignments" in Chapter 10.

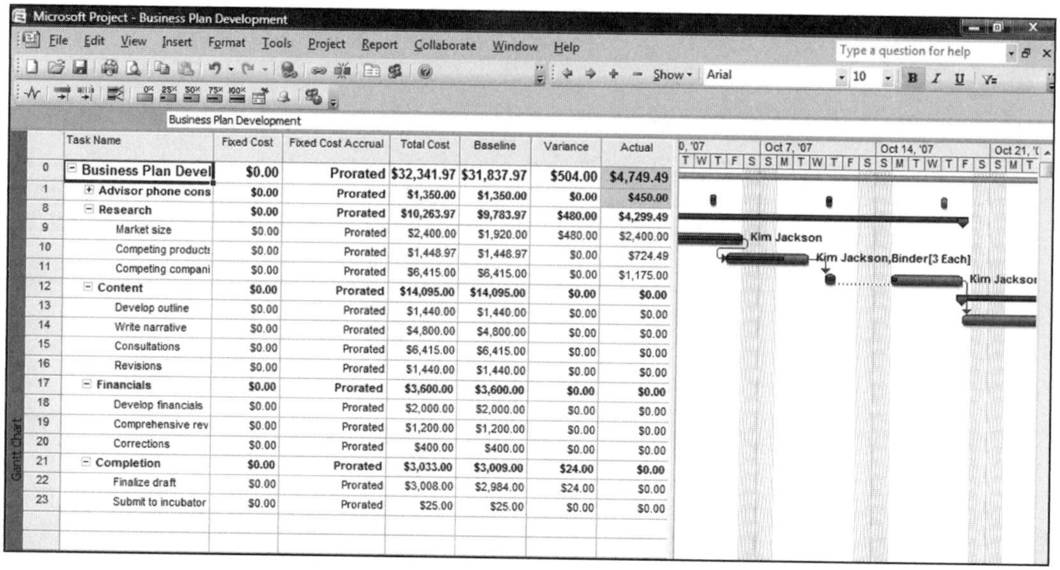

| | Task Name | Fixed Cost | Fixed Cost Accrual | Total Cost | Baseline | Variance | Actual |
|---|---|---|---|---|---|---|---|
| 0 | Business Plan Devel | $0.00 | Prorated | $32,341.97 | $31,837.97 | $504.00 | $4,749.49 |
| 1 | Advisor phone cons | $0.00 | Prorated | $1,350.00 | $1,350.00 | $0.00 | $450.00 |
| 8 | Research | $0.00 | Prorated | $10,263.97 | $9,783.97 | $480.00 | $4,299.49 |
| 9 | Market size | $0.00 | Prorated | $2,400.00 | $1,920.00 | $480.00 | $2,400.00 |
| 10 | Competing products | $0.00 | Prorated | $1,448.97 | $1,448.97 | $0.00 | $724.49 |
| 11 | Competing compani | $0.00 | Prorated | $6,415.00 | $6,415.00 | $0.00 | $1,175.00 |
| 12 | Content | $0.00 | Prorated | $14,095.00 | $14,095.00 | $0.00 | $0.00 |
| 13 | Develop outline | $0.00 | Prorated | $1,440.00 | $1,440.00 | $0.00 | $0.00 |
| 14 | Write narrative | $0.00 | Prorated | $4,800.00 | $4,800.00 | $0.00 | $0.00 |
| 15 | Consultations | $0.00 | Prorated | $6,415.00 | $6,415.00 | $0.00 | $0.00 |
| 16 | Revisions | $0.00 | Prorated | $1,440.00 | $1,440.00 | $0.00 | $0.00 |
| 17 | Financials | $0.00 | Prorated | $3,600.00 | $3,600.00 | $0.00 | $0.00 |
| 18 | Develop financials | $0.00 | Prorated | $2,000.00 | $2,000.00 | $0.00 | $0.00 |
| 19 | Comprehensive rev | $0.00 | Prorated | $1,200.00 | $1,200.00 | $0.00 | $0.00 |
| 20 | Corrections | $0.00 | Prorated | $400.00 | $400.00 | $0.00 | $0.00 |
| 21 | Completion | $0.00 | Prorated | $3,033.00 | $3,009.00 | $24.00 | $0.00 |
| 22 | Finalize draft | $0.00 | Prorated | $3,008.00 | $2,984.00 | $24.00 | $0.00 |
| 23 | Submit to incubator | $0.00 | Prorated | $25.00 | $25.00 | $0.00 | $0.00 |

**Figure 11.20** Redisplay the Cost table to compare baseline (budgeted) versus actual costs for completed work.

- **Ask the outside vendor to substitute a resource with a lower rate.** If you're working with an outside vendor for which you've set up multiple cost tables because the vendor offers multiple individuals with different skill and experience levels, you can ask the vendor to help you conserve costs by using a less costly individual for some tasks. For example, if you're working with a legal firm, see if more tasks can be handled by an associate rather than a full partner. This technique can save tens of dollars per hour of work. See "Using a Different Cost Table for an Assignment" in Chapter 8 to see how to apply the lower rates to affected assignments once you have the vendor's agreement.
- **Cut deliverables and tasks.** Perhaps the most drastic measure to pursue for a project running way over budget is to revisit overall expectations for the schedule and deliverables. If the stakeholders agree, you may need to eliminate some of the deliverables and tasks from the project plan to set them aside and return to them later as part of a new project with a new budget.

## Authorizing Overtime

A task may require more work than you originally anticipated. If the schedule is more crucial than the budget, you may want to authorize hours of overtime work for the resource. This enables Project to assign additional hours of work for the resource on a particular date and to use the resource's Ovt. Rate (entered in the Resource Sheet) to calculate the cost of the authorized overtime work. You authorize overtime in the Task Entry view using the following steps:

1. Click **View** and then click **More Views**.

2. Click **Task Entry** in the Views list and then click **Apply**.

3. Scroll the top pane of the view and click the task for which you want to authorize overtime. Information about the task appears in the lower pane.

4. Right-click the lower pane and click **Resource Work** in the shortcut menu. The fields of information in the lower pane change.

5. Select the **Ovt. Work** field entry for the resource for which you want to authorize overtime, type in the number of hours of authorized overtime, and then click **OK** in the pane (see Figure 11.21).

6. Click **Window** and then click **Remove Split** to close the bottom pane of the Task Entry view.

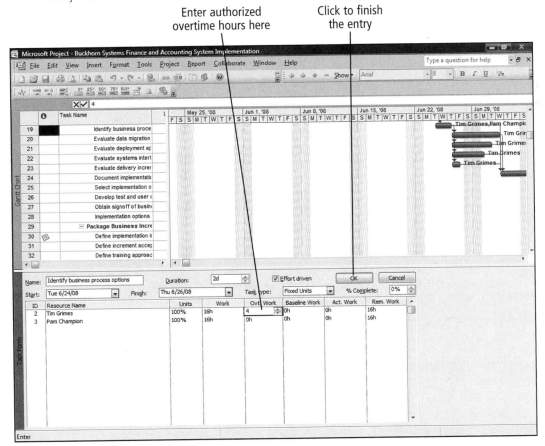

**Figure 11.21** Use the Resource *Work* fields in the bottom pane of the Task Entry view to authorize overtime.

You can change to the Task Usage or Resource Usage view and select the assignment that you just changed to view the impact of the authorized overtime on the resource's schedule for the task.

 When you authorize overtime for a task whose schedule already falls within the working hours for the current day, Project shortens the duration for the task, which may or may not be what you intend. For example, if you have a 1d task under the Standard calendar, 8h of work are calculated for the task when you assign the resource. If you then authorize 8h of overtime work for that assignment, Project reduces the task's duration to 0 and makes it a milestone, even though 8h of overtime work are still assigned. So, watch out for the impact of assigning overtime on your schedule.

## Overriding an Actual Cost

Sometimes the actual costs for a resource's assignment don't reflect the final cost for a resource's work on a task. For example, you may agree to pay an external resource more for an assignment if the resource incurred unexpected costs in completing the assignment (added travel or materials expenses, for example). Or, your costs for completing the assignment may not have increased even when the task took more time to complete. In situations like these, you can override the actual cost value for the assignment to make sure the final project costs reflect the real final expenses. Use the Task Entry view, again, to make this change:

1. Mark the task as 100% complete. Project won't calculate a final actual cost to override until the task is complete.

2. Click **View** and then click **More Views**.

3. Click **Task Entry** in the Views list and then click **Apply**.

4. Scroll the top pane of the view and click the task for which you want to override a calculated assignment cost. Information about the task appears in the lower pane.

5. Right-click the lower pane and click **Resource Cost** in the shortcut menu. The files of information in the lower pane change.

6. Select the **Act. Cost** field entry for the resource for which you want to enter a different actual cost, type the cost, and then click **OK** in the pane (see Figure 11.22).

7. Click **Window** and then click **Remove Split** to close the bottom pane of Task Entry view.

Enter actual
cost here

Click to finish
the entry

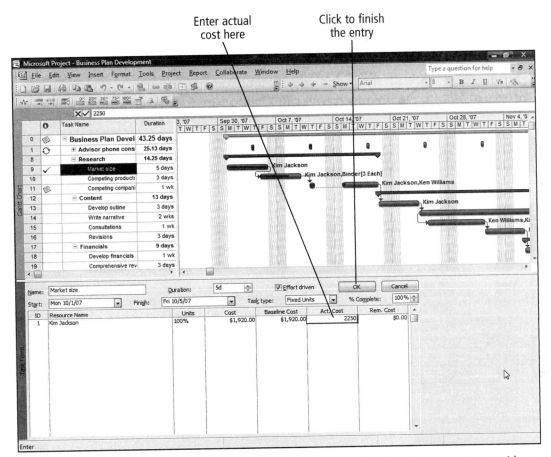

**Figure 11.22** Use the Resource *Cost* fields in the bottom pane of the Task Entry view to override an actual assignment cost.

## Accelerating the Finish Date

Of course, if you're asked to increase the project scope or deliverables or accelerate the project finish date, those actions will typically add cost to the finished project plan. It will be up to you to choose the most cost-effective and achievable way to accelerate the project finish, also called crashing the project, again using Project to test the impact of various approaches:

- **Authorize overtime.** If your organization allows you discretion in asking resources to work overtime, you can authorize overtime work for more assignments. Focus on tasks on the critical path, and make sure that the authorized overtime has a positive impact on the task duration; in other words, it may not be the best choice to add overtime for one resource assigned to a task if you can't do so for other resources, because the task would still have a later finish date.

- **Add more work resources.** Adding more resources into the project plan, particularly to tasks on the critical path, will reduce the schedule. However, this method is likely to add the most cost, as well as increasing the complexity of managing the ongoing project. You'll suddenly have more resources to deal with, and you'll need to integrate the efforts of those resources into the ongoing activities of the project.

- **Cut tasks and deliverables.** As when reducing costs, this remains an alternative for reducing the project schedule when the project is running long. With stakeholder approval, you can eliminate some deliverables and tasks with the intent of returning to them under the auspices of a new project, if the need for that work continues in the organization.

# Chapter Review

This chapter ushered you into the executing and controlling phases of project management and presented some of Project's tools for assisting you with those responsibilities. You learned how to save the baseline before work begins for later tracking purposes, as well as how to clear the baseline or use an interim plan. You learned to use the Tracking toolbar and other methods for tracking work, as well as how to specify Actual Start and Actual Finish Dates for a task, how to automatically update or reschedule work, and how to work with a single resource's work. You moved on to learn about some of the ways you can view information about project progress. Finally, you looked at methods for viewing, cutting back, and overriding costs; authorizing overtime; and reducing the duration for a project that's running behind.

## Review Questions

Write your answers to the following questions on a sheet of paper.

1. Saving the _____ saves initial information about the project plan for later comparison.

2. True or False: You can save more than one baseline.

3. The _____ toolbar includes buttons for marking work as complete on tasks.

4. Use the _____ dialog box to enter Actual Start and Finish dates for tasks.

5. True or False: Project only reschedules the entire task when you use the Reschedule Work button.

6. The _____ dialog box shows baseline, actual, and variance data after you save starting information and begin tracking work.

7. Display different _____ in the left portion of the Gantt Chart view to see various fields with calculated tracking information.

8. The _____ view displays two Gantt bars for each task: one for the original schedule and another for the current or actual schedule.

9. Name at least one way to reduce project costs.

10. Use the _____ view to authorize overtime or override an actual assignment cost.

## Projects

 To see the solutions file created by completing the projects in this chapter, go to www.courseptr.com, click the **Downloads** link in the navigation bar at the top, type **Microsoft Office Project 2007 Survival Guide** in the search text box, and then click **Search Downloads**.

### Project 1

1. Open the file named *Site Search Review* that you worked with in the projects for Chapter 10.

2. Save the file as *Site Search Track*.

 Create a folder named *PSG Exercises* in your *Documents* or *My Documents* folder and save your exercise practice files there.

3. Click **View**, point to **Table: Entry**, and then click **Variance**. Or, right-click the **Select All** button and click **Variance**.

4. Drag the divider bar between the two sides of the view to the right so that you can see the *Baseline Start* and *Baseline Finish* fields.

5. Click **Tools**, point to **Tracking**, and then click **Set Baseline**.

6. Leave the default settings in the Set Baseline dialog box selected and click **OK**.

7. Observe how change highlighting highlights the new information in the *Baseline Start* and *Baseline Finish* fields.

8. Click **Tools**, point to **Tracking**, and then click **Clear Baseline**.

9. Leave the default settings in the Clear Baseline dialog box selected and click **OK**.

10. Notice that the *Baseline Start* and *Baseline Finish* fields now read NA again.

11. Click **Tools**, point to **Tracking**, and then click **Set Baseline**. Click **OK**. This resaves the baseline.

12. Click **View**, point to **Table: Variance**, and then click **Entry**. Or, right-click the **Select All** button and click **Entry**.

13. Click **Project** and then click **Project Information**.

14. Click the **Statistics** button. Notice that the dialog box now shows Baseline information for Start, Finish, Duration, Work, and Cost.

15. Click **Close** to close the Project Statistics dialog box.

16. Save your changes to the file and keep it open for the next project.

## *Project 2*

1. Click **View**, point to **Toolbars**, and then click **Tracking**. Or, right-click any toolbar and click **Tracking**.

2. Click *task 2*, **Infrastructure**, in the task sheet portion of the view.

3. Click the **100% Complete** button on the Tracking toolbar.

4. Click *task 3*, **Space**, in the task sheet portion of the view.

5. Click the **100% Complete** button on the Tracking toolbar.

6. Click *task 4*, **Parking**, in the task sheet portion of the view.

7. Click **Tools**, point to **Tracking**, and then click **Update Tasks**. Or, click the **Update Tasks** button on the Tracking toolbar.

8. Enter **25** in the % Complete text box. In the Actual section of the dialog box, specify an actual start date of **2/4/09** by typing the date in the Start text box or using the drop-down calendar. Click **OK** to close the dialog box and apply the completion percentage and actual start date.

9. Click **Tools**, point to **Tracking**, and then click **Update Project**.

10. Specify a status date of **2/6/09** by entering the date in the Update Work As Complete Through text box in the upper-right corner or by using the drop-down calendar. Leave the rest of the options as is and then click **OK**.

11. Click **View** and then click **Task Usage**.

12. Double-click the Jane Black assignment under *task 5*, **Expansion**.

13. Click the **Tracking** tab in the Assignment Information dialog box. Change the % Work Complete text box entry to **100** and then click **OK**.

14. Click **View** and then click **Gantt Chart**. Notice that the progress bar for *task 5*, **Expansion**, now expands beyond the 2/6/09 status date specified in Step 10 based on the individual resource assignment that you marked as completed.

15. Save your changes to the file and keep it open for the next project.

## *Project 3*

1. Click the **Project Statistics** button on the Tracking toolbar.

2. Review the information that appears in the Project Statistics dialog box. Note that the Current Finish date now is two days later than the Baseline Finish, with a Variance of two days (2d). Note also that the Current Duration is two days longer than the Baseline Duration, while the Current and Baseline Work and Cost amounts remain the same.

3. Click **OK** to close the Project Statistics dialog box.

4. Click **View** and then click **Tracking Gantt**.

5. If needed, scroll the chart portion of the view to display the Gantt bars. Notice the scheduling changes that have resulted in the work tracking so far.

6. Choose **View, More Views**. Click **Task Entry** in the Views list of the More Views dialog box and then click **Apply**.

7. In the top pane of the view, click *task 2*, **Infrastructure**.

8. Right-click the bottom pane and click **Resource Cost**.

9. Click the Act. Cost column entry for the Smith Todd resource, type **2000**, and click **OK**.

10. Click **Window** and then click **Remove Split** to close the bottom pane of the Task Entry view.

11. Click **View**, point to **Table: Entry**, and then click **Cost**. Or, right-click the **Select All** button and click **Cost**.

12. Observe how change highlighting shades cells in the *Total Cost* field based on the change you made in Step 9. Compare those *Total Cost* field entries with the corresponding *Baseline* field entries.

13. Click **View**, point to **Table: Cost**, and then click **Summary**. Or, right-click the **Select All** button and click **Summary**.

14. Scroll the left side of the view to see all the Summary table information.

15. Click **View**, point to **Table: Summary**, and then click **Entry**. Or, right-click the **Select All** button and click **Entry**.

16. Click the **Project Statistics** button on the Tracking toolbar.

17. Note that the Current Cost amount is less than the Baseline Cost amount, and then click **OK** to close the Project Statistics dialog box.

18. Save your changes to the file and close the file.

# PART FOUR

# Reviewing and Sharing Results

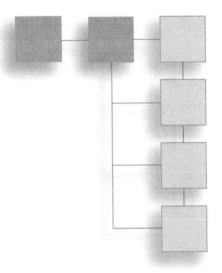

# CHAPTER 12

# USING AND PRINTING VIEWS

This Chapter Teaches You How To:

- Find and display any available view
- Check out the new and improved Calendar view
- Control information in a sheet by filtering or sorting
- Zoom or adjust the Gantt Chart timescale
- Change formatting for Gantt bars
- Build a custom view and its components
- Make a custom view available for all your projects
- Set up a printout and print

Throughout the phases of managing your project—from circulating a hard copy of the preliminary plan to stakeholders for approval to the point when you're closing down the project and archiving the final documentation—you'll need to be able to provide the project information in hard copy when required. In working through the last few chapters, you've seen the many views Microsoft Office Project 2007 offers and how specialized the information in each view can be. This chapter gives you even more information about working with views, including finding the view you need, adjusting what the view shows, creating your own custom view (and supporting elements), and finally sending what you need to the printer. Don't yawn, folks. You'll appreciate what this chapter has to teach you when crunch time comes.

# Finding the View You Need

Because you can't get far in building your project plan without changing views, you've already worked quite a bit with selecting a view from the View menu. The top of the View menu lists eight views by default, with the first five being task-related views (Calendar, Gantt Chart, Network Diagram, Task Usage, and Tracking Gantt) and the next three resource-related views (Resource Graph, Resource Sheet, and Resource Usage). To change to any of those views, click the **View** menu and then click the view name.

During the process of creating a custom view, described later in this chapter, you have the option of adding your custom view to the View menu.

Project includes even more views, though, and it's important to know how to find them so that you can see, change, and print the information you need. (Remember, Project always prints the current view.) If you click **View, More Views**, the More Views dialog box shown in Figure 12.1, appears. You can use this dialog box to open one of the two dozen views included in Project by default. Click the view to use in the **Views** list and then click **Apply**.

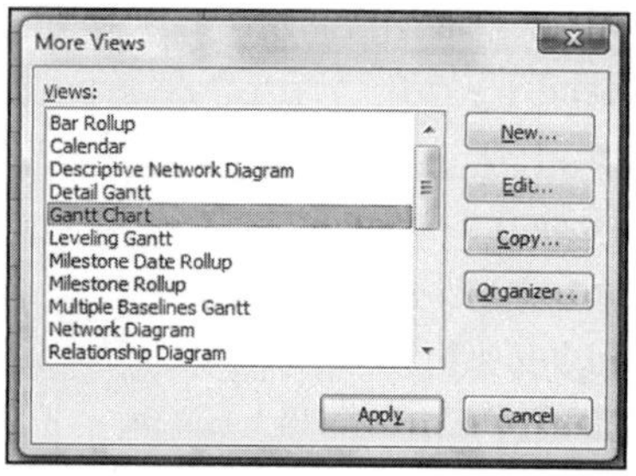

**Figure 12.1** Open, create, and edit views in the More Views dialog box.

Here are the predefined views you'll find in Project:

- **Bar Rollup, Milestone Date Rollup, and Milestone Rollup.** Use these views after you run the Rollup_Formatting macro that comes with Project to roll up the Gantt bars for subtasks onto the summary task Gantt bar. Each view provides slightly different formatting for the rolled up tasks.

You can access the default macros that come with Project 2007, such as the Rollup_Formatting macro, by using the **Tools, Macro, Macros** command (shortcut: **Alt+F8**).

- **Calendar.** This single-pane view displays tasks on a monthly calendar, using a bar and label to indicate each task duration. The next section covers this view in a bit more detail.

- **Descriptive Network Diagram.** Displays a flowchart-like diagram of tasks, such as the Network Diagram view described later, but the nodes in the Descriptive Network Diagram view offer slightly different information, such as identifying the resource(s) assigned to the task.

- **Detail Gantt.** In this variation of the Gantt Chart view, the task sheet includes delay information and the Gantt bars indicate slack time and any task slippage (a delay in a task's schedule since you saved the baseline). Figure 12.2 shows the Detail Gantt view.

- **Gantt Chart.** This is the default view in Project, showing the task sheet at the left and the chart portion with Gantt bars at the right.

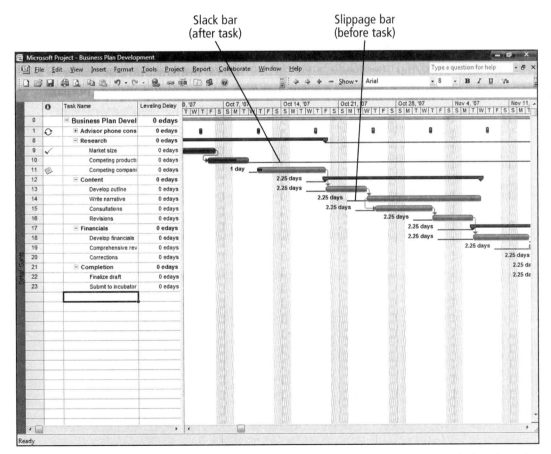

**Figure 12.2** The Detail Gantt view illustrates slack and slippage for another way to look at how the schedule has evolved.

- **Leveling Gantt.** In this variation of the Gantt Chart view, the task sheet includes a *Leveling Delay* column to indicate any tasks that Project delays when you use automatic resource leveling (a feature covered in Chapter 10). The Gantt bars are split: the upper bar shows the task's original schedule and the lower bar shows its current schedule.

- **Multiple Baselines Gantt.** This view charts the first three baselines using colored bars on the Gantt chart portion of the view. You can use this view to compare how the project plan has evolved based on the first three baselines you've saved.

- **Network Diagram.** The Network Diagram view displays tasks in a format resembling a flowchart (see Figure 12.3). You can drag to link tasks or right-click a task and click Task Information to adjust the task schedule and resource assignments. The Descriptive Network Diagram view resembles the Network Diagram view; the nodes in the Descriptive Network Diagram view offer slightly different information, such as identifying the resource(s) assigned to the task. The Relationship Diagram shows a more simplified diagram of how tasks flow.

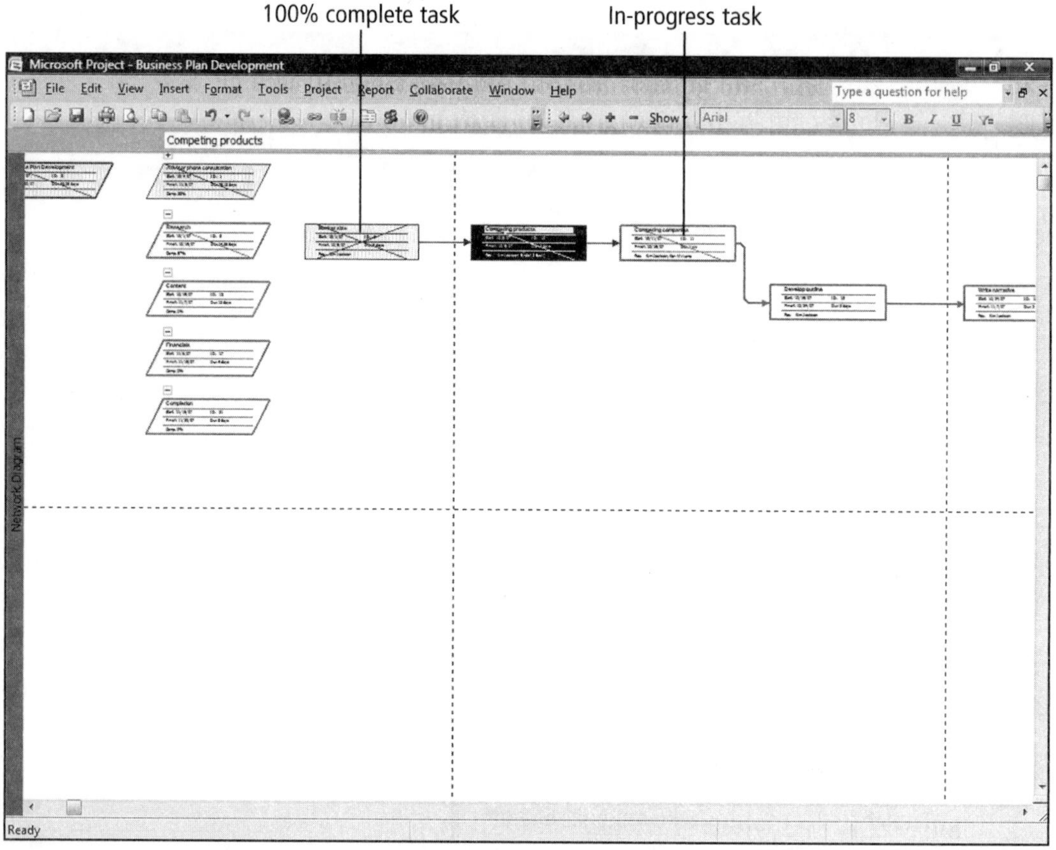

**Figure 12.3** The Network Diagram view gives an idea of task flow.

- **Relationship Diagram.** This view shows a more simplified diagram of how tasks flow.

- **Resource Allocation.** This view presents the Resource Usage view in the upper pane and the Gantt Chart view in the lower pane.

- **Resource Form.** This is a form you use to enter and edit information about a specific resource. It lists all the tasks assigned to that resource, resource cost information, and more.

- **Resource Graph.** This view, which you also worked with in Chapter 10, can graph information about a resource's daily and cumulative costs, scheduled work and cumulative work, overallocated times, percentage of work allocated, and availability.

- **Resource Name Form.** This abbreviated version of the Resource Form lists the resource name and its assigned tasks.

- **Resource Sheet.** Use the fields in this view to add resources to your project plan file, as described in Chapter 7.

- **Resource Usage.** This view, covered in various earlier chapters, combines a resource sheet on the left that identifies the assignments for each resource with a timephased grid on the right that you can use to enter daily actual costs, daily scheduled work and completed work, and more.

- **Task Details Form.** Similar to the Resource Form, this full-screen form displays task scheduling information, constraints, assigned resources, and more.

 You can right-click any timephased grid, chart, or form in Project to open a shortcut menu in which you can modify what the view displays.

- **Task Entry.** This view displays the Gantt Chart in the upper pane and the Task Form in the lower pane. Detail task edits made in the lower pane appear immediately in the Gantt Chart.

- **Task Form.** This form (shown in Figure 12.4) enables you to change the task name, schedule, work completion information, and assigned resources.

- **Task Name Form.** This variation of the Task Details Form view enables you to change the task name and assigned resources.

- **Task Sheet.** This view shows the task sheet at full-screen size rather than in combination with the Gantt Chart or timephased information.

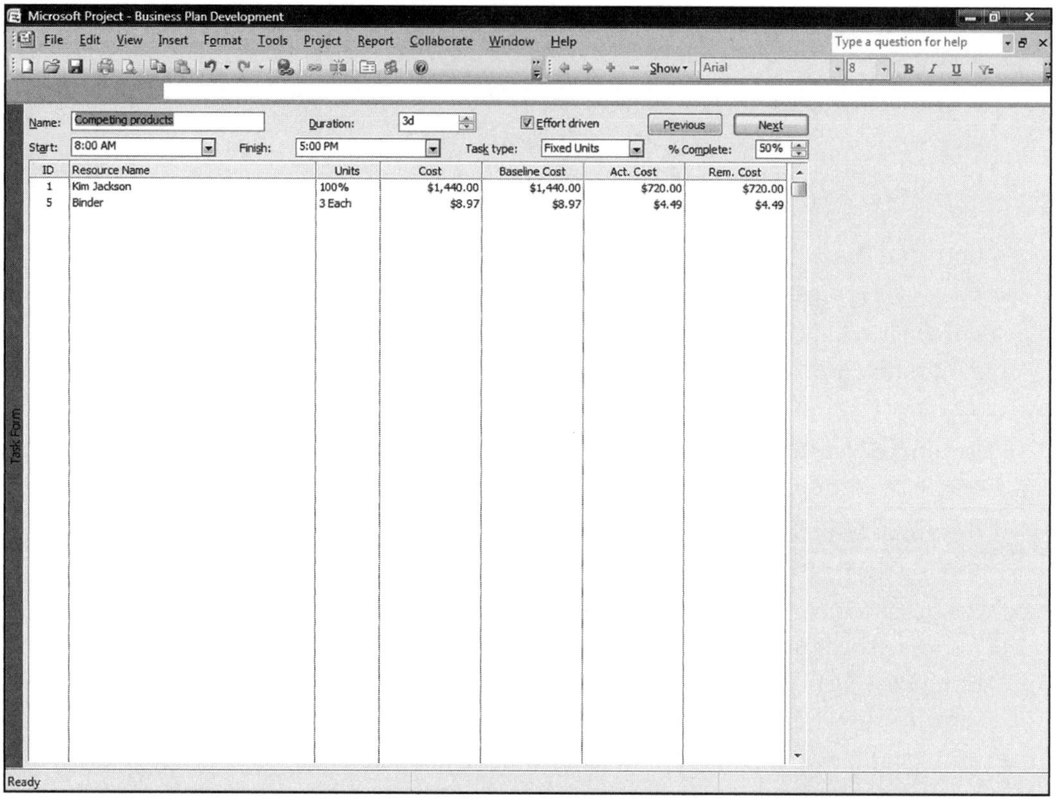

**Figure 12.4** Work with detailed task and assignment information in the Task Form view.

- **Task Usage.** This view groups assignments by task, and you can use the timephased grid at the right to view and enter daily work and cost values.
- **Tracking Gantt.** In the Tracking Gantt view, the Gantt bars are divided, with the lower portion of each bar showing the task's original (baseline) schedule and the upper portion showing the task's current or actual (finished) schedule. You learned more about this view in Chapter 11.

## Looking at the Improved Calendar View

Although the Gantt Chart view does lay out the schedule for tasks along the timescale, many users still prefer to see activities laid out in a more traditional calendar format. To serve these individuals, Project has long offered a Calendar view that by default presents information in a familiar monthly calendar layout. You can display the Calendar view by clicking **View** and then clicking **Calendar**.

Microsoft has made some improvements to the Calendar view in Project 2007. For starters, as shown in Figure 12.5, the task bars have more of a 3D appearance, just as the task bars on the Gantt Chart do.

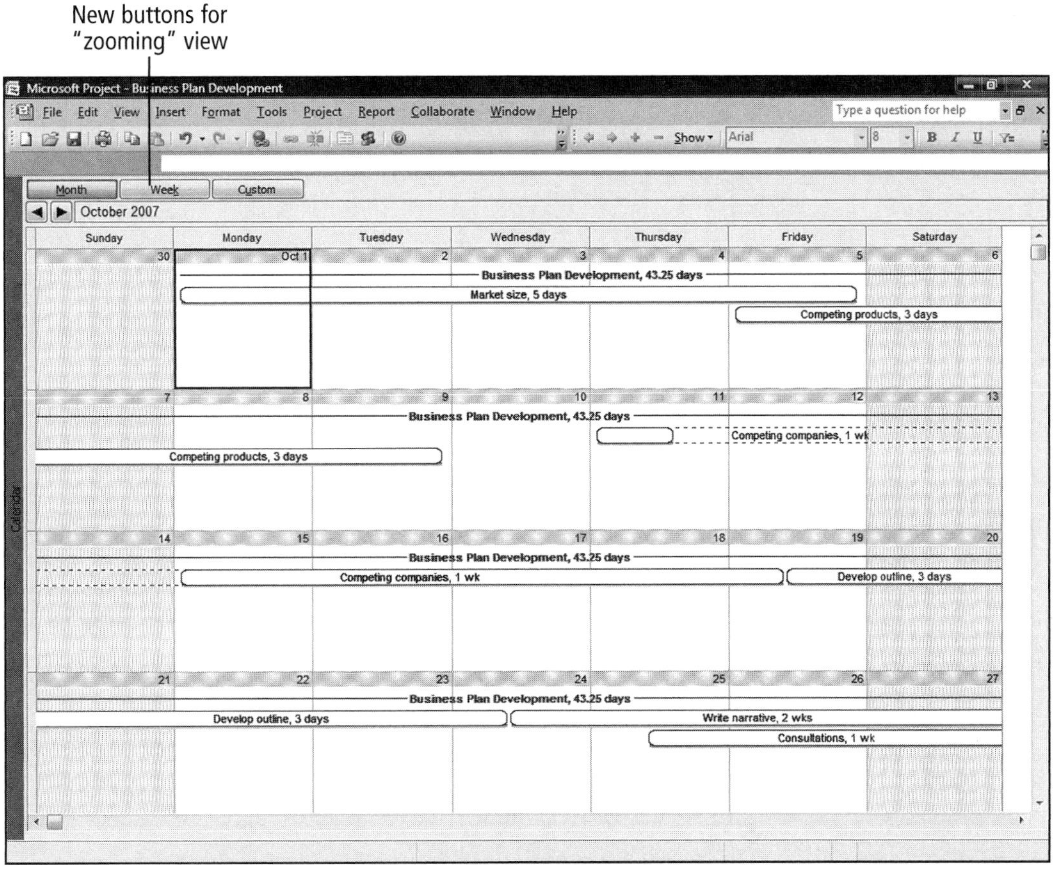

New buttons for "zooming" view

**Figure 12.5** Use a familiar schedule layout in the Calendar view.

Choose **View, Calendar** to change to the Calendar view. Changing the timeframe shown in the Calendar view or any chart portion of a view in Project is also known as *zooming* the view.

The largest improvement in the view appears in the upper-left corner. You can click the **Month** and **Week** buttons to change quickly between viewing the calendar in a monthly format to a weekly format onscreen. If your project plan has a short overall duration with many tasks active on any given day, you might find the weekly calendar quite useful. If you click the new **Custom** button that also appears at the top of the view, Project displays the Zoom dialog box shown in Figure 12.6. Use this dialog box to control the number of weeks or days of information that appear in the calendar. You can leave the **Number of Weeks** option selected and change the value in the accompanying text box to have the calendar display more or fewer weeks. Or, if you want the calendar to display a more specific timeframe, click the **From** option button and use the From and To calendar drop-downs to specify the interval that you want.

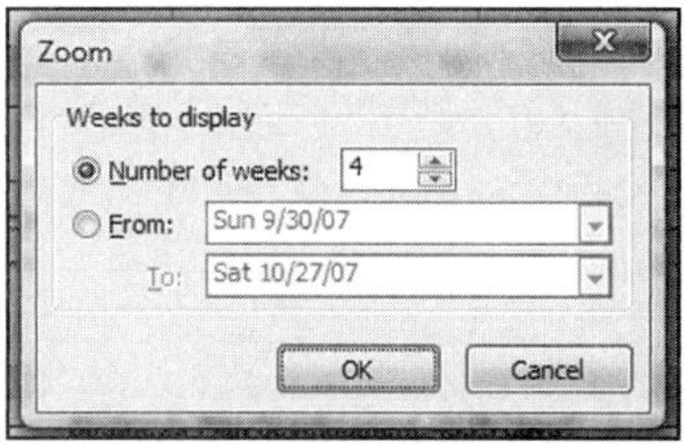

**Figure 12.6**  Zoom to change the number of days or weeks that appear in the Calendar view.

 The Calendar view is a notable exception to the overall behavior that Project generally prints each view as it appears onscreen. Even if you change the Calendar view to show a week at a time onscreen, the view still prints in monthly format. To control the print appearance, you have to use the View tab in the Page Setup dialog box before printing, which is discussed in the later section called "Working with Page Setup Choices."

To see a dialog box that lists the tasks happening on a particular date, right-click the date on the Calendar and click **Go To**. This displays the Tasks Occurring On dialog box, in which you can see the tasks for that date and even double-click a task to open its Task Information dialog box.

## Filtering and Sorting Sheet Data

When you're working with a list of information, you might want to view that information in a different order or eliminate some of the displayed information to see only what you need. That's why you can sort lists of information in Access, Excel, and even Word and why you can filter information in Excel and query information in a database.

Project also gives you the ability to sort or filter information in a sheet. If that information is part of a view that shows Gantt bars, those, too, will appear in the sorted or filtered order. Most often, you'll want to sort and filter information in the simpler sheet views (Resource Sheet and Task Sheet), but sometimes sorting or filtering a view like Gantt Chart can help you see the information you need in a project.

*Sorting* changes the order of the information in a list. In Project, you can sort by up to three fields. Project reorders the task rows or resource rows according to the first field first and then reorders any matches within that sort according to the next field specified. And then, if there are additional matches at that second level, Project reorders those matches according to the third field.

Follow these steps to sort information:

1. Change to the view in which you want to sort information.

2. Choose **Project, Sort** to open the Sort submenu.

3. You can click **By Cost, By Name,** or **By ID** (task ID or resource ID, as shown in the sheet row number) to sort immediately by one of those criteria. To choose another sort field or apply a multi-field sort, click **Sort By** to open the Sort dialog box.

4. Choose the field to sort by from the **Sort By** drop-down list and click either the **Ascending** (A to Z, smallest to largest, or earliest to latest) or **Descending** sort order.

5. Choose additional sort fields and orders as needed using the **Then By** drop-down lists and accompanying order option buttons.

The lower-left corner of the Sort dialog box has a check box named Permanently Renumber Resources (when sorting resources) or Permanently Renumber Tasks (when sorting tasks). If you check this check box, Project renumbers the resource or task ID numbers. While this might be what you want when sorting a list of resources to place them in alphabetical order by name, you almost never want to check the dialog box when sorting tasks because it can make the project links difficult to follow and possibly disrupt some of the chronology. If you use this check box and don't like the result, you can click the Undo button on the Standard toolbar or press Ctrl+Z to undo the damage.

When Keep Outline Structure is checked, Project sorts tasks only within or under each summary. If you want Project to sort all tasks together, ignoring the summary tasks, clear the Keep Outline Structure check box.

6. Click **OK**. Project applies the new sort order to the list. Figure 12.7 shows a list of resources that have been sorted by the *Group* and *Type* fields, along with how the settings for that sort appear in the Sort dialog box.

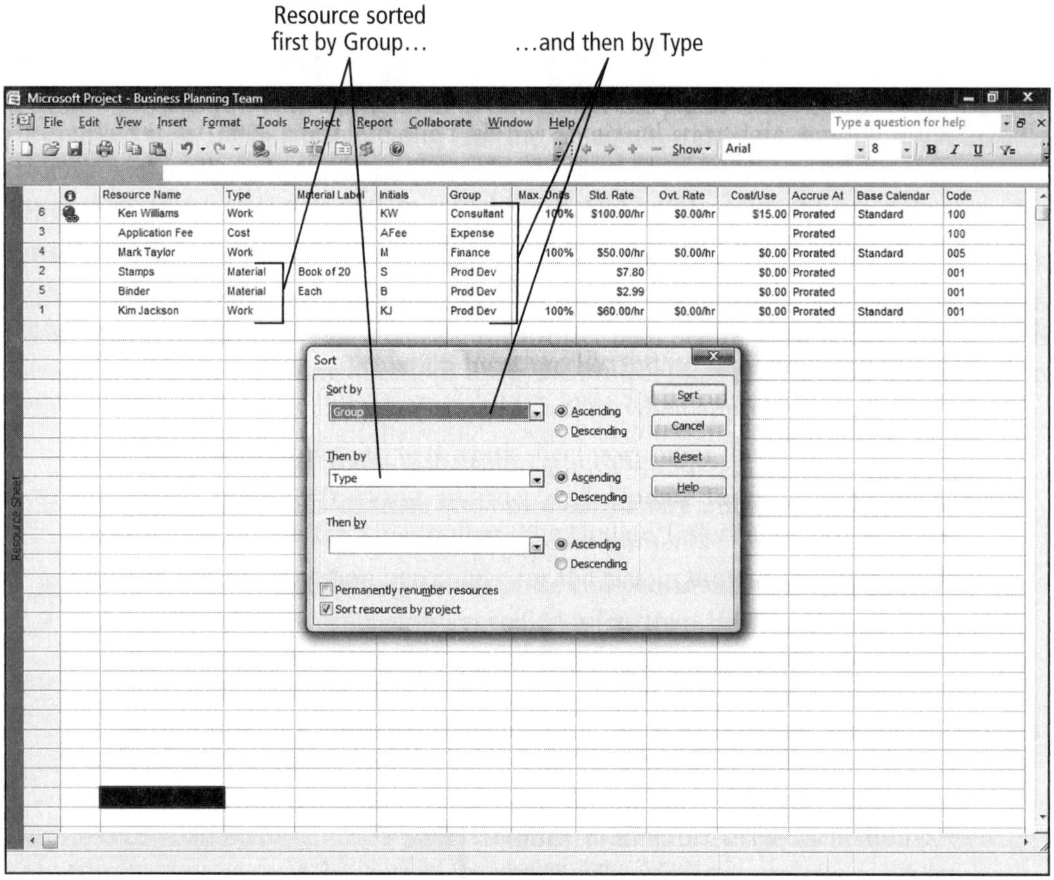

Resource sorted
first by Group...                    ...and then by Type

**Figure 12.7** Sort dialog box settings and the resulting sort.

To remove any sort, choose **Project, Sort, By ID**. This returns the list of resources or tasks to its original order based on the resource or task IDs.

> Project's group feature works similar to applying a sort. Instead of merely rearranging the list of tasks or resources, grouping also adds a summary item that subtotals information within each set of matching tasks or resources. (The group summary task is also called a *roll-up*.) Use the **Project, Group by:** *Group Name* submenu to apply and remove grouping.

Just as a table controls the columns that appear onscreen, *filtering* controls which rows appear onscreen. When you filter the list of tasks or resources in a sheet, you tell Project to display only those rows that match the specified criteria. Think of it this way: Filtering helps you to "look for" the information you want by eliminating from view the information you don't want. You can filter in two main ways in Project:

- **Use a built-in filter.** Project includes a number of filters that limit the list of tasks to match one or more criteria. Click the **Project** menu and then click **Filtered for: *Filter Name*** to see several available filters and a More Filters choice that opens a dialog box where you can apply or create filters. The filters that appear on the Project, Filtered for: *Filter Name* submenu vary depending on whether you're viewing a task- or resource-oriented view. For example, when you are viewing tasks, the filters include Incomplete Tasks, Summary Tasks, and Milestones. When you are viewing resources, the available filters include Cost Overbudget, Group, and Resources-Material. To apply a filter, click the filter in the **Project, Filtered for: *Filter Name*** submenu. If the name of a filter has an ellipsis (…) after it, Project will prompt you to specify additional filter criterion, such as a resource name or dates for task filtering. To remove a filter, choose **Project, Filtered for: *Filter Name*** and then click **All Tasks** or **All Resources**.

- **Use AutoFilter.** The AutoFilter feature enables you to filter by using the table column headings. Choose **Project, Filtered for: *Filter Name*, AutoFilter** or click the **AutoFilter** button on the Formatting toolbar. A drop-down list button appears to the left of each field name. You can click the arrow and then click one of the entries in the list to show only rows which have that entry in the specified field. For example, clicking the **Ken Williams** resource, as shown in Figure 12.8, would filter the Gantt Chart view to show only tasks to which the *Ken Williams* resource has been assigned. After you make a selection from a field AutoFilter drop-down list, the field name turns blue to indicate the field is filtered. You can filter as many fields as needed with AutoFilter to zero in on the data you need. To remove the filtering from a single field, click the AutoFilter drop-down list arrow and click **All**. To turn off AutoFilter overall, choose **Project, Filtered for: *Filter Name*, AutoFilter** or click the **AutoFilter** button again.

You also can filter a task-oriented view to show the tasks for a particular resource using the Resource Management toolbar. Right-click a toolbar and then click **Resource Management** to display that toolbar. Then, click its **Using Resource** button, which has a funnel picture on it. Type or select the resource to use in the **Show Tasks Using** text box of the Using Resources dialog box that appears and click **OK** to apply the filter.

*Sorting* changes the order of tasks or resources in a sheet. *Filtering* hides tasks or resources that don't match specified field criteria.

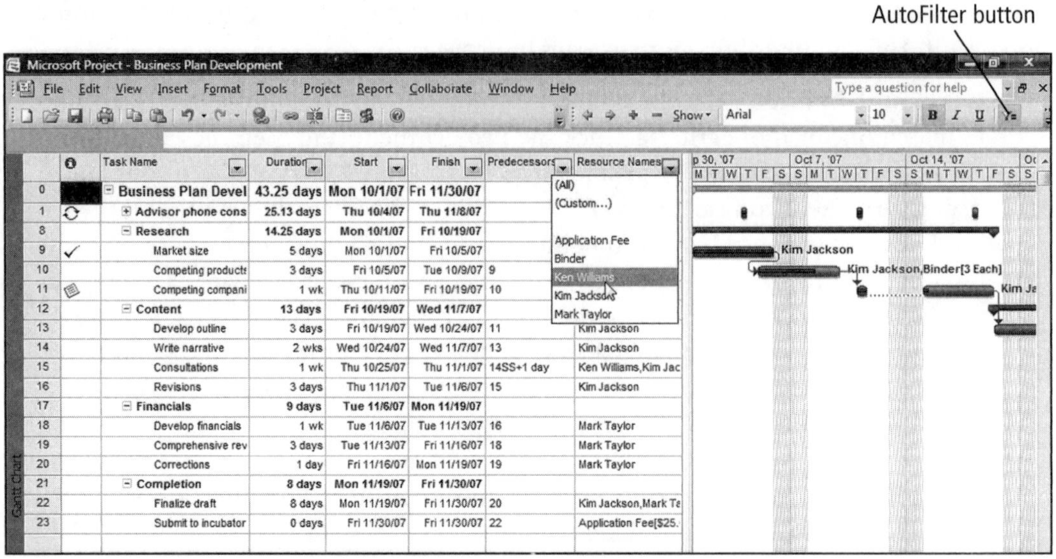

AutoFilter button

**Figure 12.8** AutoFilter adds a filtering drop-down list to every field in the sheet.

## Adjusting the Gantt Chart Timescale

Many users struggle to get the chart portion of the Gantt Chart view to provide information at the appropriate scale. In a short project with a lot of tasks that are a few hours long, the default setup for the Gantt Chart makes the bars look so small that they're almost meaningless. On the other hand, if you're viewing a long-term project with many long tasks, you might wish to compress more information into view on the chart. You can use the two methods presented here to wrangle the Gantt Chart's chart into the scale you need.

The techniques you learn here work in any other view with a timescale (except Calendar view), such as Tracking Gantt.

### Zooming

The first, less precise way to adjust the Gantt Chart is to zoom it. The Gantt Chart view doesn't offer a separate button or shortcut for zooming, so to start the process, click the **View** menu and then click **Zoom** to open the Zoom dialog box. You can zoom the chart portion of the Gantt Chart view to show data based on the timeframe you select in the dialog box: 1 Week, 2 Weeks, 1 Month, 3 Months, Selected Task, Entire Project, or a Custom time period that you specify. Choose the setting you want in the Zoom dialog box and then click **OK**. Figure 12.9 shows a project you've seen in earlier chapters zoomed to show the

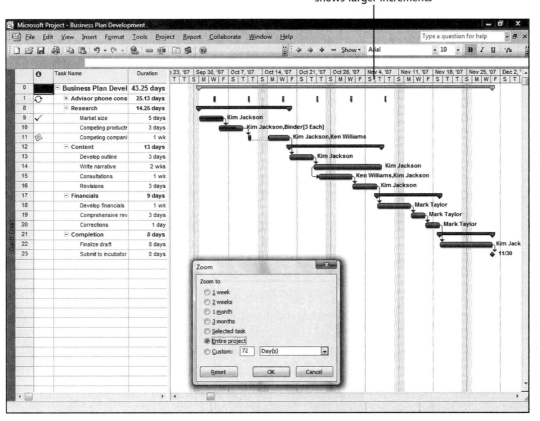

**Figure 12.9** Zooming enables you to display more or less information in the chart portion of the Gantt Chart view.

entire project onscreen at once, along with the Zoom dialog box. Notice in the figure that the bottom band of the timescale has been compressed to show three-day increments rather than the default of one-day increments.

## Changing the Time Units

The other method for controlling how the information appears in the chart portion of the Gantt Chart view is to change the time units shown in the timescale; the Gantt bars then adjust automatically to reflect the new timescale you set up. To open the Timescale dialog box, where you can change timescale formatting, either double-click the timescale itself or right-click the chart and click **Timescale**.

The timescale can display up to three bands, and the Timescale dialog box displays a tab for each band: Top Tier, Middle Tier, and Bottom Tier. The two bands that appear onscreen by default are actually set on the Middle Tier and Bottom Tier bands, so work on those tabs to adjust the bands that already appear onscreen and work on the Top Tier tab to add a third band after changing the Show drop-down list on any tab to **Three Tiers** (**Top, Middle, Bottom**).

Each of the band tabs offers the same settings, as shown in Figure 12.10. The Units setting impacts the scale of the timescale. For example, if you change the Units setting to **Days** on the Middle Tier tab and **Hours** on the Bottom Tier tab, the Gantt bars will be charted on an hourly basis using the scale shown in the Preview at the bottom of the dialog box.

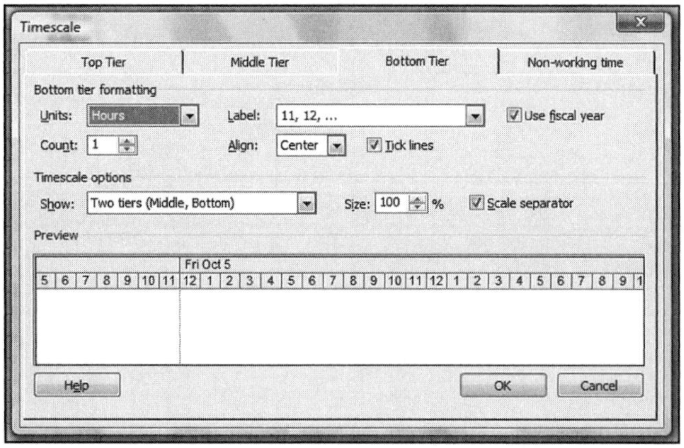

**Figure 12.10**
Adjust the timescale's band (tier) Units to change how the timescale displays information.

If you want the chart to shade the (custom) project calendar's nonworking hours and days, click the **Non-working** time tab, open the **Calendar** drop-down list, and click the name of the (custom) project calendar to apply. When you finish adjusting settings in the Timescale dialog box, click **OK** to apply them.

The higher tier of the timescale has to have a larger Units setting than any lower tier. If you try to choose a setting that violates this requirement, Project displays an error message.

## Formatting Chart Elements

When you right-click the chart portion of any view, a shortcut menu appears with commands that lead to the options for formatting that particular chart. For example, if you right-click Calendar view, your choices include changing Gridlines, Text Styles, and Bar Styles. If you right-click the right portion of Task Usage or Resource Usage views, the shortcut menu lists additional rows of information you can show and hide in the view. And in the Gantt Chart and its similar views, you can work with Gridlines, Bar Styles, and Layout details such as whether to show or hide link lines. The commands available on the short-cut menu also appear on the Format menu.

> **GOTTA KNOW**
>
> The commands and choices for editing a chart vary depending on the chart type. To find what's available, right-click the chart or open the **Format** menu. You also can change form contents by right-clicking any form in a view.

Given the number of views and the breadth of the formatting possibilities, I can't cover them all in this book. So, let's take a look at two popular changes: adjusting gridlines and changing bar styles in the Gantt Chart view.

One of the best uses for gridlines in the Gantt Chart view is to add horizontal gridlines every several tasks or so to help your eye "track" which Gantt bars match up with the tasks in the task sheet at the left. To work with gridlines, right-click the chart (right) side of the Gantt Chart view and click **Gridlines**. In the **Line to Change** list at the left side of the Gridlines dialog box (see Figure 12.11), click the gridline to change. In the case of lining

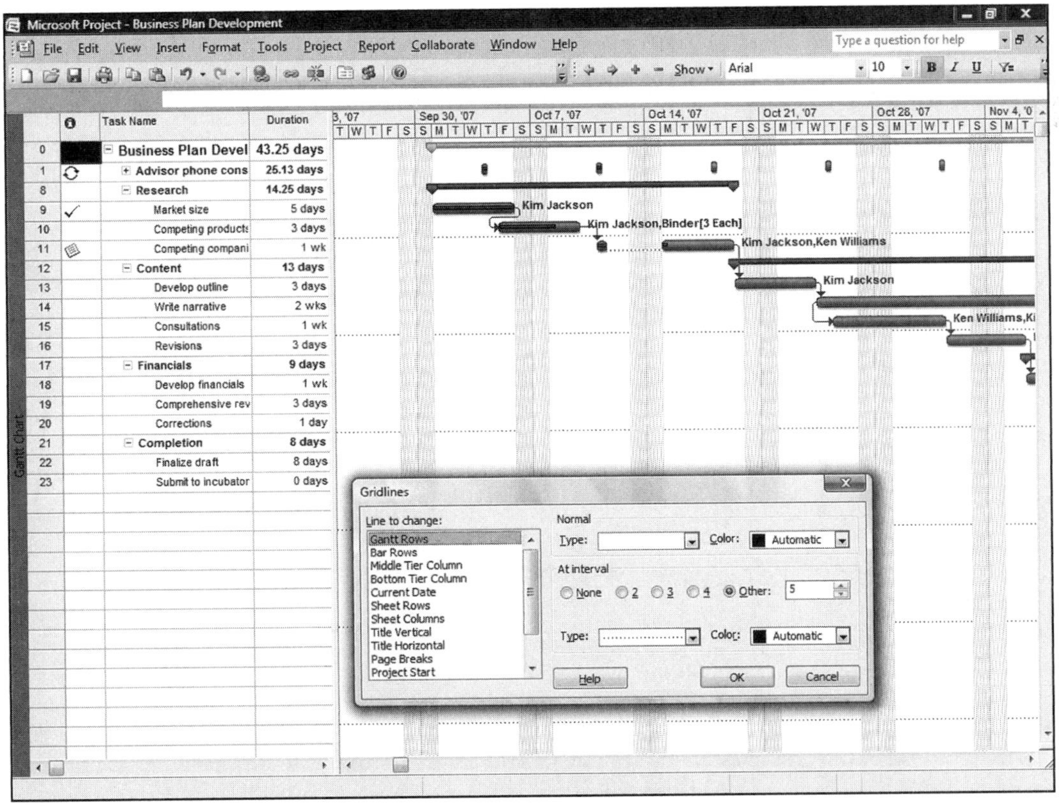

**Figure 12.11** These Gridlines dialog box settings add gridlines every five rows, as shown in the chart.

up tasks and Gantt bars, you can leave **Gantt Rows** selected. Then, in the At Interval section of the dialog box, use a numbered option button to specify the number of rows between gridlines (click **Other** and change its value to set a custom number). In the same section of the dialog box, specify the line appearance by making choices from the **Type** and **Color** drop-down lists. Then click **OK** to display the gridline you set up. Figure 12.11 illustrates settings used to display gridlines at a five-task interval in the Gantt Chart.

Another popular change is to edit the appearance of the Gantt bars themselves. If you double-click a Gantt bar on the chart, you can use the Format Bar dialog box that appears to adjust the bar's appearance. The changes you make will apply to that single Gantt bar.

If you want to change the appearance of all Gantt bars of the same type, such as all bars for regular tasks or all summary task bars, you have to change the *bar style*. Right-click the chart and click **Bar Styles**. In the list of different bar styles at the top of the Bars Styles dialog box (see Figure 12.12), click the type of bar that you want to edit; leave **Task** selected

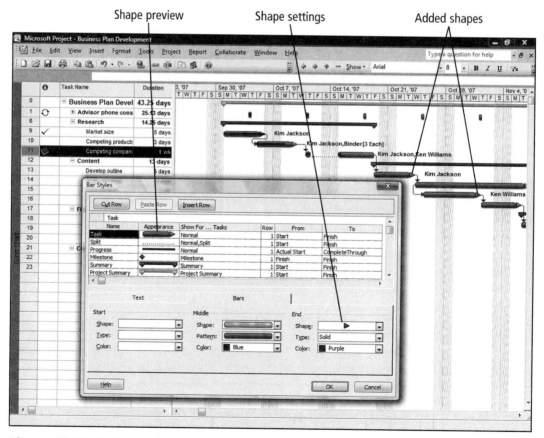

**Figure 12.12** Settings on the Bars tab added a purple arrow shape to regular Gantt bars.

to edit the default Gantt bars. Then, use the choices on the **Text** and **Bar** tabs at the bottom to work with the bar. The Text tab controls what text appears for the bar on the chart, and the Bars tab controls the appearance of the bars themselves. For example, Figure 12.12 shows the settings used to add a purple arrow shape to the right end of every regular, non-split Gantt bar. Click **OK** to close the dialog box and apply your bar style changes.

# Understanding and Creating Views

Even though you can change views by clicking a single menu command, a number of separate elements can go into each view. For a view that includes a sheet, for example, the view will include a table that defines which columns (fields) of information appear in the view. Furthermore, a filter and group can be applied to the table within a particular view. Some views consist of a chart alone, such as the Network Diagram views. But other views include a sheet at the left and a chart at the right, such as Gantt Chart and Tracking Gantt views.

If you want to create a custom view, you have to bring all the necessary pieces together. But you might be surprised to learn that you need to work in an order that's different from what you might think: You need to start from the smallest element and work your way up. If the view needs to include a custom field, create it first. Then, build the custom table that the view needs to include. Add the custom table to the view, and then customize the chart portion of the view as needed.

As has been mentioned previously in the book, it's a good practice to create your own custom tables and views rather than editing the default views in Project. That's because any changes you make to a table or view onscreen are saved as changes to that table or view in the current project plan file. While it's possible to work your way back to the default view, that change causes you to lose your custom changes. Creating your custom table/view enables you to retain the ability to switch between the custom information you need to see today and the default information a stakeholder might request tomorrow.

## Setting Up Custom Fields

Project enables you to customize many types of custom fields. If you've worked with fields in tables much on your own, you probably noticed that Project includes several series of numbered fields that contain no data, such as the *Text1* through *Text30* fields, the *Cost1* through *Cost10* fields, and the *Number1* through *Number20* fields. There are also numbered fields whose names start with Date, Duration, Finish, Flag, Outline Code, and Start. All of these fields are empty placeholders that you can set up to indicate custom data you need to show in your project plan.

You set up the custom field in the Custom Fields dialog box. For a straightforward field where you want to assign a custom name and enter text (one of the custom *Text* fields), a numeric value (a custom *Number* field), *Cost* (a custom *Cost* field), or a date (one of the custom *Date* fields), you select the field to use and rename it in the dialog box. For example, you could set up the *Text1* field as a *Last Name* field to add to a variation of the Resource Sheet view so that you can sort the sheet by the resource last names.

 Some of the placeholder fields limit you to what you can enter or specify. For example, a Flag field will offer a Yes/No drop-down list, while any of the date-related fields will let you enter dates or use a date drop-down calendar to enter dates.

Use these steps to set up a basic custom field:

1. Click **Tools**, point to the **Customize** command, and click **Fields**. The Custom Fields dialog box appears (see Figure 12.13).

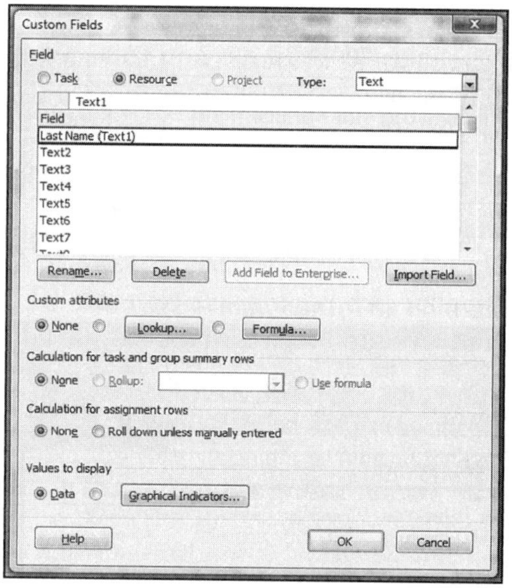

**Figure 12.13**
Convert placeholder fields to custom fields in this dialog box.

2. At the top of the dialog box, click the **Task** or **Resource** option button to specify whether the custom field will hold information about tasks or resources.

3. Open the **Type** drop-down list and click the placeholder field that you want to customize.

4. Click the **Rename** button.

5. Type the custom field name in the **New Name For** text box of the *Rename* field dialog box and click **OK**. Project displays the new field name in the Field list with the original name in parentheses beside it.

6. Click **OK** to close the dialog box. Your custom field is now ready and available to add to a custom table, as described shortly.

After you rename a field to customize it in the Custom Fields dialog box, you can choose to add another customization to make the field even more suited to your needs. For example, you could format a *Text* or *Number* field to offer a lookup list or pick list of choices. When the user clicks such a field, a drop-down list arrow appears so that the user can open a drop-down list and pick one of the field entry choices. To create a lookup list after you've renamed the field using the preceding steps, click the **Lookup** button in the Custom Fields dialog box. The Edit Lookup Table for *Field Name* dialog box appears. Type the entries for the field drop-down list in the **Value** column. To set up one of the values you've entered as the default for the field, click the **Use a Value from the Table as the Default Entry for the Field** check box to check it. Then click one of the values and click the **Set Default** button. Figure 12.14 shows the list settings for a custom lookup field, with the first entry set as the default for the field. Click **OK** to close this dialog box after you finish using it.

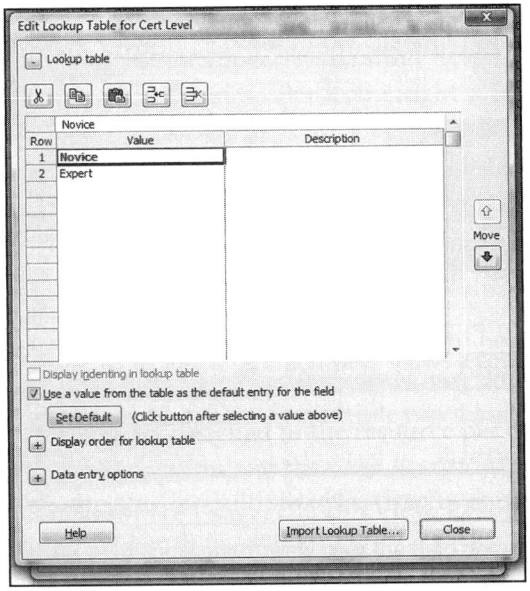

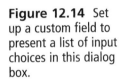

**Figure 12.14** Set up a custom field to present a list of input choices in this dialog box.

Entering a title for a field in the Column Definition dialog box (which appears when you double-click a field column header in a sheet or right-click a field and then click **Insert**) does *not* rename the field as described above. Entering a title in the Column Definition dialog box merely displays that new field title in the current table. Renaming the field in the Custom Fields dialog box changes the field name and title for any table or other instance for which it is used in the current project plan file (or all project plan files if you copy the files to Global.MPT).

Similarly, you can click the **Formula** button after renaming a field—typically a *Text* or *Cost* field, although you can choose a *Number* field or can perform some calculations on *Date* fields—to open the formula dialog box, where you can create a calculated field. Use the **Field** and **Function** drop-down lists to insert fields and functions for the calculation and click various operator buttons to enter the mathematical operators. Click **OK** when you finish building your formula. Note that any time you use a *Number* field, it will display a **0** onscreen for any task or resource that doesn't have another calculated amount; if this is not what you want, use a *Text* field as the basis for the calculated field, instead.

Finally, if you're customizing a *Yes/No* field or want to create an input list that shows colored dots rather than text, you can click the **Graphical Indicators** button. For each item you want to appear in the drop-down list, select a Test from the drop-down list (such as **equals**), enter the Value(s) the entry must match to pass the test (such as **Yes** if you're setting up a *Yes/No* field), and then click the Image to display when an entry passes the test. Click **OK** when you finish setting up the list of indicators.

## Creating a Table

When you want to display a particular set of fields in a sheet, you can create a custom table to present those fields. A custom table can include any combination of default fields that come in Project and custom fields that you've already set up. While you can add a large number of fields, as a practical matter, you want to limit the fields to the number that can display onscreen at one time, which may only be three or four if you plan to use the table in combination with a chart in a view.

Follow these steps to create a custom table:

1. Choose **View, Table:** *Table Name,* **More Tables**.

2. Click **Task** or **Resource** at the top of the dialog box to specify whether the table will display task or resource information.

3. Click the name of the table that most resembles the table to create in the **Tables** list and then click **Copy**. The Table Definition dialog box appears.

4. Type a name for the table in the **Name** text box. Consider using ALL CAPS or some other shorthand to remind you that the table is custom.

5. Each row in the list at the center of the dialog box represents a field. To remove a field, click the field in the Field Name column and click the **Delete Row** button. To add a row within the list, click the position where you want the field to appear and click **Insert Row**.

6. To specify the field that will appear in a blank row (either one you've inserted or one at the end of the list), click the **Field Name** cell, open the field list using the drop-down arrow that appears, click the field to use, and press **Enter**. You can change additional settings on the row defining the field as desired.

7. Repeat Steps 5 and 6 to add and remove other fields as needed. Figure 12.15 shows a customized version of the default Entry table for resources with some fields removed and custom *Last Name* and *Cert Level* fields added.

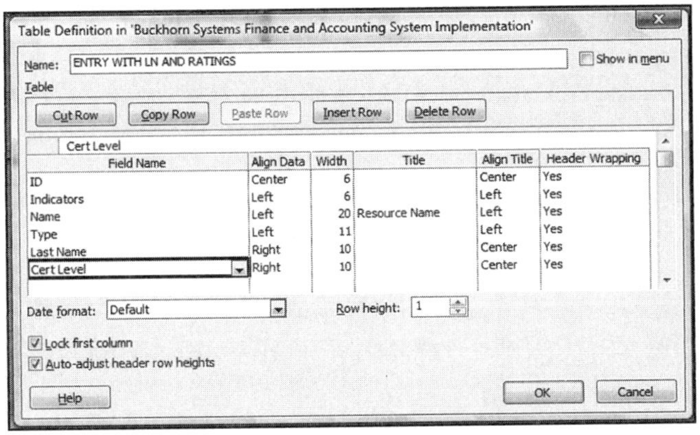

**Figure 12.15** Add and remove fields (rows) to define a custom table.

8. Click **OK** to finish setting up the table and close the Table Definition dialog box, and then click **Apply** or **Close** to close the More Tables dialog box. If you click Apply, Project displays the custom table in the current view.

After you create a custom table using those steps, you can apply it at any time using the More Tables dialog box (**View, Table: *Table Name*, More Tables**) or include it in a custom view that you create. Figure 12.16 shows how the table being defined in Figure 12.15 appears when displayed in the Resource Sheet view with dates entered into the custom fields.

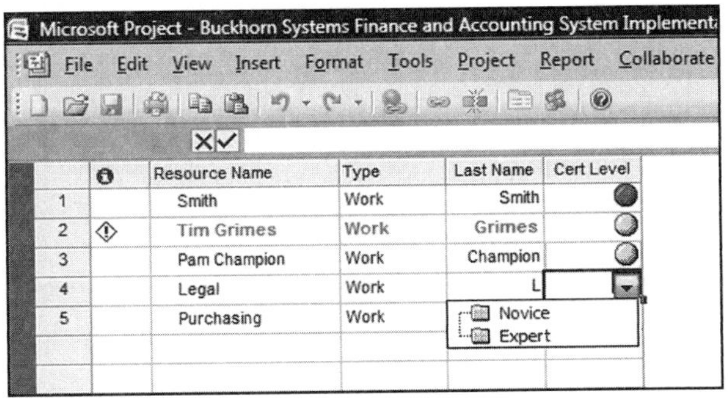

**Figure 12.16** Here's a custom table with custom fields in action onscreen.

When you want to display a custom table, first make sure you're in a view that holds the right type of information. Project won't let you display a table that holds resource information for a task view, and vice versa.

## Creating a View

Now that you have the building blocks—any needed custom fields and/or tables—in place, you can bring them and any other elements together in a custom table. Creating the custom table ensures that you can display and print the data you want but still return to the original default views in Project.

As when you created a table, you can copy an existing view that's close to the one you want. Note that if you copy a view that includes a chart (also called a *screen* when building views), you won't be able to change the chart shown. Still, copying is usually the best approach to create a view, using these steps:

1. Choose **View, More Views**.
2. Click the view that's closest to the view you want in the **Views** list of the More Views dialog box.
3. Click **New**.
4. Type a name for the view in the **Name** text box of the View Definition dialog box. Consider using ALL CAPS or some other shorthand to remind you that the view is custom.
5. Select the table to use, such as a custom table that you've previously created, from the **Table** drop-down list (see Figure 12.17).
6. If you want to apply a filter to the table, select one from the **Filter** drop-down list. While the selected table controls what fields appear in the resulting view, the filter controls whether all rows or only a selection appear.
7. If you want your custom view to appear on the View menu along with the eight Project views that appear there by default, leave the **Show in Menu** check box checked in the lower-left corner of the dialog box.

> When you add a custom view to the View menu, it is added in alphabetical order within either the task (top) or resource group of views. If you want your custom view to appear at the top of the list, begin its name with an underscore character.

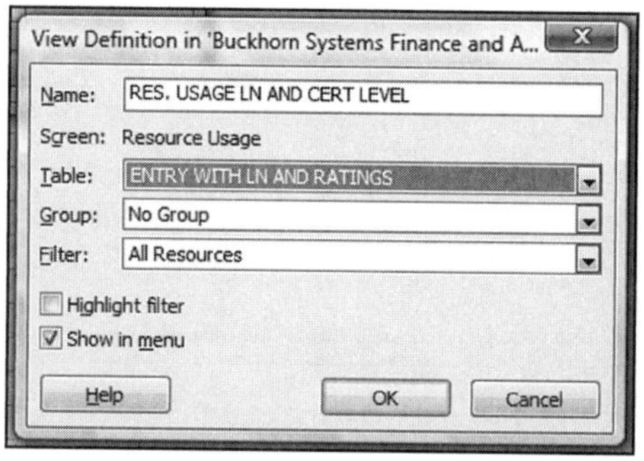

**Figure 12.17**
Specify the components of a custom view in this dialog box.

8. Click **OK** to finish setting up the view and close the View Definition dialog box, and then click **Apply** or **Close** to close the More Views dialog box. If you click **Apply**, Project displays the custom view.

After you create a custom view using those steps, you can apply it at any time using the More Views dialog box.

 If you click the **New** button in the More Views dialog box, you have the option of creating a single (one pane) or combination (two pane) view and then choosing what view appears in each pane.

## Reusing Fields, Tables, and Views with the Organizer

If you want your custom calendars, fields, tables, views, and so on to be available in all of your project plan files, rather than the current file only, you need to move those custom elements into the master template for all Project files—Global.MPT. Project provides a tool called the *Organizer* that enables you to move a custom item you create into Global.MPT in mere moments. This way, when you invest a lot of time in creating a custom setup in a file, you don't have to repeat the process over and over for each new project file.

Click **Tools** and then click **Organizer** to open the Organizer dialog box. Each tab in the dialog box represents a type of custom element that you can create in Project. Click the tab for the type of item to copy into Global.MPT and then click the **Task** or **Resource** option button at the top, if needed, to indicate the type of data managed by the custom element. Then, click the custom item in the list for the current file at the right (see Figure 12.18) and click the **Copy** button to copy the item into the Global.MPT. Repeat the process for custom items on other tabs and then click **Close**.

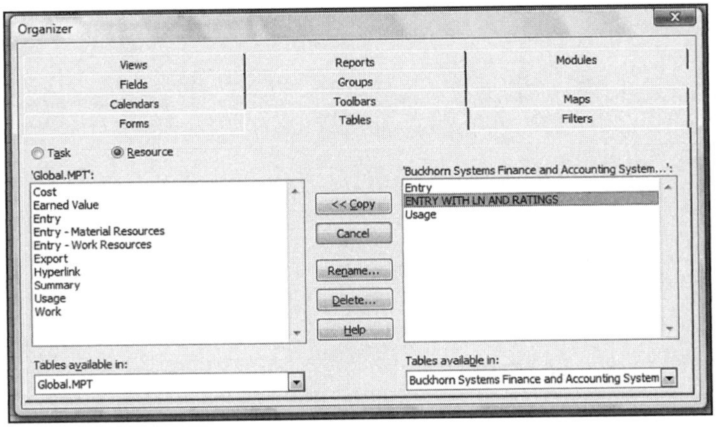

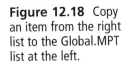

**Figure 12.18** Copy an item from the right list to the Global.MPT list at the left.

If you've created a custom view that includes a custom table that in turn includes custom fields, remember that you have to copy the custom item(s) from each "layer" of the view to Global.MPT in order for the view to display properly. If you forget to copy the table for a view, you'll get an error message when you try to display the view. If you forget to copy custom fields, the original placeholder fields will appear when you display the table. Also, consider using similar naming for each of the individual items that are part of the custom view so you can find them more easily. For example, you'll easily be able to tell that LB_COSTPLUS_FIELD, LB_COSTPLUS_TABLE, and LB_COSTPLUS_VIEW go together.

## Choosing Print Settings and Printing

The traditional method of sharing information, via a printout, continues to be a common means of informing others about project planning and execution. With Project, you may find yourself printing even more than with other applications because many of the project stakeholders and team members may not have the Project program with which to open Project files. Printing in Project works much like in any other application, so this section presents an overview of the process and highlights key settings that are unique or more important in Project.

Always keep in mind that in Project, the first step to printing is to choose the view that you want to print.

The Page Setup, Print Preview, and Print commands on the File menu present the options you need to prepare and make a project plan printout.

### Working with Page Setup Choices

Checking the page setup before you print helps you avoid printed boo-boos in any application. As in other applications, you click **File** and then click **Page Setup** to open the Page Setup dialog box (see Figure 12.19).

The Page Setup dialog box offers six tabs of choices, many of which resemble settings available in other programs:

- **Page.** Change overall page orientation, scaling, and paper size. The **Fit To** choice in the Scaling section of the dialog box can be particularly helpful in Project, enabling you to control how many pages the printout contains, thus eliminating pages that print with little information on them, which is a common problem in Project.

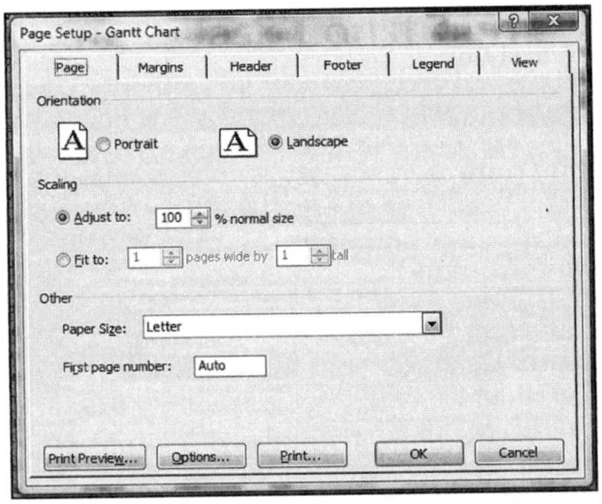

**Figure 12.19**
Control printout appearance using choices available in the Page Setup dialog box.

- **Margins.** Change the size for the margin on each edge of the page and specify whether to add a border to the page. Be sure you specify margins that are at least as wide as the minimum size required by your printer or an error message will appear when you try to print.

- **Header and Footer.** These two tabs offer the same choices, but the Header tab settings define a header to print at the top of the pages while the Footer tab settings define a footer to appear at the bottom of the pages. Enter the header or footer information to print in the text boxes on the tabs in the Alignment section of the dialog box. You can make choices from the **General** or **Project Fields** drop-down list and then click **Add** to include field information in the header or footer.

- **Legend.** This tab enables you to control how the printed legend (the key to the chart bar styles) appears or to turn off legend printing. Use the Alignment tabs to edit the descriptive text for the legend. To print the legend on a single page rather than every page, click the **Legend Page** option button, or to turn the legend off, click the **None** option button.

You can prevent a chart bar style from printing in the legend. To do so, right-click the chart (such as the Gantt chart in Gantt Chart view), and then click **Bar Styles**. In the Bar Styles dialog box, add an asterisk (*) to the beginning of the name for any bar style that you do not want to appear in the legend. This technique gives a smaller legend that prints only the bar styles that you believe are needed.

- **View.** The settings on this tab vary depending on the selected view. For views like the Gantt Chart, you can change such settings as specifying how many columns of the sheet part of the view appear in the printout or whether to print notes. For other views, such as the Calendar view, the View tab offers more detailed settings. As shown in Figure 12.20, for the Calendar view you can specify a **Months Per Page** or **Weeks Per Page** setting to control how much information prints on each page. The Details area enables you to set up other appearance aspects of the printout.

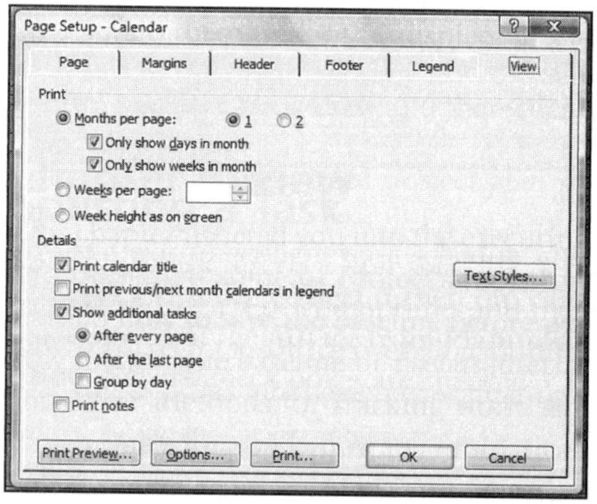

**Figure 12.20** The View tab of the Page Setup dialog box offers print appearance settings pertaining to the selected view; this example shows the Calendar view settings.

Notice that the bottom of each tab of the Page Setup dialog box includes Print Preview, Options, and Print buttons. The **Print Preview** and **Print** buttons take you to the Print Preview view and Print dialog box, respectively, each of which you'll learn about shortly. Clicking the **Options** button opens a Properties dialog box where you can choose settings for your printer.

When you finish making your page setup choices, click either **Print Preview** or **Print** to move on or **OK** to close the Print Setup dialog box.

## Using Page Breaks

Project does enable you to have a little finer control over printouts by specifying a *page break*, the location where one page should end and the next should begin in a printout. You can't specify page breaks in certain views such as the Calendar view, so you'll use this feature most often in a view that consists of or includes a sheet.

To insert a page break, click a cell in the task sheet row that you want to be the first row of a new page. Click **Insert** and then click **Page Break**. As shown in Figure 12.21, a dashed line appears in the sheet to show you that the page will end just above the row with the selected cell. To remove a page break, click in the row just below the dashed line for the page break and click **Insert, Remove Page Break**.

| 24 | | Document implementatic | 4 days | Wed 7/2/08 | Tue 7 |
| 25 | | Select implementation o | 2 days | Tue 7/8/08 | Thu 7/ |
| 26 | | Develop test and user a | 0.5 days | Thu 7/10/08 | Thu 7/ |
| 27 | | Obtain signoff of busine | 1 day | Fri 7/11/08 | Fri 7/ |
| 28 | | Implementation options | 0 days | Fri 7/11/08 | Fri 7/ |
| 29 | | ⊟ Package Business Incre | 8 days | Mon 7/14/08 | Wed 7/ |
| 30 | | Define implementation ir | 1 day | Mon 7/14/08 | Mon 7/ |
| 31 | | Define increment accep | 2 days | Tue 7/15/08 | Wed 7/ |

Ready

**Figure 12.21** A dashed line in the sheet identifies the location in which you've inserted a page break.

## Previewing the Printout

Because the nature of the views in Project does lead to some printouts with mostly blank pages and other unexpected glitches, you should always preview a printout in Project. There are several ways to open the Print Preview: click the **Print Preview** button in the Page Setup dialog box; choose the **File, Print Preview** command; or click the **Print Preview** button if it appears on the Standard toolbar (use the Toolbar Options button to find it, if needed).

In the Print Preview (see Figure 12.22), you can check the status bar in the lower-left corner to see how many pages the printout will have. Use the arrow buttons in the upper-left

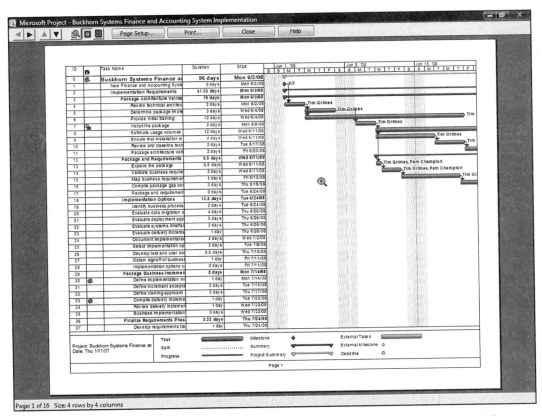

**Figure 12.22** Previewing a printout gives you the opportunity to save paper by finding glitches before you print.

corner to move between various pages, and you can click the page with the magnifying glass mouse pointer to zoom in and out. If you need to tweak the page setup, click the **Page Setup** button; otherwise click **Print** to go to the Print dialog box and send a printout or **Close** to close the Print Preview.

## Sending the Job to the Printer

Clicking the **Print** button on the Standard toolbar in Project sends a printout directly to the printer, bypassing any opportunity to make any last print adjustments. If you do want to change print settings, such as specifying how many copies to print, open the Print dialog box. To do so, click the **Print** button in the Print Setup dialog box or Print Preview; click **File** and then click **Print**; or press **Ctrl+P**.

In the Print dialog box, you can change to another printer using the **Name** drop-down list. To print only selected pages in the project plan, use the **Page(s) From** setting in the Print Range section or the **Dates** options in the Timescale section. You also can specify the **Number of Copies** to print. Click **OK** when you finish making your choices to send the printout to the printer (see Figure 12.23).

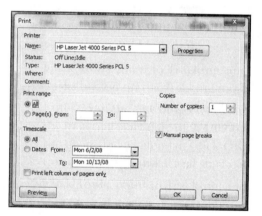

**Figure 12.23** Nail down a few last print choices here and then click **Print**.

# Chapter Review

This chapter presented information you need to know about using views in Project. The chapter kicked off with a review of the available views highlighting the new features of the popular Calendar view. From there, you learned to sort and filter data in a sheet, how to adjust the timescale to chart data using the proper timeframe, and how to format chart elements. From there, you learned how to set up custom fields and custom tables and how to combine them in a custom view that you can reuse in other project plan files. Finally, you learned the essential settings for making printed output in Project. In the next chapter, you'll learn about another key way to communicate about project status—reports.

## Review Questions

Write your answers to the following questions on a sheet of paper.

1. Open the _____ dialog box to access all of Project's available views.
2. True or False: The Calendar view can only appear in a monthly format.
3. To change the order of tasks or resources, _____ the sheet.
4. To hide non-matching tasks or resources, _____ the sheet.
5. _____ the chart timescale to open the Timescale dialog box with formatting choices.
6. Project offers a number of _____ fields that you can rename and customize.
7. True or False: You can create a custom field that calculates values.
8. A custom _____ defines a set of fields to appear in a sheet.
9. True or False: You can't add a custom view to the view menu.
10. Click the _____ command on the File menu to start the process for creating a hard copy output of the project plan.

## Projects

To see the solutions file created by completing the projects in this chapter, go to www.courseptr.com, click the **Downloads** link in the navigation bar at the top, type **Microsoft Office Project 2007 Survival Guide** in the search text box, and then click **Search Downloads**.

### Project 1

1. Open the file named *Site Search Track* that you worked with in the projects for Chapter 11.
2. Save the file as *Site Search Views*.

Create a folder named *PSG Exercises* in your *Documents* or *My Documents* folder and save your exercise practice files there.

3. Click **View** and then click **More Views**.

4. Click **Descriptive Network Diagram** and then click **OK**.

5. Scroll through the view to review its appearance.

6. Right-click the chart in the view and then click **Box Styles**. (This type of chart has box style settings rather than the bar style settings you saw for the Gantt Chart view.)

7. Click **Project Summary** in the Style Settings For list, if needed. Open the **Color** drop-down list under Background, click **Yellow**, and click **OK**.

8. Scroll if needed to see the project summary task box, which should have a blue outline and yellow background.

9. Click **View** and then click **Resource Sheet**.

10. Click **Project**, point to **Sort**, and then click **Sort By**.

11. Select the **Group** field from the Sort By drop-down list, leave **Ascending** selected, and make sure that Permanently Renumber Resources is unchecked. Click **Sort**.

12. To return the list of resources to its original order, click **Project**, point to **Sort**, and then click **By ID**.

13. Click the **AutoFilter** button on the Formatting toolbar.

14. Click the filter drop-down list arrow for the **Type** field and then click **Work**. Only work resources now appear in the Resource Sheet.

15. Click the filter drop-down list arrow for the **Type** field and then click **(All)**. This redisplays all resources.

16. Click the **AutoFilter** button on the Formatting toolbar.

## *Project 2*

1. Click **View** and then click **Gantt Chart**.

2. Right-click the **Rating** column heading and click **Hide Column**.

3. Click **Tools**, point to **Customize**, and click **Fields**.

4. Leave Task selected at the top of the dialog box. Open the **Type** drop-down list and click **Number**.

5. With the **Number1** field selected in the Field list, click **Rename.** Type **ACCT. CODE** in the Rename Field dialog box, and click **OK**.

6. Click **Lookup.** In the Edit Lookup Table for the dialog box that appears, enter **102**, **105**, and **110** into the Value column. Click the **Use a Value from the Table as the Default Entry for the Field** check box, click **102** in the Value list, and then click **Set Default.** Click **Close** and then **OK** to finish creating the field.

7. Click **View**, point to **Table:** *Table Name*, and then click **More Tables**.

8. Leave Task selected at the top of the dialog box, click **Entry** in the Tables list if needed, and then click **Copy.**

9. Type **ENTRY WITH CODES** as the table name.

10. Use the **Cut Row** button to delete the *Start, Finish, Predecessors,* and *Resource Names* fields.

11. Use the Field name drop-down list for the next two blank field name rows to insert the **ACCT. CODE** custom field and the **WBS** existing field.

12. Click **OK** and then **Close** to finish creating the custom table.

## *Project 3*

1. Click **View** and then click **More Views.**

2. With **Gantt Chart** selected in the Views list, click **Copy.**

3. Click **OK** to close the Project Statistics dialog box.

4. Click **View** and then click **Tracking Gantt.**

5. Type **GANTT WITH CODES** in the Name text box of the View Definition dialog box.

6. Open the **Table** drop-down list and click **ENTRY WITH CODES**, the custom table that you created.

7. Click **OK** to finish creating the custom table.

8. Click **Apply** in the More Views dialog box to display the custom view.

9. Make the Duration column wider so that you can see all the entries, and drag the divider between the two parts of the view to the right so that all fields are visible.

10. Use the custom ACCT. CODE field drop-down list to specify **102** as the field entry for tasks *2, 3,* and *4.* (The default entry did not appear because you applied the new view to a project with existing tasks.)

11. Click **View** and then click **Zoom.**

12. Click the **Entire Project** option button and then click **OK.** The new zoom becomes part of the custom view.

13. Click **File** and then click **Print Preview.** Notice in the bottom left corner that the printout will be two pages. If you click the right arrow button in the upper-left corner, you can view the information that will print on the second page.

14. Click the **Page Setup** button at the top of the preview.

15. Click the **Page** tab, click the **Fit To** option button under Scaling, and then click **OK.** The Print Preview changes to reflect the single-page printout.

16. Click the **Print** button and then click **OK** to print the custom view of your project. This also closes the Print Preview.

17. Save your changes to the file and close the file.

# CHAPTER 13

# REPORTING PROJECT INFORMATION

This Chapter Teaches You How To:

- Know what reports you can use
- Open and print a report
- Create a custom version of a report
- Check out the new visual reports
- Display a Visio visual report
- Display an Excel visual report
- Add your own visual report template

Team members and stakeholders have different information needs, as do you, the project manager. For this reason, Microsoft Office Project 2007 enables you to provide information in a number of different ways. In addition to printing views, which you learned about in the last chapter, you also can print and distribute different types of reports. This chapter introduces you to what's old and what's new in Project reporting. You'll learn how to select and display a report, print a report, create a custom report, and take a crack at displaying one of the new visual reports.

# Traditional Reports in Project

The *reports* long offered in Project present different types of information that are generally organized in a list or tabular format. Each report identifies the information to be included—whether a table of resource information, a table of cost information, or information selected from specific fields—and whether to sort or filter the information. The report also defines details about the appearance of the information.

Reports provide a fast, attractive, and sometimes easier to understand alternative to a printed view. For example, Figure 13.1 shows the Resource Usage report. This report presents the same information as the Resource Usage view but summarizes the work by week and adds a useful *Total* field at the right. While Project doesn't offer a report that matches each default view, many of the reports offer information that would be time-consuming to reproduce in a custom view.

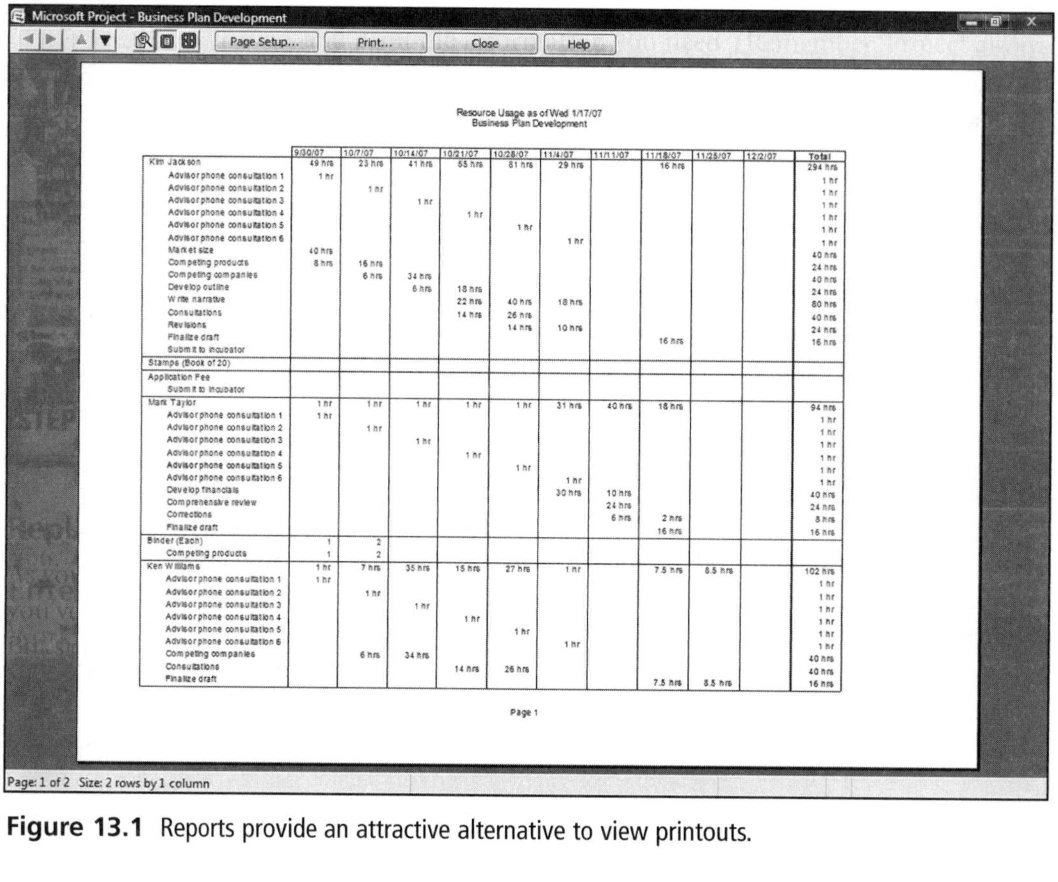

**Figure 13.1** Reports provide an attractive alternative to view printouts.

## Reviewing Available Reports

Project 2007 offers 22 reports organized into five categories. Table 13.1 lists the available reports by category to give you a head start in finding a report that presents the information you need.

**Table 13.1**  Standard Reports in Microsoft Project 2007

### Overview Category

| Name | Description |
|---|---|
| Project Summary | Presents the same information shown in the Project Statistics dialog box, as well as additional information about task and resource status |
| Top-Level Tasks | Lists the tasks at the top outline level, as well as the project summary task, and includes notes assigned to any of those tasks |
| Critical Tasks | Presents a list of the summary and critical tasks in the project, including notes and successor information for each task, if applicable |
| Milestones | Lists the tasks marked as milestones in the project |
| Working Days | Gives the schedule information for the Standard calendar |

### Current Activities Category

| Name | Description |
|---|---|
| Unstarted Tasks | Lists the tasks that haven't started, the resource(s) assigned to each, and any notes |
| Tasks Starting Soon | Prompts you to enter a date range and then lists tasks starting in that date range, along with the assigned resource(s) and notes |
| Tasks In Progress | Lists tasks with a completion percentage between 0% and 100%, along with the assigned resource(s) and notes |
| Completed Tasks | Lists information about tasks marked as 100% complete |
| Should Have Started Tasks | Prompts you to enter a date and then displays tasks that should have started by that date, along with assigned resource(s) and notes |
| Current Slipping Tasks | Lists tasks that might not be completed when scheduled, along with assigned resource(s) and notes |

### Costs Category

| Name | Description |
|---|---|
| Cash Flow | Shows how costs accrue for each task on a weekly basis, including weekly and task totals |
| Budget | Shows fixed and total costs per task, as well as baseline, variance, and remaining information |
| Overbudget Tasks | Lists tasks that have a positive cost variance (overage) based on actual tracking information entered |

**Table 13.1** Standard Reports in Microsoft Project 2007 (continued)

| Name | Description |
| --- | --- |
| Overbudget Resources | Lists resources that have a positive cost variance (overage) based on actual tracking information entered |
| Earned Value | For each task, compares the budgeted expenses saved in the baseline with the cost of the actual work performed |

### Assignments Category

| Name | Description |
| --- | --- |
| Who Does What | Provides a list of assignments by resource |
| Who Does What When | Lists assignments by resource and shows hours of work assigned by day |
| To-Do List | Prompts you to enter a resource name and then lists the tasks assigned to that resource during each week of the project |
| Overallocated Resources | Lists each overallocated resource and the tasks assigned to that resource |

### Workload Category

| Name | Description |
| --- | --- |
| Task Usage | Provides an alternative version of the Task Usage view listing each task, the resources assigned, and the total hours of work per task, assignment, and week |
| Resource Usage | Provides an alternative version of the Resource Usage view listing each resource, the tasks assigned, and the total hours of work per resource, assignment, and week |

## What the Heck Is Earned Value?

*Earned value* is a technical form of analysis used to determine how the project's progress and costs compare with the baseline. You don't have to worry about making any of the calculations—Project makes them for you. But behind the scenes Project calculates values like the BCWP (budgeted cost of work performed), ACWP (actual cost of work performed), and BCWS (budgeted cost of work scheduled). Project also calls the *BCWP* field the *Earned Value* field in the Earned Value report.

Project uses these values and others to calculate indexes and variances of schedule and cost performance. The Earned Value report includes the *SV* (schedule variance) and *CV* (cost variance) fields, which give an indication of progress and cost versus the plan. Unlike the variance values shown in the Project Statistics dialog box and Project Summary report, for the *SV* and *CV* fields, positive (greater than 0) values mean the project is ahead of schedule or under budget and negative (less than 0) values mean the project is behind schedule or over budget.

The names and descriptions in Table 13.1 should give you a decent idea of when to use a particular report. For example, if a project is running behind, you might print the Critical Tasks Report to focus your attention there. Or, if you're looking for which resources may need some assistance to stay on track, the Overallocated Resources report could be useful. For reporting to financial stakeholders, the Cash Flow and Budget reports might present much of what you need to communicate.

## Viewing and Printing a Report

The regular reports in Project appear as a print preview. You display the desired report onscreen, change any page setup and print settings as needed, and send the report to the printer. In previous versions of Project, the user accessed reports via the View menu. Project 2007 moves reports to their own menu, not surprisingly called the Report menu. Any regular report you display opens in Print Preview. Accordingly, you can't change the fields it contains and you can't save the data it displays on a particular date.

This sounds odd, but you have to display all subtasks for a report you run to make sure that the report includes information from the subtasks. For example, if you have a recurring meeting task set up, you need to expand all its subtasks before you generate the report to ensure that information gets included in the report. For that reason, you may want to get in the habit of clicking the **Show** button on the Formatting toolbar and then clicking All Subtasks before you display and print any report.

You have to select the printer to use to print the report before displaying the report. Choose **File, Print**. Select the desired printer from the **Name** drop-down list and click **Close**. If the printer you select is a black-and-white printer, the report preview will appear in black and white only.

Once you've displayed a report, the process for selecting page setup and print settings works just as described for views in Chapter 12, so we won't rehash those details here and you can refer to the previous chapter, if needed. Follow these steps when you're ready to get that report on paper:

1. Click the **Report** menu and then click **Reports**. The Reports dialog box, shown in Figure 13.2, appears.

A *report* presents selected project data in a nice format for printing. Choose **Report, Reports** to open the Reports dialog box. First double-click a category and then double-click the report to display.

2. Double-click the category that holds the report you want to display.

3. In the dialog box that appears showing the reports available in the selected category, double-click the desired report.

4. If the report prompts you to specify dates or select a resource (as shown in Figure 13.3), type or use the drop-down calendar or list to make your choice and then click **OK**. If you see a second dialog box prompting for a date, enter it or choose it from the drop-down calendar and then click **OK**. The report appears onscreen as a print preview, like the example shown in Figure 13.4.

**Figure 13.3** A report
with a filter assigned
may prompt you to
specify additional criteria
for the filter.

5. You can use the navigation buttons to move through the pages in the report to review it for potential changes.

6. To change page setup features such as a zoom percentage, margins, header, or footer, click the **Page Setup** button, make the desired changes, and then click **OK**. Navigate through the report to view the impact of your changes and return to the Page Setup dialog box, if necessary, to make changes.

7. When the report is ready to print, click the **Print** button. Make any desired changes in the Print dialog box, such as specifying the number of copies to print, and then click **OK**.

Navigation          Printout              Magnifying
buttons            dimensions              pointer

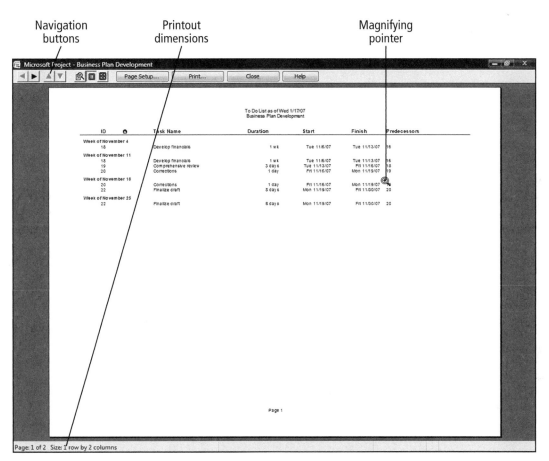

**Figure 13.4** Like all reports, this To Do List report appears as a print preview.

While the reports as they stand will meet a typical user's needs, there are just a couple of glitches that you should be aware of and check for when you print a report:

- The fonts you see in the preview aren't always a precise match for what prints. This discrepancy is due to the difference between screen fonts and the fonts used by many printers.

- Like views, reports can have an issue with including nearly blank pages. For example, navigating to the second page of the report in Figure 13.4 shows that the second page of the report only includes a single field column. To remedy this problem, you can click the **Page Setup** button in the preview, decrease the **Adjust To** percentage entry under Scaling on the Page tab, and then click **OK**. In the example shown, scaling the report to 90% size fit all the columns on a single page.

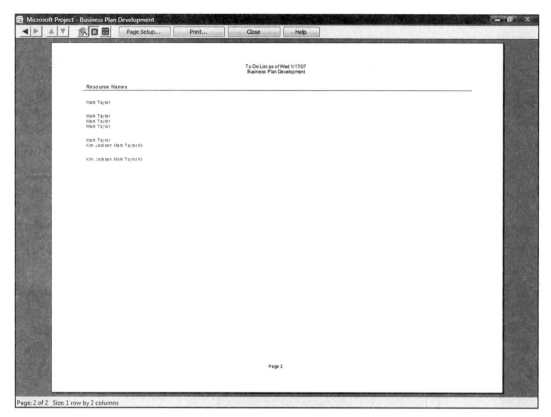

**Figure 13.5** Check your report for issues like mostly blank pages.

■ Finally, make sure that your report shows all the labels and identifiers necessary to make the information understandable for your audience. For example, if you look at the To Do List report, shown in Figures 13.4 and 13.5, you can see there's no heading or label telling you what resource the To Do List is for. (You could identify the resource by looking at the Resource Names column, but that may not be obvious to the report's recipient.) In a case like this, consider clicking **Page Setup**, clicking the **Header** tab, and editing the header information to include the resource name.

 If you're using Project with Windows Vista, you can select Microsoft XPS Document Writer as the printer in the Print dialog box *before* displaying the report. (Choose **File, Print**. Select **Microsoft XPS Document Writer** from the Name drop-down list and click **Close**.) You cannot make this change after you open the report. Then, when you display and print the report, you will be prompted to save the file as an XPS document. You can then e-mail the XPS file to any other Vista user. The recipient can double-click the file to view it in Internet Explorer.

## Creating a Custom Report

As with a view, you can make changes to a report to help it better suit your needs. If you double-click the **Custom** category in the Reports dialog box, the Custom Reports dialog box appears (see Figure 13.6). Simply click a report in the Reports list and then click the **Edit** button to open a dialog box where you can change it.

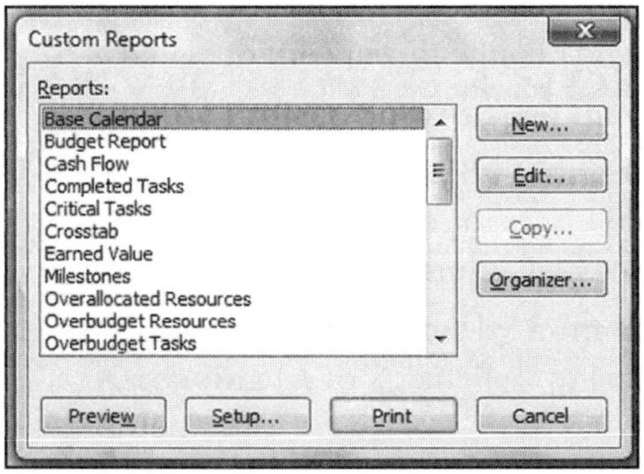

**Figure 13.6** Select a report for editing or create a new report here.

But, once again, if you want the original reports offered with Project to remain available in their unaltered state, you should instead create a new report. Project enables you to create four different types of reports, and the dialog box with the settings for creating the report will vary depending on the type of report you choose to create:

- **Task.** Provides information about tasks. Existing reports with the word "task" or "what" in the name are task reports.
- **Resource.** Provides information about resources and work. Existing resource reports include "resource" or "who" in the report name.
- **Monthly Calendar.** Creates a report that resembles the default appearance of the Calendar view.
- **Crosstab.** Summarizes information in a grid of rows and columns. The existing Cash Flow report is an example of a crosstab report.

To create a new report in Project:

1. Choose **Report, Reports**.
2. Double-click **Custom** in the Reports dialog box.
3. Click the **New** button in the Custom Reports dialog box. The Define New Report dialog box shown in Figure 13.7 appears.
4. Click the type of report you want to create in the **Report Type** list and click **OK**. A dialog box with settings for creating the report will appear. The report type you selected in Step 4 determines the name and available settings in this dialog box.

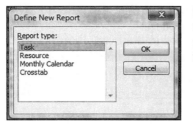

**Figure 13.7**
Choose which type of
report to create in
this dialog box.

5. Enter a name for the report and choose its settings. The example in Figure 13.8
   shows the dialog box that appears for a new resource report with the report **Name**
   entered and a custom **Table** selected.

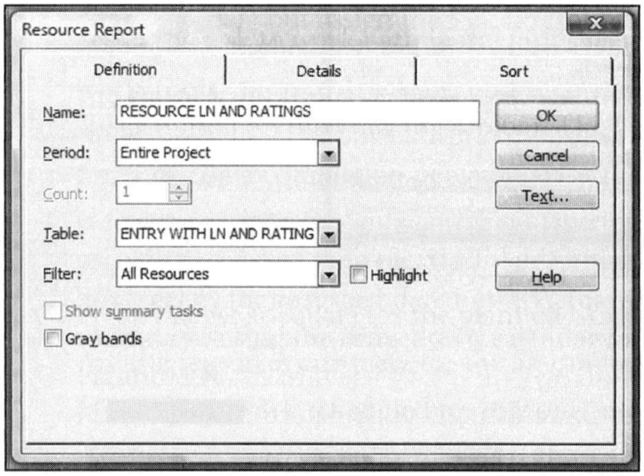

**Figure 13.8** Name
the new report and
set up its contents
and appearance.

6. Click **OK**. The dialog box for defining the report closes and the report appears in
   the Reports list in the Custom Reports dialog box. From there, you can display the
   report with the **Preview** button or close the dialog box and the Reports dialog box.

## New Visual Reports

One of the most exciting new features in Project 2007 is its ability to work with Microsoft
Office Excel and Microsoft Office Visio Professional 2007. None of the reports in Project
offer any visuals, and the new *visual reports* feature presents information in either a chart
or flowchart format that can be edited outside of Project.

To start working with visual reports, click the **Report** menu and then click **Visual Reports**.
The Visual Report - Create Report dialog box, shown in Figure 13.9, appears. The **All** tab
lists all of the available reports, but if you want to limit the list to reports about a specific
topic, you can click one of the category tabs. Click the report template to use in the selected

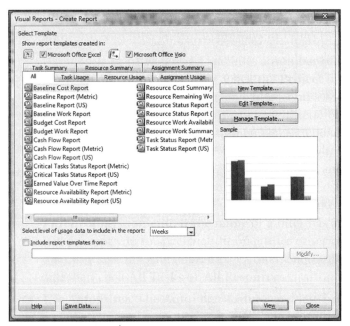

**Figure 13.9** Project offers 22 visual report templates for Excel and Visio.

tab. If you want to include more or less detail in the report, open the **Select Level of Usage Data To Include** in the Report drop-down list and click an alternate timeframe. Then click **View** to create the report, which will appear in Excel or Visio.

A *visual report* exports information to Excel or Visio Professional 2007, where you can manipulate it. Choose **Report, Visual Reports** to open the Visual Reports dialog box. Click category tab, click a report template, and then click **View** to create the visual report.

If you don't have Excel or Visio installed and want to hide the reports for the application you don't have, clear the **Microsoft Office Excel** or **Microsoft Office Visio** check box under Show Report Templates Created In at the top of the Visual Reports - Create Report dialog box.

## Reporting in Visio

Visual reports that you send from Project to Visio appear as PivotDiagram views. This means that you can use the tools in Visio to add, remove, and rearrange information in the diagram. For example, if I click the **Actual Cost** check box under Add Total in the task pane in Figure 13.10, Visio would add data from the *Actual Cost* field to the shape data box for

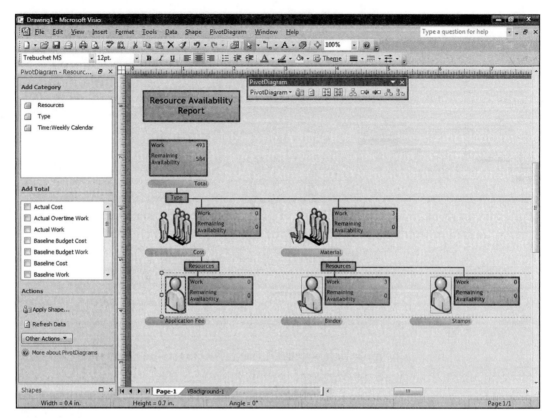

**Figure 13.10** Visio visual reports appear as PivotDiagrams that enable you to change the data displayed and rearrange the layout.

each resource and summary item. You can manipulate a Visio visual report quite extensively to ensure it displays the data you want. And, of course, you can use all of Visio's other cool features, like the ability to apply different shapes to the items in the diagram to customize the report to meet your needs.

After you create a visual report in Visio or Excel, don't forget to save the file! Note that you need to change the Save As Type entry in the Save As dialog box to **Excel Workbook** for Excel 2007 to ensure that all functionality is preserved.

## Reporting in Excel

Each visual report that you send from Project to Excel creates a workbook file with data on two worksheets. The first worksheet, named *Chart1,* shows a chart of the reported information. The second worksheet, labeled according to the type of data used in the report, holds a PivotTable of the charted information. If you click either the chart on the chart sheet or the PivotTable on its sheet, the PivotTable Field list pane appears at the right (see Figure 13.11) so that you can add, move, or rearrange the data in the report.

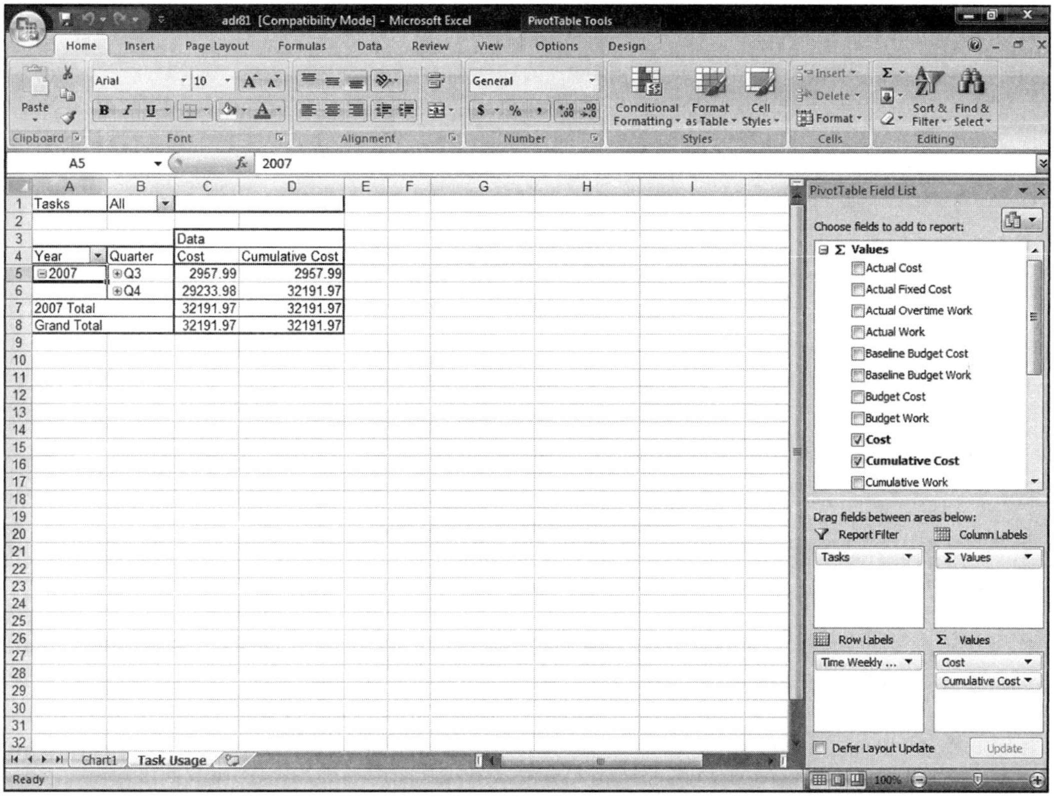

**Figure 13.11** Excel visual reports appear as PivotTables that enable you to change the data displayed and rearrange the layout; the PivotTable information is charted on a separate sheet.

## Creating Your Own Visual Reports Template

You can create your own visual report template from the Visual Reports - Create Report dialog box. Clicking **New Template** there opens the Visual Reports - New Template dialog box, shown in Figure 13.12.

**Figure 13.12**
Specify the data for a new visual report template in this dialog box.

Click the application to use under 1. Select Application in the dialog box. Under 2. Select Data Type, open the **Choose the Data on Which You Want to Report** and click one of the data choices: Task Usage, Resource Usage, Assignment Usage, Task Summary, Resource Summary, or Assignments Summary. After you select the data type, click the **Field Picker** button under 3. Select Fields. In the Visual Reports - Field Picker dialog box, click any field to include in the report from one of the two lists at the left and then click the **Add** button. To remove a field from one of the right-hand lists of selected fields, click the field and then click the **Remove** button. Click **OK** twice to close the dialog boxes for designing the report. The PivotDiagram (Visio) or PivotTable (Excel) appears onscreen so that you can finish designing the report in the destination application.

## Chapter Review

In this chapter, you took on reporting in Project, a vital area to understand when you need to review project information for execution and control purposes, as well as when you need to communicate with team members and stakeholders. You learned what reports Project offers, how to display and print a report, and how to create a custom report when you need it. You learned about the new visual reports that Project can create with Excel and Visio and how to start the process for setting one of those up yourself. The next chapter will build on the sharing and communication information you learned about here.

## Review Questions

Write your answers to the following questions on a sheet of paper.

1. Project includes this number of built-in regular reports.
2. Use the _____ menu to access both regular and visual reports.
3. True or False: A report you create appears in its own separate window.
4. Use the _____ button and dialog box to change settings for the printed report, such as margins and headers.
5. _____ the report to fit more information on each page.
6. True or False: The report always prints exactly as shown onscreen.
7. True or False: You can change the fields contained in a regular report.
8. A visual report appears as a PivotDiagram in this application.
9. A visual report appears as a chart and PivotTable in this application.
10. True or False: You can change the data shown in a visual report.

## Projects

 To see the solutions file created by completing the projects in this chapter, go to www.courseptr.com, click the **Downloads** link in the navigation bar at the top, type **Microsoft Office Project 2007 Survival Guide** in the search text box, and then click **Search Downloads**.

### Project 1

1. Open the file named *Site Search Views* that you worked with in the Projects for Chapter 12.
2. Save the file as *Site Search Reports*.

 Create a folder named *PSG Exercises* in your *Documents* or *My Documents* folder and save your exercise practice files there.

3. Make sure your printer is turned on. If needed, choose **File, Print**; select your printer from the **Name** drop-down list; and then click **Close**.
4. Click **Report** and then click **Reports**.
5. Double-click the **Costs** category.

6. Double-click the **Cash Flow** report.

7. Click the right navigation arrow button (**Page Right**) twice to view the two other pages of the report.

8. Click the left navigation arrow button (**Page Left**) twice to return to the first page of the report.

9. Click **Page Setup**.

10. Under Scaling on the Page tab, change the **Adjust To** zoom percentage entry to **90**. (That's 90% of normal size.) Click **OK**.

11. Now scroll through the report. Notice that it has been reduced to two pages.

12. Click **Print** and then click **OK** to print the report.

13. Click **Close** to close the Reports dialog box.

14. Leave the file open for the next exercise.

## *Project 2*

1. Click **Report** and then click **Reports**.

2. Double-click the **Custom** category.

3. Click the **New** button.

4. Click **Task** in the Report Type list of the **Define New Report** dialog box, if needed, and then click **OK**.

5. Type **COMPLETED TASKS WITH WBS** in the **Name** text box.

6. Open the **Table** drop-down list and click **ENTRY WITH CODES**. This is the custom table you created in Chapter 12.

7. Open the **Filter** drop-down list and click **Completed Tasks**.

8. Click the **Sort** tab. Open the **Sort** drop-down list, type a **W** to scroll, and then click **WBS**. Click the **Descending Option** button.

9. Click the **Text** button. Choose another font from the **Font** list. Also choose alternate **Font Style**, **Size**, and **Color** settings and then click **OK**.

10. Back in the Task Report dialog box, click **OK** to finish defining the new report.

11. Leave the new report selected in the Reports list of the Custom Reports dialog box and click **Preview**.

12. After you finish reviewing your custom report, click **Close** to close the Print Preview, click **Close** again to close the Custom Reports dialog box, and click **Close** a third time to close the Reports dialog box.

### Project 3

1. Click **Report** and then click **Visual Reports**.

2. Make sure that **Microsoft Office Excel** is selected under Show Report Templates Created In.

3. Click the **Cash Flow Report** on the All tab.

4. Make sure the **Select Level of Usage Data To Include in the Report** remains set to Weeks.

5. Click **View**. Excel opens and the visual report appears.

6. Scroll down to view the chart. Notice that it displays just two columns, one for each quarter.

7. Click the **Task Usage** tab. This displays the PivotTable for the chart.

8. Click the **plus (+) icon** beside **Q1** in cell B5 and beside **Q2** in cell B6. This expands the weekly detail in the PivotTable.

9. Click the **Chart1** tab to return to the chart sheet. Note that the chart now shows the cost information on a weekly basis.

10. Save the Excel visual report file as *Site Search Visual Report*, and then click the window **Close (X)** button to close Excel. (Note that you need to change the Save As Type entry in the Save As dialog box to **Excel Workbook** for Excel 2007 to ensure that all functionality is preserved.)

11. Save your changes to the *Site Search Reports* file and then close the file and Project.

CHAPTER 14

# OTHER WAYS TO SHARE AND COMMUNICATE

This Chapter Teaches You How To:

- Understand the import and export concept
- Understand how maps properly identify data during an import or export
- Import data from Excel into Project
- Use more detailed information from Outlook in Project
- Export information from a project plan file
- Copy project plan information and use it in Word
- Create a Web page (HTML file) based on project information
- Discover and try the Copy Picture to Office Wizard
- Link data from an Excel worksheet to a sheet in a project plan file

Just as a screwdriver is a better choice than a hammer for screwing in a screw, using only Microsoft Office Project 2007 to communicate and analyze your project plan information may not always be the right tool for the job. As part of the Office family of applications, Project offers numerous ways to share information with the other Office applications and even other applications that can save to a supported file format. This chapter teaches you some key ways to bring data from another application into Project, as well as how to use information from Project in other applications.

# Understanding Importing, Exporting, and Data Maps

When you *import* information into Project, you're opening a file created by another application to use that data in Project. *Exporting* from Project is the opposite, where you're saving specified data from Project for use in another application. Project's built-in Import Wizard and Export Wizard walk you through the process of importing and exporting information.

Project supports a specific list of file formats for importing and exporting. Table 14.1 details those formats and notes whether Project is limited to either importing or exporting a particular format.

 If an application that you want to share data with doesn't support one of the file formats listed in Table 14.1, chances are it can import and/or export the Text (.txt) or Comma-Separated Values (.csv) formats, which are commonplace. So, for example, if you need to use some information from a database program with a file format not supported by Project, you could export to a .txt or .csv file from the database and then import into Project from that .txt or .csv file.

**Table 14.1** Supported File Formats for Import and Export in Project 2007

| Program/Format | Extension | Description |
| --- | --- | --- |
| Microsoft Project 2000–2003 | .mpp, .mpt | Project plan files and templates from earlier versions |
| Microsoft Project 98 | .mpt | Project plan files from that earlier version (Import only) |
| Microsoft Project Exchange | .mpx | A format used by various project management programs for exchanging data (Import only) |
| Microsoft Excel Workbooks | .xls | The format used by Excel versions 2000–2003 |
| Microsoft Excel PivotTable | .xls | Data set up as an Excel PivotTable in the format used by the 2000–2003 versions of Excel (Export only) |
| Microsoft Project Database | .mpd | A format that stores an entire project database (Import only) |
| Microsoft Access Database | .mdb | The format used by prior Access versions (Import only) |
| Open Database Connectivity | | SQL Server databases that are ODBC compliant (Import only) |
| Text-Only (ASCII) | .txt | A format used by many types of programs that uses tab delimiters to separate text |
| Comma-Separated Values | .csv | A format used by many types of programs that uses comma delimiters to separate text |
| Extensible Markup Language | .xml | A format in increasing use by a variety of programs for structuring and standardizing data |

The process for importing a file starts just like opening a file. You choose **File, Open**. In the Open dialog box, open the Files of Type drop-down list (which isn't labeled when using Project with Vista) that appears near the **File Name** text box and click the type of file you want to open. Navigate to the location for the file to import, click the file when you see it, and then click **Open**. The Import Wizard will start and lead you through the import.

There are two important issues to be aware of when you want to import files in Project:

- In some instances, Project 2007 considers opening files in older formats to be a security risk. If you have not changed an option to allow opening these files using *legacy* formats, Project displays an error message and stops the import process. To make sure you'll be able to import files in older application formats, choose **Tools, Options**. Click the **Security** tab, click **Allow Loading Files with Legacy or Non Default File Formats** under Legacy Formats, and then click **OK**.

- Word, Excel, and Access files in Microsoft Office 2007 use different file formats and file name extensions for their files than older versions of those applications. As such, Project might not display those files in the Open dialog box when you select the applicable file type. To make sure that you can see the Office file you want to import, click **All Files** in the file type drop-down list. If a message box asks whether you want to open the file as text only, click **Yes**. If the file does not import correctly, you can use the Save As command to save the file to be imported into an older file format, such as Excel 97–2003 Workbook in Excel. Then Project will be able to import the file directly.

The export process starts just like saving a file under a new name. Choose **File, Save As**. Choose the format to save to from the **Save As Type** drop-down list, navigate to the destination folder for the save, enter a name in the **File Name** text box, and click **Save**. At that point the Export Wizard takes over and walks you through the process of exporting the file.

 *Exporting* saves data from Project in another file format for use in another application. *Importing* brings data from a file saved by another application into Project. A *data map* defines the fields of information to be exchanged and matches up the source and destination fields for data during an import or export.

Because data in an import or export process is moving between two files that typically will not use the same column or field names, Project needs a way to define which fields hold the data to be copied and to match the data from each source field to the destination. To do this, the Import Wizard or Export Wizard uses a *data map*. You can create a custom data map when you import or export or use an existing map defined in Project.

When the Import or Export Wizard reaches the point in the process where it needs you to determine how to map information, it will ask: Create a New Map or Use Existing Map? If you want to use one of Project's predefined maps, click the **Use Existing Map** option button, click a map in the wizard dialog box that lists the maps (see the example in Figure 14.1), and then click **Next** to continue the wizard.

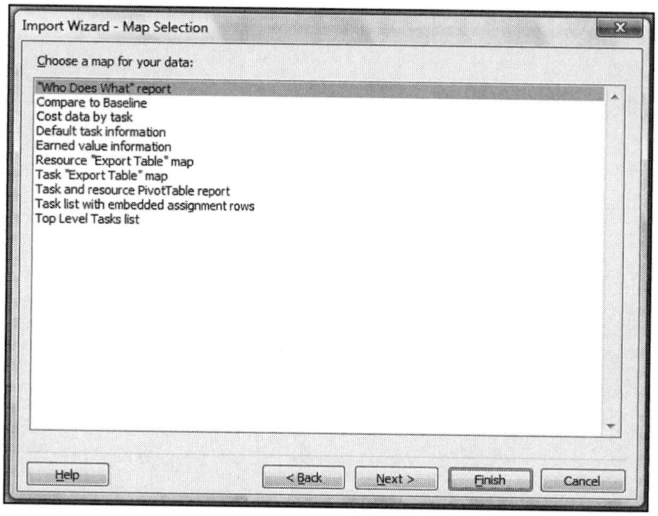

**Figure 14.1** Project offers several predefined data maps for imports and exports.

You might instead need to create your own custom map to set up the fields to import and export. In addition, when you're creating a map to import information from Excel or Access, the map specifies which worksheet or table holds the information to be imported. To create a map, click the **New Map** option button in the wizard screen that asks whether to create a new map or use an existing one and then click **Next**. If you're importing information, in the next screen click an option to specify where to place the imported information (**As a New Project, Append the Data to the Active Project, Append the Data to the Active Project, Merge the Data Into the Active Project**) and click **Next**. (Exporting always creates a new file.) The next step of the wizard presents Map Options, as shown in Figure 14.2.

At the top, click **Tasks, Resources,** or **Assignments** to determine the type of information to be imported or exported. Also determine whether the imported data has a header row with field names or whether to create a header row in the exported file by checking the appropriate check box. Click **Next** again; you'll see the wizard dialog box where you can create the map. As shown in Figure 14.3, if you're importing from a workbook or database, select the worksheet or table using the drop-down list at the top of the dialog box. When exporting, you specify a name for the destination worksheet or table. Then, map the fields using the columns in the middle of the dialog box. When importing, select the Project fields

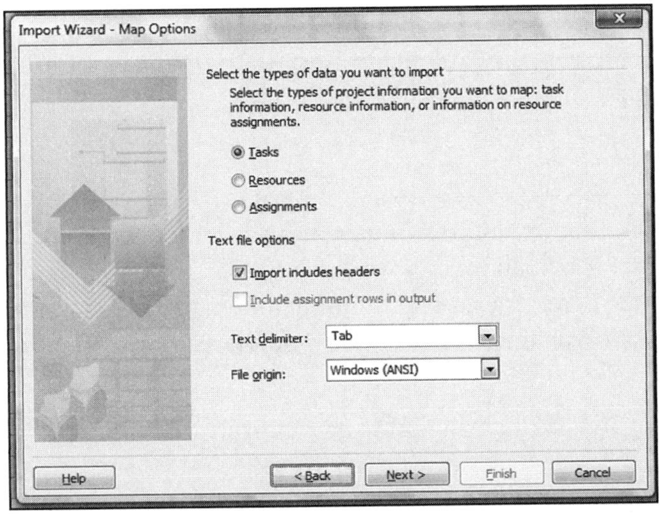

**Figure 14.2** Specify here what type of information the map will import.

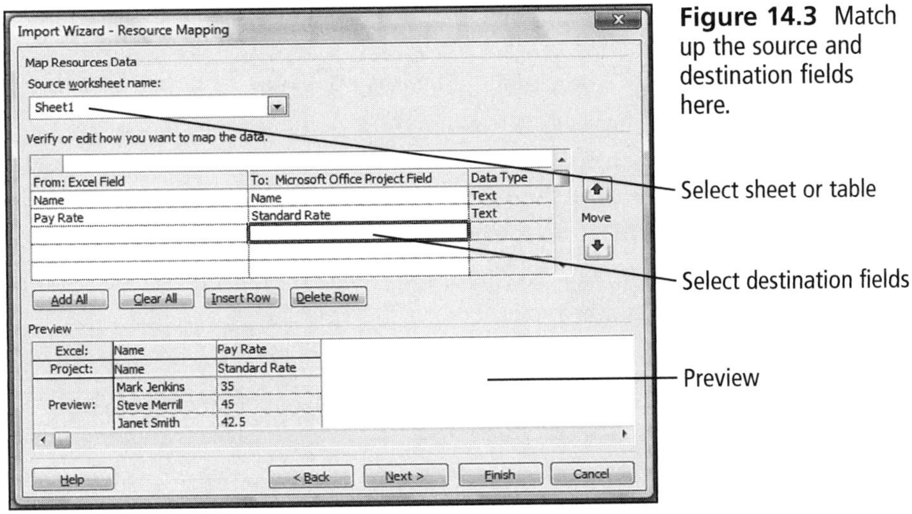

**Figure 14.3** Match up the source and destination fields here.

Select sheet or table

Select destination fields

Preview

into which to place the data in the To: Microsoft Project column. When exporting, type in a field name for each field to create in the destination document. Before continuing, check the Preview area at the bottom of the dialog box to ensure information is mapping as you wish.

To exclude a field of information from being imported or exported, leave it set to **(not mapped)** in the To: column. You also can click a row and click the **Delete Row** button to remove that field from the map.

After you click **Next**, you can use the **Save Map** button to save the custom map that you created. To use a custom map in other project plan files, use the Organizer (**Tools, Organizer**) to copy it into Global.mpt.

## Importing from Excel

You already saw in Chapter 7 how to import resource information from an Excel workbook file into Project. You use that same overall process whenever you import from Excel to Project, so I won't rehash it in detail here. One important thing to remember is that the data being imported must be the right type for the field where you place it. For example, you need to import numeric information into a cost field.

Just follow these overall steps when you want to bring information from an Excel file into Project:

1. Make any necessary changes and save the Excel file to import. If you're working in Microsoft Office Excel 2007, save the file in the Excel 97–2003 Workbook format to ensure that Project will recognize it as an Excel file.

2. Click **File** and then click **Open**. The Open dialog box appears.

3. Click the file type drop-down list near the lower-right corner of the dialog box (it looks like a button reading Microsoft Project Files) and then click **Microsoft Excel Workbooks**. (You'll have to click All Files if you're attempting to import an Excel 2007 file, but that process doesn't always work.)

4. Navigate to the folder holding the file to import, click the file, and then click **Open**. The first Import Wizard dialog box appears.

5. Click **Next** to move to the next step of the wizard.

6. Specify whether to create a new data map and where to place the imported data. Create the map if needed.

7. When you have all the field mapping properly specified and the Preview area at the bottom of the dialog box shows the correct mapping, click **Finish**.

## Exporting Outlook Tasks and Then Importing Them

Chapter 5 showed you the **Tools, Import Outlook Tasks** command, which enables you to import tasks that you've entered into your Outlook To-Do list. That process limits you to importing only three fields of information into Project: Task Name, Notes, and Duration. But Outlook tracks additional information about tasks such as Start Date and Due Date.

To be able to import all the data you want from Outlook, you need to first export the data from Outlook to create a file that Project can import. In Outlook, choose the **File, Import and Export** command. In the Import and Export Wizard dialog box that opens, click **Export to a File** in the Choose an Action to Perform list and then click **Next**.

In the next wizard dialog box, click the desired file format in the **Create a File of Type** list. The Comma Separated Values (Windows) and Tab Separated Values (Windows) options work well. Click **Next**. In the next wizard dialog box, click a choice in the **Select Folder to Export From** list. If you want to export task information, you should click **Tasks** here, as shown in Figure 14.4.

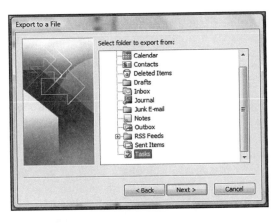

**Figure 14.4**
Exporting Outlook task information to a file format Project can import enables you to import more details into Project.

Click **Next**, specify a name and location for the exported file, and then click **Next** again. Click **Finish** in the final wizard dialog box. The Set Date Range dialog box prompts you to specify the time period within which the exported tasks fall. Change the dates shown, if needed, and then click **OK**. The export finishes and creates a file that you can then import into Project by displaying the Open dialog box, selecting the All Files file format, and then navigating to and selecting the file with the exported Outlook data to start the Import wizard.

## Exporting Project Information

As with the import process, when you export data from a project plan file, an Export wizard appears to lead you through the process, which includes selecting or creating a data map. The overall steps are the same no matter what type of file you want to export your data to:

1. Make any needed changes and save the project plan file you want to export.
2. Click **File** and then click **Save As**. The Save As dialog box appears.

3. Click the **Save As Type** drop-down list and then click the desired format for the exported file. Edit the **File Name** and save location, if desired, and click **Save**. The first Export Wizard dialog box appears.

4. Click **Next** to move to the next step of the wizard.

5. Click the **Selected Data** option button and then click **Next**.

If you instead click the other option button presented (its name varies depending on the file format selected in Step 3), Project exports all the data. This gives you more data to work with in the exported file, but keep in mind that the data might not be set up in a way that works for you. For example, if you choose **Project Export Template** when exporting to Excel format, the data is divided between several different worksheets in the exported file.

6. Specify whether to create a new data map or use an existing map. Create the export map if needed.

7. When you have all the field mapping properly specified and the Preview area at the bottom of the dialog box shows the correct mapping, click **Finish** to export the file.

If you prefer to enter resource information in Excel, consider exporting a blank file with the Resource Sheet fields to create a "template" for your resource spreadsheet. Then, you can more smoothly import the information into Excel or simply copy from Excel and paste in the Resource Sheet view in Project.

## Copying Project Data and Pasting It into Word

When you select information from a sheet in Project, you can paste it into a Word document. Drag over the cells you want to copy, press **Ctrl+C** to copy them, click to position the insertion point at the location where you want to paste the data in a Word document, and press **Ctrl+V** to paste.

The pasted data appears in rows in Word, with tabs separating the entries that came from different fields. The data will look better if you convert it to a table. Select the data. Then, in Word 2007, click the **Insert** tab, click the **Table** button, and then click **Convert Text to Table** (see Figure 14.5). (In Word 2003, the command is **Table, Convert, Text to Table**.) Verify the correct **Number of Columns** entry in the Convert Text to Table dialog box that appears and then click **OK**.

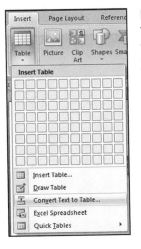

**Figure 14.5** Use this command to convert pasted Project data to a table in Word.

# Creating and E-Mailing an HTML File via Excel or Word

Previous versions of Project included the ability to save (export) Project information as a Web page (HTML) file. I loved this feature and I'm sad to see it go. You could easily e-mail the HTML files and all a user needed to have to view the HTML file was a Web browser program, which nearly every computer offers these days.

You can still offer your Project data in HTML format, but you have to take a little detour through Word or Excel:

1. Export the Project data to an Excel file or copy and paste it into Word.

2. In Excel or Word, format the data as desired.

3. Use the **Save As** command on the **File** menu (click the Office Button in the 2007 versions).

4. Open the **Save as Type** drop-down list in the Save As dialog box and select **Single File Web Page** or **Web Page**.

5. Enter a **File Name** and select the folder to save to and then click **Save**.

# Using the Copy Picture to Office Wizard

The Analysis toolbar in Project 2007 offers a Copy Picture to Office Wizard button that you can use to export information from Project to a nice, graphical document for PowerPoint, Word, or Visio. Figure 14.6 shows an example of a PowerPoint slide created with this feature.

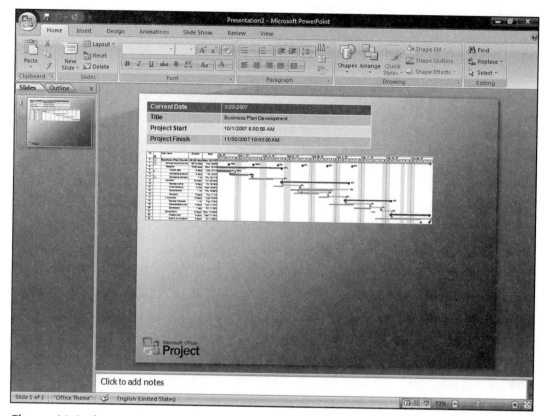

**Figure 14.6** The Copy Picture to Office wizard enables you to create graphical versions of Project information for PowerPoint (shown here), Word, and Visio.

Follow these steps to use the Copy Picture to Office wizard:

1. Right-click any toolbar and click **Analysis** to display the Analysis toolbar.
2. Change to the view that you want to show in the picture.
3. If you want to include only selected tasks or resources, select the tasks or resources.
4. Click the **Copy Picture to Office Wizard** button on the Analysis toolbar.
5. Click **Next** to move past the wizard's welcome dialog box. The Copy Picture to Office Wizard - Step 1 of 4 dialog box appears.
6. If you want to show a different level of detail in the picture, click **Modify My Outline Level,** click the **Show** check box, and choose the outline level to show from the accompanying drop-down list. Otherwise, just leave **Keep My Original Outline Level** selected. Click **Next**. The Copy Picture to Office Wizard - Step 2 of 4 dialog box appears.

7. Under Copy, click an option to specify which information to include in the picture. **Rows on Screen** includes only the rows presently visible. If you selected specific tasks or resources for the picture in Step 3, click **Selected Rows in View**. To include all rows, click **All Rows in View**.

8. Under **Timescale**, select how much of the chart portion of the view to include. **As Shown on Screen** captures the chart information or bars exactly as they currently appear on the screen. **Entire Project (Start Date to Finish Date)** includes all the chart information in the picture. Click **From** and enter starting and ending dates if you want to include only information falling within a particular timeframe (see Figure 14.7).

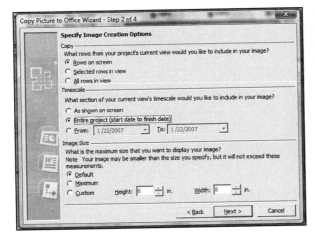

**Figure 14.7** The settings here control which information appears in the copied picture.

9. Under Image Size, you may optionally change the size of the finished picture. Click **Maximum** to make the picture as large as possible or click **Custom** and then enter custom measurements.

10. Click **Next**. The Copy Picture to Office Wizard - Step 3 of 4 dialog box appears.

11. Click the option button for the application in which you want to create the picture: **PowerPoint**, **Visio**, or **Word**. If it becomes active based on your application choice, you also can click **Portrait** to change to a tall image orientation.

12. Click **Next**. The Copy Picture to Office Wizard - Step 4 of 4 dialog box appears.

13. Determine which fields will appear as "titles" above the picture. To add a field, click it in the left **Microsoft Office Project Fields** list and then click **Add**. To remove a field, click it in the right **Fields to Export** list and click **Remove**.

14. Click **Finish**. The Copy Picture to Office Wizard - Complete dialog box appears.

15. Click **Close**. The wizard closes and the new picture document opens in the application you specified in Step 11. You can save, edit, and print the document there.

TIP  Project offers the Copy Picture button on the Standard toolbar. You can use this button to copy a picture of selected tasks for pasting in another application or to save the pictures as an image file in the .GIF format for use elsewhere.

# Linking Info from Excel into Project

Copying and pasting is fine, but that technique can result in many different "versions" of data floating around in different files. If a value changes, you have to change it in its original file and every other file to which you copied it.

If you have cost or other information in Excel that you want to use in Project but you know that the information is subject to change, you can paste it as a linked cell in Project. For example, a client of mine in the construction business has developed extensive material pricing lists in Excel. He wanted to use the same prices for the corresponding material resources in Project but didn't want to have to update both files each time a price changed. So, we copied each price from Excel and pasted it as a link into the *Std. Rate* field of the Resource Sheet.

When a cell's information is linked, changing the cell entry in Excel updates the value in Project, and vice versa.

Here's how to set up a link between a cell in an Excel worksheet and a cell in a Project sheet:

1. In Excel, select the cell that holds the information to link.

MIS-STEP  This process only works if you select and paste one cell at a time.

2. Press **Ctrl+C** to copy the cell or use the copy command in your version of Excel.
3. Open the Project file into which you want to paste and link the copied information.
4. Display the view that holds the sheet and cell into which you want to paste and link the information. (Change tables if needed.)
5. Click the destination cell in the sheet.
6. Click **Edit** and then click **Paste Special**. The Paste Special dialog box appears.
7. Click the **Paste Link** option button at the left and then click **OK**. The pasted linked data appears in the sheet.

A small green triangle appears in the lower-right corner of any linked cell, as shown in Figure 14.8. If you want to open the Excel file and view the linked cell there, double-click the linked Project cell.

---

**NOTE** If you link information from Excel to Project, the usual caveats about links apply. For example, moving or renaming either of the files can break the link.

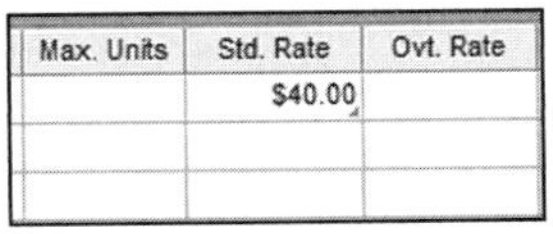

---

| Max. Units | Std. Rate | Ovt. Rate |
|------------|-----------|-----------|
|            | $40.00    |           |
|            |           |           |
|            |           |           |

**Figure 14.8** A green triangle appears in the lower-right corner of any linked cell.

# Chapter Review

This chapter taught you the most common methods of bringing information from another application into Project and reusing information from Project in other programs. You saw how to use the Import or Export Wizard by using the Open or Save As commands and choosing a different file type and how to create a map to determine the fields that will hold the imported or exported information. You also learned how to paste information into Word; save Project information as a Web page; use a wizard that creates a picture of schedule information in Word, PowerPoint, or Visio; and link a Project cell to an Excel worksheet cell. The next chapter moves on to view and use information from multiple project plans for higher-level planning and execution.

## Review Questions

Write your answers to the following questions on a sheet of paper.

1. True or False: Project can import or export virtually any file format.
2. Use the _____ command on the File menu to start an import.
3. Use the _____ command on the File menu to start an export.
4. Create a _____ to match fields between the source and destination files.
5. The _____ lists the field names that appear in the source or destination file.
6. True or False: You have to import or export all fields.
7. True or False: Data pasted into Word appears as a Word table.

8. Name one of the two programs that enable you to save Project information as a Web page once you've copied or exported the data to that application.

9. The _____ toolbar holds the Copy Picture to Office Wizard button.

10. Name one of the three applications for which the Copy Picture to Office wizard can create a file.

## Projects

To see the solutions file created by completing the projects in this chapter, go to www.courseptr.com, click the **Downloads** link in the navigation bar at the top, type **Microsoft Office Project 2007 Survival Guide** in the search text box, and then click **Search Downloads**.

### *Project 1*

1. Open the file named *Site Search Reports* that you worked with in the Projects for Chapter 13.

Create a folder named *PSG Exercises* in your *Documents* or *My Documents* folder and save your exercise practice files there.

2. Choose **File, Save As.** Select **Microsoft Excel Workbook** from the **Save As Type** drop-down list, change the **File Name** entry to *Site Search Export,* and then click **Save.**

3. Click **Next** at the first Export Wizard dialog box.

4. Leave Selected Data selected and click **Next.**

5. Click **Use Existing Map** and then click **Next.**

6. Click **Default Task Information** in the Choose a Map for Your Data list and click **Next.**

7. Leave the **Tasks** and **Export Includes Headers** check boxes checked in the next wizard dialog box. Click **Next.**

8. Review the mapping in the next Export Wizard dialog box and then click **Finish.**

9. Close the *Site Search Reports* file in Project. Do not save changes.

10. Go to Excel and open the *Site Search Export* file to review its contents. After doing so, you can close the file and Excel.

## Project 2

1. In Project, click **File** and then click **Open**.

2. Open the file type drop-down list in the Open dialog box and click **Microsoft Excel Workbooks**. Click the *Site Search Export* file (navigate to the folder where you saved it, if needed) and then click **Open**.

3. Click **Next** at the first Import Wizard dialog box.

4. Click **New Map** and then click **Next**.

5. Leave the **As a New Project** option selected and click **Next**.

6. In the next wizard dialog box, click the **Tasks** check box to check it and leave **Export Includes Headers** checked. Click **Next** to move to the next wizard dialog box.

7. Open the **Source Worksheet** drop-down list and click **Task_Data**.

8. In the list of mapped fields, select each of the following fields and then click the **Delete Row** button below the list of fields to delete it: **Start_Date, Finish_Date, Predecessors,** and **Resource_Names**.

9. Click **Finish**. The newly imported file appears.

10. Save this file as *Site Search Export* and leave it open for the next exercise.

## Project 3

1. Use the **Indent** button on the Formatting toolbar to indent the following tasks:

   2 through 6

   8 and 9

   11 through 13

   15 through 21

2. Use the Link Tasks button on the Standard toolbar to link the following tasks:

   2 through 6

   8 and 9

   11 through 13

   15 through 21

   6 and 8

   9 and 11

   13 and 15

3. Right-click a toolbar and then click **Analysis**.

4. Click **Copy Picture to Office Wizard** on the Analysis toolbar and then click **Next**.

5. Leave **Keep My Original Outline Level** selected and then click **Next**.

6. Click **Entire Project (Start Date to Finish Date)** under Timescale and then click **Next**.

7. Click the **Word** option button in the next dialog box and then click **Next**.

8. Leave the field selections as is and click **Finish** and then **Close**.

9. Save the Word file as *Site Search Export.*

10. Close any open files, as well as Word and Project.

# CHAPTER 15

## ENHANCING EXECUTION WITH RESOURCE POOLS AND MASTER PROJECTS

This Chapter Teaches You How To:

- Understand and create a resource pool
- Share resources from the pool
- Refresh resource information
- Understand how a master project works
- Build the master project
- Display, hide, and link subprojects
- View resources that are overbooked between projects
- Add a master project task

Often you will find yourself managing multiple projects that use many of the same resources and overlap in time. Coordinating the details within a project can be challenging enough; coordinating details *between* projects can ramp up the complexity level significantly. Fortunately, Microsoft Office Project 2007 provides functionality that enhances your ability to plan and execute multiple projects that share resources. The techniques covered in this chapter help you bump your perspective up to a higher level while retaining your access to detailed project information.

## Sharing Resources from a Pool

When you use basically the same list of resources for a number of different projects, there's no need to rebuild the list of resources in every project plan file. Even importing or copying the resource information takes some time, and then you would still need to adjust calendar settings for each resource. Why spend time reinventing the wheel?

In addition, having a separate list of the resources in every project plan file leaves you with the issue of how to ensure the information is up to date in every file. For example, if the Std. Rate for a resource changes, you have to make sure you update the *Std. Rate* field entry in the Resource Sheet in every file where you list that resource. Missing the correction in a project plan file would mean that Project would be calculating inaccurate cost data. You can avoid these issues by creating a single list of resources called a ***resource pool***.

### Understanding the Resource Pool

A resource pool is a Project file that contains only a list of resources in the Resource Sheet view. While the resource pool file could technically include tasks and assignments, the best practice is to store resources only in the resource pool file. You can name the file whatever you want, but make sure you choose a name that clearly identifies the file as your resource pool.

After you create and save the resource pool file, you can share the resources from that file into other project plan files that do have task information, as illustrated in Figure 15.1. The files using the resources from the pool are called ***sharer files***. Information about each resource flows from the Resource Sheet in the pool file to the Resource Sheet in an individual sharer file. By default, the link between the two files stays live or active so that Project

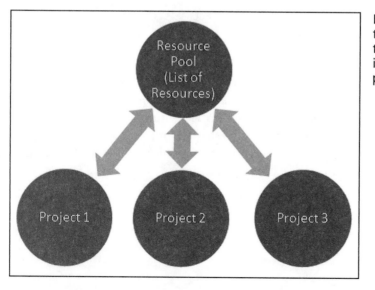

**Figure 15.1** Use the resources from the resource pool file in other individual project files.

is able to use assignment information from the individual sharer files to tell you which resources are overbooked between projects.

Use these overall steps to create a resource pool file:

1. Click the **New** button on the Standard toolbar (shortcut: **Ctrl+N**) to create a new, blank project plan file.

2. Click **View** and then click **Resource Sheet** to display the Resource Sheet view.

3. Enter as much resource information as you wish and adjust resource calendars, if desired.

4. Save and name your file (**File, Save**). An example resource pool file appears in Figure 15.2.

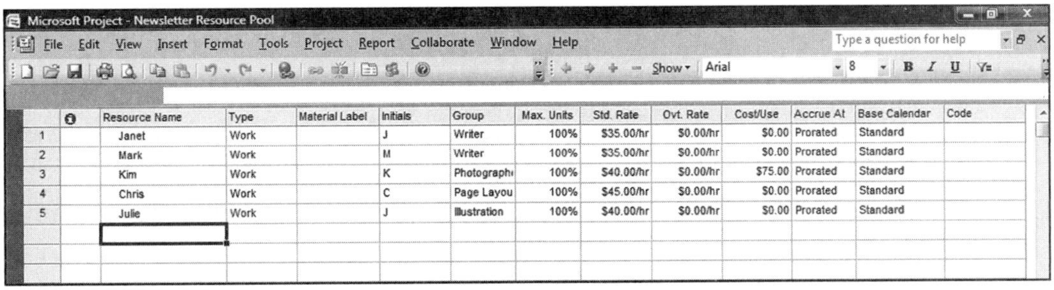

| | 0 | Resource Name | Type | Material Label | Initials | Group | Max. Units | Std. Rate | Ovt. Rate | Cost/Use | Accrue At | Base Calendar | Code |
|---|---|---|---|---|---|---|---|---|---|---|---|---|---|
| 1 | | Janet | Work | | J | Writer | 100% | $35.00/hr | $0.00/hr | $0.00 | Prorated | Standard | |
| 2 | | Mark | Work | | M | Writer | 100% | $35.00/hr | $0.00/hr | $0.00 | Prorated | Standard | |
| 3 | | Kim | Work | | K | Photographe | 100% | $40.00/hr | $0.00/hr | $75.00 | Prorated | Standard | |
| 4 | | Chris | Work | | C | Page Layou | 100% | $45.00/hr | $0.00/hr | $0.00 | Prorated | Standard | |
| 5 | | Julie | Work | | J | Illustration | 100% | $40.00/hr | $0.00/hr | $0.00 | Prorated | Standard | |

**Figure 15.2** The resource pool file lists the resources for all your projects in the Resource Sheet view.

## Sharing Resources into a Project Plan

To use the resources from a resource pool, you share the resources into the individual sharer files that hold the task information. Use these steps to share resources from the pool into an individual sharer file:

1. Open the resource pool file.

> If the pool file isn't open, you can't share its resources into another file. If you get to Step 4 and don't see the name of the pool file in the From drop-down list, start over from Step 1 of this process.

2. Open or create the sharer file with the task information. You do not need to enter any resource information into this file.

3. With the sharer file active, click **Tools**, point to **Resource Sharing**, and click **Share Resources**. The Share Resources dialog box appears.

4. Click the **Use Resources** option button under Resources for 'File Name,' and then make sure that the name of the resource pool file appears as the From drop-down list selection. Figure 15.3 shows an example.

**Figure 15.3**
Choose to use resources from a resource pool file in this dialog box.

5. Click the On Conflict with Calendar or Resource Information option that you want to use:

■ **Pool Takes Precedence.** When a conflict in resource information occurs, Project will keep the information from the pool file rather than the sharer file.

■ **Sharer Takes Precedence.** When a conflict in resource information occurs, Project will keep the information from the sharer file rather than the pool file.

6. Click **OK.** Project makes the resources from the pool available in the sharer file.

---

The *resource pool* is a separate Project file in which you enter the list of resources to be used for all your projects. You can then use the **Tools, Resource Sharing, Share Resources** command to use the resources from the pool in the current project plan file.

---

Shared resources in the sharer file look and work exactly as if you had retyped the resource information into the Resource Sheet. You can use the Assign Resources dialog box to assign the resources to the tasks in the sharer file, as shown in the example in Figure 15.4. The resources listed in the pool file shown in Figure 15.2 have been shared into the file shown in Figure 15.4.

## Viewing Resource Overallocations Between Projects

The live information link between the resource pool file and the individual sharer files enables the resource pool file to track how you've assigned resources in all the sharer files. You can use the same views in the resource pool file as you would in an individual project file to find resource overallocations and issues with assignments; the difference is that the resource pool file can show you when you've overallocated a resource between the multiple sharer projects.

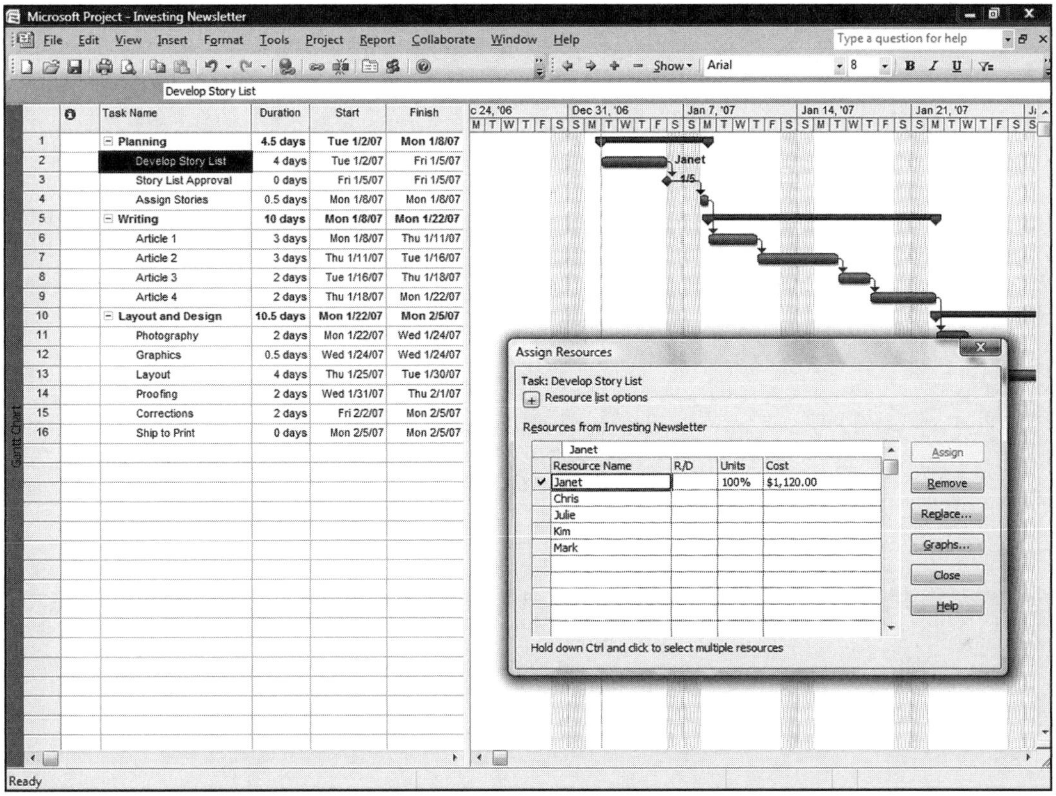

**Figure 15.4** Work with resources shared from a pool using the same techniques as resources that were typed into the Resource Sheet.

Use these steps to see when you've overallocated a resource between projects:

1. Open the resource pool file.
2. Open *all* of the sharer files. Project won't be able to include the assignment information from a sharer file in its calculations if the sharer file isn't open.
3. Click the **Window** menu and click the name of the resource pool file to change to that file.
4. Click **View** and then click **Resource Sheet**. Just as when you're working in an individual project plan file, the name for each overbooked resource will appear in red and an exclamation point indicator will appear for it (see Figure 15.5).
5. Click **View, Resource Usage**. Select the name of an overbooked resource in the left side of the view and then click **Alt+F5** to display the first date with an overallocation in the right side of the view. Figure 15.6 illustrates a resource that's overbooked between projects.

The Resource Usage view doesn't by default show you what project file the individual assignments come from, nor will the Assignment Information dialog box when you double-click an assignment in the view. You can add a task sheet field to show the project file name so that you can identify the project in which each assignment was made. This is particularly helpful when similar projects have similar task names, as in the example in Figure 15.6.

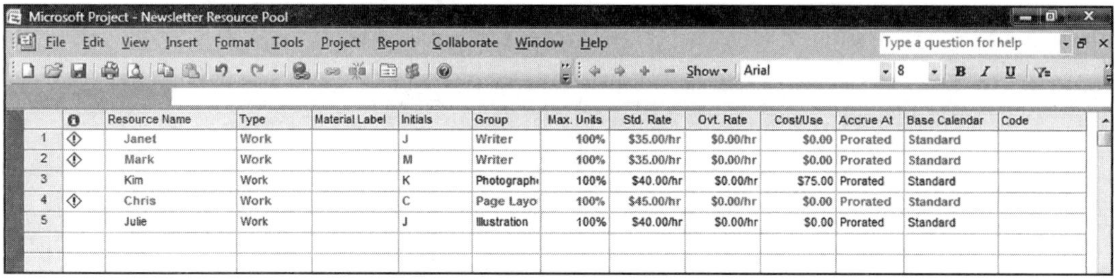

**Figure 15.5** Overallocated resources are highlighted in red in the Resource Sheet view of the resource pool file.

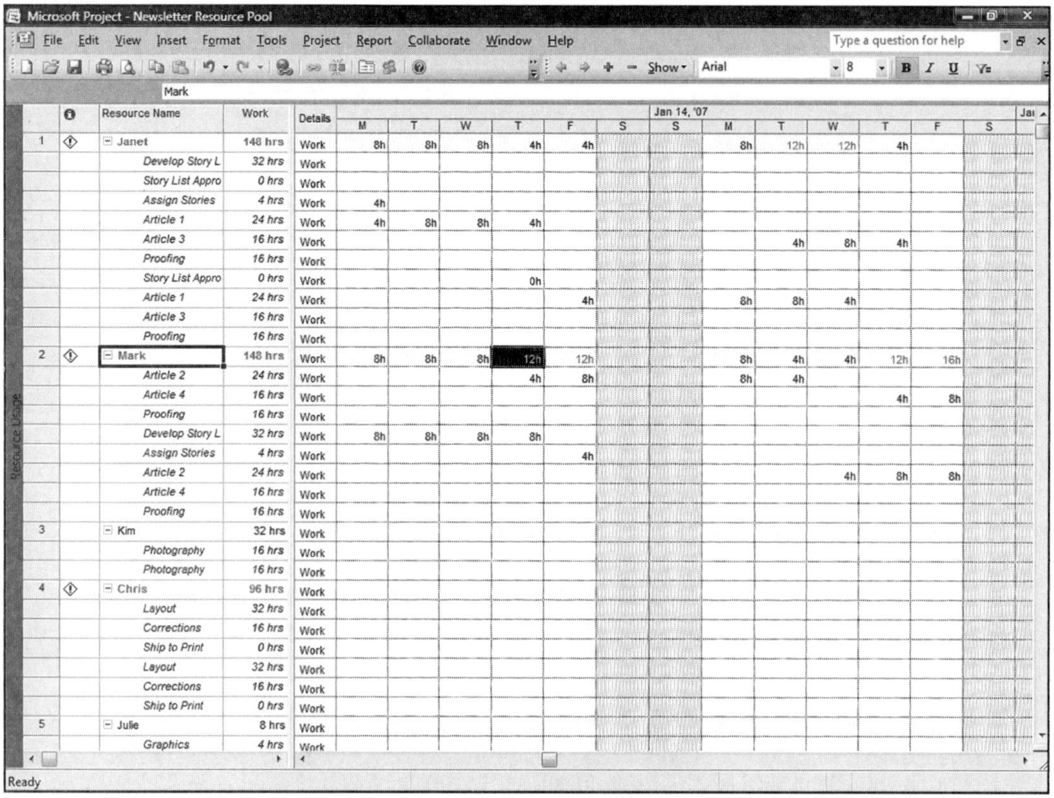

**Figure 15.6** You can find overallocated dates and assignments for a resource by displaying the Resource Usage view in the resource pool file.

Follow these steps to insert a field with the project file's name:

1. Right-click the field to the left of which you want to insert the project file name field and then click **Insert Column**.

2. In the Column Definition dialog box, open the **Field Name** drop-down list, type a **p** to scroll the list, and click **Project**.

3. Make any other changes as desired in the Column Definition dialog box and then click **OK**.

4. Resize the new column and drag the divider between the two sides of the view to display more fields as needed. As shown in Figure 15.7, you can now identify the sharer file in which each assignment was made. For example, for the first date on which the *Mark* resource is overallocated, one of the assignments creating the overallocation comes from the *Investing Newsletter* file, while the other assignment for that date comes from the *Insurance Newsletter* file.

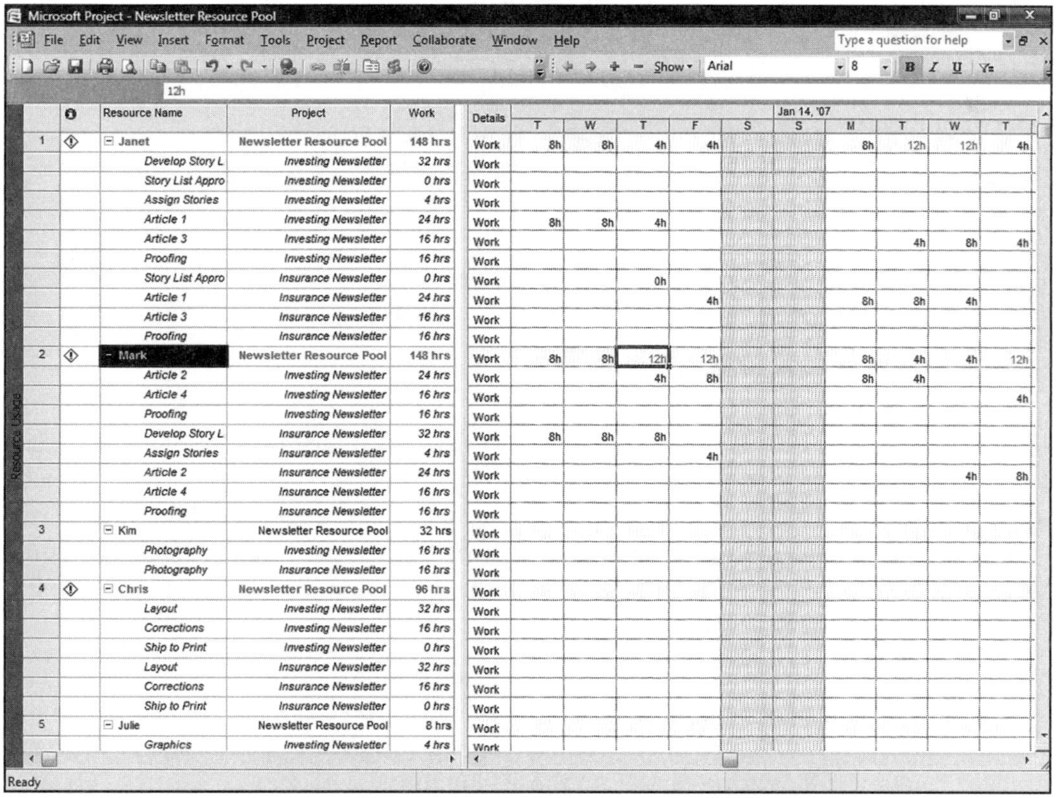

**Figure 15.7** Add the *Project* field into the task sheet to identify the sharer file that holds each assignment.

> **NOTE** Ideally, you want to create a new table that includes the inserted column, as explained in the "Creating a Table" section of Chapter 12. I just gave you the quick method for editing the Entry table here to save steps and show you more quickly which field to add and how it looks when added.

## Working with Updates

The resource pool file remains linked to the individual project files sharing its resources by default. When you open the file containing the link to resource information, Project must also open the resource pool file. It displays the Open Resource Pool Information dialog box asking if you want to open the resource pool or not, as shown in Figure 15.8. Leave the top option button selected, as shown in Figure 15.8, and then and click **OK**. If you've made changes to the resource information in the shared resource pool file, those changes appear in the open sharer file. The only time you want to click the Do Not Open Other Files choice in the Open Resource Pool Information dialog box is if you don't want pool changes to flow into the sharer file.

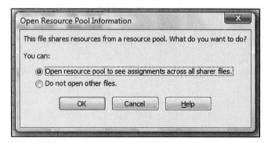

**Figure 15.8** Project reminds you that the file has shared resources and asks you to verify that you want to open the resource pool file.

If you reopen the resource pool file rather than a sharer file, the Open Resource Pool dialog box presents a few options (see Figure 15.9). You can open the resource pool as read-only, open the resource file normally so that you can make changes to it (although if you choose this option and your files reside on a network, other users won't be able to change the resource pool), or open the file with the resource pool and any other files using the resource pool in a new master project file.

When resource information changes, such as when a resource's cost rate changes or when you need to add vacation days into a resource's calendar, you can make the changes in the Resource Sheet view of the resource pool file. When you then open the sharer files, the updated resource information flows into those files, too.

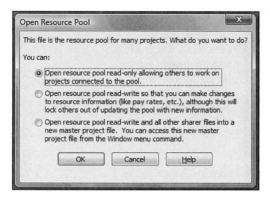

**Figure 15.9** When you open the resource pool file, specify whether or not you want to be able to make changes to it.

If the resource pool file is stored on a network and others can make changes to the pool file, and if you have left a sharer file using that resource pool open for several hours, the resource information in the sharer file won't reflect the changes that other users may have made to the resource pool file. In this situation, you can refresh the resource information (to get the latest pool information) without closing and reopening the sharer file. Instead, choose **Tools, Resources, Refresh Resource Pool** to pull the latest changes from the resource pool file into the individual sharer file.

If you make changes in any sharer file and want to make sure that the resource pool file is updated with those changes, choose **Tools, Resources, Update Resource Pool**. This "pushes" any new assignment or resource information to the resource pool file, helping prevent problems with overallocating resources between projects.

## Breaking a Pool Link

You can use the Share Resources dialog box for the resource pool file to open a sharer file or break the link between the pool and the sharer. The following steps explain how to perform either of these operations:

1. Open the resource pool file.
2. Choose **Tools, Resource Sharing, Share Resources**. The Share Resources dialog box opens.
3. Click the file to open or unlink in the Sharing Links list, as shown in Figure 15.10.
4. Click **Break Link** to break the link between the pool and the sharer file, or click **Open** to open the sharer file.

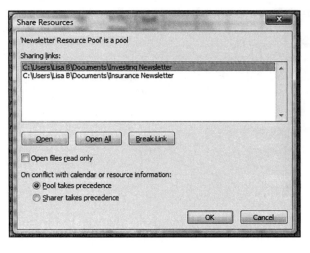

**Figure 15.10** You can break a link between a sharer file and the resource pool file by clicking the sharer and then clicking **Break Link**.

# Viewing a Master Project

Managing multiple projects demands that you have the ability not only to manage the workflow at a more "micro" level within projects but also to take the "macro" view of how priorities play out between multiple projects.

You learned earlier that using a resource pool file enables you to see resource overallocations and assignments for the multiple projects sharing the pool's resources. When you manage multiple projects, you also might want to see information like the following:

- A Gantt Chart view printout that shows the schedule for the tasks from more than one project
- A list of in-progress tasks or tasks starting soon for all projects to jog your memory about things that you need to follow up on
- A view that enables you to specify when a task from one project might be the predecessor for a task in another project
- A view that enables you to insert administrative tasks that pertain to a number of project files

## Understanding Master Projects and Subprojects

Project offers a solution to enable you to manage priorities between projects: *consolidating projects*. To consolidate two or more project plan files, you insert the information from each of the selected files (called *subprojects*) into a single container file called the *master project*. Then you can change the view, print, and otherwise work with the combined information. You can consolidate up to a thousand different project schedules (assuming your system has the horsepower to do so) in a single master project file, but in the real world, you'll only consolidate the projects that are currently underway and relevant to your team and stakeholders.

Although it's not necessary that the subproject files share resources from a resource pool, doing so ideally will ensure consistent resource rate and scheduling information in the individual subproject files and within the master project file. By default, each inserted subproject file is linked to the master project file so that updates flow back and forth between the files, just as updates flow back and forth between the resource pool and linked sharer files. Figure 15.11 illustrates how this arrangement results in a system of linked files that update one another so that any change you make in one file can flow to impacted tasks, resources, and assignments in the affected linked files.

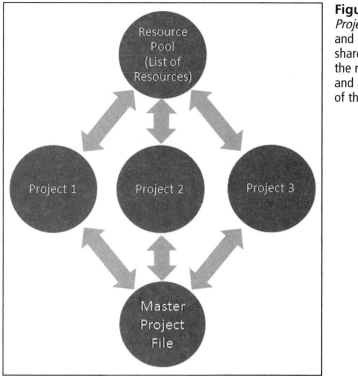

**Figure 15.11**
*Project 1*, *Project 2*, and *Project 3* each share resources from the resource pool file and are subprojects of the master project.

## Creating a Master Project and Inserting Subprojects

The primary method for consolidating files in Project 2007 is to insert each subproject file into a new, blank file that then becomes the master project file. Each inserted subproject file is linked to a single task sheet line in the master project. You have to create the source or subproject files before you add them to the consolidated project file. This makes sense because generally speaking, you'll plan your individual projects and then see how they compare.

To create a master project file and insert subprojects, follow these steps:

1. Create, save, and close the subproject files, linking each to a resource pool file, if desired.

2. Click the **New** button on the Standard toolbar (shortcut: **Ctrl+N**) to create a new, blank project plan file. This file will become the master project file.

3. Click **Project, Project Information**. Select a **Start Date** that's the same as the earliest start date for any of the files that will be inserted as subprojects and then click **OK**. This step prevents any potential scheduling errors or constraint violations when you insert the subproject files.

4. Click the first blank cell in the *Task Name* field of the task sheet. This is the row where the inserted subproject will appear.

5. Click **Insert** and then click **Project**. The Insert Project dialog box appears.

6. If needed, navigate to the drive and folder that contain the file to insert.

7. Click on the file you want to insert (see Figure 15.12). If you want to insert more than one file stored in the same drive and folder, you can click on the first file and then press and hold Ctrl and click on additional files to select them.

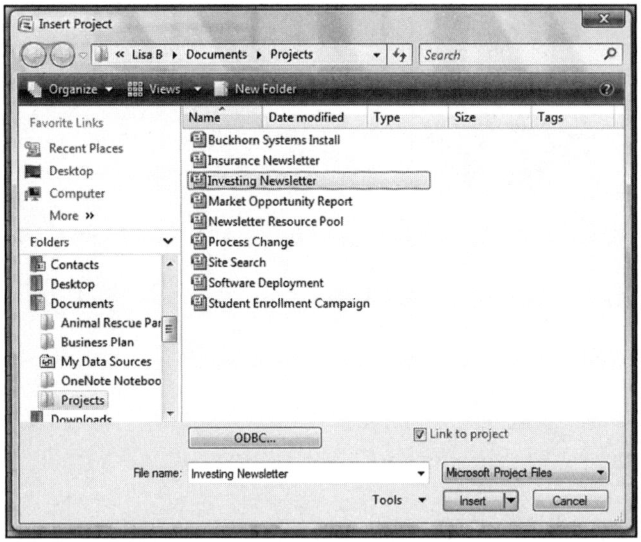

**Figure 15.12**
Choose the subproject file(s) to insert in this dialog box.

8. By default, the inserted subproject file is linked to the master project file, so the Link to Project check box will be checked. If you do not want the files to be linked (meaning that changes you make in one of the files will not appear in the other), click the **Link to Project** check box to clear it.

9. Click **Insert.** The inserted subproject appears in the file. As shown in Figure 15.13, the inserted subproject appears as a collapsed project summary task. (You'll see how to expand and collapse the subprojects next in this chapter.)

To insert a project file as read-only (preventing you from making any changes to the original subproject file from the consolidated file), click the drop-down list arrow to the right of the **Insert** button and then click the **Insert Read-Only** choice in the submenu that appears.

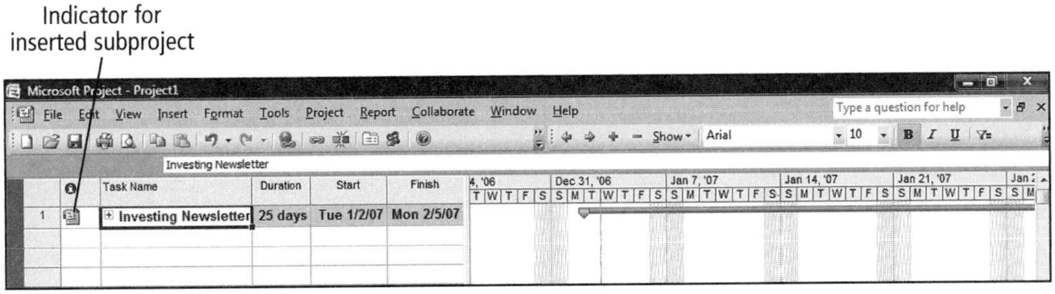

Indicator for
inserted subproject

**Figure 15.13** The inserted subproject looks like a collapsed project summary task.

10. Repeat Steps 4 through 9 to insert additional subproject files as desired.

When you insert a subproject into a master project file that already contains other subprojects, be sure that all the subprojects are collapsed so that only the subproject summary task appears. Otherwise, you may inadvertently insert a new subproject file at the wrong outline level. Of course, if you want to insert the subproject at a lower outline level, you may do so.

11. Choose **File, Save** (shortcut: **Ctrl+S**), choose a save location, type a **File Name**, and click **Save** to name and save the master project file.

A *master project* file consolidates inserted *subproject* files. Use the **Insert, Project** command to insert a subproject file into the master project file.

You can use one of two other methods to create a master project file "on the fly," without choosing a new project start date or specifying the order in which the inserted subprojects should appear. Use one of these two methods to do so:

- If you're opening a resource pool file, you can click the third option button in the Open Resource Pool dialog box (refer to Figure 15.9), **Open Resource Pool Read-Write and All Other sharer Files Into a New Master Project File.** When you then click **OK**, Project creates a new master project file with the resource pool file and each of its sharer files inserted as subprojects.

- If you've already opened the files that you want to insert as subprojects into a new master project file, click **Window** and then click **New Window.** In the New Window dialog box that appears (see Figure 15.14), Ctrl+click each of the files to insert as a subproject. Choose the view in which you want to see the new master project from the **View** drop-down list and then click **OK**.

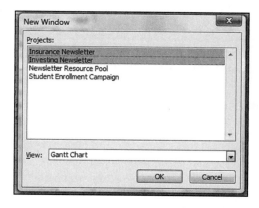

**Figure 15.14** You can combine already-opened files into a new master project from this dialog box, displayed by choosing **Window, New Window**.

When you close a master project file that has unsaved changes, Project displays numerous prompts to ask whether you want to save changes to the master project file and the subprojects. When you see the first prompt about saving the subprojects, like the one shown in Figure 15.15, you can click **Yes to All** or **No to All** to save all the subprojects or not and close more quickly.

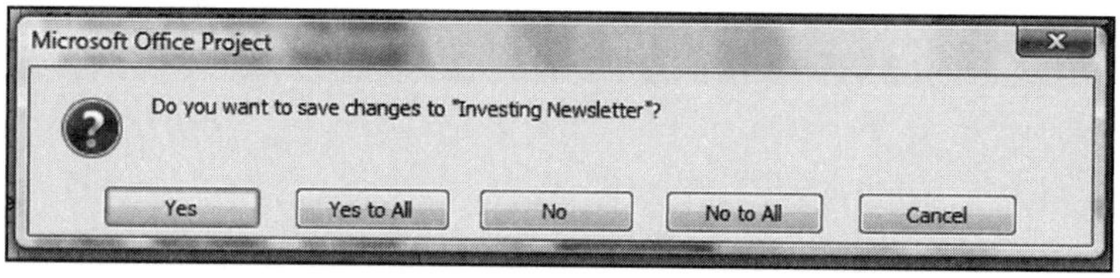

**Figure 15.15** Project asks exactly which changes to save when you close the master project.

## Viewing and Hiding Subprojects

When you first create a master project by inserting subprojects, you don't see all the tasks for the inserted subproject files; instead, you see a single project summary task and a corresponding Gantt bar summarizing the inserted project. The subproject information works like any other outlined information in Project: You can expand (view) or collapse (hide) levels of detail as needed by clicking the plus (+) and minus (-) outline symbols beside the name of any summary task or by using the tools on the Formatting toolbar.

If you click the plus icon beside the name for an inserted subproject and that project is a sharer of a resource pool file that isn't open, Project displays the Open Resource Pool Information dialog box, shown in Figure 15.16. Leave the top option button selected and then click **OK** to expand the tasks and open the resource pool.

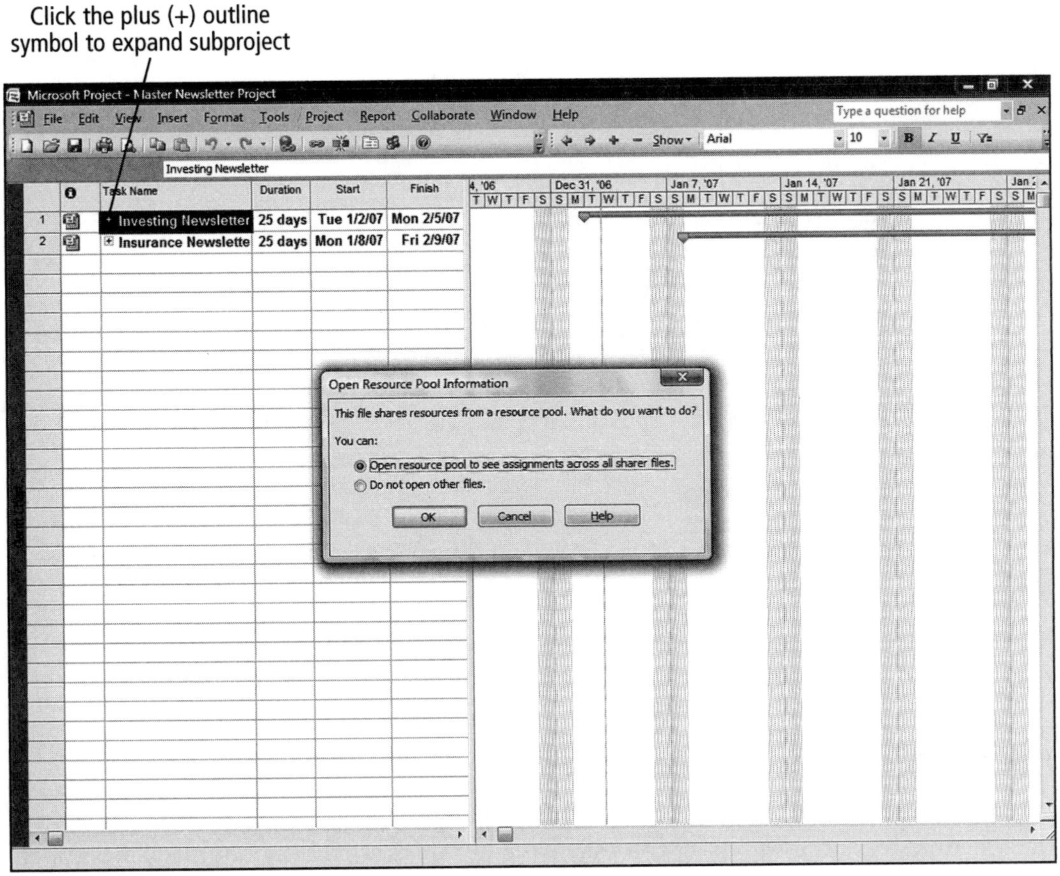

Click the plus (+) outline
symbol to expand subproject

**Figure 15.16** When you expand a subproject that shares resources, Project prompts you to open the resource pool file.

In addition to being able to expand and collapse the inserted subprojects in a master project file, you can view the consolidated information in any of Project's views just like you would any other project plan file. For example, if you display the Calendar view (see Figure 15.17), it shows the subproject name above the tasks from that subproject. If you change to the Task Usage view, you'll be able to see details about the tasks and assignments from each of the inserted subprojects. If you change to the Resource Usage view, you'll be able to see each resource's assignments in all the subprojects, as well as which resources are over-allocated.

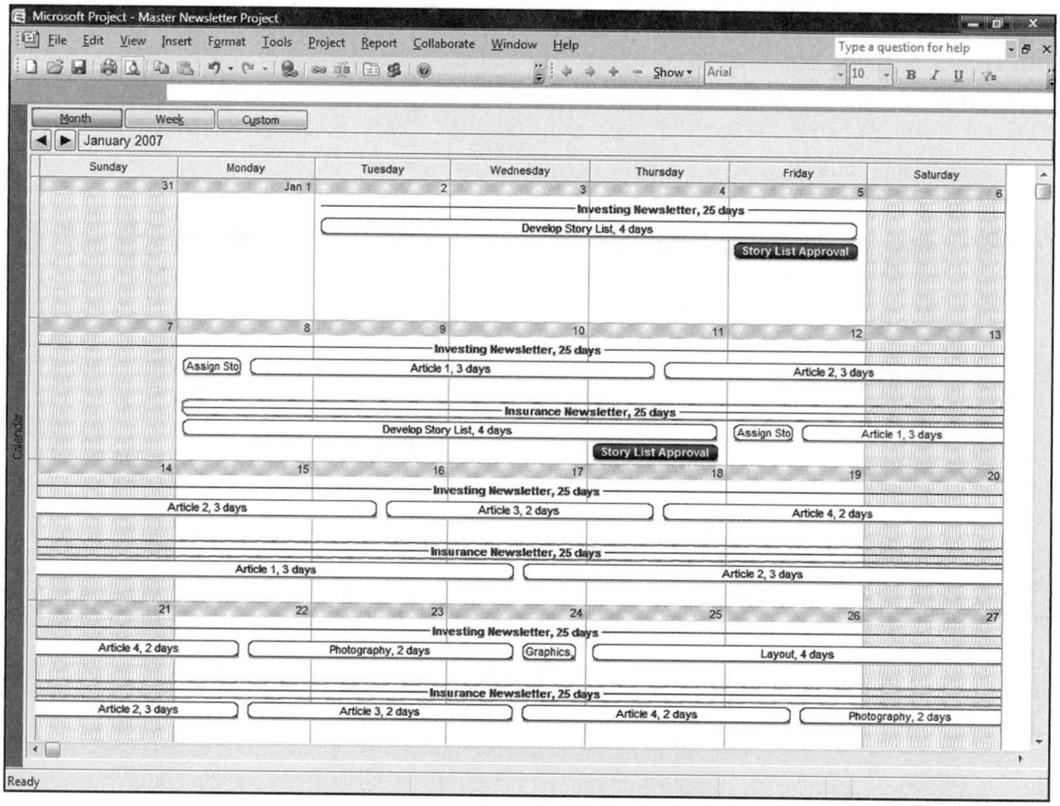

**Figure 15.17** The Calendar view identifies the name of the subproject that contains each task.

## Linking Tasks Between Subprojects

Just as you use links within a project plan file to identify which tasks have an impact on the schedules of successor tasks, you may have instances where the boundaries between your projects are somewhat fuzzy, and a task from one project drives the schedule for a task in another project. To reflect this relationship, you can insert both of the affected projects into a master project file and then add a link between the two tasks. Such a link lets you ensure that the tasks happen in the proper order even when they're in different project plan files.

Creating a link between tasks in a master project file works just like creating a link in a single project file:

1. Open the master project file and display the subtasks as needed.

2. In the task sheet, click the Task Name cell entry for the earlier task, which will be the predecessor task for the link.

3. Press and hold the **Ctrl** key and click the Task Name cell for the second task to link, which will be the successor task.

4. Click the **Link Tasks** button on the Standard toolbar. (Shortcut: **Ctrl+F2**) Project links the tasks and adjusts the schedule for the successor task and any tasks linked to it as needed to honor the new link. Figure 15.18 shows such a link.

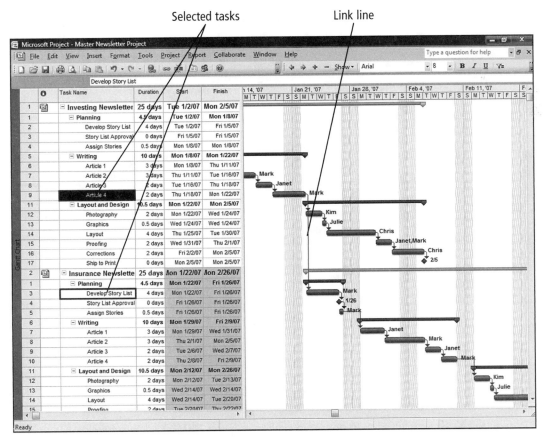

**Figure 15.18** Linking tasks in the master project file reschedules other tasks in the successor's subproject as needed.

Notice the task ID numbers in Figure 15.18. Each inserted subproject has a task ID number; under it, the subtasks use their individual task numbers.

If you then open a project plan file that has a link to another project created within a master project file, you'll see that a special task has been inserted to identify the *external predecessor* or *external successor* task. For example, Figure 15.19 shows the external predecessor task for one of the consolidated files linked in Figure 15.18. The external task's name is dimmed, which means that you can't edit it. Its Gantt bar is gray as well because you can't move or otherwise reschedule the task.

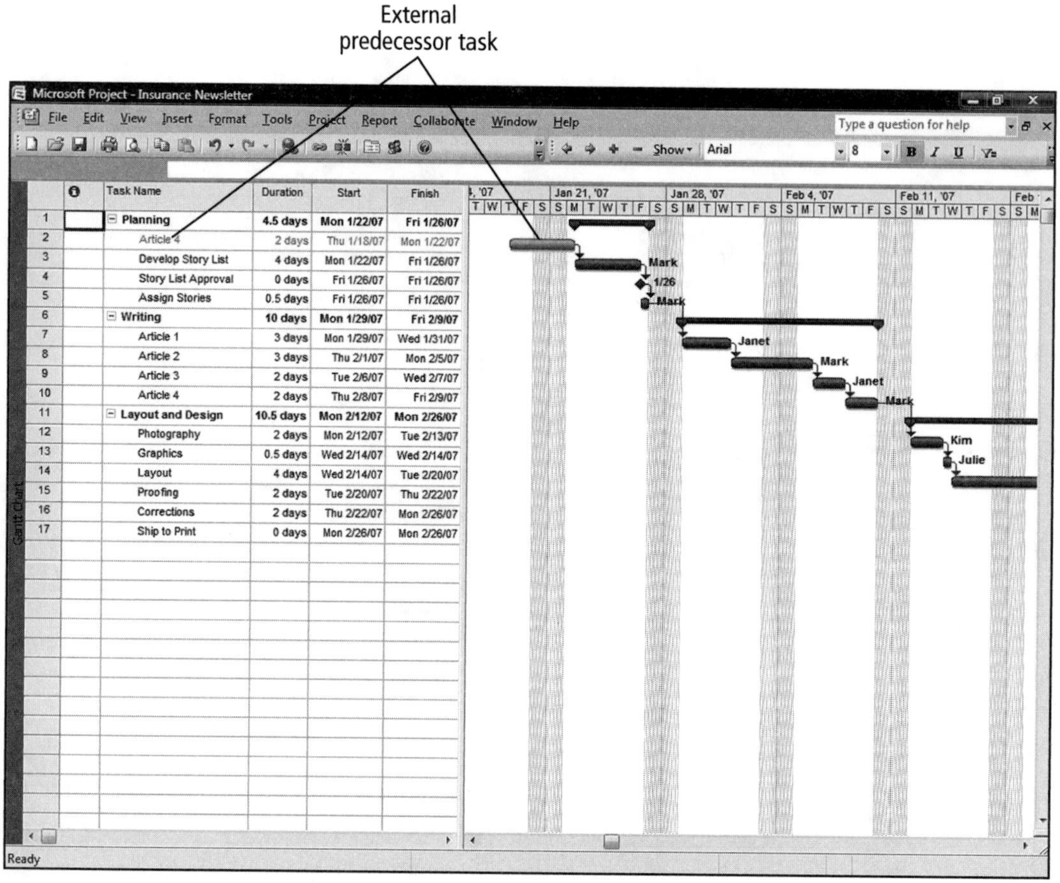

**Figure 15.19** External linked tasks appear gray when you open the individual subproject file rather than viewing it in the master project.

If you look at the *Predecessor* field entry for an external predecessor task, the field entry identifies the full path and file name of the file holding the predecessor task, followed by a backslash and the task ID number. For example, the entry might look like C:\Users\John\Doucments\New Product.mpp\10, to identify a link to *task 10* in the *New Product* file stored in C:\Users\John\Documents.

> To view more details about external predecessor or successor tasks in the current project file, click **Tools** and then click **Links Between Projects**. In the Links Between Projects dialog box that appears (see Figure 15.20), you can view and delete links as needed.

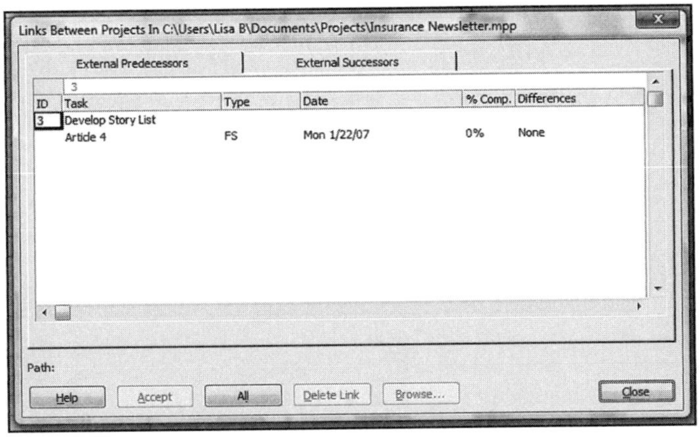

**Figure 15.20**
Choose **Tools, Link Between Projects** to open this dialog box and work with links to external tasks.

## Adding Tasks in the Master Project File

Because the inserted subprojects in a master project file behave just like outlined tasks in an individual file, you have to be careful if you want to insert new tasks into the master project rather than into one of the subprojects.

The trick is to collapse all the subproject files before you add any other regular tasks or recurring tasks. This tells Project to add the task into the master project only, whether you insert the new task above or below the collapsed subprojects. You can expand the collapsed subproject and link the task in the master project to any subproject task as needed.

Also, as shown in Figure 15.21, if you simply click the Assign Resources button to try to assign resources to the added task, none will be available by default. (The master project was a blank file when you inserted the subprojects, remember?) So, you can type resources into the Assign Resources dialog box or the Resource Sheet view of the master project file, or you can share resources from a resource pool file using **Tools, Resource Sharing, Share Resources**.

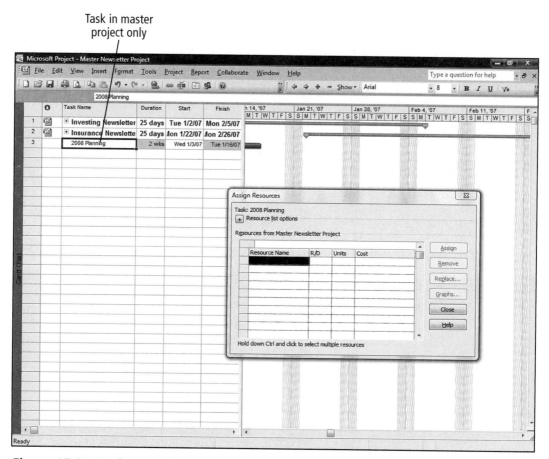

**Figure 15.21** You have to add resources to the master project file before you can make an assignment to the master project's task.

## Making Changes to the Subproject

You also can make changes at the subproject level for any inserted subproject. If you want the master project file to display another name for an inserted subproject file, want to change the subproject file's start date, want to break the link between the master project and subproject files, or want to make another change, you can use the Inserted Project Information dialog box.

Double-click the inserted subproject summary task or click the task and then click the **Task Information** button on the Standard toolbar. The Inserted Project Information dialog box appears (see Figure 15.22). It offers six tabs of options. You'll probably work with two options on the General and Advanced tabs most often. On the General tab, you can change the display **Name** for the inserted subproject. You can clear the **Link to Project** check box on the Advanced tab to break the link between the master project and inserted subproject.

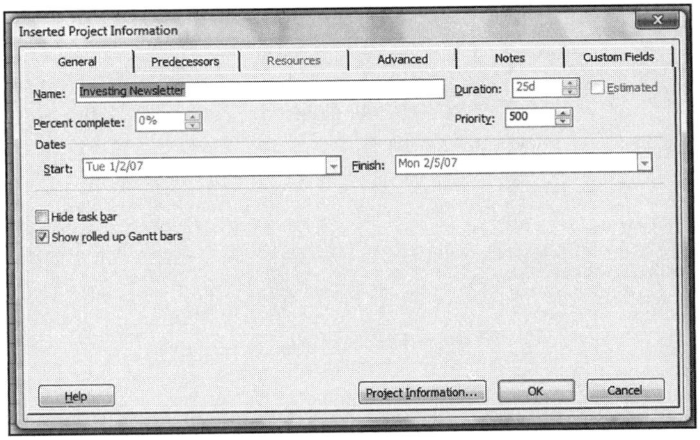

**Figure 15.22**
Change information about the inserted subproject in this dialog box.

---

If you break the linking between an inserted subproject file and the master project file, the tasks from the subproject remain as tasks in the master project file, but they no longer update based on changes made in the original subproject file. You can't reinstate the link between the master project and subproject. You instead have to delete the tasks that were originally part of the subproject and then reinsert the subproject file. Also, breaking the link affects the task numbering within the master project file, treating the tasks remaining from the unlinked subproject like tasks you typed directly into the master project. A better choice might be to leave the projects linked but check the **Read Only** check box on the Advanced tab of the Inserted Project Information dialog box. This option tells Project to retrieve the most current information from the subproject file each time you open the master project, but changes you make in the master project won't flow back to the subproject.

---

The first five tabs in the Inserted Project Information dialog box display a Project Information button at the bottom. Click that button to open the subproject's Project Information dialog box, in which you can change such key settings as the Start Date for the inserted project or the Calendar it uses, just as if you opened the Project Information dialog box from within the subproject file rather than the master project.

If you want to delete a subproject, right-click its row number and then click **Delete Task**. If the Planning Wizard is enabled, a dialog box appears asking you to confirm the deletion (see Figure 15.22). To finish the deletion, leave the **Continue** option button selected and click **OK**. If you made changes to any of the inserted project's information in the master project file, you'll also be prompted to specify whether or not to save those changes to the subproject file before the subproject is removed from the consolidated project. Click **Yes** to do so or **No** to remove the inserted subproject without saving changes. Deleting the subproject from the master project file as described above does not delete the standalone subproject file from your system's hard disk. You can still open and change that file just as you could before you inserted it into the master project.

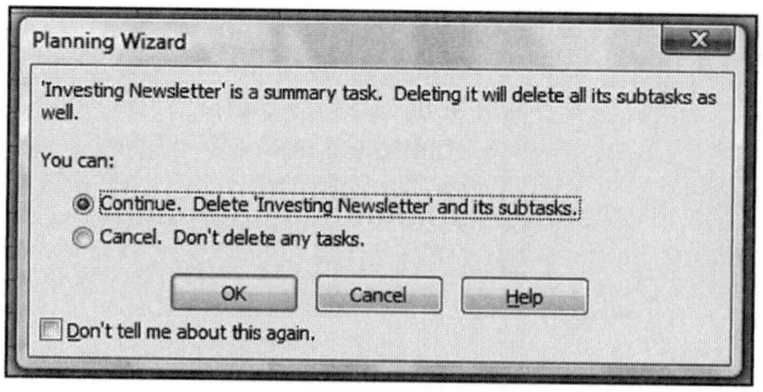

**Figure 15.23** The Planning Wizard asks you to verify whether to delete the inserted subproject.

# Chapter Review

While you might not use the techniques described in this chapter the first few times you use Microsoft Office Project 2007 to plan and execute projects, as your responsibilities and proficiencies expand, you may want to try what you've just learned. This chapter showed you how to set up a resource pool file, share resources from the pool, view assignments and overallocations between projects, and keep everything up to date. From there, you moved on to learn how to consolidate multiple individual project files into a master project, where you can see how the schedules from your various projects compare and even link activities between projects.

Although this is the final chapter of the book, the Appendixes provide some bonus information that you might find helpful, including highlights of the differences between the XP and Vista versions of Windows, help for special situations you may encounter when using Project, and answers for the chapter review questions.

## Review Questions

Write your answers to the following questions on a sheet of paper.

1. Enter resources for the resource pool file in the _____ view.
2. True or False: The resource pool file must be named *Resource Pool*.
3. Use this command to share resources from a resource pool file into a sharer file.
4. True or False: The resource pool file is linked to sharer files by default.
5. To see overallocations between sharer files as well as individual assignments, display the _____ view in the resource pool file.
6. A master project file holds inserted _____ files.
7. Use this command to insert a file into the master project.
8. _____ the subtasks in a master project file so that you can link them.

9. To add tasks that exist only in the master project file, do this first.

10. Double-click an inserted project to display the _____ dialog box, where you can make overall changes.

## Projects

 To see the solution files created by completing the projects in this chapter, go to www.courseptr.com, click the **Downloads** link in the navigation bar at the top, type **Microsoft Office Project 2007 Survival Guide** in the search text box, and then click **Search Downloads**.

### *Project 1*

1. Create a new, blank project file.

2. Save the file as *New Company Resources*. This will be your resource pool file.

 Create a folder named *PSG Exercises* in your *Documents* or *My Documents* folder and save your exercise practice files there.

3. Click **View** and then click **Resource Sheet**.

4. Enter the following five work resources into the *Resource Name* field:

Jean

Max

Art

Phil

Lynn

5. Save the resource pool file and keep it open for the next project.

6. Create another new, blank file.

7. Choose **Project, Project Information**, specify a Start Date that's about two weeks in the future, and click **OK**.

8. Enter the following task names and durations:

| | |
|---|---|
| Identify and Reserve Domain | 4d |
| Write Contents | 6d |
| Develop Design | 4d |
| Scripting | 4d |
| Testing | 3d |

9. Link all the tasks in sequence with default links.

10. Save the file as *Web Site* and keep it open for the next project.

11. Create another new, blank file.

12. Choose **Project, Project Information**, specify the same Start Date as for the *Web Site* file, and click **OK**.

13. Enter the following task names and durations:

| | |
|---|---|
| Develop Theme | 2d |
| Identify Media | 3d |
| Write Copy | 4d |
| Design | 6d |
| Placement | 2d |

14. Link all the tasks in sequence with default links.

15. Save the file as *Advertising* and keep it open for the next project.

## *Project 2*

1. Click **Window** and then click **Web Site** to change to the Web site project file.

2. Click **Tools**, point to **Resource Sharing**, and click **Share Resources**.

3. Click the **Use Resources** option button, open the From drop-down list and click **New Company Resources**, and then click **OK**.

4. Click the **Assign Resources** button on the Standard toolbar, use the Assign Resources dialog box to make the following assignments, and then click **Close**:

| | |
|---|---|
| Identify and Reserve Domain | Lynn |
| Write Contents | Jean |
| Develop Design | Max |
| Scripting | Phil |
| Testing | Phil |

5. Click **Window** and then click **Advertising** to change to the advertising project file.

6. Click **Tools**, point to **Resource Sharing**, and click **Share Resources**.

7. Click the **Use Resources** option button, open the From drop-down list and click **New Company Resources**, and then click **OK**.

8. Click the **Assign Resources** button on the Standard toolbar, use the Assign Resources dialog box to make the following assignments, and then click **Close**:

   Develop Theme     Art

   Identify Media     Art

   Write Copy     Jean

   Design     Max

   Placement     Art

9. Save your changes to the file.

10. Click **Window** and then click **New Company Resources** to change to the resource pool file. You should see that two resources are overallocated in the Resource Sheet view.

11. Click **View** and then click **Resource Usage**. Scroll to the right so that you can see assignment information. You can see that the *Jean* resource is overbooked between her two assignments, as is the *Max* resource.

12. Click **View** and then click **Resource Sheet** to change back to Resource Sheet view.

13. Save your changes to the *New Company Resources* file.

14. Close all three files, saving again if prompted to do so.

## *Project 3*

1. Create a new, blank file.

2. Save the file as *New Company Master*. This will become the master project file. You need not specify a project start date, as the subprojects you will be inserting already have future start dates.

3. Click **OK** to close the Project Statistics dialog box.

4. Click the Task Name cell in the first row.

5. Click **Insert** and then click **Project**.

6. Click **Web Site** in the Insert Project dialog box and then click **Insert**.

7. In the top pane of the view, click *task 2*, **Infrastructure**.

8. Click the Task Name cell in the next blank row.

9. Click **Insert** and then click **Project**.

10. Click **Advertising** in the Insert Project dialog box and then click **Insert**.

11. Click the **plus** (+) outline symbol beside each subproject name to display its sub-tasks. When the Open Resource Pool Information dialog box appears during the process, leave the default option button selected and click **OK**.

12. You need to link a task between subprojects to resolve the *Jean* and *Max* resources' overallocations. Click *task 2*, **Write Contents** in the first subproject; press and hold the **Ctrl** key; click *task 3*, **Write Copy** in the second subproject; and release the Ctrl key. Then click the **Link Tasks** button on the Standard toolbar.

13. Click **View** and then click **Resource Usage**. Scroll to the right so that you can see assignment information. You can see that the overallocations you saw in the last project have been resolved by linking the two tasks to which **Jean** was assigned.

14. Click **View** and then click **Gantt Chart** to change back to the Gantt Chart view.

15. Save the master project file and close it, clicking **Yes to All** to save changes to the subproject files and click **OK** to update the resource pool file when prompted. If the resource pool file remains open, close it as well.

# APPENDIX A

# SLIGHT DIFFERENCES BETWEEN WINDOWS VERSIONS

Y ou can run Project 2007 on Windows XP or Windows Vista. If you're using good ol' XP, then you're probably familiar with the ins and outs of the Start menu and the Save and Open dialog boxes. Vista tweaks those elements, so knowing a few more details about how you can work with the Start menu and dialog boxes for working with files will save you time and trouble.

## Start Menu Changes

The sequence of choices you use to start Project from the Start menu is the same in both XP and Vista: click **Start**, click **All Programs**, click **Microsoft Office**, and then click **Microsoft Office Project 2007**. One key difference occurs between the versions. In XP, choosing **Start, All Programs** displays a pop-up All Programs menu. In Vista, the left-hand column of the Start menu changes to reflect each choice you make. For example, Figure A.1 shows how the left column of the Start menu looks when you click **Start** and then **All Programs**.

Chapter 2 explains how you can type **Project** into the Start Search text box at the bottom of the Start menu to jump right to the Project startup command. You can make Project even more convenient to access by adding it to the Quick Launch toolbar on the taskbar or by pinning it to the Start menu so that it appears as an unchanging choice at the top of the left column. To add Project to the Quick Launch toolbar or pin it to the Start menu, right-click the **Microsoft Office Project 2007** choice on the **Start** menu (see Figure A.2) and then click either **Pin to Start Menu** or **Add to Quick Launch** in the shortcut menu that appears.

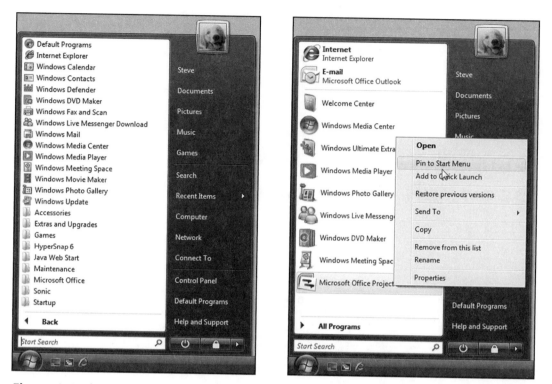

**Figure A.1**  The contents of the left column of the Start menu change in Vista.

**Figure A.2**  Add Project to the Quick Launch toolbar or pin it to the Start menu.

## Save and Open Changes

Another important new area of functionality to get comfortable with under Windows Vista is the new layout for file-oriented dialog boxes: Save As and Open. In XP, these dialog boxes feature a My Places bar along the left. You can click an icon in that bar to jump quickly to a location such as My Documents or My Computer. You also can use a Look In drop-down list at the top of the dialog box to navigate to any folder.

Vista replaces the My Places bar with Favorite Links and Folders lists. The first time you open the Save As dialog box in Project, the dialog box doesn't even display folders. You have to click the **Browse Folders** button (see Figure A.3) in the lower-left corner of the Save As dialog box to browse folders.

Even after you do that, you may need to click the **More** double-right arrow (see Figure A.4) to find the Favorite Links item that you want, or you can click the up arrow to the right of Folders to expand the dialog box to show the Folders list.

Click here to browse

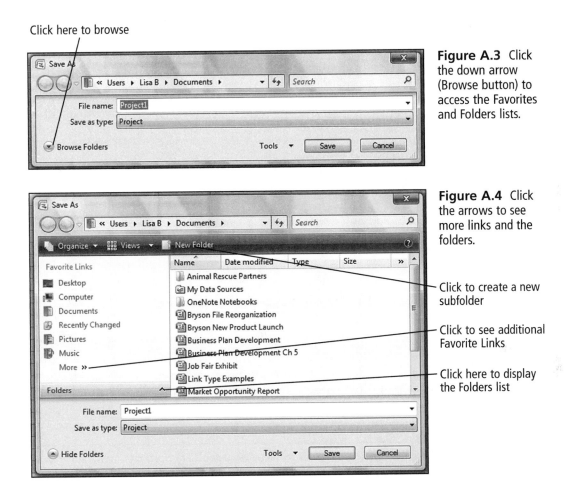

**Figure A.3** Click the down arrow (Browse button) to access the Favorites and Folders lists.

**Figure A.4** Click the arrows to see more links and the folders.

Click to create a new subfolder

Click to see additional Favorite Links

Click here to display the Folders list

Once you expand the Folders List in a Save As or Open dialog box, you can expand and collapse folders as in any other folder tree you've used in an earlier Windows version or in an application. As shown in Figure A.5, you can move the mouse over a folder and click the small triangle that appears to the left of the folder name to expand or collapse the folder. You also can double-click the folder icon itself to expand and collapse the folder.

 Once you've selected a folder, you can click the **New Folder** button to create a new folder. Type a name for the new folder and press **Enter** to finish creating it.

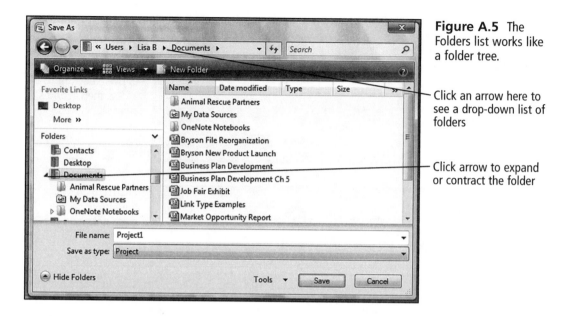

**Figure A.5** The Folders list works like a folder tree.

Click an arrow here to see a drop-down list of folders

Click arrow to expand or contract the folder

The Address box at the top of a Save As or Open dialog box replaces the Look In list under XP. The Address box shows the full path to the current folder. If you click an arrow button in the Address bar, a menu of folders (or other locations) appears so that you can click one to display it. Clicking the double left arrow at the far left displays a menu of common locations like the hard disk, Computer, or Network.

In Windows Vista, the *Documents* folder replaces the default *My Documents* working folder from Windows XP. Vista also uses the name *Computer* rather than *My Computer*.

# APPENDIX B

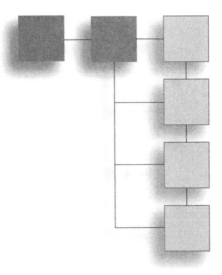

# SPECIAL SITUATIONS

Y ou've seen throughout the book that Project has dozens of options and settings and often offers multiple ways to accomplish a particular action. In many cases, you need to learn not only what a particular setting does individually but also how to use settings in the right combination to achieve the scheduling outcome you expect. This appendix addresses some of those real-world combinations. What you'll learn here is based on actual problems and requests I've worked on with clients over the years.

> Although there are workarounds for updating your project plan if you need to make a scheduling change like one of those described in this appendix, you should always think ahead and make the types of scheduling changes described here before you add tasks into the project plan file. If you do have a problem and need to start the schedule over from scratch, keep in mind that you can copy and paste task names and durations from one Project file to another.

## Making Sure the Calendar and Schedule Options Are In Synch

If you've gone to the trouble of creating a custom calendar, you want to make sure that Project actually follows that calendar. Many users aren't aware of it, but if you want Project to start scheduling from a particular hour of the day, you have to change Project's Calendar options to match the working hours you defined for a custom calendar assigned to the project. (See the later section called "Setting Up the Gantt Chart to Display an Hourly Schedule" if you want to see how you can verify the results of setting these options.)

Change the Default Start Time, Default End Time, Hours Per Day, Hours Per Week, and Days Per Month settings on the Calendar tab of the Options dialog box to match the calendar assigned to the project and ensure proper daily scheduling.

For example, say you create a custom calendar that has a 7 a.m. to 4 p.m. workday with an hour for lunch. You use the Project, Project Information command to assign the calendar to your project file. Even though you don't know it, when you start adding tasks, Project schedules them from 8 a.m. rather than 7 a.m. because the Calendar options override the calendar assigned to the project.

So, *before* you add any tasks to the project plan, take the following steps to synch the Calendar options that affect how Project schedules tasks with the calendar applied to the project file in the Project Information dialog box:

1. Click the **Tools** menu and then click **Options**.

2. Click the **Calendar** tab.

3. Change the **Default Start Time**, **Default End Time**, and **Hours Per Day** text box entries to match the times you will later create in your project calendar. For example, if your calendar starts at 7 a.m. and ends at 4 p.m., you need to enter **7:00 AM** and **4:00 PM**, respectively (but you won't need to change the Hours Per Day entry). Figure B.1 illustrates these example settings.

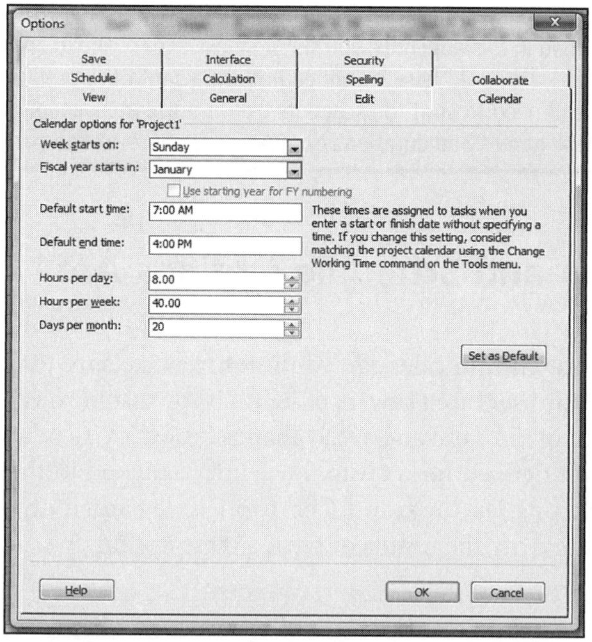

**Figure B.1** Make entries on this tab to synch the project calendar with Project's defaults.

4. (Optional) Also change the **Hours Per Week** and **Days Per Month** entries if needed for consistency with your project calendar.

5. Click **OK** to close the dialog box.

6. Click **Project** and then click **Project Information**.

7. Click to the right of the *Start Date* field entry, type the needed starting time of day (such as **7 AM**), and then press **Tab**. You won't be able to see your change (unless you've included hours of the day in the date display, as described later in this appendix), but you have changed the starting time for the project.

8. Click **OK**. You can now enter tasks and they should schedule from the correct starting time each day.

## Setting Up a Project with Fixed Task Durations

For some Project users, the default functionality wherein Project decreases a task duration when you pile on more resources adds too much complexity to the planning process. These folks just need to know when tasks occur and who will be handling them, and they may not even be tracking hours of work associated with tasks. For example, a construction company might not care how many hours it takes to frame the house. They just know that they want three carpenters to get it done in three weeks.

If you need to simplify the planning process and want to set up your project plan so that the durations you enter remain the same no matter how many resources you assign, use these steps *before* you add any tasks to your project plan:

1. Click the **Tools** menu and then click **Options**.

2. Click the **Schedule** tab.

3. Open the **Default Task Type** drop-down list and click **Fixed Duration** (see Figure B.2).

4. (Optional) Click the **New Tasks Are Effort-Driven** check box to clear it. If you leave this check box checked, whenever you assign another resource to a task, Project will leave both the duration and total hours of work for the task unchanged, in effect reducing the hours of work allocated to each resource by decreasing the resource's Units for the assignment. If you clear the **New Tasks Are Effort-Driven** check box, Project leaves the duration fixed but piles on more hours of work for each resource assigned. Figure B.3 illustrates this behavior by showing two Fixed Duration tasks in the Task Usage view.

5. Click **OK** to apply the changes. All new tasks added to the project plan file will use a fixed duration.

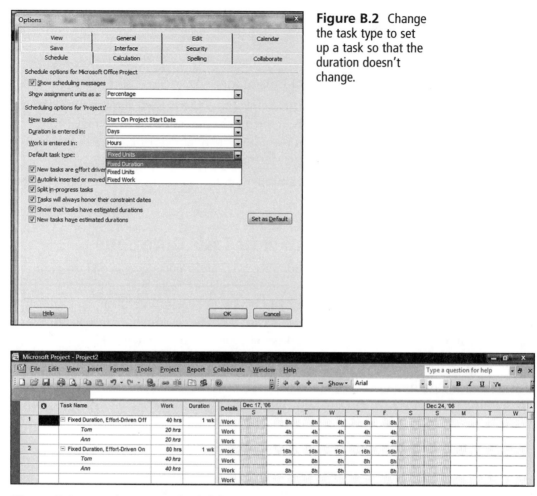

**Figure B.2** Change the task type to set up a task so that the duration doesn't change.

**Figure B.3** For task 1, Project divided the original 40h of work between the two resources. For task 2, where effort-driven scheduling was turned off, Project doubled the hours of work when a second resource was assigned.

# Using Templates and Generic Resources and Units Settings

In the section called "Replacing a Resource" in Chapter 8, you learned how to replace a resource throughout the project plan by typing over an existing resource name in the Resource Sheet view. This is a valuable skill to know if you intend to use templates, either Project's or those you create on your own. Many of Project's templates, like the one shown in Figure B.4, include generic resource names that are intended to be placeholders.

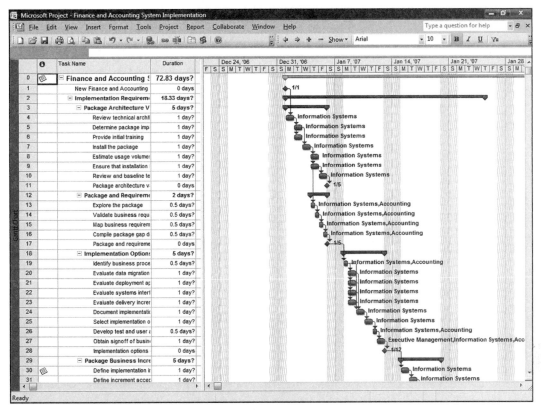

**Figure B.4**  This Project template uses generic resource names.

When you create a new project file based on a template, you can follow these overall tips for adjusting the template content to suit your planning needs.

- First, use the **Project, Project Information** command to open the Project Information dialog box and choose a future Start Date and a Calendar for the project.

- Go to the Resource Sheet view (**View, Resource Sheet**) and replace the Resource Name for any generic resource that you want to convert to a named resource.

- Back in the Gantt Chart view (**View, Gantt Chart**), adjust any task durations and links as needed.

- Display the Assign Resources dialog box (click the **Assign Resources** button on the Standard toolbar) and edit individual assignments and units settings as needed.

If you compare Figure B.5 to B.4, you can see how the preceding techniques have been used to adapt a generic Project template for use in managing a real project.

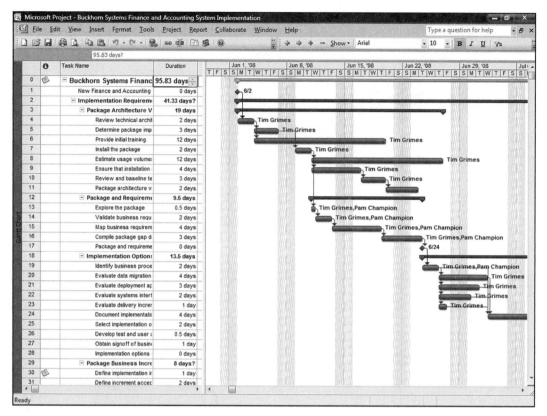

**Figure B.5** The generic template information has been updated to produce a real project plan.

## Setting Up the Gantt Chart to Display an Hourly Schedule

In some cases, a project might need to be scheduled on an hourly basis. For example, if you're performing a critical software installation that makes the network inaccessible for some period of time, you may want to schedule that installation in hourly detail to make sure you've planned thoroughly and covered all the bases.

These steps explain how to set up a project file and the Gantt Chart view to chart the schedule hourly:

1. Click the **Tools** menu and then click **Options**.

2. Click the **View** tab, if needed.

3. Open the **Date format** drop-down list and then click one of the formats that includes the day or date and time (such as **Jan 28 12:33 PM**).

In a scenario like this, if you also want Project to assume your *Duration* field entries are in hours rather than days, choose **Tools**, **Options**. Click the **Schedule** tab, change the **Duration Is Entered In** drop-down list setting to **Hours**, and then click **OK**.

4. Click **OK** to close the Options dialog box.

5. Double-click the timescale band at the top of the Gantt Chart.

6. On the Middle Tier tab, open the **Units** drop-down list, and click **Days**.

7. Click the **Bottom Tier** tab, open the **Units** drop-down list, and click **Hours**.

8. If you've applied a custom calendar to the project and want its hours charted correctly, click the **Non-Working Time** tab. Open its **Calendar** drop-down list and click the custom calendar assigned to the project. It will be identified with (**Project Calendar**) appended to its name.

9. Click **OK** to close the dialog box and apply the changes.

Then, when you enter tasks, you can see the schedule on an hourly rather than daily basis. For example, Figure B.6 shows a simple project scheduled to occur between 7 a.m. and 4 p.m. If you needed to, you could click in the Start field for any task and edit its starting time as well as the starting date.

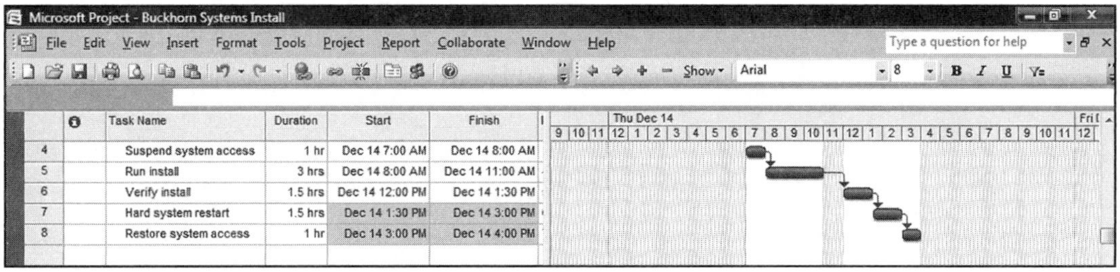

**Figure B.6** Project has scheduled and can now display these tasks on an hour-by-hour basis.

## Use a Constraint to Emphasize a Finish Date

Whether you set up the final task in your project as a regular task or a milestone, you can add a constraint to the task (see Chapter 9) to help it work for you as a warning flag if any changes to the project will cause you to miss that final date. Here's how to set that up:

1. Display and double-click the final task in the project.

2. Click the **Advanced** tab in the Task Information dialog box.

3. Open the **Constraint Type** drop-down list and click **Must Finish On**. Then enter the drop-dead finish date for the project in the accompanying **Constraint Date** text box, or use the drop-down calendar to enter the date.

4. Click **OK**.

Now, any duration change or task finish delay to an earlier linked, critical task will cause a warning message to appear (see Figure B.7) as long as the Planning Wizard is turned on. To make sure that the Planning Wizard is turned on, choose **Tools, Options**, click the **General** tab, and make sure that **Advice from Planning Wizard** and **Advice About Scheduling** underneath it are both checked.

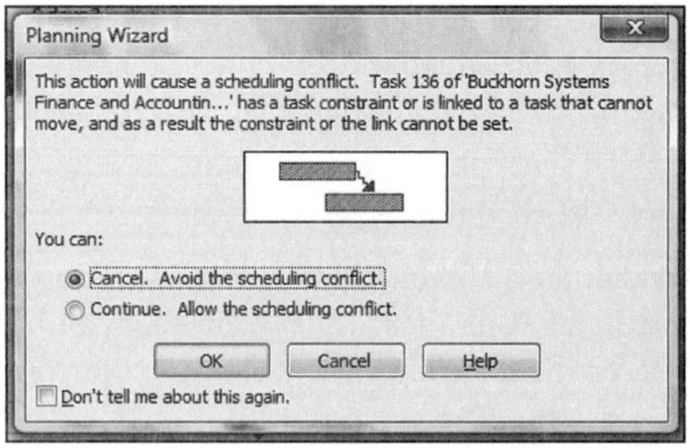

**Figure B.7** Here's the Planning Wizard warning that appears if you try to make a change that will violate the Must Finish On constraint for the final task.

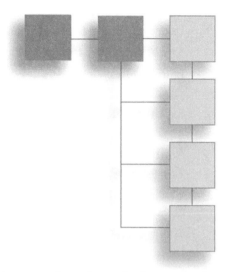

# CHAPTER REVIEW SOLUTIONS

This appendix presents the answers for the review questions for each chapter in the book. After you finish each set of questions (don't peek!), you can look here to grade your own work.

## Answers to Chapter 1 Review Questions

1. What's the difference between a To Do list and a project plan?

   **A To Do list provides a list of activities that may not be related to a single purpose or outcome. The items on the To Do list might not have specific starting or ending dates. A project plan lists related activities that, when completed, will yield specified goals and deliverables. The project plan and the activities within it all have specific starting and ending dates/times.**

2. What are the overall steps in managing a project?

   **Initiating, Planning, Executing, Controlling, Closing**

3. What is a task?

   **A task is an activity with a specific starting point and ending point.**

4. What is a resource?

   **A resource is a person, piece of equipment, or quantity of consumable material used to complete one or more tasks.**

5. What is an assignment?

   **An assignment occurs when you apply a resource to a task, indicating that the resource is responsible for or will be used in completing the task.**

6. Name one phase or part of the project management process that Microsoft Office Project 2007 can help with.

**Any of the following four answers are acceptable:**

**Planning. Project helps a project manager build a more detailed and accurate project plan.**

**Executing. Project provides tools for tracking work and communicating progress.**

**Controlling. Track and reschedule work as needed with tools in Project. Review views and reports to help identify when corrective actions may be needed.**

**Closing. Refer to previous project plans to review lessons learned.**

### Answers to Chapter 2 Review Questions

1. Name one way each to start and exit Project.

**For starting Project, any of the following are acceptable:**

**Click** Start, **click** All Programs, **click** Microsoft Office, **and then click** Microsoft Office Project 2007.

**Click** Start **and then click** Microsoft Office Project 2007 **if it appears on the left side of the Start menu.**

**Click** Start, **type** Project, **and then click** Microsoft Office Project 2007.

**For exiting Project, any of the following are acceptable:**

**Click** File **and then click** Exit.

**Click the Project window** Close (X) **button.**

**Press** Alt+F4.

2. One or more _____ appear below the menu bar and offer buttons you can click to perform actions in Project rather than having to choose menu commands.

**Toolbars**

3. To show or hide a toolbar, do this:

**Right-click any toolbar and then click the toolbar name in the shortcut menu.**

4. The _____ appears at the top of each column in a sheet view.

**Field Name, Column Name, or Title (Partial credit can be given for Column Heading).**

5. When you add a task, its _____ appears in the row header cell to the left of the task name.

**Task ID Number or ID Number**

6. Access one of the eight most-used views on the _____ menu.

   **View**

7. What is a table in Project?

   **The specific collection of fields that appears in a sheet view.**

8. The _____ can walk you through the procedures for creating and executing your project plan file with Project.

   **Project Guide**

9. The text box where you can enter a phrase or topic to search for in Help is found here:

   **c. Menu bar**

10. Name one new feature in this version of Project.

    **Any of the following are acceptable:**

    **Multiple-level undo**

    **Cell highlighting**

    **Task drivers**

    **Visual reports**

    **Cost resources**

    **Top-down budgeting**

    **Enhancements to the Calendar and Gantt Chart views**

## Answers to Chapter 3 Review Questions

1. True or False: The calendars that come with Project have holidays marked.

   **False**

2. The information you specify to define overall project parameters include the _____ and the _____.

   **Project start date**

   **Project calendar or base calendar**

3. To define each task, enter its _____ and _____.

   **Task name**

   **Duration**

4. To enable Project to calculate task schedules, _____ the tasks.

   **Link**

5. Change to the _____ view to enter resources.

   **Resource Sheet**

6. What is a material resource?

   **A resource that is consumed in quantity when completing a task.**

7. What is effort-driven scheduling?

   **The task scheduling method that Project uses by default, where Project will recalculate the task duration, making it shorter, if you add more resources to a task to which you've already assigned one or more resources.**

8. Use the _____ dialog box to add resources to tasks.

   **Assign Resources**

9. Save the _____ so that you can track work against the original schedule.

   **Baseline**

10. For each task, the Tracking Gantt view shows:

    **d. Both a and b.**

### Answers to Chapter 4 Review Questions

1. Why do you store each project plan in a separate file?

   **Every project has a specific starting and ending point, with specific tasks, goals, and deliverables. Storing each project in a separate file ensures that you can review the data about a single project without having to consider information from other projects.**

2. Do I have to start every new project from scratch?

   **No, you can use a template that supplies basic information, such as the list of tasks and estimated durations. You can use one of the dozens of templates that installs with Project, save your own templates, or find more templates online.**

3. My employer doesn't follow an 8 a.m. to 5 p.m. schedule. How do I match my project schedule to the real work schedule?

   **You can create and apply a custom calendar using the** Tools, Change Working Time **command. Also be sure to adjust the settings on the** Calendar **tab of the** Options dialog box (Tools, Options) **to match your calendar.**

4. Why do I enter a project start date?

   **Because the assumption is that you are planning your projects in advance of the actual work. Use the Project Information dialog box** (Project, Project Information) **to set the project's start date and calendar.**

5. True or False: Calendar options must match the custom calendar applied.

   **True. If you don't change the calendar options to match the calendar, Project might not schedule the work to begin at the hour of the day needed for your purposes.**

## Answers to Chapter 5 Review Questions

1. Where do you enter the list of tasks?

   **In the task sheet, usually in the default Gantt Chart view.**

2. What two pieces of information should you enter to create each new task?

   **The Task Name and Duration field entries.**

3. Why should you not type dates for a task in the *Start* or *Finish* fields?

   **Because Project will add constraints that may prevent it from rescheduling the task when needed.**

4. What's the duration you enter to have Project mark a task as a milestone, and when would you use a milestone?

   **0 (zero). Use a milestone task to mark an event that doesn't have associated work.**

5. What is the task ID number for the task named *Competing products* in Figure 5.8?

   **3**

6. Insert a _____ for any task that repeats over the duration of the project.

   **Recurring or repeating task**

7. In an outline, _____ tasks summarize the data for the _____ tasks under them.

   **Summary Tasks**

   **Subtasks**

8. Use the _____ button on the Formatting toolbar to demote tasks to the next lower outline level.

   **Indent (right arrow)**

9. _____ subtasks hides their task names and Gantt bars.

   **Collapsing**

10. What is the WBS code for the task with task ID 20 in Figure 5.26?

    **4.3**

## Answers to Chapter 6 Review Questions

1. Why do you skip typing in Start and Finish dates for tasks?

   **Because you want Project to retain the ability to reschedule tasks as needed.**

2. How do you instead build the task schedules?

   **After entering task durations, link the tasks. Project uses the durations you enter and the dependencies (links) between tasks to calculate start and finish dates for tasks.**

3. The _____ task drives the schedule of its _____ task.

   **Predecessor**

   **Successor**

4. Name the default task type and its abbreviation.

   **Finish-to-start (FS)**

5. How do you link two tasks using the Standard toolbar?

   **Select the tasks by dragging over the task names or Ctrl+clicking on them, and then click the** Link Tasks **button.**

6. How do you display the Task Information dialog box?

   **Double-click a cell in the task's row on the Task Sheet.**

7. What tab in the Task Information dialog box do you use to change the link type?

   **Predecessors**

8. How do you display pop-up information about a link?

   **Point to the link line with the mouse pointer**

9. Enter lead time as a _____ value and lag time as a _____ value.

   **Negative**

   **Positive**

10. Enter lead or lag time in the _____ text box in the Task Dependency dialog box.

    **Lag**

## Answers to Chapter 7 Review Questions

1. What menu and command do you choose to change to the Resource Sheet view?

   **View, Resource Sheet**

2. Name the three main types of resources.

   **Work, material, and cost**

3. A _____ resource has neither associated work nor consumed quantity.

   **Cost**

4. Make an entry in the _____ field of the Resource Sheet if the resource charges a fee every time you use or assign it.

   **Cost/Use**

5. The entry in the _____ field of the Resource Sheet indicates whether the resource will be working full time or part time on the project or whether multiple persons will be used for each assignment.

   **Units**

6. How do you replace a resource throughout the project plan?

   **Click in the** Resource Name **field for the resource to replace in the Resource Sheet, type a new resource name, and press** Enter.

7. How do you display the Resource Information dialog box?

   **Double-click a resource in the Resource Sheet**

8. What tab in the Resource Information dialog box do you use to specify a rate increase or set up cost tables?

   **Costs tab**

9. True or False: Project always follows the project's base calendar, no matter when a resource actually works.

   **False. If you make changes to a resource's calendar, then the resource's calendar will override the project base calendar if needed any time you assign the resource to a task.**

10. When a resource can only work on your project during a fixed time period, specify that resource's _____ in the Resource Information dialog box.

    **Availability**

### Answers to Chapter 8 Review Questions

1. What button on which toolbar do you use to open the Assign Resources dialog box?

   **The Assign Resources button on the Standard toolbar**

2. Briefly describe how to make an assignment for a work resource once the Assign Resource dialog box is open.

   **Click the task in the Task Sheet portion of the Gantt Chart view, click the resource in the Assign Resources dialog box, and then click Assign.**

3. Briefly describe how to make an assignment for a material resource once the Assign Resource dialog box is open.

   **Click the task in the task sheet portion of the Gantt Chart view, click the resource in the Assign Resources dialog box, enter the quantity of the resource to consume in the Units column, and then click** Assign.

4. After you assign a cost resource to a task, change to the Task Usage view and double-click the assignment to open the _____ dialog box, where you can enter the expected cost for using the cost resource.

   **Assignment Information**

5. To take off a resource assigned to a selected task, use the _____ button in the Assign Resources dialog box.

   **Remove**

6. To replace a resource throughout the entire project, type a new Resource Name in the _____ view.

   **Resource Sheet**

7. True or False: An assignment with a 50% units setting is a full-time assignment.

   **False. That is a part-time assignment.**

8. If a resource such as an outside vendor or another department will be supplying two people full time for an assignment, what should the units setting for that assignment be?

   **200%**

9. The _____ and _____ views list project assignments.

   **Resource Usage and Task Usage**

10. If a resource charges different rates and you need to specify which rate to use, choose another _____ in the Assignment Information dialog box.

**Cost rate table**

## Answers to Chapter 9 Review Questions

1. True or False: You apply formatting to sheet text and shading to cell backgrounds in different dialog boxes.

   **False. You choose settings for both the text and a background color (fill) to shade the cell in the Font dialog box** (Format, Font).

2. Drag the _____ to wrap text in a cell.

   **Bottom border of the row header**

3. To open the Information dialog box, do this to a task, resource, or assignment.

   **Any of the following are acceptable:**

   **Double-click it.**

   **Click it and press** Shift+F2

   **Click it and click the** Task Information, Resource Information, **or** Assignment Information **button on the Standard toolbar.**

   **Click it, click the Project menu, and click Task Information, Resource Information, or Assignment Information.**

4. Type in extra information on the _____ tab of the Task Information, Resource Information, or Assignment Information dialog box.

   Enter added information in the Notes tab. **(If related information exists in another document, hyperlink to it instead.)**

5. Do this to see what an indicator means.

   **Move the mouse pointer over an indicator, and a pop-up box or tip appears to tell you what the indicator is alerting you about. Or, for a note indicator, the pop-up shows you the note's contents.**

6. When a task follows a different schedule than the overall project, assign a _____ to the task.

   **Calendar (You can apply another task calendar on the Advanced tab of the Task Information dialog box. The task's assigned calendar will then override the project base calendar.)**

7. A _____ reduces Project's flexibility in rescheduling a task.

**Acceptable answers include:**

**A constraint assigned to a task**

**An assigned task calendar**

**An assigned resource's calendar**

8. If you add a _____ to a task, a white down arrow on the task's Gantt bar appears and an indicator appears when the task runs late.

**Task deadline**

9. Unlike other costs associated with resources, you enter a _____ for a task.

**Fixed cost (Project then adds the fixed cost to any resource-related costs to arrive at the total cost for the task.)**

10. Do this to a column header to begin the process for hiding or inserting a field.

**Right-click it and then Click Hide Column or Insert Column.**

**(Alternate answer: click the column heading, and press the Delete or Insert button on the keyboard.)**

## Answers to Chapter 10 Review Questions

1. True or False: You can use various views and features in Project to perform a review of your project plan.

**True: You need to perform a thorough last check of your plan to identify schedule problems and resource overallocations and to ensure that the plan is thorough and realistic.**

2. Access project statistics via the _____ dialog box.

**Project Information**

3. A task is _____ when delaying it will delay the finish of the project as a whole.

**Critical**

4. Taking steps to make the _____ shorter will have the greatest positive impact on the project schedule.

**Critical path**

5. Use the _____ to format (display) the critical path in the project.

**Gantt Chart Wizard**

6. A resource with too much work assigned is _____.

   **Overallocated or overbooked**

7. The name for a resource with too much work appears in this color in resource-related views.

   **Red**

8. Name at least one view in which you can see more detail about resource overallocations.

   **Resource Usage or Resource Graph**

9. Name at least one way to fix a resource overallocation.

   **Acceptable answers include:**

   **Remove the resource from the task and assign another resource.**

   **Level the resources in the project plan.**

   **Make manual changes to the resource's assignments in Resource Usage view.**

   **Split the task yourself.**

10. A _____ inserts a nonworking period within a task.

    **Split**

## Answers to Chapter 11 Review Questions

1. Saving the _____ saves initial information about the project plan for later comparison.

   **Baseline**

2. True or False: You can save more than one baseline.

   **True. You can save the initial baseline plus 10 more. You also can save up to 10 interim plans.**

3. The _____ toolbar includes buttons for marking work as complete on tasks.

   **Tracking**

4. Use the _____ dialog box to enter Actual Start and Finish dates for tasks.

   **Update Tasks**

5. True or False: Project only reschedules the entire task when you use the Reschedule Work button.

   **False: If the task has some percentage of work marked as complete, that actual work will not be rescheduled. Project will only reschedule the uncompleted portion of the task.**

6. The _____ dialog box shows baseline, actual, and variance data after you save starting information and begin tracking work.

   **Project Statistics**

7. Display different _____ in the left portion of the Gantt Chart view to see various fields with calculated tracking information.

   **Tables**

8. The _____ view displays two Gantt bars for each task: one for the original schedule and another for the current or actual schedule.

   **Tracking Gantt**

9. Name at least one way to reduce project costs.

   **Acceptable answers include:**

   **Identify the most expensive tasks and see if you can reduce the work (and therefore costs).**

   **Substitute less expensive resources.**

   **Ask the outside vendor to substitute a resource with a lower rate.**

   **Cut deliverables and tasks.**

10. Use the _____ view to authorize overtime or override an actual assignment cost.

    **Task Entry**

## Answers to Chapter 12 Review Questions

1. Open the _____ dialog box to access all of Project's available views.

   **More Views**

2. True or False: The Calendar view can only appear in a monthly format.

   **False. You can use the new Week button at the top of the calendar to change to a weekly format or click the Custom button to choose another display timeframe. And, you can use the View tab of the Page Setup dialog box to control how much calendar information prints per page.**

3. To change the order of tasks or resources, _____ the sheet.

   **Sort**

4. To hide non-matching tasks or resources, _____ the sheet.

   **Filter**

5. _____ the chart timescale to open the Timescale dialog box with formatting choices.

   **Double-click**

6. Project offers a number of _____ fields that you can rename and customize.

   **Placeholder, numbered or custom. Also acceptable are the types of specific numbered fields: Text, Cost, Date, Duration, Finish, Flag, Number, Outline Code, and Start.**

7. True or False: You can create a custom field that calculates values.

   **True**

8. A custom _____ defines a set of fields to appear in a sheet.

   **Table**

9. True or False: You can't add a custom view to the view menu.

   **False. You can check the** Show in Menu **check box in the View Definition dialog box to have a custom view appear on the View menu.**

10. Click the _____ command on the File menu to start the process for creating a hard copy output of the project plan.

    **Print**

## Answers to Chapter 13 Review Questions

1. Project includes this number of built-in regular reports.

   **22**

2. Use the _____ menu to access both regular and visual reports.

   **Report**

3. True or False: A report you create appears in its own separate window.

   **False. A report you create appears as a print preview rather than its own window. (In other words, Project changes to a print preview view and prevents you from viewing any other files.) You have to close Print Preview to close the report.**

4. Use the _____ button and dialog box to change settings for the printed report, such as margins and headers.

**Page Setup**

5. _____ the report to fit more information on each page.

**Acceptable answers include:**

**Scale**

**Adjust percentage**

**Zoom**

6. True or False: The report always prints exactly as shown onscreen.

**False. There may be slight discrepancies between the screen fonts shown in the print preview and the fonts in the printout.**

7. True or False: You can change the fields contained in a regular report.

**False. Once the report has been defined, such as if you create a custom report, you cannot change the data without editing the report definition. Some reports prompt you for information to filter the data, but you can't control which fields appear.**

8. A visual report appears as a PivotDiagram in this application.

**Microsoft Office Visio Professional 2007**

9. A visual report appears as a chart and PivotTable in this application.

**Microsoft Office Excel**

10. True or False: You can change the data shown in a visual report.

**True. You can edit the contents of the PivotDiagram in a Visio visual report or the PivotTable in an Excel visual report.**

## Answers to Chapter 14 Review Questions

1. True or False: Project can import or export virtually any file format.

**False. Project supports a limited number of file formats for data exchange.**

2. Use the _____ command on the File menu to start an import.

**Open**

3. Use the _____ command on the File menu to start an export.

**Save As**

4. Create a _____ to match fields between the source and destination files.

   **Map or data map**

5. The _____ lists the field names that appear in the source or destination file.

   **Header row**

6. True or False: You have to import or export all fields.

   **False. When creating the data map, you can exclude fields by leaving them set to (not mapped) or you can use the Delete Row button to remove a field.**

7. True or False: Data pasted into Word appears as a Word table.

   **False. You have to convert the data after pasting it.**

8. Name one of the two programs that enable you to save Project information as a Web page once you've copied or exported the data to that application.

   **Either of these is acceptable:**

   **Excel**

   **Word**

9. The _____ toolbar holds the Copy Picture to Office Wizard button.

   **Analysis**

10. Name one of the three applications for which the Copy Picture to Office wizard can create a file.

    **Any of these is acceptable:**

    **PowerPoint**

    **Word**

    **Visio**

### Answers to Chapter 15 Review Questions

1. Enter resources for the resource pool file in the _____ view.

   **Resource Sheet**

2. True or False: The resource pool file must be named *Resource Pool*.

   **False. The resource pool file can have any name that you prefer, as long as you remember what you named it. And, although you can enter tasks in the resource pool file, standard practice is to enter resources only in that file.**

3. Use this command to share resources from a resource pool file into a sharer file.
   **Use the** Tools, Resource Sharing, Share Resources **command.**

4. True or False: The resource pool file is linked to sharer files by default.
   **True. Changes to resource and assignment information that you make in sharer files flow back to the resource pool file, and vice versa.**

5. To see overallocations between sharer files as well as individual assignments, display the _____ view in the resource pool file.
   **Resource Usage**

6. A master project file holds inserted _____ files.
   **Subproject**

7. Use this command to insert a file into the master project.
   **Use the** Insert, Project **command.**

8. _____ the subtasks in a master project file so that you can link them.
   **Expand (Click the plus (+) outline symbol beside the subproject name to display its tasks.)**

9. To add tasks that exist only in the master project file, do this first.
   **Collapse the subprojects. Click the minus (-) outline symbol beside each subproject name to hide its tasks.**

10. Double-click an inserted project to display the _____ dialog box, where you can make overall changes.
    **Inserted Project Information**

# INDEX